£1.00 ✓

Gift
7/12/82

P.C.Pettit.
   Cambridge.

        from Ken

THE IMPRISONED SPLENDOUR

THE IMPRISONED SPLENDOUR

An approach to Reality, based upon
the significance of data drawn from
the fields of Natural Science, Psychical
Research and Mystical Experience

Raynor C. Johnson
M.A. (Oxon), Ph.D., D.Sc. (Lond.)
Master of Queen's College
University of Melbourne.

HODDER AND STOUGHTON
LONDON · SYDNEY · AUCKLAND · TORONTO

Ninth impression 1971

ISBN 0 340 01076 2

First published April 1953. Printed in Great Britain for Hodder and Stoughton Limited, St. Paul's House, Warwick Lane, London, E.C.4 by Compton Printing Ltd., London and Aylesbury.

TO

MY WIFE

best of fellow-seekers,

in gratitude

CONTENTS

PART IV—THE SIGNIFICANCE OF THE WHOLE

FOREWORD

By the Rev. LESLIE D. WEATHERHEAD, M.A., Ph.D., D.D.

IT is a joy and a privilege to me to introduce to a new type of reader my friend of nearly a quarter of a century, Dr. Raynor C. Johnson. Dr. Johnson is, of course, well known already as a physicist in his own branch of science, and has two books to his credit.

In this book he breaks ground that will be new to many readers, but is not new to him. For years he has been a deep student of psychology, psychical research and mysticism, and here, in the clear form we expect from a scientist, and in a fascinating literary style, he presents some conclusions at which he has arrived : conclusions as thrilling as they are timely.

It is a strange and significant thing that the physicist, who works in the realm of physical matter, is more and more interpreting the universe in terms of mind. The psychologist—with some out-standing exceptions—is tending to interpret the phenomena of mind in terms of matter.

Here is a book in which a competent scientist, without dogmatism, hints at an interpretation of the nature of Man which seems to me to be in harmony with, and in some ways to carry forward, Christian faith, Oriental philosophy and psychical research. Concerning the last named, I have long felt that the interpretation given by even the best spiritualists was far too crude and shallow. Dr. Johnson not only sees far greater significance in the findings of serious psychical research, but advances some original interpretations which commend themselves to me as the most reasonable and likely of those yet put forward.

It was my privilege, during my three months as guest in the home of my old friend at Queen's College, Melbourne University, of which he is the Master, to sit by the fire with his wife, members of his family, and my own daughter, while Dr. Johnson read to us the manuscript of this enthralling and stimulating book. He was generous in allowing us to criticise, and we took advantage of his generosity, often sitting up into the late hours while he expounded and clarified the views which follow.

I trust that many as they read will get the intellectual stimulation, enjoyment and enlightenment which we got as we listened. For myself, the book offers just the help I needed in this most difficult field of human enquiry—a field which is more and more engaging the attention of thoughtful men and women. With immense enthusiasm and without reserve, I commend the book to the public.

LESLIE D. WEATHERHEAD.

The City Temple,
  London, 1953.

PREFACE

THE author of a book in his preface is traditionally allowed a freedom which would be a personal intrusion if included in his subject-matter. I am going to take advantage of this to say that for some years I have wanted to write this book. I am glad to have had the discipline of Physics as a background to my thinking and the familiarity which comes from having lectured to students in this field for about thirty years. In other sciences and in philosophy I have no professional qualifications, but can claim the interest of an ordinarily intelligent person in the developing thought of his colleagues in these fields. Psychical research has seemed to me an important, vast and much-neglected field of enquiry, to large tracts of which the scientific method is applicable, and to other tracts of which apply the methods of analysis of testimony used in disciplines such as Law and History. I can claim to have read fairly widely and investigated a little in this field. The field of Mysticism is one which deeply interests me, although my temperament has so far excluded me from any impressive first-hand experience. It is in this domain that we may hope to find the answers to those problems about which we are most hungry to have real knowledge and certainty.

I have endeavoured to take selected and representative scientific data, and to say in effect to my reader : if these things are accepted as true, what can we then infer about the nature of the world we live in and the nature of human life ? My survey of the data of psychical research and the data of mysticism has been undertaken with a similar end in view. If these data also have to be accepted, what more can we infer about our environment, our nature and our destiny ? These three fields of enquiry seem to me to take us into regions of deepening significance. The questions I have tried to illuminate—it would seem almost a presumption to say " tried to answer "—are the age-old questions which return to haunt every generation, in spite of all the volumes of philosophers and all the sermons of divines. These questions revolve around the nature of Man, his origin and his destiny, and the nature of the cosmic drama of which he seems so small a part.

I have endeavoured constantly to find reliable data and to make reasonable deductions therefrom ; but I hope I have made clear my sense of the limitations of reason, and of the existence of a deeper intuitive faculty perhaps most markedly developed in the poet and the religious genius.

An author should, I think, say for whom he has written. I have had several types of people in mind. One cannot be responsible for a residential university college for many years without knowing a little of the questing minds of university students, the questions they constantly ask, and in particular the materialistic tendencies created in their thinking by the disciplines of Medicine and Science. These students have often little time to correct them by wider reading and study. I have lectured also for some years under the auspices of the Adult Education Movement. Here, again, many people from all sections of the community—thoughtful people, though not university educated—have posed their questions and problems, and I have had them also in mind. Not all my readers will be interested equally in the different sections of the book. May I suggest that, in first reading, if a chapter is found too difficult, it should be passed over and the thread picked up at the next chapter.

What I have written must necessarily be a personal philosophy of life : it can be no other. One may aim at detachment : one knows that one has failed. I think the only safe claim is of sincerity, within the limits of one's present understanding.

I have many acknowledgments to make. Where poems or lengthy passages have been quoted I have sought and received permission from the publishers or authors. My indebtedness to those who have contributed to my thinking cannot easily be stated, for it is very wide, but I think the quotations and references made in footnotes will clearly indicate these persons. I would particularly like to mention, however, Mr. G. N. M. Tyrrell's book *Grades of Significance*. In a more immediate way I am here, as always, indebted most of all to my wife for her frequent helpful discussions of these subjects and for reading through the whole manuscript. My friends Dr. Leslie D. Weatherhead of London and Mr. Arthur W. Osborn of Melbourne have also placed me in their debt, the former by his generous foreword and by valuable suggestions when reading through the manuscript and proofs, and the latter by his book *The Superphysical*, and also through many friendly chats we have enjoyed together on these subjects of mutual interest.

R. C. JOHNSON.

Queen's College,
University of Melbourne,
1953.

ACKNOWLEDGMENTS

I SHOULD like to thank Messrs. George Allen and Unwin, Ltd., for extracts from *Letters to a Friend* by C. F. Andrews, and from *The Drama of Love and Death*, and *The Art of Creation*, by Edward Carpenter; Edward Arnold and Co. for extracts from *The Human Situation* by W. Macneile Dixon; G. Bell and Sons, Ltd., for an extract from *Some Cases of Prediction*, by Hon. Mrs. Alfred Lyttelton; Ernest Benn, Ltd., and Rupert Hart-Davis, Esq., for the extract from *My Religious Experience*, by Hugh Walpole; Basil Blackwell and Mott, Ltd., for the extract from *Beyond the Five Senses*, by Miss L. M. Bazett; The Bobbs-Merrill Co., Inc., for extracts from *Experiences Facing Death*, by Mary Austin; Cambridge University Press for extracts from *Man on his Nature*, by Sir Charles Sherrington, from *The Universe Around Us*, by Sir James Jeans, and from *The Causal and the Casual in History*, by John Buchan; Wm. Collins, Sons and Co., Ltd., for the extract from *Thirty Years of Psychical Research*, by C. Richet; Cassell and Co. and the author's agents for extracts from *Pain, Sex and Time*, by Gerald Heard; Country Life, Ltd., for the extract from *Poltergeist over England*, by Harry Price; Miss Geraldine Cummins for extracts from *The Road to Immortality* and *Beyond Human Personality*; J. M. Dent and Sons, Ltd., for extracts from *The Essentials of Mysticism*, by Evelyn Underhill; E. P. Dutton and Co., Inc., for extracts from *Cosmic Consciousness*, by R. M. Bucke and from *My Brother's Face*, by D. G. Mukerji; Faber and Faber, Ltd., for extracts from *The Psychic Sense*, and *This World and That*, by Payne and Bendit, and also from *The Timeless Moment* and *The Happy Issue*, by Warner Allen, and from *Apparitions and Haunted Houses*, by Sir Ernest Bennett; Faber and Faber, Ltd., and Curtis Brown, Ltd., for extracts from *The Supreme Identity*, by Alan W. Watts; Faber and Faber, Ltd., and Walter de la Mare for the quotation of " All That's Past " and a verse of " Farewell "; Hodder and Stoughton, Ltd., for extracts from *Goodbye for the Present*, by Eleanor Lady Acland, and from *Good News of God*, by Canon C. E. Raven; Hodder and Stoughton, Ltd., and the Tweedsmuir Trustees for extracts from *Memory-hold-the-Door*, by John Buchan; Hutchinson and Co., Ltd., for the extract from *Mysticism in Religion*, by W. R. Inge, and also, with the executors of the late Mr. H. G. Wells, for the extract from *The Bulpington of Blup*, by H. G. Wells; Jonathan Cape, Ltd., for the extract from *Diagnosis of Man*, by Kenneth Walker; John Lane The Bodley Head, Ltd., for an extract from *The Earthen Vessel*, by

Lady Pamela Glenconner; Longmans, Green and Co., Ltd., for
extracts from *The Most Haunted House in England*, by Harry Price;
Sir Francis Meynell for quotation of Alice Meynell's poem "I am the
Way", and some lines of Francis Thompson; Macmillan and Co.,
Ltd., for extracts from *Holism and Evolution*, by J. C. Smuts, and from
Testament of Friendship, by Vera Brittain; also with the Trustees of
Rabindranath Tagore for extracts from *Poems of Kabir* and *Creative
Unity*; and with Mr. Diarmuid Russell for several extracts from
Song and its Fountains and *The Avatars* by Æ (George Russell);
Mr. E. McLysaght for quotations from the poems of Sidney Royse
Lysaght; Methuen and Co., Ltd., for extracts from *The Survival of
Man*, by Sir Oliver Lodge, and from *The Unknown Guest*, by M.
Maeterlinck, and from *Supernormal Faculties in Man*, by Eugene
Osty; John Murray (Publishers), Ltd., for extracts from *The Silent
Isle*, by A. C. Benson; A. W. Osborn, Esq., for extracts from his
book *The Superphysical*; Clarendon Press, Oxford, for extracts from
Eastern Religions and Western Thought, by S. Radhakrishnan;
Penguin Books, Ltd., for an extract from *The Personality of Man*, by
G. N. M. Tyrrell; Rider and Co., for extracts from *Grades of
Significance*, by G. N. M. Tyrrell, from *Practical Astral Projection*,
by Yram, from *Man Outside Himself*, by H. F. P. Battersby, and from
The Nameless Faith, by Lawrence Hyde; John Farquharson, for
an extract from *Varieties of Religious Experience*, by William James;
Routledge and Kegan Paul, Ltd., for an extract from *Thoughts of a
Modern Mystic*, by C. C. Massey; Sidgwick and Jackson, Ltd., for
an eztract from *Evidence for Telepathy*, by Mrs. W. H. Salter; Mrs.
F. S. Smythe and Hodder and Stoughton, Ltd., for an extract from
The Spirit of the Hills, by F. S. Smythe; the Secretary of the Society
for Psychical Research for numerous extracts from the *Proceedings*
and *Journal* of the Society, and Mr. G. N. M. Tyrrell's *Myers
Memorial Lecture*; John M. Watkins for an extract from *Contemplations*, by W. L. Wilmshurst; T. W. Laurie and Co., for an extract
from *Mental Radio*, by Upton Sinclair; Sidgwick and Jackson, Ltd.,
for a quotation from a poem of Rupert Brooke; and Burns, Oates
and Washbourne, Ltd., for quotations from poems of Francis
Thompson.

Chapter

1

INTRODUCTION

" In the great matters it is now common knowledge that we have
no knowledge, unless it be sufficient to advise us of the utter folly
of all dogmatism. Reason, for all the flourishing of her trum-
pets, has had no greater success in illuminating the grand problems
than the imagination. From the central keep of the world's
mystery its arrows fall idly back, as from the walls of the medieval
castle the bolts of the archers. . . . Our business is not to solve
problems beyond mortal powers, but to see to it that our thoughts
are not unworthy of the great theme."

W. MACNEILE DIXON.

" By wonder are we saved."

PLATO.

" Jesus, on Whom be peace, has said : wonder at the things
before you, for wonder is the beginning of knowledge."

THE OXYRHYNCHUS PAPYRI.

I. ADAPTATION TO ENVIRONMENT

IN the Darwinian picture of the evolution of living things no aspect
is more impressive than the variety and ingenuity of the methods by
which these have adapted themselves to their environment. Living
things have conquered the air, the dry land, fresh water and the sea
from its shallow fringe to its six-mile depths, and in every case they
have modified their structure to suit the conditions of their habitat.
In the deep sea, conditions differ enormously from those on other
parts of the Earth's surface. The pressure for each mile descended
is over one ton to the square inch—the equivalent of about 160
atmospheres—a pressure which would certainly crush and destroy
any of our own tissues. The deep-sea creatures adapted themselves
to this situation by developing very permeable, spongy structures in
order to equalise the pressure within and without. No sunlight can
penetrate to depths of the sea greater than half a mile, but many of
these creatures contrive to manufacture their own light by intricate
chemical processes. Furthermore, they have their own distinct
luminescent patterns (dare we suggest for purposes of mutual
recognition !). In this cold, dark and almost silent world the sense
of touch has naturally been greatly exploited.

The success of the amphibians in emerging from the water some

300 million years ago and establishing themselves on dry land presents as remarkable a group of new adaptations as can be found anywhere. The water was a medium of approximately the same density as they were themselves : it supported them without effort. The air was eight hundred times less dense ; the problem of self-support and balance became acute, and had to be met by special muscular development and great elaboration of the balancing mechanism of the brain. Fins became legs to make movement possible with the minimum of friction, and lungs had to be devised to deal with respiration in the new environment. The new range of temperatures to which these creatures were subject made it necessary to alter the whole outer surface of their bodies—hence the devices of thickened skin, fat layers, fur and hair, and the seasonal variations of which these devices are capable.

From time to time some great challenge seems to surge out of the vast Unconscious of Nature, " Capture a new area for Life ". As though in response, we see experiments taking place and novelties constantly arising. Some seem to last a few million years and then fail. Others succeed, and from these, again, new experiments arise always to achieve greater adaptation to, and sometimes to provide greater awareness of, the environment. As we look at the evolutionary picture, our attention is naturally attracted to these aspects of change ; but we must remind ourselves of the vast time-scale involved. Far from there being anything dramatic about the change, we can affirm that from the viewpoint of hundreds of generations of creatures all must have seemed sunk in the complacency and stagnation of complete adaptation to their own world.

When we come to Man we see the apotheosis of adaptive mechanisms.* His body has innumerable devices the functioning of which is largely below the level of consciousness, to ensure that, however stormy and changeable his environment, his physical body shall adapt itself and remain at peace. It is the exceptional event for these adaptive functions to be unequal to their task and for a state of disease to supervene. Even when it does, and the first line of defence has broken down, the body is not without its resources, and, given a reasonable chance, will marshal its reserves and throw them skilfully into action. If it were not so, neither medicine nor surgery would exist within the respectable aura which our civilised society accords to them. The human body has achieved to a superb degree the ability to adapt itself automatically to a changing environment, and thereby has freed the psyche to a large extent to devote itself to its own proper field of exploration and development.

* Alexis Carrel : *Man the Unknown*, Chapter VI.

The ability of Life on the physical level to preserve the *status quo* and maintain itself in a comfortable relationship with its surroundings is clearly reflected on other levels also. It is commonly said that one can get used to anything. Time, we say, heals all wounds. The sharp edge of grief is softened. Things which once were fearful or shocking become accepted without emotional stress through use and familiarity. The medical student who felt faint at the first contact with operational technique becomes the competent surgeon who undertakes his task with no qualms. The young nurse of delicate nurture and upbringing acquires a familiarity with suffering, disease and death which allows her to take these things as all part of the day's work. The peasant who lives where Nature has been lavishly beautiful takes it for granted as the setting of his toil, nor stops to wonder at

> The grass, the thicket, and the fruit-tree wild,
> White hawthorn, and the pastoral eglantine;
> Fast fading violets covered up in leaves. . . .

The miles and miles of drab streets, with houses all in rows and all alike, with little back-yards behind and a smoke-pall above, do not house any greater proportion of the discontented or unhappy than the flats of the West End. Indeed, the social reformer is often surprised to discover that those he would gladly transport to villas in suburbia would not thank him for the exchange. Another pound or two on the wages and greater security for the future would be far more often preferred. The fact is that our emotional and mental life can be " conditioned ", so that we come to accept without pain or dissatisfaction things which shock the individual who meets them for the first time ; and, conversely, we come to accept without wonder or gratitude things the value of which we appreciate only when we have lost them. This process of " conditioning ", or, in biological terminology, " adaptation to environment ", is constantly operative below the level of consciousness. We can see its biological utility : it is, we may think, in some aspects of its operation, a merciful provision to secure an harmonious correspondence of the creature with the environment. It is equally clear, however, that all progress really depends on the stimulus which produces disharmony. The law of entropy has its equivalent on intellectual, emotional and spiritual levels. Energy, as we know from physics, is constantly degrading into heat and running down into forms of less availability. The points of significance in the physical world are living creatures, where for the time being Life is operative to reverse the flow and create centres of self-activity. The Hebrew poet who wrote, " Every valley shall be exalted, and every mountain and hill shall be made low ", may have intended it as a prophecy (a rather dismal prospect, and nothing, we should have thought, to sing about), but he was in fact describing not only a phenomenon of geological interest, but a commonplace contemporary activity on all human levels—the tendency to complacency, uniformity and harmonious inactivity. Leave Nature alone, and the lowest common level will inevitably be found : there will be nothing to wonder at; all will be accepted. That which Life is doing in the physical world to create significant centres of self-activity, happily has its counterpart on other levels.   A higher order seems to touch the lower creatively at various times and places, and then, through poet, artist, scientist and religious genius, the stagnant waters are effectively troubled.   However uncomfortable this process may be, we must be courageous enough to recognise it as another opportunity given to us to develop.   Such supreme appearances are the basis of the Hindu belief in the Avatar, an incarnation from time to time of the Divine, as a Krishna, a Buddha or a Christ.   In the Gita, Krishna is pictured as saying to Arjuna, " I, unborn and soul eternal, Lord of all creations, taking upon me mine own nature, I arise by mine own power.   For whensoever righteousness decays and there is a rising up of evil, then myself do I create, for the protecting of the good and the overthrow of evildoers : for the setting up of righteousness am I re-born from age to age." *

We are born, then, into this world, and to a very large extent are conditioned by it on all levels, physical, emotional and intellectual. To very few does it occur seriously and persistently to ask why they themselves exist, what kind of a world they live in, or indeed why there is a world at all.   These questions are supposed to interest the academic philosophers, to which select band I have no qualifications to belong.   For me, however, they are not academic questions : they are central to all my thinking and living.   I would rather have trustworthy and satisfying answers to these questions than all the gold of the Indies.   To *know*—not to believe, not to hope, not to have faith, but to *know* that the universe is friendly, that our feet are set on an intelligible pilgrimage, and that there is Love at the heart of things : this is knowledge for which I am still questing and for which I would gladly barter, as for the pearl of great price, all other knowledge.   I am writing this book for the few " unconditioned ", for those constantly troubled by the divine discontent of thought who share the same hunger *to know*.

* *Bhagavad Gita*, IV, 6–8.

2. THE STRANGENESS OF EXISTENCE

Once the mind is awakened from its conditioned state and looks around with wide-open eyes at the world, it is shocked by the things it formerly took for granted. The warp of the tapestry of life may be of our own making, but the woof is complete mystery.

Let us start with ourselves. We came into the world, so far as we know, without being consulted, and we shall be bundled out of it likewise without choice. We came into a particular family of a particular nationality in a particular place at a particular point of history—and no other. What if we had been born to Esquimaux or Arabian or Tibetan or African parents? How different would have been our physique and our cultural interests, our friends, our thoughts, our dreams and our opportunities; we might have been born 1,000, 500 or 100 years ago, instead of into the twentieth century at this particular point of time. Our whole outlook and attitude would then necessarily have been so different that it is not unreasonable to ask if we should have been the same person.

Let the reader look back reflectively over his own life, and observe at how many points where alternative paths appeared, the particular way taken was determined by what we are disposed to call the " merest accident ". A headache, a missed train, a shower of rain, a chance walk or meeting, a slight accident or delay, a casual word— these are the things by one of which, or by a series of which, the pattern of life seems to have been radically affected. Are we, then, the playthings of chance, the sport of Destiny? And, if not, what is our philosophy of accident? We are reasonable beings : we believe in cause and effect. All our Western science is based upon the reliability of this fundamental law. Do we not, in fact, regard this law as applying to the physical world, but hesitate to regard it as applying equally in the moral world? As soon as we start to think of these things we are prisoners of philosophy. How far, indeed, are we free? The longer we reflect on experience, the more overwhelming appears the " givenness " of things and the more circumscribed the area of our freedom, important though that area may be. Looking at some momentous trifles which have affected the course of history, John Buchan * has said :

> " The movement of mankind is not by a single-gauge track ; there is a network of tracks, and the one actually taken may owe its choice to the blindest chance. Rationalise the facts as much as you please— and you can often carry the process a long way—there will remain things which you cannot rationalise, things which you can only call

* *The Causal and the Casual in History*, the Rede Lecture, 1929 (C.U.P.).

accidents and which cannot be explained by any logical terms. Instead of the causal we find the casual. I do not for one moment argue that these incomprehensible factors are incapable of rationalisation by some higher intelligence than our own; I only say that we cannot fit them into any mortal scheme of effects and causes."

Consider the strangeness of existence from the individual's standpoint. There are those who seem the favourites of fortune: they have good health, able minds, all the advantages of a cultured environment and training and the blessings of friendship. Opportunity knocks on their door at the right time. For others the race of life is one long struggle against handicap, suffering and tragedy. These inequalities are strange and baffling from the individual's standpoint. A young surgeon has qualified himself to begin his work and is then stricken with blindness. A young mother is attacked by cancer and her children are left orphans. A youth is accidentally shot through the spine and must lie in bed for the rest of his life. A tile is lifted from the roof by a gust of wind and kills or blinds a young child below. This is the raw material of human life in one of its aspects: tragedy which no sort of vigilance or conduct on the part of the victims could have averted. It is good to take a balanced view of life, and it may be that, on the whole, for humankind the happiness outweighs the suffering. The real issue raised, however, is that of justice *to the individual*: is there a moral order, and is it fundamentally just to the individual?

More than 2,000 million human beings inhabit this Earth of ours: every day more than 100,000 of them die and a similar number is born. This colossal drama has gone on for tens of thousands of years: perhaps for hundreds of thousands of years, of which history retains no record. The endless procession of humanity has come out of the unknown, crossed the lighted stage of human life and disappeared again into the unknown.

> The Worldly Hope men set their Hearts upon
> Turns Ashes—or it prospers; and anon,
>   Like Snow upon the Desert's dusty Face
> Lighting a little Hour or two—is gone.

The transiency of all human achievement and the brevity of the human span are part of the unalterable pathos of life.

> One Moment in Annihilation's Waste,
> One Moment, of the Well of Life to taste—
>   The Stars are setting and the Caravan
> Starts for the Dawn of Nothing—Oh, make haste!

We may disagree with Omar Khayyám's conclusions, but we share with him the poignancy of the spectacle, for each one of these passing millions was a human being with loves and fears, hopes and dreams like our own. To what goal and what purpose is all this? What has become of this vast procession which has disappeared into the past: where are they now? They have disappeared from the eyes of their successors as though they had never been—us, who for a few short years try to weave our own dreams into realities on the same spinning orb. And what strange dreams men have! They know they, too, will die. How, then, do they spend the years vouchsafed to them? Some seek power, and lust after action: these are the soldiers, the statesmen and rulers, the merchants, the pirates, the adventurers and the conquerors. Others seek a hermitage from which to contemplate the world: these are the artists and poets, the writers and philosophers, the musicians and the ascetics. Of most people it can be said that they live lives caught in a routine, not of their choosing, but from which they cannot escape: that their minds are conditioned by an environment which they have never seriously questioned or supposed could be substantially other than it is. Of all, it can be said that they are seeking for happiness, but few—very few—know how to find it, or where to look for it. It is a moving, thrilling, fascinating spectacle, full of human tears and human laughter; but has it any meaning? It is strange, desperately strange, and when the thinker has put the last ounce of himself into his thinking to unravel the mystery, he may well feel like

> An infant crying in the night
> And with no language but a cry.

3. HOW FAR CAN REASON TAKE US?

Reason may be regarded as the highest function of the mind. The mind is itself a complex instrument of Man, just as is his body, and while Mind in its higher reaches has its own peculiar purpose to serve, in its lower reaches it is closely linked to the body. To the closeness of this interaction the whole of psycho-somatic medicine bears testimony. If Mind on its lower levels is concerned, like engineer officers below deck, with the maintenance of the ship of the body as a smoothly running unit, Mind on its higher levels is concerned, like the deck officers, with the ship's relation to its environment. Reason is one of these deck officers—some would like to think the first officer—but the fact is that his advice is not always accepted by the captain, although the captain likes to pretend that it is. The methods of reason are deductive and inductive logic, respectively the drawing of specific applications from a general principle, and the discovery of a general principle to embrace specific cases. Pure mathematics is an impressive array of machinery to assist the mind in these activities. It bears the same relationship to the unaided mind that optical instruments such as the microscope, telescope and spectroscope bear to the naked eye, extending its power and efficiency enormously. In the absence of light, these optical instruments would have no value, and in the absence of reliable data in the form of facts or ideas, the mind, whether aided or unaided, cannot approach truth. Thus all our codified knowledge of the material world, which is described as Natural Law, has been derived from experimental data of observation. There is no value in arguing about the sort of world it would be if light had such and such a velocity, or electricity had such and such properties. We must find out these primary data of observation from Nature, and then the ingenious mind can get busy to build upon them a consistent scheme of thought : that which we call a science.

We are accustomed to say we " understand " a thing when we see it as a particular illustration of a general principle or law. Thus we say that we " understand " the motions of the planets around the sun because we recognise that these are special cases of a universal law of gravitation : but we are prone to forget that this law was itself inferred from the observed data, so that we are really talking in a circle, and not " understanding " anything. The fact is that when we find a simplifying hypothesis—one which embraces within itself a large number of diverse phenomena of observation—this unification is assumed to be evidence that we are approaching some facet of universal truth. If we proceed to ask " why " there is such a law of gravitation as the one we know, the only sort of answer which would give us any satisfaction is one which would show it to be a deduction from a still more general or unifying principle. It is very interesting and significant to note that this *feeling of satisfaction*, of which all the most advanced minds are apparently capable, seems itself the ultimate warrant for the belief that along the road of science we can approach Truth.

If it be asked, can Reason tell us anything really *new*—something not itself contained in the data of observation ?—the answer is surely " No ". As long as we have got all the data, everything is there latent but unrecognised, and Reason is the instrument which reveals it to us. Reason, then, is an instrument created to manipulate symbols and discern relationships. It is an extraordinarily flexible instrument, but it can operate to discover truth only if raw material of observation is fed into it. For the symbols in question we then substitute data of observation in scientific enquiry, or ideas in philosophic enquiry.

There do, however, seem to be certain basic or background

symbols which cannot be defined, but which are always present. These are Space, Time and Energy. Without these, Reason does not seem able to operate. What they are in themselves, Reason cannot tell us : they are the great indefinables, conditions or aspects under which Mind appears to view the world of matter. Reason has had remarkable success in formulating relationships between physically observed quantities, and of this success the edifice of modern science is the evidence. To the degree, however, in which Reason has been applied beyond the fields of physics and chemistry to that of biological enquiry its successes have been less spectacular, and this is because a new element, Life, is now involved. Life I shall regard as a state of organic association of Mind with matter : dissolve this association and the organism loses the characteristics of Life and is no more than a complex aggregate of chemical substances. The aspects of the biological sciences where most progress has been made are those where the techniques and principles of physics and chemistry have been applicable ; the aspects where least achievement has resulted are just those which are specifically characteristic of the new and seemingly unaccountable factor of Life. That this should be so is natural enough, for in the field of inanimate things, Mind, which is clearly something of a different and, indeed, a higher order than matter, has, through its function of Reason, been very successful. The higher order has illuminated and provided " understanding " of the lower. As soon as we ask Reason to do this for living things— the characteristic of which is that they are expressions of Mind—we are really asking Mind to explain itself : a task which it may well be beyond its power to do. It is true that we have regarded Reason as the highest function of Mind, a function which we may suppose does not even dawn until the higher mammalian level is reached. The spider constructs its web, the peacock its magnificent coloured feather-patterns, the bird builds its nest and migrates at a certain time to a particular place, bees and ants have a well-developed organisation— these all doubtless occur without any *reasoning*, but it is impossible to consider them as other than evidences of Mind, lower mind if you will. Higher mind, with its function of Reason, may be able to throw much light on the functioning of lower mind, but we shall find that it is only from the standpoint of a different and higher order than Mind that we can hope to gain real " understanding " of Mind itself—and therefore, I submit, of living things. This conception of different orders of reality or ascending grades of significance is one of the utmost importance. The higher order can substantially " explain " the lower, and perhaps in some measure illuminate the lower sub-levels of its own order, but the task constantly being attempted of understanding the higher (usually the less familiar) in terms of the lower (usually the more familiar) is, as we shall see, hopeless. From it arise all the mechanistic theories in biology and psychology, and all the anthropomorphic concepts of religion. G. N. M. Tyrrell * has said, in a book to which we shall refer later :

> " Our usual mode of procedure is to attempt to explain higher levels of significance in terms of lower, as when we take the living organism and try to explain it in terms of physics and chemistry. On a certain significant grade this explanation is possible, but when we become dissatisfied and press for fuller meanings, it becomes necessary to view the thing on a higher significant level. Then the physical explanation breaks down, and we are forced to admit it to be the abstraction it really is. Henceforth we are obliged to adopt the higher conception, and then we find that the lower flows from it."

If Reason, applied in the biological field, the region of lower mind-in-matter, is likely to meet with only limited success, it is likely to meet with even less in the psychological field, where it is called upon to consider feeling, thinking and willing. Success here, so far as any deep and real understanding is concerned, will be impossible ; for we cannot expect to lift ourselves by pulling on our shoe-laces. I do not suggest that the application of Reason on this (its own) level is of no value, but that it will be able to go only a limited way in the matter of understanding, and that there will remain a hard core of mystery resolvable or intelligible only from a higher level or stand-point. In the same way, physics and chemistry applied in the biological field have had their successes on their own level and have given us bio-physics and bio-chemistry, but on the phenomena most characteristic of Life they have thrown no explanatory light. When we turn to the things which are most significant in human life, to which the greatest of the human race have contributed most, and in which our real wealth consists—the love of truth and beauty, the inspirations which have led to great art, music and sculpture, and that simple goodness of character to which we pay involuntary tribute whenever we meet it—the capacity of Reason to explain them is almost negligible. Reason may help us to discover truth, but it cannot explain the hunger of men to discover it

> . . . the deep passion of enduring hours
> And endless seeking after endless Truth.

Reason cannot tell us why beauty exists or what is beautiful. It cannot fathom or understand the sources of inspiration or tell us how to produce a great statue, a poem, a concerto or a painting. It

* G. N. M. Tyrrell : *Grades of Significance*, p. 28 (2nd ed., Rider & Co.).

cannot tell us what love is, the spring from which it arises or the direction of its outflowing. It cannot understand the nature and origin of goodness, unselfishness and self-sacrifice. These things appear to have their source in a deeper level of our being than Mind, or, to use the terminology we have previously employed, they belong to a higher significant level of reality. It is rather in terms of this higher level that we may hope ultimately to find understanding of some of the mysteries of Mind, and I think particularly in this connection of Space, Time and Energy, the mind's modes of perception of the outer world.

These things of the higher significant level—truth, beauty and goodness—are the " values " of philosophy, and we must ask ourselves the question whether the *mind* can rightly be expected to make any valid judgments in this field. The question may seem absurd at first, for is not philosophy itself full of such judgments ? Do we not every day distinguish the beautiful from the ugly, right from wrong, the true from the false, the higher way from the lower way ? We do, but we are wrong in assuming that it is the mind which makes these judgments of value. Reason clothes these judgments in language, it orders them and presents them to us ; but the judgments and evaluations themselves come from a higher level of ourselves than Mind. To facilitate discussion I propose to call this higher level buddhi (coming from a Sanskrit word meaning " wisdom "). Buddhi apprehends Truth directly—fragments of Truth only, of course. It offers no reasons for its perceptions, but it makes no mistakes, and this wisdom is passed through the level of Mind, to be there clothed in intelligible form. The clothing is commonly language, but it may be music or colour or any other art form. It is in the process of clothing, in the expression of Truth in symbolic form, that distortion may take place. It is, however, the characteristic of great Art that it reveals the true form shining through, so that another person whose mind and buddhi approximate to the same degree of development involuntarily and immediately recognises the authentic message. This response of conviction, which is accompanied by a feeling of inner satisfaction, may possibly arise because the truth has found its way home again, just as the echo returns to its source or the electric current from one pole of a battery passes round a circuit and back again to the battery. For we shall see later that at the buddhic level there is a unity of selves far more intimate than at the mental level, just as at the mental level there is a closer degree of association than on the physical level. Indeed, the descent through the levels or orders of significance within ourselves is accompanied by increasingly marked separateness.

If on the buddhic level there is immediate and intuitive knowledge of Truth—fragments of Truth—which are clothed by the mind and appear as judgments of value, it may be asked why such judgments, made by apparently honest and sincere people, differ so widely and often clash so violently ? The principal cause is without doubt the distorting mechanism of Mind, which, as we have seen, is so easily and generally " conditioned ". Whether we turn to political theory or economics, to theology or psychology, to religious denominational-ism or philosophy—in almost every field of human enquiry and association we find conditioned minds. In more respectable circles they are called " schools of thought ". Truth cannot filter through conditioned minds without suffering a greater or lesser degree of distortion. That which supports the preconceptions is retained and stressed, that which does not is unexpressed or distorted. It is as though all wells sunk to the buddhic level find the pure water of Truth in greater or lesser amount, but as it is drawn up to the surface the intervening strata introduce some contamination. It may be very little, or it may be so much that the water is unfit for human consumption.

The second cause of differing value-judgments is doubtless the differing degrees of buddhic development in people. The well, as we have said, may have very little or may have much to yield. The fragments of Truth presented to Mind may be small and isolated and so much out of relationship with other truths that they may in themselves (though still true) be misleading. Thus it is, as Lowell says, " Time makes ancient good uncouth ". Slavery was once accepted by good and kindly people as a part of the natural order of society : now it is no longer tolerated. Such people had grasped the isolated truth that the eye, the ear, the hand and the foot had not the same function to fulfil, but they had not grasped it in relation to the wider truth that these were parts of one body, and that no one part was less honourable than another. A truth in isolation may be almost as dangerous as an error.

The greatest spiritual leaders of mankind have always had well-developed buddhi, and a clear, flexible, unconditioned mind as the perfectly attuned vehicle of the buddhi. From them Truth has come in its original purity, and according to men's capacity to respond (i.e., according to their measure of freedom from conditioned prejudice) have recognised the voice of authority. Unfortu-nately, the records which we possess of all the great teachings have suffered distortions just because of these limitations on the part of those who heard them and passed them on. The great teachers, recognising this, have therefore always entrusted Truth with most confidence to parables, which, because of their simplicity, picturesqueness and association with everyday life, are a thought-form most likely to be remembered and least likely to be corrupted. Each man, then, according to his buddhic development and freedom of mind, can perceive that depth of Truth to which he has a capacity to respond. If he is reasonably well developed, at least beyond the point of those who recorded the teachings, he discovers within himself the power infallibly to separate the wheat from the chaff.

Most of us must have met occasionally in the course of our life persons of simple, clear and almost unconditioned mind. They are always humble and un-self-conscious, never critical of others, in whom they always seem to find the good. Sometimes in obscure circumstances and not highly educated in the technical sense, their buddhic development is obviously considerable on the side of love and compassion, although the range of Truth they can command is limited. Their mind is, however, a simple, undistorting medium of the truth they have, and we listen with respect when they speak, for we recognise it is their deeper self speaking, and it strikes the authentic note. It is of these that Dean Inge was probably thinking when he said, " The saints do not contradict each other ".

We accord, then, to the mind in its highest function of reason a superb power to manipulate symbols and discern relationships—the techniques of logic and mathematics, which, applied to the world of material things, have given us the orderliness and achievements of Natural Science. We accord to Mind in both this and in its other functions of feeling and imagination the power to clothe in the symbolic dress of language, music, form and colour, the value-judgments of buddhi. It may be interesting to consider, then, what is the nature of doubt. Within the limited range of its apprehension we have attributed to buddhi an intuitive and infallible knowledge of what is true. One obvious source of doubt is therefore the knowledge possessed by buddhi (or perhaps by some still higher level of the self) that its apprehensions, though true so far as they go, are limited. This sense of limited knowledge may be passed on into the mind as a vague feeling of doubt or disquiet that its value-judgments, though not wrong, are imperfect.

The other source of doubt is probably due to the imperfection of the expression given by Mind to buddhi's intuitive knowledge, and buddhi's awareness that the instrument of Mind is too inflexible to render any truer expression possible. Doubt may come from a vague feeling finding its way into consciousness that buddhi and Mind are not quite at one in the formulation made.

Macneile Dixon has said,* " Even when we have doubts, it is the mind that doubts. All criticism of the mind is done by the mind itself." It will be apparent, from what has been said, that our view is rather different, and that doubt, when it arises in the mind, is rather due to an interpolation from the buddhic level. But we are in thorough agreement when he goes on to say of Mind that " no doubt its present powers may expand, that they are prophetic of higher powers to come ". There is no good reason for supposing that even the best representatives of twentieth-century man have minds developed to the point at which they can perceive all the clues to the riddle of existence. It is good that we should keep this constantly before us in our speculations. The function of Mind, then, is to express the wisdom of a higher order, and to understand and learn to manipulate a lower order. In so far as it does the latter it grows and develops, and thereby fits itself more effectively to do the former. Its achievements in the latter direction may seem remarkable (as we shall see in Part I of this book), but they do not touch more than the fringe of things (as we shall see in Part II).

4. REVELATION AND THE SOURCE OF AUTHORITY

We have said that one of the functions of Mind is to express the wisdom of a higher aspect of ourselves, a task which, in most of us, is carried out with varying degrees of distortion and imperfection. This is the chief source of the strange miscellany of value-judgments and the clashing of consciously sincere minds. We have seen that Mind, in its function of Reason, has answered many of our questions about the physical order, and with increasing development may perhaps go on to answer them all, but that it is powerless to answer those questions to which we are most eager and hungry to find answers. We have seen that our value-judgments are the imperfect expression of our buddhi—and we have already discussed the origin of the feeling of doubt. Who, indeed, at some crisis, in the face of some sorrow or anguish, being desperate to understand the meaning of events, has not craved for an infallible guide through the labyrinth, or some beam of authentic illumination from a higher source ? This is the mood in which men turn to religion (often to be disappointed) —or, should we say, more correctly, that this is the religious mood ? It is important to distinguish between the intellectual formulations of religion, the necessarily symbolic and imperfectly apprehended expression of the insight of some great soul, and the essence of the

* W. Macneile Dixon : *The Human Situation*, p. 70 (Edward Arnold & Co., 1937).

religious experience, which is mystical. Men are like children. It is good that they should listen to the voice of external authority and submit to its guidance in the days of their spiritual childhood; but all real development thereafter depends on the individual's own untrammelled search, his " endless seeking after endless truth ". The fact is that objective formulations of spiritual truth can never be a substitute for experiencing the truth in one's self. These formulations, which are contained in all the scriptures of the world and the commentaries on them, are guides and signposts to the discerning mind. But no belief in historic persons or historic events has in itself power to satisfy the once-awakened hungering soul. The answers which alone will satisfy him cannot be another person's answers; they must be his own. Occasionally something he reads may become vividly alive for him—not because the source was august, but because from his own buddhic level a response leaped out to meet it. In the words of Coleridge, he has chanced

> . . . from outward forms to win
> The passion and the life, whose fountains are within.

Somewhere in the long past he had made the discovery of this truth for himself. It has been stored away at the buddhic level, where no wisdom is ever lost, and the chance stimulus from without, coinciding with a favourable disposition of mind, has permitted it to come forth as something he *knew*. There is a vital difference between belief and knowledge. Belief is that to which we assent intellectually as the most probable working hypothesis, and we do so usually because some other person whom we respect as an " authority " has proposed it. For every human being it is probably true to say that they have *knowledge* of the fact of gravity, for they have constant daily acquaintances with it. The overwhelming majority of people, however, can only have *belief* in a law of universal gravitation based on their confidence in the integrity and ability of those very few men who have had the opportunity to make astronomical observations of planetary orbits and delicate laboratory experiments. For *practical purposes* the difference between knowledge and belief, so far as impersonal things are concerned, is not of great importance. I shall not be greatly troubled if my *belief* that light travels with a speed *in vacuo* of 186,000 miles a second is some day disproved; such beliefs do not concern the things that matter most to me.

> But oh to *know* not while with friends I sit
> And while the purple joy is passed about
> Whether 'tis ampler day, divinelier lit
> Or homeless night without.

You would not be content to " believe ", you would require to
" know ", whether your best friend in another place was alive or
dead. Of all the profounder questionings of Man the same is true.
Belief is all that can be acquired from all outward sources and testi-
monies ; knowledge must well up from within. When it does so it
carries its own authenticity. The conditions favourable to the
appearance of this " knowing ", this wisdom of the innermost pre-
existent self, we shall have to consider later. The restless mind
requires normally to be stilled before such knowledge can make its
appearance. There do, however, occur moments, unprepared for
and memorable, sometimes of emotional stress, when some great
loss or shaking of the foundations of life occurs, when knowledge of
this convincing kind emerges. I give two examples.

Hugh Walpole * writes :

> " On this occasion I was quite certain [of death], and I remember
> thinking of things and people that I was going to leave ; I remember
> feeling sorry that I hadn't written a masterpiece, that I must leave
> two people whom I dearly loved, but most of all that I must abandon
> so many beautiful things, tiny things, the sound of running water,
> birch trees in the sun, a hot day by the sea, music, reading a good book
> by the fire, a walk over the hills, and so on. Then, *with absolute
> conviction* I was aware that I would be leaving nothing, that whatever
> I had found lovely and of good report I should still enjoy."

A friend of mine, an educated and religious-minded man in his
fifties, who held a key position in University administration and was
interned by the Japanese in Stanley Camp, Hong Kong during the
war, had the following experience. The Japanese did not fly planes
at night, but were fond of night bombardments. During one of
these he was sleeping in a small bedroom at Morrison Hall overlooking
the harbour when shells began to whine and drone, and some to fall
quite close. The account is taken from his camp diary of 1942.

> " I had always wondered how I would stand up to imminent
> danger. . . . Now this is the experience I had. I got up in something
> I can only describe as a thrill, as shell after shell approached, and
> thanked God for the revelation which came to me in that hour quite
> unsought, that whatever might be on the other side, should I be
> knocked out, it was a good something, something to look forward to,
> something not in the least to dread or draw back from. . . . After this
> I don't think I was conscious of danger. I didn't want to be killed.
> I hated the idea of being hurt, and anyway I longed for the day when
> you and the youngsters and I would all be reunited. But I knew
> that if I were killed it would be absolutely all right, not because there
> would be nothingness, but because there would be goodness and
> richer experience beyond the grave."

* Hugh Walpole : *My Religious Experience* (Ernest Benn, Ltd.).

Describing the same experience in a letter written three years later to relatives and friends when he had returned to Australia he said :

> " I woke up apparently from a dream, and was conscious of the most amazing sense of exhilaration, peace and well-being. I felt as though some unseen power were about me, wholly friendly, and I knew without the shadow of doubt, that at the back of this strife was sheer goodness, and that though this did not imply immunity from danger or death, these things somehow were insignificant and irrelevant. The realisation of this sent the blood tingling through my body with a strange glad kind of anticipation. It didn't seem to matter what happened—it was all right beyond. So thrilling was this experience that I exclaimed again and again, ' Oh, if A—— could only know how I feel now, how at rest her mind would be about me '. This experience coloured every experience during the blitz and much in the camp afterwards, and I realised that the things that were happening were things that could not harm, but which might enrich my life."

Such occurrences are of the nature of mystical experiences which we shall have to consider more fully later. Such may be, and probably are, an out-flowing into awareness of something from a higher level of the self even than the buddhic. Observe in each case the authority which it has for the recipient, who becomes aware " with absolute conviction " or who knows " without the shadow of doubt ".

> Truth is within ourselves ; it takes no rise
> From outward things, whate'er you may believe.
> There is an inmost centre in us all,
> Where truth abides in fulness ; and around,
> Wall upon wall, the gross flesh hems it in,
> This perfect, clear perception—which is truth.
>
> A baffling and perverting carnal mesh
> Binds it, and makes all error : and to *know*,
> Rather consists in opening out a way
> Whence the imprisoned splendour may escape,
> Than in effecting entry for a light
> Supposed to be without.*

So wrote Browning : most of the great poets, and certainly all the great mystics, agree with him. It has seldom, however, been viewed generally as a proposition of other than academic interest, and obviously it is uncomfortable teaching for those who delight in the organisation of belief, or desire to repose under the wing of external Authority. There is a story † told of how the devil and a friend of his were walking along the street, when, some distance away, they saw a man stoop down, pick something up and put it in his pocket.

* Browning : *Paracelsus*.   † Carlo Suarès : *Krishnamurti* (1933).

The friend said to the devil, " What did that man pick up ? " " He picked up a piece of Truth," said the devil. " That is a bad business for you, then," said his friend. " Oh, not at all," the devil replied. " I am going to let him organise it."

Keeping in mind the distinction between knowledge and belief, two questions may be asked. What kind of authority should we accord to the recorded teachings of the world's great spiritual geniuses ? What value, if any, is to be ascribed to organised systems of belief based upon them ?

The answer to the first question would technically involve us in a decision as to the measure of historical veracity attached to records which were built upon oral traditions and compiled in their present forms many years after the events. Such decisions are for experts only, and unfortunately the experts do not speak with one voice. Let us therefore adopt a middle path and assume as regards the teachings of the sages that the spirit of their teaching has survived, together frequently with easily remembered parables, and in some cases even actual statements which must have staggered the first hearers and are too unexpected to have been invented. The numerical devices adopted in Buddhism, where we have " four " noble truths and an " eightfold " path, probably also assisted to secure a fairly reliable oral transmission. Let us also assume that in the course of the centuries, especially in the period before the earliest manuscripts, a considerable amount of error and misrepresentation crept in. On such assumptions what kind of authority should we accord to the recorded teachings ? A Christian might say, " I believe the teaching of Jesus Christ because I believe in the historic person and his unique spiritual status ". A Buddhist might say something similar of the Buddha. But there is a vast gulf between this affirmation of " belief " and the mystical affirmation of " knowledge " : " I know the teaching of Jesus Christ is true because it expresses my own experience ". The first is trusting in another's formulation of his mystical insights, and how much the learner can grasp of the experience behind them depends on his own intellectual and buddhic development. The second has the infallible inner authority of first-hand experience. The kind of authority to be ascribed to a great spiritual leader's recorded teachings is therefore that which we might give to a map, a signpost or a guide-book. We may believe in them, we may trust them, they point out a way and can help us to travel wisely and profitably on our spiritual journeyings, but they are no substitute for our own first-hand experience and discovery.

The answer to the second question, " What value, if any, is to be attached to organised systems of belief based upon them ? " recalls to us the supreme irony of the history of religions. Writing of Kabir,* the fifteenth-century Indian mystical poet, Evelyn Underhill says :

> " His fate has been that of many revealers of Reality. A hater of religious exclusivism, and seeking above all things to initiate men into the liberty of the children of God, his followers have honoured his memory by re-erecting in a new place the barriers which he laboured to cast down."

Is there a single revealer of Reality who has not in some measure met this fate ?

It is the tragedy of all " belief " that sooner or later it is codified and organised into a system. The intentions of the early enthusiasts are doubtless good ; the zeal for intellectual clarity and consistency may be regarded as in the best traditions of science. But what results is invariably in the worst traditions of nationalism. People get together in a common defensive posture against those who do not accept their creed and their outlook. If the posture were wholly defensive it would be tragic enough, but it has all too often been offensive and contemptuous. The creed doubtless intended at first by honest men to be a useful working basis—the highest common factor, as it were, of intelligible belief—becomes a touchstone of orthodoxy, and departures from it a ground for bitter persecution. Macaulay described the theory of one great branch of the Christian Church as " I am in the right and you are in the wrong. When you are the stronger, you ought to tolerate me, for it is your duty to tolerate truth : but when I am stronger, I shall persecute you, for it is my duty to persecute error." It is the supreme irony of history that great mystical geniuses who have reverenced human freedom as perhaps few others have done, who have taught the brotherhood of all men, and the supremacy of Love, whose presence on earth has been a benediction, and whose teaching has enriched our common life beyond measure, should come to be regarded as founders of systems of religious belief and doctrine which have divided men from each other and been the causes of hatred, persecution, intolerance and bloodshed on a vast scale.

It might be thought, as we reflect on this picture, that the verdict should properly be given against all organised systems of belief. Let us consider, however, that the alternatives for the majority of people are either adherence to some such system, or no religious belief at all. The large majority of people are as yet insufficiently developed on the buddhic level to be capable of a sustained voyage of spiritual discovery—of that effort of self-discipline and meditation

---

* *Poems of Kabir*, trans. by Rabindranath Tagore (Macmillan).

B

capable of yielding indubitable insights and knowledge. For these, an organised framework of religious belief having symbolic expressions on a still lower level of significance, as in ritual and ceremonial, may be the most appropriate and satisfactory expression of religious feeling. To deplore this is to quarrel with the time-process. We do not complain that a baboon has no appreciation of beauty, that primitive man has left us no legacy of mathematics or music, or that Central African tribes are not conversant with the finer shades of courtesy or self-sacrifice. The limitations and the tragedy of the contending religious systems of belief may be the growing pains of humanity on its spiritual pilgrimage.

Bondage to these systems has to be transcended by the person who seeks " knowledge ", for this can only be found within. I am of the opinion that in our day there are increasing numbers of people hungry for this knowledge and unsatisfied by systems of belief, who are not willing to exchange the lonely quest for enlightenment for the contentment of accepted authority. Those who tell us that if only we will believe certain things, and " have faith ", all will be well and our spiritual questing will be over, do not understand either the importance of intellectual integrity or the true religious attitude. For such a one there is no rest from the striving to see what he cannot yet see, and to become what as yet he is not.

" God offers to every man ", says Emerson, " the choice between truth and repose. Take which you please ; you can never have both."

PART I
THE DATA OF NATURAL SCIENCE

Chapter

2

MACROCOSM AND MICROCOSM

"Thou, Lord, in the beginning hast laid the foundation of the earth, and the heavens are the work of Thy hands. They shall perish, but Thou remainest; and they all shall wax old as doth a garment; and as a vesture shalt Thou fold them up and they shall be changed; but Thou art the same, and Thy years shall not fail."

PSALM 102.

"Around the ancient track marched, rank on rank,
The army of unalterable law."

MEREDITH.

I TAKE up a text-book of philosophy and I read, "Space is not a conception which has been derived from outward experience; it is a necessary representation *a priori* which serves for the foundation of all external perceptions". Again I read, "Time has no real existence of its own but serves for the representation of internal states".

I seem to recall that when I was a boy persons who were older, and thought to be wiser than myself, occasionally encouraged the taking of medicine from a spoon with the words "Open your mouth and shut your eyes"—an attitude making singular demands upon faith. If the philosopher's medicine is held out to us with the assurance that it will quench the fever of confused thinking, we shall probably take it also; but we must claim first the right of one little peep at the size of the dose we are called upon to swallow.

I. THE UNIVERSE OF SPACE

From time immemorial Man has looked up at the midnight sky. On a clear night with the naked eye some 2,000 or 3,000 stars can possibly be distinguished, apart from the unresolved light of the Milky Way. There can be few thoughtful people who have not at some time been stirred by the sublimity of this spectacle and found themselves wondering what it all means. Such emotions must have been entertained for half a million years—ever since Man first emerged from his ape-like ancestry and began to contemplate his environment. It was, however, in 1610—when Galileo first pointed a telescope at the night sky—that the age of modern scientific astronomy may be

37

said to have begun.   The work of his successors with more powerful instruments has disclosed a Universe beyond the wildest dreams of the imagination.   The account of this has been presented so well and authoritatively in recent years by Jeans, Eddington, Hoyle and others, that a brief summary here will suffice.   The use of large telescopes such as the 100-inch reflector of Mt. Wilson shows that the galaxy consists of stars to an estimated number of perhaps 10,000 million.   In this galaxy our own sun is but a single star intermediate in size, luminosity, temperature and other general characteristics. The density of stars in the field of a telescope depends on the direction in which it is pointed, and indicates that the general shape of the galaxy is something like that of a huge bun or convex lens.   In this distribution the sun lies apparently fairly close to the galactic plane, but by no means near to its centre.   (The light-year is the unit of distance used in astronomy and, as its name suggests, is the distance light travels in a year.   Since the speed of light is 186,000 miles a second, the light-year is about six million million miles.)   In these units the dimensions of the galaxy are about 60,000 light-years along a diameter—that is, from one extreme edge of the Milky Way to the other—but only comparatively few light-years in thickness—that is, along an axis perpendicular to the plane of the galaxy.   The appearance of the Milky Way thus arises from the layers upon layers of stars which are observed if the telescope is pointed in the galactic plane outwards towards the edge of the " bun ", as compared with the more limited depth if the telescope is pointed perpendicular to the galactic plane.

One of the most naturally occurring questions is this : how do astronomers form any idea of the dimensions of the galaxy ?   How can they tell how far away from us a particular star may be ?   Everyone knows that as we change our position in space—e.g., by travelling in a train—nearer objects appear to move relative to the more distant ones.   In six months the earth moves 185,740,000 miles from one side of its orbit round the sun to the opposite side, and as a result of this a few of the nearer stars show minute displacements relative to the distant ones.   From this displacement it can be calculated that the nearest star to us, Proxima Centauri, is twenty-five million million miles—or about 4·27 light-years—distant.   The brilliant star Sirius, so prominent in the night sky, is about 8·65 light-years. Only an extremely small fraction of stars are, however, near enough to make this method of calculation possible.   Several other methods have been devised to take us farther.   There is a class of star called " Cepheid Variables ".   These are characterised by regular fluctuations of brightness, the cause of this being unknown.   In the so-called Magellanic Cloud a considerable number of these stars is found, which may all be assumed to be at approximately the same distance from the Earth. The discovery was made that the periodic time of light fluctuation depends on the apparent brightness, and since the Cepheids in the Magellanic Cloud are all at the same distance, this means that the period of light-fluctuation depends on their *intrinsic* brightness. Cepheid variables are therefore like lighthouses, whose intrinsic brightness or luminosity is known from their periodicity. Knowing that the apparent brightness of any star falls off inversely as the square of its distance from us, it follows that wherever a Cepheid variable appears in the Universe, its distance can be estimated from an observation of its apparent brightness and its period of light fluctuation. Other methods are available, and taken all together they give us the approximate scale of the galaxy, which we have already mentioned. Moreover, observations of stellar motion show that the whole galaxy is in rotation like a giant catherine wheel, making a complete revolution about every 200 million years.

Far outside the galaxy, as we now know, are the spiral nebulæ, which Herschel first picturesquely called " island universes ". It is clear that these are huge aggregations of matter in rotation, condensing into stars, and that they are comparable in mass with our own galaxy, although naturally in various stages of evolution. The nearest of these, the Andromeda nebula, is found to be about 700,000 light-years distant and to have a mass equivalent to about 3,500 million stars. It is therefore clearly well outside our own system of stars. The large telescopes of Mt. Wilson and Palomar have recorded many millions of these galaxies distributed through space, at an average distance apart of about 1,500,000 light-years. The most distant of these observed up to the present is about 1,000 million light-years away, but there seems no reason to doubt that as bigger telescopes are built with greater light-gathering power the number of such galaxies known to us will increase. Does this go on to infinity, or is there any limit ? We do not know—but there have been some interesting scientific speculations. According to a theory of Eddington, the total number of galaxies may be of the order of 100,000 million, for this Universe which would then contain matter equal to about $1 \cdot 08 \times 10^{22}$ stars of the average mass of the sun would cause light to bend on its path and return ultimately to its starting point. Such space would, as mathematicians say, be "finite but unbounded ", much as the surface of a globe is finite and unbounded, so that if you walked far enough in a straight line over the globe you would return to your starting point.

Figures such as these are so far beyond our imagination that even illustrations on a reduced scale can help us only a little to grasp the basic facts. Instead of 1.08×10^{22} stars, let us think of this number of grains of sand. Taking about 5,000 grains to the cubic centimetre, this quantity of sand would cover the whole land-surface of the Earth to a depth of about 1 cm. If instead it formed a beach 2 metres deep and 100 metres wide, the beach would need to be about 6,000 million miles long.

The spectroscope is another instrument which, when used in conjunction with a large telescope, has played a most important part in our knowledge of the world outside us. The spectroscope analyses light which falls upon its slit into its component colours or wave-lengths. Every chemical element has certain characteristic wave-lengths of light which it can emit—so that the appearance of these in a specific part of the spectrum is an infallible indication of the presence of that element in the source of light. Applied to the light of the Sun, the spectroscope has shown that most of the chemical elements known on earth occur also in the Sun. Applied to starlight it has shown us that the same chemical elements are there, too, though often under vastly different conditions of temperature, and this has permitted a valuable temperature classification of the stars.

When a source of light is moving in an observer's line of sight (i.e., towards or directly away from him), this causes a displacement of the spectral lines according to a well-known principle of Döppler. The spectroscope thus makes it possible to determine whether any star is moving towards us or away from us, and also at what speed. When the light of the spiral nebulæ was studied in this way, a most surprising observation was made. With the exception of the few nearest nebulæ, all of them were found to be receding from us, and the rate of recession was found to be proportional to the distance the nebulæ were away. For each million light-years distance the speed of recession is about 100 miles per second, and this remarkable feature led Eddington to formulate his theory of an expanding Universe. From the observed data it would seem that all the galaxies would double their distances apart every 1,300 million years. The familiar law of gravitation which we owe to Newton expresses the force of *attraction* between one mass and another, and it may be asked : Why, then, are the spiral nebulæ moving farther apart ? Einstein's formulation of the Law of Gravitation includes a new term which represents a force of cosmical repulsion proportional to distance apart. While this term is inappreciable for inter-stellar distances, it becomes important for inter-nebular distances, and appears to account for the observed recession of the spiral nebulæ. If the only evidence for the cosmical constant which governs this term was this achievement, it might not seem very impressive: we might be tempted to regard it wholly as a mathematical device to account for observed data. Professor Weyl, however, used it to show that the two great and hitherto independent fields of gravitation and electro-magnetism could be correlated through its agency. Eddington has in fact written: " I would as soon think of reverting to Newtonian theory as of dropping the cosmical constant." * In the development of brilliant, and indeed most remarkable, speculations of his own, Eddington has given grounds for supposing that this same cosmical constant may control the scale of structure inside the atoms of matter. If this should ultimately be accepted by scientists, it will fittingly link together the almost inconceivably great and inconceivably small in the material Universe.

There is one other feature which should be noted in our survey: this is the extraordinary emptiness of space. When we recall that our own galaxy contains perhaps 10,000 million stars, we must also recall the vast extent of space over which they are dispersed. Jeans has picturesquely said that if Waterloo Station contained six micro-scopic specks of dust, of about $\frac{1}{3000}$ inch in diameter, it would be more crowded with dust than space is with stars. We may use another scale, and suppose the Sun, with its diameter of 860,000 miles, to be reduced to the size of a dried pea, say $\frac{1}{4}$ inch in diameter. The Earth would then be a minute speck of dust circling round it about 27 inches away, while the nearest star would be another dried pea about 115 miles away. We should scarcely regard space in which dried peas were at this distance apart as crowded with matter.

2. THE UNIVERSE IN TIME

It is obvious from what has been said that our knowledge of what the Universe is like is inextricably mixed up with time. If tonight we look through a large telescope at the most distant nebulæ, the light by which we see them left its source many millions of years ago. The light from Andromeda left its source 700,000 years ago, the light from Sirius over eight and a half years ago, the light from the Sun a little over eight minutes ago. It is clear that we can never know what the Universe is really like at what we call the present moment, and that our knowledge of space and our knowledge of time are inevitably mixed up together, because of the finite velocity of light. All we are concerned to do at present is to form an impression of the time-scale involved in astronomy and how it has been constructed.

Let us start with our own planet, the Earth. Geologists can

* Eddington : *The Expanding Universe.*

measure the average depths of different strata, and by observing how
rapid is the rate of deposition today, can form an approximate idea
how long the whole process must have taken.   Of course a great
source of error may arise in assuming that this rate has always been
the same ; but at least it is clear that a time-period of some hundreds
of millions of years is involved.   Physics fortunately provides another
method of estimating the Earth's age, picturesquely called the radio-
active clock.   The heavy element uranium breaks down spontaneously, changing into other unstable chemical elements on its way to
the stable element lead.   The time involved in each of these stages
has been determined with some accuracy, so that it is only necessary
to find the ratio of uranium to lead in a mineral sample to say how old
it is.   This and similar methods suggest that the age of the Earth
is about 2,000 million years, and that it must certainly be less than
3,000 million years.

The age of the stars is estimated in a different way, into the detail
of which we need not enter, but in the result the stars in the galaxy
are believed to be many thousands of millions of years old.

Anyone reflecting on this enormous time-scale must n turally be
intrigued by the source of energy in the stars.   Our Sun must
presumably in the past have radiated heat and light at not less than
the present rate, and this has, according to previous calculations, been
going on for thousands of millions of years.   Energy cannot appear
from nowhere.   What, then, is its source ?   It cannot be chemical.
If the Sun were a solid mass of coal burning, it could not have lasted
more than a few thousand years.   Helmholtz advanced the theory a
century ago that the Sun was contracting and that the potential energy
made available by this process generated the observed heat and light.
Kelvin showed, however, that with the Sun at its present size this
would only account for the past fifty million years of its energetic
life.

There is, in fact, no adequate source of the Sun's enormous energy
output other than the conversion of some of its mass into energy.
The relationship between mass and energy has become familiar
through Einstein's work ($E = mc^2$).   Here E is the quantity of
radiation which appears when m grammes of matter disappear,
while $c = 3 \times 10^{10}$ cm. per second is the velocity of light.   Matter
and radiation seem to be different forms of the fundamental energy
of the material Universe.   Matter is a kind of " frozen " static form
of this energy, and radiation its elusive ethereal form which cannot
stay still, but is compelled to move about at the enormous speed of
light.   The energy output of the Sun is adequately accounted for if
four million tons of solar matter are converted into radiation every

second. This amounts to the impressive figure of about 130 million million tons per year, an amount which is, however, almost negligible compared with the mass of the Sun itself—2×10^{27} tons. It makes clear that this source of energy is adequate even to cover the long life of the Sun.

In recent years the fission of uranium and plutonium by neutrons has been used to make available " atomic energy ". Such energy results from the fact that a small equivalent amount of matter disappears in the process. This fission process is, however, an artificial one, in the sense that it almost certainly has no natural occurrence in the stars. The basic process in the stars is believed to be the synthesis of helium from hydrogen, for this nuclear change involves the disappearance of mass, and the consequent production of energy. We may ask what becomes of the enormous amount of energy radiated away by the stars into space. No one can answer the question. All we can say is that, so far as we can see, in some distant future the whole process of transforming matter into radiation must come to an end with a kind of " heat-death ", when the whole temperature of space and the residual matter in it cannot remain much above the absolute zero of temperature.* Looking back into a distant past before the birth of the spiral nebulæ from some large and possibly uniform dispersion of matter can offer us no further understanding. Sir James Jeans † says very suggestively :

" Travelling as far back in time as we can, brings us not to the creation of the picture but to its edge ; the creation of the picture lies as much outside the picture as the artist is outside his canvas. On this view, discussing the creation of the universe in terms of time and space is like trying to discover the artist and the action of painting by going to the edge of the picture. This brings us very near to those philosophical systems which regard the universe as a thought in the mind of its Creator, thereby reducing all discussion of material creation to futility."

3. LIFE IN THE MATERIAL UNIVERSE

From the scientific point of view (i.e., keeping to deductions which may be reasonably drawn from sense data) it would seem that living things like those we know must be comparatively rare in the Universe. First as to the stars themselves. The great majority have surface temperatures ranging from 20,000° C. down to 2,500° C., and there

* In Hoyle's fascinating book *The Nature of the Universe* (Blackwell, 1950), this conclusion is avoided by the postulate of a continuous creation of hydrogen.
† *The Universe Around Us* (C.U.P., 1929).

are so few stars with temperatures below this that we may assume cold, dark stars to be rare. At stellar temperatures solids and liquids cannot exist. It seems that matter in the Universe is almost everywhere at a high temperature, except where planetary systems have been born and small globes have had a chance to cool. Jeans' theory of the formation of a planetary system by the near approach of two stars showed that such an event as a near-collision must be very infrequent. Jeans suggested that perhaps one star in 100,000 may have planets; Eddington suggested that not one in 100 million has planets under the right conditions for life to appear. Jeans * commented on this:

> " It seems incredible that the Universe can have been designed primarily to produce life like our own; had it been so, surely we might have expected to find a better proportion between the magnitude of the mechanism and the amount of the product."

Eddington † commented:

> " We know the prodigality of Nature. How many acorns are scattered for one that grows to an oak ? And need she be more careful of her stars than of her acorns ? "

Hoyle,‡ on the modern view that planetary systems arise from the debris following the explosion of a super-nova when the latter is a member of a binary system, calculates that there may be as many as 10 million stars with planetary systems in our own galaxy. He suggests that perhaps one in ten of these may be habitable by living things.

Even so, it is the extreme rarity of the experiment which is the most impressive feature. When we consider our own family of planets from this standpoint, the likelihood of life on any of them does not seem very great—or should we say, more accurately, life *like our own*; for one of the most remarkable aspects of Life is the degree of its adaptability to varied environments.

From Mercury, the planet closest to the Sun, the solar disc would have an area seven times as great as if seen from the Earth. The planet is not independently rotating, and therefore turns the same side always towards the Sun. This side is probably at a temperature of about 350° C., while the dark side, which receives no heat and light, is probably extremely cold. In any case, the planet is too small to retain any atmosphere.

Venus has an atmosphere which, according to spectroscopic

* Jeans : *The Mysterious Universe* (C.U.P., 1930).
† Eddington : *The Nature of the Physical World* (C.U.P., 1928).
‡ Hoyle : *The Nature of the Universe* (Blackwell, 1950), p. 88.

evidence, contains abundant carbon dioxide—several hundred times the amount in the Earth's atmosphere—but very little oxygen and water-vapour. It is considered that the huge mass of carbon dioxide would exert a " greenhouse " effect, and probably raise the temperature beneath it to that of boiling water : a condition not favourable for life as we know it. The surface detail of Mars has probably been studied more closely than that of any other planet. There is a substantial atmosphere containing some oxygen and water-vapour, though by no means as much as on Earth. The polar caps are believed to be frozen water, and the reddish colour of much of the surface suggests oxides of iron, in which form much of the former free oxygen in the atmosphere may now be combined. The surface does show seasonal changes of colour which suggest that in the Martian spring there is an awakening of vegetation. We must admit that conditions on Mars do not completely rule out life as we know it.

On Jupiter the solar disc will only have about one-fifth the apparent diameter it has on the Earth. Calculations of the surface temperature, based on the amount of heat it will receive from the Sun and also direct radiometer observations, suggest the extreme cold of — 120° C. The spectrum of the planet shows evidence of ammonia and methane in its atmosphere. The temperatures of Saturn, Uranus and Neptune will be lower still, and methane appears to be increasingly abundant. On these distant planets the Sun will have apparent diameters of respectively a tenth, a twentieth and a thirtieth the diameter which we see on Earth. We can sum up this survey by saying that on none of the other planets of our solar system could the human body as we know it survive. On the other hand, we know of the extraordinary adaptive mechanisms found among living things, and we obviously cannot rule out the possibility that Mind may under widely different environmental conditions be using the same chemical elements to make very different experiments in Life. We do not know, and perhaps cannot hope to know, except by a much deeper knowledge of the powers of Mind.

The Universe which astronomy discloses to us is one completely outside Man's control—one of which he can only hope to be a remote spectator. However large may be his future telescopes and equipment, his data will necessarily still be very limited and his conclusions can only be drawn from the interpretation of visual sense-data. The greatest instrumental advances can but give Man more visual sense-data, and therefore knowledge *of the same kind*. It is by exploring the world of causes rather than effects, of purposes rather than achievements, that we may hope to discover the deeper significance of our environment. It is in the first instance to that mysterious entity, Mind, which is the instrument of these purposes, and which, while not spatio-temporal itself, is so clearly interested in, and equipped to interpret our world of space, time and matter, that we shall have to turn for clues. It is not by the interpretation of more and more visual sense-data that we can expect to discover the meaning of the cosmic drama, but by discovering more of the nature and powers of the interpreter.

4. THE ATOMIC WORLD

If the relationship of Man to the starry Universe should lead him to a fitting humility in the light of his material insignificance, he might lay claim to the status of a whole galaxy in relation to the world of atoms and molecules. It is to this world we must now turn our attention. It is a world of small-scale processes, our knowledge of which we owe to modern physics, and it is not a whit less impressive in its character than the large-scale processes revealed by astronomy. A good microscope will magnify about 3,000 times, but this will not help us to see the molecules of matter. The smallest particle of common salt which such a microscope could reveal still contains something of the order of a million molecules. A cubic centimetre of water—half a thimbleful—contains $3 \cdot 3 \times 10^{22}$ molecules, but the diameter of each of these molecules is only about $4 \cdot 6 \times 10^{-8}$ cm. This really conveys nothing to our imagination, nor perhaps does it convey much more to say that if they were spread uniformly over the whole surface of the Earth there would be about sixty-five of them on every square millimetre of the Earth's surface. We are clearly in a world as remote from normal experience as the conditions in the interiors of stars. It is the collisions of such molecules moving at speeds of about 500 yards a second which create the pressure in gases. It is the forces between them which give to solid bodies their stability of form and account for the varied properties of matter. No physicist or chemist has the slightest doubt in his mind of the existence of matter in the form of molecules, although they must remain for ever beyond our visual perception.

Molecules in their turn are synthesised from atoms, of which ninety-two natural varieties are known, hydrogen being the lightest and simplest, and uranium the heaviest and most complex. Some molecules, like common salt, contain only two atoms—one of sodium and one of chlorine—others, like hæmoglobin, the red pigment in blood, contain many thousands of atoms. The study of all these is the province of chemistry. It is strange, with our present knowledge, to reflect that from the time of the speculations of Democritus up to 1911, when Rutherford published his "planetary theory" of atomic structure, it was assumed without question that atoms were the ultimate particles of matter, and in their nature indivisible. It is now commonplace belief that the typical atom is something like a solar system in miniature. The central sun, which has a positive charge and carries almost all the mass, is called the nucleus, while the negatively charged electrons move in planetary orbits around it. The gravitational force which operates in the solar system is here negligible compared with the powerful electrical forces of attraction. The simplest atom, hydrogen, consists of one negative electron circulating round a positive nucleus called a proton, the latter being about 1,850 times as massive as the former. The most complex atom, uranium, has ninety-two electrons circulating in orbits of various sizes and shapes round a central nucleus which has a positive charge sufficient to neutralise and hold in their orbits these ninety-two electrons.

This planetary model of the atom, suggested by Rutherford in 1911 and developed mathematically by Bohr in 1913, represented a remarkable step forward in our fundamental conceptions of matter. It brought order into chaos and helped us to account, among other things, for the vast wealth of data of spectroscopy. We shall see later that the truth is really embodied in the mathematics, not in the model, and that in constructing models to illustrate the mathematics, we are transposing our ideas of the familiar large-scale world into a region where they probably have no validity. For purposes of simple exposition, however, we must necessarily continue to write in terms of the model which illustrates the mathematical truth. The most impressive feature of the model from a general standpoint is that it reveals what we had hitherto supposed to be "solid substance" as practically empty space. Consider the electron of the hydrogen atom which moves in an orbit having a diameter just over 10^{-8} cm. The electron itself is a negative particle with a diameter of about 2×10^{-13} cm. This is only $\frac{1}{50,000}$ the size of its orbit, and the positive nucleus is somewhere about the same size. We may visualise the degree of emptiness by regarding the nucleus and the electron as dried peas of $\frac{1}{4}$ inch diameter. Their distance apart would then be about 175 yards; in other words, one of them circles round the other (regarded as stationary because of its high mass) in a circle of 175 yards radius.

Atoms do not differ greatly in size, and this same "emptiness" is characteristic of them all. If all the nuclei and electrons in a man could be somehow collected together, they would constitute a speck which might just be discerned by the naked eye. The substantiality of matter is thus an appearance only, and depends on the scale on which we are built, and in particular on the sensitivity range of our special senses. The sizes of atoms and molecules are of the order of a thousand times smaller than the wave-lengths of light to which our eyes respond. Material objects therefore scatter and reflect light-waves back to our eyes, and in so doing give no indication of their porous structure. On the other hand, as is well known, X-rays which have a wave-length of the same order as molecular sizes reveal to the photographic plate the " granular " structure of matter. If we had eyes sensitive to X-rays instead of visible light, we should have a strangely different impression of the material world. A razor-edge would look like a saw, and much that we describe as opaque would be transparent, or porous. In so far as we want to understand the nature of the physical world, it is most important to bear in mind how relative is all appearance. The properties or qualities which are ascribed to a material object depend on the selectivity or power of the instruments used to examine it—and among these instruments we must include the five special senses. We might look at a picture from a reasonable distance and appreciate its beauty and significance. If we looked at it through a magnifying glass, we might learn something more about the pigment and its dispersal, but we should lose our awareness of the picture as such. If we used X-rays and photography, we might discover something of the molecular constitution of the pigment and canvas, but all colour would have vanished. On the other hand, we might walk so far away from our picture that it is indistinguishable from any other picture, and in this way its qualities are unperceived and its significance lost for us. The range of physical conditions within which the picture retains significance for us as a picture is of course determined by the particular structure of our eyes : the focal length and aperture of the eye-lens, and the density of rods and cones on the retina. If we could imagine a person with eyes insensitive to visible light, but sensitive only to ultra-violet or infra-red, then for him the canvas would hold no picture. Depending on the range of his sensitivity, he might not even see frame, canvas or any part of it, although his senses of touch and smell might reveal its presence. A race of such persons would have a very different conception of the appearance of the world from ours, and it is cogent to ask ourselves whether our world-picture can claim any greater validity than theirs. Are we going to suppose that we, who have eyes sensitive to wave-lengths of light lying between 7×10^{-5} cm. (red) and 4×10^{-5} cm. (violet), have, because of this peculiar selectivity, a truer perception of the world as it is than any other ? There can obviously be no logical justification for such an idea. The picture familiar to us because of our special senses would not necessarily exist for another race with different special senses, and vice versa. It might be thought that perhaps these different races, prone to quarrel about the appearance of the world, could come to some common agreement based upon their sense of touch. The possibility of doing so would depend on the relative degrees of sensitivity of this sense. To a highly sensitive touch the canvas surface might be rough and irregular, to a less sensitive touch smooth and plane, and to a person whose sensation of touch required high pressure to excite it the canvas would perhaps not be there at all. The canvas might break before the pressure of the observer's hand reached the necessary minimum to reveal it.

It is not easy to imagine the conception of the material world which would be possessed by a blind person who had simultaneously no sense of ordinary touch. It is, I think, doubtful if any conception of space would have arisen at all, for he would have no awareness of material objects around him, and therefore no need to picture space in which they were located. He would, moreover, have no sense of movement from one place to another. His only chance of inferring the existence of space might be to account for changes in the intensity of sounds and smells.

It is an interesting exercise to consider how different our picture of the world would be if one or other of the special senses had never been created. Without an organ of vision, for example, there would be no astronomy, very little chemistry, biology and geology, and only a small fraction of physics left to us. All the visual arts would go— or at least the two-dimensional ones. But we need not pursue this line of thought further. We are each rather like a prisoner in a round tower permitted to look out through five slits in the walls at the landscape outside. It is presumptuous to suppose we can perceive the whole of the landscape through these slits—although I think there is good evidence that the prisoner can sometimes have a glimpse out of the top !

We have seen that to our ordinary vision matter presents the appearance of colour, solidity and substantiality. In the scientist's picture it is an assemblage of nuclei with their planetary electrons, producing by the speed of their motion and the play of their electrical forces the hardness, the opacity and other qualities which we normally recognise. We must bear in mind that these two descriptions, as we have already said, are two among many possible descriptions of appearance, and that they are all abstractions from the background. The scientific picture is constructed by abstracting the metrical data (viz., those properties of matter which can be measured and related to each other mathematically), and then trying to find a model which would illustrate these properties. It does so by ignoring the subjective elements of experience, such as colour, sound and scent, because these are all the things which differ supposedly with the type of special sense available for recording them. In so far as science correlates the metrical data mathematically it is on safe ground, but as soon as it presumes to present us with a model of " what an atom would *look* like " it places itself in the ranks of all those hypothetical observers with special organs of vision who also have their own ideas of what things *look* like. Of all these, we have seen that no picture can claim to be truer than another. Each observer has seen things through his own tinted glasses from a slit in his own round tower.*

* In an appendix will be found a continuation of this chapter intended for those with a training in physics. The ordinary reader need not trouble with this.

Chapter

3

LIFE: PATTERN AND PURPOSE

Here they have wrought a thousand years to dower
With lovelier form the unbeholden flower,
To hide the moonlight in a gem, or bring
A subtler motion to an insect's wing,
Or to a bird's song add a note that tells
The joy that in their lonely labour dwells.
Here they have striven, age by age, to write
In things that perish, tidings infinite ;
In things that change, the wonder that abides,
The hope that beckons, and the love that hides.

SIDNEY ROYSE LYSAGHT.

I. THE NATURAL UNIT OF LIFE

THE most notable differences between living and non-living things, between organisms and chemical substances, are probably two in number. First, there is what we may describe as maintained co-ordination. An organism is distinguished as being a centre of co-ordinated activity, and it maintains itself as such by interactions with its environment. A mineral remains what it is through no interaction with its environment. Although the matter of which the organism is composed gradually changes, the organism retains its form and composition. If it is injured (not too badly), processes of healing are initiated to restore the normal state. If its environment is changed (but not too much), it adapts itself actively to meet the change. This effort and ability to maintain its structure and function as a whole are most characteristic of living things. Secondly, there is the phenomenon of reproduction, by which a process initiated in a part of itself gives rise to another complete organism of the same kind. There are other differences between the living and non-living world, but the two we have mentioned seem fundamental and unquestioned. They are characteristic not only of plants and animals which are highly complex organisms, but also of the individual cells of which they are composed. We shall therefore consider first the structure and function of a typical cell, for it is here that we may expect to find this new factor of life manifesting in its simplest form.

Under the microscope all plant and animal tissues are seen to be composed of cells. The cell is the natural unit of " life ", and plays much the same fundamental part in biology as the atom does in chemistry. Cells are of many and varied types, according to the functions they have to perform, but certain general characteristics which they possess in common will be first described. Every cell is bounded by a thin wall or membrane which contains within it a mass of jelly-like substance, and in this floats a nucleus. The nucleus is obviously of prime importance, for it plays a dominant part in reproduction, and if it is removed the cell dies. The jelly-like surrounding substance, called cytoplasm, is a reticulated structure, and has scattered throughout its volume a large number of minute protein particles. On these internal surfaces, which are of considerable area, scores of complex chemical processes proceed continuously. There is a constant movement or streaming of the cell-contents hither and thither, so that the whole process conveys the impression of persistent and purposeful activity. What are these activities? The cell membrane does not wholly isolate the cell from its surroundings. It is semi-permeable—that is, it allows a selective passage of substances through its meshes. Oxygen is taken in and carbon dioxide excreted—the process known as respiration. Food-stuffs are taken in and waste products excreted. In animal cells the foodstuffs are absorbed usually as sugars, fats and proteins : these are broken down into simpler forms, and then synthesised into the complex materials from which the cell is made (or which perhaps other distant cells of the organism may require). In plant cells the process is essentially one of synthesis from carbon dioxide and water using the energy of sunlight, together with other substances absorbed from the soil. This immense variety of complex chemical activities, in which material is absorbed in one form, transformed, and rebuilt into an enormous variety of other complex forms, is characteristic of living cells. The term metabolism is used to describe it. The whole of these processes of oxidation, hydrolysis, rearrangement and synthesis take place within a very limited temperature range— all facilitated and controlled by colloidal catalysts like chlorophyll and by other enzymes. The elegance of these methods is most apparent when they are compared with the techniques designed to reproduce them in the laboratory. Moreover, it must be remembered that all the catalysts and enzymes which work this magic are themselves the product of the life-activity of the original cell. The microscopic living cell is a physico-chemical laboratory in which simultaneously, and without interfering with each other, scores of complex processes are constantly proceeding. It is a self-maintaining system, which, from the point of view of its energy interchanges with its environment, conforms to the laws of physics and chemistry (notably the principle of conservation of energy). The mystery of life lies not at this point, nor even in the elegance and complexity of its chemical processes, but in the fact that the living cell always acts (and reacts to changes) as though with the purpose or intention of maintaining itself on some basic pattern or design. Its processes of repair and healing are a commentary on this.

When we look at the reproductive activity of cells—the process of cell division—we observe a series of remarkable events found in all plants and animals above those of the very lowest grade. The cell nucleus within its own membrane begins to undergo change. A coiled, thread-like structure forms, and subsequently breaks up into a number of segments, known as chromosomes. These are characteristic in number and structure for each animal and plant, and are believed to be the carriers of all inheritable qualities. Another tiny structure, the centrosome, which we have not previously mentioned, also becomes active. This is normally a small, specialised body which lies quiescent just outside the nucleus and is distinguished by the curious feature that filaments appear to radiate from it. It now splits into two and these halves move to opposite sides of the nucleus, being apparently connected with each other by radiating filaments or streamers. The nuclear membrane gradually disappears, and the threads from the two centrosomes attach themselves to the chromosomes, which now split lengthwise. The centrosomes, acting as though they were attracting centres, cause the threads to contract, so that one set of chromosomes is drawn to one side and the other set to the opposite side. Two separate nuclei now form from these groups, and at the same time the parent cell forms a constriction and divides into two daughter cells. This intricate pattern of changes is going on in countless myriads of cells of every living thing, yet we know virtually nothing of its causation or control. This most commonplace and fundamental phenomenon of living cells is wrapped in mystery, and nothing that we at present know of the properties of matter and the laws of physics and chemistry is likely to offer a solution.

The cell, then, is the smallest unit manifesting life. This it has in virtue of its own nature, and not merely as part of an organism. Fragments of living tissue have in fact been kept alive in a suitable culture medium for many years after their separation from the organism of which they were originally a part. The culture medium provides the nourishment necessary for this, but unless the cells are transferred at intervals to fresh media, they are poisoned by their own excretory products. It is interesting to observe that specialised cells, such as muscle, nerve, etc., after much cell division under these conditions lose their specialised character and revert to a simpler generalised type of cell. Their specialised structure and function would appear to have arisen from, and been maintained by, the overriding control of the greater organism of which they were a part. It is as though the cell has its own simple and generalised life-pattern which, however, is modified and made specialised by the overruling life-pattern of the organism.

2. CELLS AND ORGANISMS

Unicellular organisms are found in both the plant and animal kingdoms. Advance in structure and function arises with multicellular organisms, where groups of cells become specialised to fulfil particular tasks. Thus in plants we have roots, stem, leaves and reproductive organs. All the cells of the plant then come to depend on the green cells of the leaves for their carbohydrates, for these alone can synthesise them. Similarly all the cells depend for their water supply and salts on the root-cells and the vascular bundles which convey the sap. Other cells secrete woody substances to strengthen the whole structure : in short, we have a complex but co-operative and co-ordinated whole. What is true of plants is true in a still more marked degree of animals, where the specialisation of cells is enormous. In the adult man there must be close on a thousand billion cells : what is it that makes all of these co-operate in the interests of the whole ? The behaviour of the single cell seems to have something of intelligence about it ; but when we consider a vast organism, we appear to see intelligence and faculty enormously transcending those of the individual cell. The cell, so to speak, can have no conception whatever of the function of the huge structure of which it is so small a part. Innumerable questions arise as soon as we start to ponder on these things. Does Life imply Mind, and is it Mind such as we know in ourselves ? How far are intelligence and purpose operative in all living things, from cells to organisms : or, may we suppose that under favourable conditions physico-chemical laws account wholly for the phenomena of Life ? What is Life ? It is better to defer any attempt at answering these until we have a fuller picture of that which we have to account for.

It is, I think, true to say that the process by which a single fertilised ovum becomes, in the course of nine months, a human child is the most remarkable of all the remarkable things within the experience of Man. It is at this process we should glance if we would know what Life can achieve and what we have to explain. Almost as soon as it is formed, the cell begins to divide into two, then each daughter cell into two again, and so on. At first the cells in the cluster are all alike, but slowly differentiation begins to appear and primitive structures are created from which, later, organs will form. It is a process of the most amazing co-ordination, in which cells go to their appointed places at the right time and develop the right properties for carrying out the function of that part of the structure. All the billions of cells have come from one progenitor, yet in the end

> " some will have changed their stuff and become rigid bone, or harder still, the enamel of a tooth ; some become fluid as water, so to flow along tubes too fine for the eye to see. Some become clear as glass, some opaque as stone, some colourless, some red, some black. Some become factories of a furious chemistry, some become inert as death. Some become engines of mechanical pull, some scaffoldings of static support, some a system transmitting electrical signs. . . ."

More still, the cell has done so as though it knew the minute local conditions of the particular spot in which its lot is cast.

> " Each cell we remember is blind ; senses it has none. It knows not ' up ' from ' down ' ; it works in the dark."

Sir Charles Sherrington, the eminent physiologist, from whose book * we have quoted, surveying this, says : " It is *as if* an immanent principle inspired each cell with knowledge for the carrying out of a design ".

The variety of the chemistry in the cells of various parts of the body, bearing in mind that they all come from one cell, is something to ponder over. Why should the position in space within the foetus determine whether a cell shall manufacture adrenalin, thyroxin or play a humble role as muscle ? It is quite true that chemical substances have been isolated from certain parts of the growing embryo, and have been called " organisers ". These appear to have growth-stimulating and growth-controlling properties wherever they are found. All this is another example of the remarkable chemical activity which occurs in the whole process of physical growth, from ovum to adult. But what organises the " organisers " ? How are these chemical substances produced in the right place, *and at the right time*, so that the end result is not a chemical monstrosity, but an organically functioning whole ?

Do not let us overlook the importance of correct timing in the development of the embryo. Should a process be a little late or a little early, should an aperture not close here or a fold form there when required, an imperfect human being—a " freak "—is formed. Such failures are rare enough to create interest. Consider, as one example, the large number of changes which must occur immediately following the birth of a child. The foetal circulation has provided

* Sherrington : *Man on his Nature*, Gifford Lectures, 1937–38 (C.U.P.).

for purification of the blood through the placental membrane (the intermediary between the fœtus and the mother). After birth, when the lungs start to function, a new circulation arises, and the old one must stop. It is then most important that an aperture between the auricles of the heart should close and certain vessels become obliterated. This is all usually completed within eight to ten days of birth. The whole process of development of the embryo is linked up with Time in an intimate way. Many structures laid down provide for what *will* be required of them at some distant date, not what is at *that* time essential. If it be supposed that form and structure should be chemical responses to the environment as it *then* exists, how can this account for lungs which *will* at some future day be needed, for eyes which *will* at some future day respond to light, for ears which *will* some day respond to sound-waves in air, for a larynx which *will* some day be used to talk, and so on ? If the building of so complex a structure, capable of response to an environment which it will some day meet, is not evidence of purpose—highly intelligent purpose such as highly developed Mind might formulate—I confess I do not know the meaning of the word " purpose ".

Sherrington, viewing the whole data, says : " All seems to argue prospective knowledge of the needs of life which are not yet, but are foreknown." Again : " The shaping of the embryo taken at its face value is an amazing ' becoming' which carries ' purpose ' even as the wing of the insect or the streamlining of the whale." Yet Sherrington, and other physiologists of the mechanistic school, are unwilling to concede purpose or Mind as causative of all this. They would argue " we do not speak of electrons as *for* producing atoms. Yet molecule-producing and atom-producing would seem as purposive as limb-producing. Our concept of an atom treats an atom as a deterministic necessity. To describe atomic behaviour, science makes no appeal to purpose. In physics science would gain nothing by that appeal. Does it in biology ? "

The answer is, it gains what is most significant—intelligibility. The processes of atom-producing on the one hand, and limb-producing on the other, have this in common : that they are the building of more complex wholes from simpler constituents. But the one critical distinction between them is that Life is involved in the latter case. We have seen that one of Life's characteristics is its capacity for maintaining itself as a going concern in relation to an environment which may be changing. If it fails in this, the living organism perishes. The process of atom-building or molecule-building does not involve such a corresponding relationship with the environment. An atom's or molecule's existence, now or in the future, does not depend on its capacity to react satisfactorily to its environment; but an organism's existence does so depend. The preparations made in order that it *will* have the capacity of response to an environment utterly unlike that which it is at present meeting in the uterus, admit of no other explanation but purpose. Sherrington toys with this idea, but appears to find the difficulties too great. Thus he says :

> " Suppose tentatively, at pause before this riddle, we allow the premise that in this developing embryo there resides some form of mind or psyche, and even in each of its constituent cells, and not inferior to what as a human individual it will ever have. Mind so present and intent on producing the child to be, would still be faced at every step with ' how '. It would be helpless." [It has no experience or memory to have recourse to for the purpose.] " It is an aggregate of cells doing what they are doing for the first time and the only time they ever will. Yet every step they take seems fraught with purpose toward a particular end."

Such a view is, I judge, considering mind a sort of epiphenomenon of matter, and attributing to it no knowledge or experience other than that which it acquires passively by its association with those particular cells. Such a concept of Mind is not based on anything evidential, and is, of course, of no assistance to an understanding of life-processes. Mind, it will be shown later in this book, is something existing in its own right : it is not born with, nor does it perish with the matter of the organism with which it is associated while the latter is " living ". Mind has, by its very nature, the faculty of memory : one without the other is unthinkable. Something of the sweep of Mind in space and time it is hoped to survey later, and the architecture of material form may then seem less difficult to account for. The mind animating and directing a growing physical form is probably, in its most fundamental aspect, not as highly individualised or separate from other minds as are physical forms from each other on the material level, and it draws on the experience of racial mind, which has done something similar a myriad times before.

As soon as we start to think of the creation of " forms "—i.e., the shapes which things grow into—we have quite as remarkable a group of facts to explain as those involved in the differentiation of chemical substance and physical structure from a single cell. In an interesting book Dr. Kenneth Walker has written : *

> " As a surgeon, I am sometimes called upon to cut away the ureter (the narrow channel that connects the bladder with the kidney)

* Kenneth Walker : *Diagnosis of Man* (Jonathan Cape).

and to implant it into another part of the bladder. When my work has been completed I am ashamed of its crudity. Compared with the job done by a plumber, my joint is a poor and botched concern. Yet when I examine it a year after I am scarcely able to tell which is Nature's joint and which is my own. Some intelligence in the patient's body has made good my failure, paring off redundant tissue here, adding new tissue there, until perfection has been attained. Does that intelligence exist only in the brain? No, for if I divide all the nerves that reach that spot from the brain, the work is performed just as well. If we concede intelligence to the body, we must also concede to it some degree of consciousness."

These observations of Walker are worthy of pondering. It would almost seem as though a three-dimensional " blue-print "—a skeleton pattern of structure—is laid down, presumably created, sustained and animated by Mind, on which matter moulds itself, and to which it is obliged to conform. If it be asked in what " substance " this pattern persists, we shall for the present reserve our answer until the data of later chapters have been presented. The observations made by Dr. Walker meet us at every turn as we contemplate the persistence and constant creation of natural forms. Why should a beech-tree always produce leaves shaped like beech leaves—never shaped like chestnut leaves? Why do anatomical features of Smith junior resemble those of Smith senior? We only marvel at growth when it fails to conform to control, as in cancer: but does this not seem strange? We take the familiar as " natural ", and our familiarity blinds us to the mystery that lies behind the physical. Surveying the brilliant developments in protein chemistry, Sherrington, having looked at all these facts, is yet prepared to say: " The body of a worm and the face of a man alike have to be taken as chemical responses." *

This is, of course, the faith and hope of mechanistic biology. To the present writer such a concept seems hopelessly inadequate, and indeed in its intrinsic nature incapable of explaining the facts of embryology. When the chemistry of growth-promotion and growth-control will have been fully unravelled, the central problem will still remain the same. What controls the local chemical controls? What organises the organisers in space and time? Where is the pattern? It has been demonstrated, for example, that if the bud of the embryo brain of a young tadpole is transplanted to another place, the skin over this new place will dip down and change its character to form the eye-lens. Conversely, if the skin over the original embryonic brain is removed, and replaced by skin from some other place, the latter skin will function in the same way. It seems

* Sherrington: *Man on his Nature*, p. 104, 2nd ed. (C.U.P.).

evident that some chemical influence emanates from the embryonic brain to cause this skin change. Substances of this kind have in fact been isolated. Sherrington says :

> "The embryo at this stage seems pervaded by some general invisible plan which compels each of its localities, whatever the provenance of the material there, to become what is demanded there as part of the immanent plan. Later on, the trend in the local part to be what it set out to be becomes too strong to permit change. Then, the rudiment beginning to be a limb, will be a limb whatever happens and wherever the experimenter puts it."

Sherrington seems unwilling or reluctant to make the critical inference. Some day all the actual *mechanism* of growth-control may be demonstrated as chemical in character, but the crucial point is the existence of an intelligent plan. We cannot have a plan without a planner. Mind is the only thing known to us with purpose, memory and intelligence, and we may infer it is the source and sustainer of the plans.

3. THE STRUCTURE OF THE EYE

Impressive as are the achievements of Life in the building of organisms, nothing, I think, is more impressive than the intricacy, accuracy and ingenuity of the building of a small specialised organ like the eye. We shall not attempt to provide any description of this here, but the reader may be interested in the fascinating and authoritative account which Sherrington * has provided in his Gifford Lectures.

The development of such a specialised organ as this only serves to emphasise again the evidence of purpose, of elaborate preparation for future functioning, which the whole organism has revealed. Because, however, the eye is a sense organ through the use of which the greater part of our knowledge of the external world is derived, we are once more driven to reflect upon the relationship between the mechanism and the knowledge. The image on the retina of the eye produces chemical changes in certain cells and these in turn send a stream of electrical pulses to a few cubic centimetres of matter in the brain. But no one has ever supposed that this pattern of electrical pulses in the cortex resembles in any way, in either distribution or nature, the objects in the outside world which are said to be " seen " by the seer. As Sherrington says :

> " Electrical charges having themselves not the faintest elements of the visual—having, for instance, nothing of ' distance ', ' right-side-upness ', nor ' vertical ', nor ' horizontal ', nor ' colour ', nor ' bright-

* Sherrington : *Man on his Nature*, pp. 105–14, 2nd ed. (C.U.P.).

ness', nor 'shadow', nor 'roundness', nor 'squareness', nor 'contour', nor 'transparency', nor 'opacity', nor 'near', nor 'far', nor visual anything—yet conjure up all these. A shower of little electrical leaks conjures up for me when I look, the landscape, the castle on the height, or, when I look at him approaching, my friend's face, and how distant he is from me, they tell me. Taking their word for it, I go forward and my senses confirm that he is there. . . . But this last, not the eye, but the 'seeing' by the brain behind the eye? Physics and chemistry there are silent to our every question. All they say to us is that the brain is theirs, that without the brain which is theirs the seeing is not. But as to how? They vouchsafe us not a word. Their negation goes further—they assure us it is no concern of theirs at all."

I invite you to ponder this admission of Sherrington—and the following statement of J. S. Mill : " That the eye is necessary to sight seems to me the notion of one immersed in matter." Sherrington pushes physics and chemistry to the limit of explanation, and it is right that we should get the utmost by way of explanation out of these well-established sciences, before we venture on novel hypotheses. At this point he stops and frankly admits that the actual business of seeing is beyond the power of science to explain.

But we *do* see. I ask you to ponder on this—and it is inevitable, therefore, to infer something which sees. We will call it Mind : a non-material entity. We must infer a little of the power of Mind, at least from this fact : that we know it is able to interpret the electrical storms in a few cubic centimetres of grey matter, and from them to construct a picture of an outer world. And what a picture ! Snow-capped mountains and torrid deserts, placid lakes and colourful flowers, cathedrals and primroses, works of art and works of steel— what a world the Mind has constructed from the electrical storms in a few cubic centimetres of grey matter which it has interpreted !

If Mind is thus a necessary hypothesis to understand seeing, it is difficult to believe that Mind, the user of this extraordinary brain-mechanism, has not had much to do with its design. If Mind is the interpreter of the electrical storms, how has it learned to interpret this complexity ? *It seems to me the most plausible of hypotheses that the immediate user of the instrument may have been intimately associated with the designer of the instrument—hence its unique facility for using it.* I do not envisage that each *individual* mind directs the construction of its own material vehicle in the sense that an architect directs construction of a house. The construction of an insect is, after all, only one degree less remarkable than that of a man. Mind itself I believe to be but an instrument of something that lies nearer to reality than itself. Perhaps we can consider a world of

Mind (just as we envisage a world of Matter) sustaining and creating (under higher direction) " forms " or patterns which are dynamic centres of influence and activity. On this higher directive level— perhaps that of Platonic " ideas "—may exist the master-plans of homo sapiens and of all other species. The consciousness of higher beings may, on the level of Mind, be making constant experiments and creating novelties, just as we ourselves make our own new forms and creations out of matter. The process of individuation we must consider later. Perhaps for the present we can regard the living physical form as a " condensation " on the level of matter of a mental form, which is in its turn a centre of activity of consciousness which is there striving to realise further expression. In the creation of these new individual instruments, whether on the mental or material level, the resources and knowledge of its myriad experiments flow through the growing embryo as light flows through the focus of a lens.

4. THE PAGEANT OF LIFE

In 1859 Charles Darwin published his book *The Origin of Species*, a book which profoundly influenced and stimulated human thought and had repercussions far beyond the biological field to which its concepts were properly applicable. The closing sentences of this book, J. C. Smuts confesses,* have always affected him deeply. They are worth reproducing :

" It is interesting to contemplate a tangled bank, clothed with many plants of many kinds, with birds singing on the bushes, with various insects flitting about, and with worms crawling through the damp earth, and to reflect that these elaborately constructed forms, so different from each other, and dependent on each other in so complex a manner, have all been produced by laws acting around us. These laws, taken in the largest sense, being Growth with Repro- duction ; Inheritance which is almost implied by reproduction ; Variability from the indirect and direct action of the conditions of life, and from use and disuse ; a Ratio of Increase so high as to lead to a struggle for life, and as a consequence to Natural Selection, entailing Divergence of character and the extinction of less improved forms. Thus, from the war of Nature, from famine and death, the most exalted object which we are capable of conceiving, namely, the production of the higher animals, directly follows. There is grandeur in this view of life, with its several powers, having been originally breathed by the Creator into a few forms, or into one ; and that, whilst this planet has gone circling on according to the fixed law of gravity, from so simple a beginning endless forms most beautiful and most wonderful have been and are being evolved."

* J. C. Smuts : *Holism and Evolution*, p. 187 (Macmillan & Co., 1926).

Here Darwin has summed up his life's work, and we have in these few sentences the methods of, and principles governing, the evolution of Life. Before discussing these, we shall very briefly look at the pageant of life as it is known to us through countless scientific observations. It is a story that has often been told, and we shall here refer to only a few salient features. The time-scale of the table must not be taken as more than a rough guide.

PERIOD	TIME-SCALE (million years)	FEATURES
Pleistocene	0–1	Last Ice Age. Man appears.
Plio- and Miocene	1–35	Advance of mammals.
Oligo- and Eocene	35–60	Higher mammals arise.
Cretaceous	60–100	Primitive mammals. Flowering plants.
Jurassic	100–125	Flying reptiles. Birds arise.
Triassic	125–175	Dinosaurian reptiles.
Permian	175–200	Rise of reptiles.
Carboniferous	200–260	Rise of insects. Giant amphibians.
Devonian	260–320	Successful invasion of land.
Silurian	320–350	First attack on land. Lung-fishes.
Ordovician	350–420	First vertebrates. Cuttlefish.
Cambrian	420–500	Sea-life increasing. Trilobites.
Pre-Cambrian	500–	No fossil records of early life.

The earliest and deepest geological strata have no fossil records of life, presumably because of the smallness and softness of living organisms, which would be destroyed by conditions of pressure and heat. Beds of limestone suggest that calcareous algæ must, however, have lived in these ancient times, and beds of graphite suggest that green plants may also have existed. We do not know how old life is on the Earth, but in round figures we might suggest 1,000 million years. The earliest life probably flourished in the shallow water near the sea-shores of the ancient world, and in Cambrian times proliferated in the seas, producing sponges, jelly-fishes, starfish, worms and creatures which protected themselves externally, like the molluscs. The Ordovician period saw the experiments with segmented or jointed armour and jointed-footed trilobites, but the most sensational development was the first appearance of vertebral columns or backbones, which occurred in the fishes. This profoundly interesting and daring experiment, in which the hard, supporting structure was put on the inside and the soft parts transferred to the outside, provided the basis of the main subsequent advance. Every new experiment Nature made was tried out in scores of variations. Some of these proved unsuccessful, and these creatures died out. Others proved successful but limiting, and these creatures, though persistent for long periods, remained substantially unchanged in the " blind alleys " of the maze of Life. Others provided an advantage on which further advance might be based.

For example, the primitive flat worms had.to be flat so that all parts could be near the food supply, but once the idea of a fluid transport system (circulation of the blood) was demonstrated as satisfactory, bulky three-dimensional animals were possible, and the flat worms remaining today are almost all degenerate parasites. In the round worms was tried out the simple experiment of a second opening (the anus) to the digestive cavity, giving the advantage of a continuous flow of food and making it possible for higher creatures later on to specialise certain parts of the intestine for digestion. Once this simple advance had been made, the idea of using the space between the body-wall and the intestine was exploited successfully, and this offered great advantages. It was a convenient cavity for other organs which might be devised, and for the blood circulatory system. It also made the body-wall and intestine independent of each other's movements. Every successful idea, once its value was established, found a permanent place in some succeeding forms of life.

Purposeful Mind had clearly laid down, some 300 to 400 million years ago, certain basic ground-plans on which to build its myriad experiments. These are the phyla of biological classification. The first great phylum was based upon the advantages of a backbone or vertebral column, and the architecture of life rose to its highest point through this ground-plan. We have the fishes, amphibians, reptiles, birds, mammals and finally Man. The second great phylum or ground-plan was that of the arthropods. These all kept their protective armour, which was their skeleton, on the outside, but they exploited in innumerable ways the possibilities of segmentation. Imagine a long chain of armoured segments each carrying a pair of appendages, and you have their general plan, capable, of course, of many modifications. All the creatures of this phylum live inside their skeletons and have a nervous system running along the front side ; some of them possess a heart, which is in the back. In such cases the blood pigment is in solution, not tied up in corpuscles, and is pale blue in colour, making use of a copper compound instead of an iron one. On this general ground-plan are built sea-creatures like shrimps, crabs, lobsters and barnacles. Others, such as spiders and scorpions, are found both in sea and on land. Centipedes are in this phylum and, most remarkable of all, the insects. Alone of the invertebrates, the insects conquered the air. They are impressive by their enormous variety : there are more species of insects than of all other living creatures taken together. They breathe by an elaborate system of air tubes running throughout their structure—a feature the limitations of which happily have prevented them growing to any great size. Equally impressive is the enormous elaboration of structure within such small creatures. Cajal, the Spanish neurologist, after microscopic study of the many-faceted insect-eye wrote :

> " Before it the mind halts abased. Peering through the micro-scope into this Lilliputian life one wonders whether what we disdain-fully term ' instinct ' is not, as Jules Fabre claims, life's crowning mental gift."

Certain classes of insects, such as ants, termites and bees, are remarkable also in their social organisation.

The third ground-plan which has sustained a huge edifice of life is that of the molluscs. These nearly all possess shells, and none of them makes use of segmentation. Such creatures as the oyster, the cockle, the snail and cuttlefish are types. Of one large class which includes land snails and slugs and marine whelks and winkles there are said to be about 6,000 land species and 10,000 known aquatic species. Such is the wealth of Nature's experiments!

Another ground-plan was that of the segmented worms, the importance of one group of which to Man has been described by Darwin :

> " The plough is one of the most ancient and most valuable of man's inventions ; but long before he existed the land was in fact regularly ploughed and still continues to be thus ploughed by earthworms. It may be doubted whether there are many other animals which have played so important a part in the history of the world as have these lowly organised creatures."

From Nature's basic patterns let us turn back to her time-table. In Silurian times the great attempt to establish life on dry land was made, and three groups of creatures appear to have succeeded in this great step. Vegetation must first have established itself as a food supply for animal life, and a group of adventurous worms were possibly the first followers. Fossilised scorpions have been found in Silurian rocks, so that some arthropods must have developed a primitive lung. The most important success was that of the amphi-bians, the first known footprints of which occur in early Devonian strata. The amphibians themselves probably came from primitive fresh-water fish which had developed an air-bladder to adapt them-selves better to life in stagnant water. One group of these ultimately

regressed and re-colonised the sea, the other went forward, transforming the air-bladder into a lung, and fins into legs, and colonised
the land. Those that did neither one thing nor the other almost
all perished. There remain today only three species of lung-fish to
remind us of this critical phase of life. The amphibians were kings
of the earth for about twenty to thirty million years in the great
coal-swamps and forests of the Carboniferous period. Some were
fantastically armour-plated and as large as donkeys : today the humble
toads and frogs are the small amphibian residues. Meanwhile insect
life was proliferating and a few small primitive reptiles were making
their appearance.

Following the Carboniferous period came a time of great terrestrial
upheaval. The antarctic continent arose, and bitter conditions of
cold and drought led to the reptiles achieving pre-eminence over the
amphibians. Their success was probably largely due to the invention
of the shelled egg. This wrapped the fertilised ovum round with its
own food supply and enclosed it in a hard, protective case, giving it a
far better chance of survival. It also implied that internal fertilisation
replaced the more hazardous external type. For 150 million years
the reptiles flourished, lasting in giant forms up to the end of
Cretaceous times. The modern survivors of the reptiles are such
creatures as snakes, lizards, crocodiles, tortoises and turtles. Some
reptiles attempted to conquer the air—an effort made about twenty
million years before the first birds. Other reptiles returned to the
sea. The most spectacular were, however, the great Dinosaurs,
some of which weighed up to 40 tons, others measured 90 feet from
head to tail and raised their heads as much as 20 feet above the ground.
Both fossil eggs and the skeletons of these enormous creatures have
been unearthed. A limit is fortunately set to the size of land
creatures by the strength of bone. A point comes when a bone's
own weight must increase more rapidly than the body-weight
supported. The Dinosaurs were certainly Nature's most ambitious
land-experiment in both size and armour-plating. They ultimately
vanished because they were unequal to changing conditions, presumably because of insufficient bodily co-ordination due to their
small brains. The average man's brain weighs about 3 lb., giving a
ratio of brain to body-weight of 1/40. The 40-ton Sauropod
had a brain of less than 2 lb., giving a ratio of 1/45,000.

About 100 million years ago the first primitive birds emerged from
a reptilian ancestor, and they specialised on the conquest of the air.
With a few modern exceptions, such as the ostrich and the penguin,
whenever birds have forsaken the air as their natural element they
have perished. Like the reptiles, birds lay eggs ; unlike the reptiles,

c

but like the mammals, they are warm-blooded creatures. The great invention of the feather must be regarded as the key to their success, combining lightness with heat-preserving qualities. Few creatures have given more pleasure to Man, a feature to which much outstanding poetry and prose bear witness. They have been closely studied in many aspects : their intelligence, social life, song, migration, plumage, courtship and mating, and their nesting habits.

The mammals evolved concurrently with the birds. They share the characteristic with the birds of being warm-blooded and, to minimise heat loss, are more or less completely covered with hair. Instead of laying eggs they bring forth their young alive, and they are, of course, unique, as their name implies, in suckling the offspring through special milk-producing glands. The long-drawn-out period of gestation and of infancy has greatly favoured better brain development, and to the superior maternal care over this long period and the superior brain resulting must be attributed their pre-eminence. They have explored widely, and so adaptable has been the ground-plan of the mammals that they are found in every variety of environment : on the earth and under the earth, in streams and on the sea-shore, in the sea and in the air.

Finally, Man diverged from Simian stock somewhere between half a million and two million years ago. The earliest known remains of Man, called *Pithecanthropus erectus*, were found in Central Java. They consist of a skull-cap, thigh-bone and two teeth, and are estimated to be half a million years old. It is suggested that this early man was about 5 feet 7 inches in height, and had a much smaller brain-capacity than modern Man. Comparing the brain-capacities of the gorilla, Pithecanthropus and modern Man, they are respectively about 650 cc., 900 cc. and 1,450 cc. When the brains of the higher apes are compared with that of man, there are found to be no absolutely new structures present, but there is found an enormous increase of the so-called " association areas ". How much this has made possible, we all know. Man has become the maker of tools, the inventor of language, the cherisher of values and the seeker after God.

Such in barest outline is the story of Life's achievement, resulting in expanding awareness alongside of, and through, specialisation of structure.

5. THE SIGNIFICANCE OF EVOLUTION

The fact of evolution stands unquestioned, but it raises in our minds many questions to which as yet we cannot claim to have satisfactory answers. Some of the more immediate questions are these. What are the factors which create and sustain the process ? Why do some species succeed and others fail ? In addition, interesting metaphysical questions are also raised. Why is the trend " upwards " at all, in the sense of leading to the creation of organisms of increasing complexity and awareness ? What is the goal of evolution ? What is its end or purpose ?

The two essential elements in Darwin's view were Variation and Natural Selection. The first of these is an internal factor. For various reasons connected with the use and disuse of organs, or the stresses created by the environment, creatures will from time to time appear which show variations or departures from the norm. The second factor is the external one. Those variations which are an advantage and assist the animal to survive will continue, while those which are disadvantageous will lead to elimination of the creatures which possess them. The conception of the " survival of the fittest ", as Herbert Spencer termed it, is a simple one, and makes the influence of the environment the dominating factor. It is easy to see that this emphasis generally supports a mechanistic picture of the world. Darwin had much less to say about the factor of Variation than about Natural Selection, but further development of evolutionary theory initiated by Weismann turned attention to this inner creative factor.

The variations which Darwin envisaged, might possibly arise from three sources : (1) Modifications due to use and disuse of organs during the organism's own life. Here of course is implied the possibility of transmission of acquired characters to the next generation (Lamarck's view). (2) Chance variations arising from inheritance from parents. (3) Distinct, sudden and unexplained " mutations " which sometimes do occur and create new species (de Vries' emphasis). It was not to these, but to the summation of a large number of small variations, such as may arise from (1) and (2) over vast stretches of time, that Darwin attached major importance. Weismann stressed the importance of the germ-cells (ova and spermatozoa) as being the place where variation occurred—the real theatre of evolutionary change. He over-emphasised, however, the isolation and independence of the germ-cells from the body-cells, maintaining that in the nature of things there could be no interaction between them. In other words, he denied the possibility of the inheritance of acquired characters, and conceived of a theory of intracellular or Germinal Selection instead of Natural Selection. Such views, however, have never received any general acceptance. It may not be possible to demonstrate the inheritance of acquired characters by experiments over a few years which involve only some hundreds of generations, but we must remember the vast time-scale of evolution and the millions of years of Nature's experiments. We have in ourselves vestigial organs, such as, for example, the cæcum and appendix, which retain an important function in lower mammals, but which in us have long fallen into disuse. Conversely, we have the much higher sensitivity to touch of our fingers compared with that of other parts of the body, which is consequent, we may suppose, upon their persistent use. In the case of bacteria which may reproduce thousands of generations in a year, we do in fact observe perceptible inherited changes, such as acquired resistance to certain drugs (e.g., penicillin) with which they have been persistently treated. One of the difficulties of the whole Darwinian concept is to understand how small modifications or minute variations, even if inheritable, can be conserved until they are marked enough to have definite survival value. Once *marked* variations have arisen, we can appreciate that Natural Selection may operate to conserve those which are favourable; but in their beginnings variations must be minute, and it is difficult to see how they would lead to selection of the organism possessing them as more favourably adapted to its environment.

From the mechanistic standpoint I do not know of any satisfactory way to meet this difficulty. J. C. Smuts, in his book *Holism and Evolution*, makes use of the concept of a " field of influence ". He writes : *

" Every ' thing ' has its field, like itself, only more attenuated ; every concept has likewise its field. It is in these fields and these fields only that things really happen. It is the intermingling of fields which is creative or causal in nature as well as in life. The hard secluded concrete thing or concept is barren, and but for its field it could never come into real contact or into active or creative relations with any other thing or concept. Things, ideas, animals, plants, persons : all these, like physical forces, have their fields, and but for their fields they would be unintelligible, their activities would be impossible, and their relations barren and sterile. The abstract intelligence in isolating things or ideas, and constituting them apart from their fields, and treating the latter as non-existent, has made the real world of matter and of life quite unintelligible and inexplicable."

Again he writes : †

" The organism and its field is one continuous structure which, beginning with an articulated sensible area, gradually shades off into indefiniteness. In this continuum is contained all of the past which

* J. C. Smuts : *Holism and Evolution*, p. 18 (Macmillan & Co., 1926).
† Ibid., pp. 114–115.

has been conserved and still operates to influence the present and the future of the organism : in it is contained all that the organism is and does in the present ; and finally in it is contained all that the organism vaguely points to in its own future development and that of its offspring. . . . The whole is there carrying all its time with it."

In this concept, which is amplified and expounded in many parts of his book, Smuts, as a philosopher, presents a valuable and illuminating contribution which I believe to be independently supported by the data of psychical research. From some such standpoint we can begin to understand the evolutionary process. The difficulty which we raised of the conservation of small useful modifications or minute variations of value, is resolved by this concept of the organism's field, " adding up and conserving whatever in the experience and development of the individual is of survival value ", until finally it is sufficiently accentuated to take marked structural form. The modern view as to how small inherited variations arise takes us back to the germ-cells. The physical basis of hereditary unit-characters is now known to be the genes. These may possibly be very complex molecules, and are strung together like beads on the threads of the chromosomes. One gene will control the length of the femur, another the colour of the iris ; one the shape of the lip, another the texture of the hair, and so on. Upon fertilisation of the ovum there is no blending of these unit characters : they are preserved intact, but there may be considerable rearrangement of the order of the genes in the chromosomes, much as the pearls on a necklace could be rearranged. It is now recognised that the effect of any gene is greatly influenced by the presence of other genes (possibly its immediate neighbours). In one genetical environment its effect may be substantially different from its effect in another genetical environment. The possibilities of inherited variations lie, then, in these changes in the gene-ordering (apart from the relatively rare gene-mutations). This seems to be an idea for which Weismann was unsuccessfully groping when he recognised the germ-cell as the theatre of evolutionary change. The vital question still, of course, remains, however detailed is our present knowledge of the mechanics of variation : What controls the gene-ordering ? We are back once more at the hypothesis of a controlling and conserving " field " which the writer conceives to be mental or psychical. It is of interest to note that Professor A. C. Hardy * has recently advanced the idea of a sub-conscious group pattern of behaviour : a sort of mental racial inheritance, linking together all individuals of that type,

* " Telepathy and Evolutionary Theory ", *Jour. Soc. Psychical Research*, May–June 1950.

and controlling the genetic environment. Telepathy, he thinks, may be the means by which an individual creature adopting different habits modifies the habits of the group and, through this, the gene-ordering, and hence the physical structure, of progeny.

Another difficulty which occurs in Darwinism, so long as we limit ourselves to the purely materialistic viewpoint, is that of the existence of small variations in co-ordinated groups. The evolutionary development of a wing, for example, implies a whole group of related variations—scales into feathers, musculature and shoulder-girdle modifications, etc.—without which a wing could not function. On the original Darwinian view we are asked to envisage a variation " A " arising accidentally and conserved as being favourable to the survival of the organism. But in fact useful variations must arise in co-ordinated groups $A + b + c + d \ldots$ and the supposition of *accidental* simultaneous arrival of a number of these is highly improbable. When related groups occur—and it is clearly only such groups which would have survival value—it is much more suggestive of planning or purpose than of accident.

Smuts' concept of the " field " of the organism in which, as he says, " the pull of the future is almost as much upon it as the push of the past "—a conception very different from that of mechanism, in which the past alone could be effective—gives a basis for understanding. The organism has vaguely anticipated its future structure, and conserves in its field those minute variations or tendencies which point in this direction, frail though they are, until they can be incorporated as a group into the material structure with good hope of the organism's survival in competition with others. What Smuts calls Holistic Selection acts within each organism in respect of all its parts, putting the resources of the " whole " behind any promising tendency. Smuts' philosophy of Holism develops the idea of the new properties and functions found in " wholes " which do not reside in " parts ". He sees the whole process of evolution as one of the formation of greater " wholes " with new functions and wider powers.

When we try to sum up in more familiar terms what we understand by the " field " which surrounds " things, animals, plants, and persons " and carries with it memory and purpose, we are irresistibly reminded of Mind. The ability to profit by mistakes, the experimental method of trial and error, the quality of inventiveness, the ability to formulate goals and plan for their realisation—these characteristics of the evolutionary process are characteristics of Mind as we know it in ourselves, or of that which lies behind Mind and uses Mind as the instrument of its realisation. Is it not reasonable to suppose that parallel with the evolution of physique we have an evolution of Mind which is seeking to realise itself in an ever-increasing degree of awareness ? We suggested earlier that Life is a state of organic association of Mind and Matter in which this concurrent evolution is proceeding. We may envisage the evolution of Mind as causal or primary, and that of the material forms as consequential or secondary, in that the former has apparently a degree of permanence not characteristic of the physical forms. Once the association is broken—which we describe as the death of the organism —the physical form disintegrates into unorganised matter. This view seems to be shared by Gerald Heard,* who says :

" Physical evolution is paralleled by, is the invariable concomitant of a psychical evolution. . . . There is a mind–body complex present from the beginning of life, and that mind is, at the source, as rudimentary and unspecific as the single cell in which it is manifested. The organism increased in awareness by a series of steps, each indicated by a corresponding alteration of physique."

Just as all mental and artistic achievements are built upon the foundations laid by scientists, mathematicians and artists in the past, so that one generation can start to build further where the last one finished, so there has been no purposeless repetition of the basic experiments in Nature's laboratory. It is the novel which is being constantly tried out. The process bears the general character of intelligent research—of countless experiments directed towards a goal : that of ever-increasing awareness and comprehension of the environment.

" Yet all this abundance of inner physical invention must not blind us to the other factor in evolution, the Time element, the fact that there is a tide when advance in physical invention can be made, and will lead to a completely new quality of consciousness, but that if that advance is not sustained and if it is then attempted at too late a time, only failure results. The ' composition ' which we call the history of life has, like a musical composition, been conducted at a certain ' tempo ', and when one movement is over, those who have failed to play their parts there, can find no place later. After the lobe-finned fishes no fish appears ever to have given rise to an amphibian, though at least two hundred million years have elapsed since then. After the amphibians of the Carboniferous period, no amphibian seems to have given rise to a reptile." †

Our conception of the significance of evolution is, then, of Mind seeking development—which means ever-increasing potentiality of awareness for the consciousness which lies behind Mind. It

* Gerald Heard : *Pain, Sex and Time*, p. 23 (Cassell & Co., 1929).
† Ibid., p. 27.

awakens from its dreaming state to its true growth or becoming by its downward plunge into the world of matter. It is as though in its dreaming state all worlds are possible and none is actual. So long as there are no rules, no game is possible : it is only within the limitations of rules that a game can be played. With a world of an infinite number of dimensions, nothing (or everything) can be done : it is only when confined within the discipline of a few dimensions (notably three) that Mind can do something effective, and, through that doing, come to know the difference between existence and non-existence. Infinite space and time are doubtless there, latent within the undifferentiated mind : it is only through limitation that it can come to know of them. Without limitation there could be nᵣ forms ; if there were no forms there would be no space postulated in which to relate them. It is only through observing change in those forms that the Mind infers Time. It is only through knowing Time that we can ever know Timelessness. Many visions, fantastic and impossible, may flow through a child's imagination, but it is only the discipline of building which will show him the possible and make him an architect.

And so we have

> This primal and ecstatic mystery
> Of chaos bidden into many-hued
> Wonders of form, life in the void create,
> And monstrous silence made articulate.*

Memory and Purpose are the distinctive characteristics of Mind on all levels : in some degree—very varying degrees, it is true—they are found over the whole range of living things. The functioning of Higher Mind also shows from time to time the two qualities of artistry and humour, and it does not require an intensive search to find both of these in evidence in the pageant of evolution. We may draw attention to some bird-songs, to the magnificently rich colora-tion of rosella parrots, to the colours and patterns of deep-sea fish (where there is practically no light) and also of butterflies, and to the perfection of colour and construction of the peacock's feathers. On the basis of sexual selection this beauty must be explained as arising from the emotional sensitivity of the peahen, which was such that it was attracted to those males who proved superior in some minute artistic creation to their neighbours. To attribute such æsthetic susceptibility to the peahen's mind seems fantastic : indeed, on the human level this sensibility only develops as a rule with the approach of maturity. The grace of form and colour of many

* John Drinkwater : *The Building*.

flowers can scarcely, I think, be for the delectation of the hymenoptera. Wherever we look in Nature we see the evidence of artistic exuberance far beyond the utilitarian requirement of survival value.

Lest a sense of humour should be thought unfitting in the serious business of the Mind's development, I commend to biologically minded students the neck of the giraffe, the girth of the hippopotamus, the nose of the elephant, and the tail of the pig for a consideration of their survival value.

There are some biologists and biochemists who take the view that the gap between the so-called living and non-living does not in fact exist : that viruses or other such forms may be in fact the bridge which makes one continuous series from mineral to mammal. If this should be established we should be prepared to extend the association of Mind with matter in the same continuous manner. There is nothing inherently improbable in the association of primitive undifferentiated " mind-stuff " with matter ; there are, indeed, some indications that we may be driven to do so by the observations of psychical research. It has, indeed, been said—not perhaps without real insight—that Mind is sleeping in minerals, dreaming in plants, awakening in animals and fully awakened in Man. From the standpoint of traditional physics and chemistry such a view may appear fantastic and imaginative. To anyone who is prepared to base his outlook and judgment upon the modern conception of matter, this need no longer be the case.

The position we have adopted may be described as that of Vitalism—but the " vital principle " or " entelechy " must be under-- stood to be Mind of the nature of which we have a wider conception than is accorded by some thinkers. The chief objection traditionally raised against Vitalism—that it is impossible to demonstrate the influence of Mind apart from physical and chemical factors—is now no longer tenable, as the evidence of Part II of this book will show.

Chapter

4

HOMO SAPIENS

All That's Past

Very old are the woods ;
  And the buds that break
Out of the brier's boughs,
  When March winds wake,
So old with their beauty are—
  Oh, no man knows
Through what wild centuries
  Roves back the rose.

Very old are the brooks ;
  And the rills that rise
Where snow sleeps cold beneath
  The azure skies
Sing such a history
  Of come and gone,
Their every drop is as wise
  As Solomon.

Very old are we men ;
  Our dreams are tales
Told in dim Eden,
  By Eve's nightingales ;
We wake and whisper awhile,
  But, the day gone by,
Silence and sleep like fields
  Of amaranth lie.

WALTER DE LA MARE.

In spite of Pope's familiar assertion,

" The proper study of mankind is Man ",

we find that anything approaching a comprehensive scientific knowledge of Man himself is still far from being realised. We may perhaps regard the early seventeenth century, which had the inspiration of Francis Bacon, Galileo and Descartes, as the beginning of the era of modern experimental science in the fields of matter and life. Of the sciences of Man : anthropology (concerned with his origins, racial characteristics, economic, political and social organisation, and his culture) and psychology (concerned with the working of his mind), it can scarcely be claimed, I think, that they represent much more than a century of effort. No attempt will here

74

be made to present any outline of the conclusions of these sciences. We shall be content to make brief reference to a few aspects of Man's nature, some of which arise from his animal ancestry and others of which point to his ultimate destiny.

1. MAN THE ANIMAL

As we look back at the long line of man's descent, the impression received is very strong that intelligent experimenting has been going on over vast stretches of time. We see the same sort of processes of trial and error and learning by experience in the great laboratory of Nature, as those which intelligent scientists themselves undertake in their own laboratory researches. During Permian and Triassic times there were a number of reptiles which approached in some degree the mammalian pattern, but they all eventually died out except one type, which managed to achieve warm-blooded characteristics. The advantages of this achievement, which allowed the creature to maintain its body temperature constant under a variety of external conditions, were so great that the further main line of advance was built upon it. Similarly, the four-chambered heart, with its independent pulmonary and bodily circulations, was so efficient that it became the standard device in mammalian development. The first mammal which was created in upper Triassic times was probably a small, mouse-like creature, and the *general* pattern seems to have suffered little change until upper Cretaceous times (a period of seventy or eighty million years). During this time, while large reptiles and birds were flourishing, experiments were obviously still proceeding with the mammals, but almost all proved unsuccessful, and died out. The price of too intensive a specialisation seems to be diminished adaptability to a changing environment, and the main line of advance always retains a degree of generality which ensures adaptability to change, and preserves to it the widest field of awareness. Only the prototheria (the platypus and echidna) and the marsupials (kangaroo, opossum, etc.) linger today as evidence of these mammalian experiments made about 100 million years ago. Somewhat later a new and successful stimulus to experiment arose, and for forty million years thereafter the generalised mammalian type threw off remarkably good specialised forms : toothless mammals, water-mammals, bats, insectivores, rodents, hoofed mammals, carnivores and, most important, the Primates. After Eocene times no new group of mammals has arisen, nor can they now ; for the generalised type has expended itself and disappeared. Nature committed herself to the more limited degree of generalisation found in the Primates. Somewhere about thirty to thirty-five million years ago the ape-like ancestors of Man diverged from the primate stem, leaving the gibbons, the orangs, chimpanzees and gorillas to develop separately. No fossil remains of this ancestor of Man belonging to the Miocene or Pliocene periods have so far been found; but in the pleistocene period, which covers the last million years, fossil remains of early Man have been unearthed in several parts of the world. We now know of Pithecanthropus (from the Java skull), Sinanthropus (from the Peking skull) and Eoanthropus (from the Piltdown skull), as well as of other offshoots of Man. Comparison of the cavities of these skulls shows the progressive development of the brain—in the same order in which these areas develop and reach maturity in the growing child.

There is a well-known adage in biology, " Ontogeny follows phylogeny ". The statement just made is one illustration of it. In the process of individual development as an embryo, all creatures pass through structural stages which recapitulate the process of evolutionary development. Thus, if the human embryo is examined at about the third or fourth week, it shows unmistakable characteristics of a fish-like structure. Its tail is broad, and comparable with the trunk. In the throat region are four pairs of clefts which, though not perforated, correspond to gill-slits, and are supported by gill arches and supplied by appropriate blood-vessels. The embryonic heart has no right and left chambers at this stage : it is like the simple pumping mechanism of the fish. By the end of the second month all these structures have become modified, and the embryo begins to look like a young mammal.

Again, if the seven-month human embryo is examined it will be noticed that it has the ape-like characteristic of the soles of the feet turned towards each other. Just as the palms of our hands are turned towards each other for purposes of grasping, so in the ape, which uses its feet for grasping, this condition is retained. In the young child the foot becomes modified to support its weight later in the erect position.

It would be possible to consider the process of development of the human embryo in detail and show how its various stages recapitulate in transient forms the long story of life's ascent. Some of these evidences, as is well known, linger with us in the adult body. We call them vestigial : they serve no useful purpose now, but they are contemporary reminders of our animal ancestry. In cold weather many fur-bearing animals erect their hair, with the obvious advantage of enclosing a bigger layer of static air, which, being a poor conductor, will cause a smaller loss of heat. We try to do the same; but the condition of goose-flesh which results has, of course, no heat-retaining value, because our body-hair is vestigial. Very few people can move their ears : the musculature for doing so is still present in us, but in a vestigial form. The tailed monkeys can still move their ears, but the great apes have lost their power of doing this. The pointed ear characteristic of most of the mammals is represented as a vestige in most human beings by Darwin's tubercle—a little projection just within the marginal fold of the ear. The third eyelid of lower mammals is represented in us by the fleshy vestige at the inner corner of the eye. Wisdom teeth and the appendix are well-known examples of variable and useless structures which, however, in other mammals fulfil an active function.

It is interesting to reflect upon these many evidences of our ancestry. If we could understand why, in the building of each individual body, there is a brief résumé or structural recollection of each of Nature's ancient discoveries which contributed to the line of ascent, we should have a valuable key in our hands. One might suppose that, having done it so often, " Nature " could construct a new human being without recapitulating the past; but in fact this is not so. Can we find any clue to this in our conception of evolution as psycho-physical : the evolution of mind-stuff being causative, and that of matter being consequential ? Mind has as its most basic characteristic memory. It is in virtue of its power to remember that its higher faculty of reason can be exercised at all, and that its power to formulate purposes is possible. Something which we may call the racial or collective mind appears to be concentrated or focused on the growing embryo, and goes through the process of recollection, building its theme into matter. Once the race-mind has done its work, it leaves as it were in the new physical form a basic mental structure, upon which will be built throughout this individual's life the higher mental pyramid of individual experience. Mind appears to achieve its own further evolution through this process of individualisation, and by watching how creative mind develops in ourselves, we may, I think, expect to find in a more evolved form the method of working of the collective Mind which constructed the body.

If you present to a mathematician a new problem to solve, he will recognise its type and know the mathematical functions or calculus by which he may hope to achieve success. His first few lines, written down on paper as the starting point, will probably be unintelligible to most of us. That, however, is *his* starting point, and from that (to him) familiar ground he proceeds to build the new. He can start there, because stored in his memory is all the ordered knowledge upon which that starting point is based, and if he had time and patience it would be possible for him to construct the whole edifice on first principles. Indeed, an intelligent non-mathematician attempting to solve the problem would have to start at the beginning and build up the solution from first principles ; for he would have no ordered system of mathematical memories on which to draw. The early stages of his attempt would probably be passed through quite rapidly ; but the later stages, when he was discovering the properties of the functions he would need to use, would be much slower and more laborious. If later on some similar problem presented itself to our non-mathematician, he could recapitulate his earlier work, quickly in its elementary parts, but more slowly in the later and less familiar parts, until he came to the point of new and creative advance. The mathematician as a specialist makes this recapitulation in a flash. His present facility is based upon innumerable recapitulations in earlier years.

The recapitulation of evolutionary progress involved in the developing embryo suggests the same sort of activity—an activity of Mind, intelligent and constructive, but not too highly specialised in one direction—drawing on the resources of memory as it prepares to attempt a new creative leap forward.

One might perhaps liken the collective or racial mind to the sea-floor which is thrust up, in response to some powerful urge beneath it, into islands dotting the surface of the sea. The sea is the world of matter which separates individual minds. Some islands are constantly awash ; the sea flows over them and they never rise fully into the air of self-consciousness. Others tower proudly out of the sea and are crowned with individual achievement. Some are impressive, rocky and forbidding ; others are green, attractive and gay with colour. Our minds emerge from the common submarine continent ; we have our basic structure of instinct and desire in common, but the part above sea level is ours, to make of it what we will.

> Yes : in the sea of life enisl'd
> With echoing straits between us thrown,
> Dotting the shoreless watery wild,
> We mortal millions live alone.*

The base upon which all higher individual mind is reared is held in common. Its deeper stratum is the animal mind, and built upon that is the savage mind. We have only to look around us to discover

* It is only fair to add that Matthew Arnold in later verses of this poem (To Marguerite), recognises the profounder truth that we are " parts of a single continent ".

how much of human behaviour and judgment is the product of these ancient levels. We need scratch the surface only a little to find the mind of a primitive savage : indeed, in our own day we have seen outcrops of these normally submerged strata. We shall look at this further in the next section.

If, as we have seen, the development of the individual body recapitulates the history of Life, we may expect to find also that the development of the individual mind recapitulates the history of Mind's evolution, and a study of the child's developing mind from this standpoint is interesting. We should expect the earlier animal phase to be passed through fairly rapidly, the primitive savage phase to take longer and the more recent phase of mind in historic times to be faintly reflected perhaps in the flowering of æsthetic appreciation and inventive interests in adolescence. Certainly there is in many growing boys a phase in which the propensities of the hunter and those of the fighter are apparent, in which they tend to move in groups—an echo, perhaps, of the nomadic period of early Man. There is a later phase of the collector (whether it be butterflies, birds' eggs, stamps or cigarette-cards)—an echo again, perhaps, of food-collecting and the necessity for storage in early agricultural communities. The nightmares to which growing children are prone, as well as some of their inborn fears, such as fear of the dark—all of which become less frequent and usually disappear in adolescence—are possibly echoes of ancestral memory of the menace of wild beasts and of the terror of these marauders after darkness fell. It is certainly noticeable that the highest and latest cultural activities of Man, such as the appreciation of natural scenery, art, music and religion, are the last to awaken in the individual mind—not because they are intrinsically of a difficult or complex nature, but because hitherto interest in them has been lacking.

Professor J. H. Robinson in his book *The Mind in the Making* has said :

> " We are all born wholly uncivilised. If a group of infants from the best families of today could be reared by apes they would find themselves with no civilisation. How long it would take them and their children to gain what now passes for even a low savage culture it is impossible to say. The whole arduous task would have to be performed anew, and it might not take place at all."

This is undoubtedly true. Those higher and later acquisitions which constitute civilisation can be little more than acquired *tendencies* in the adolescent mind, and whether they will issue in achievement and realisation depends on the favourableness of environment.

2. MAN THE THINKER

Gerald Heard * has expressed some interesting views on the evolution of Man. He takes the view that the evolutionary urge has substantially spent itself so far as the production of *physique* is concerned. Following this throughout the period of pre-history and history, mind has evolved by, and been substantially concerned with, the mastery of the environment through the development of *techniques*. The achievements of science and engineering are a witness to the success with which this has been done. Heard sees signs that this phase of evolution, though not yet spent, has passed its zenith, and believes that the next phase of evolution will be wholly on the level of Mind itself, and that because of this it must be consciously and deliberately undertaken. He says:

> " Now that evolution takes a further turn, and is stepped up to a higher intensity, his (Man's) mental evolution (which through the pre-historic periods was certainly sub-conscious, and which through the historic periods has still in the main been unintentional and unapprehended) must henceforth become conscious. If we are to advance to the achievement and mastery of new faculties, we must do so deliberately, and by a scientific technique understand how to enlarge our apprehension."

With this the present writer is in complete agreement, but the way is not easy, and not many as yet are ready to take it. How this may be done we shall consider later.

The pyramid of mind, in so far as it is an individual achievement, is based, we have claimed, on the substrata of the animal mind and the mind of primitive man. From these levels we have constant irruptions into consciousness, which deflect the judgment of higher Mind. These are levels of extreme physical adaptation and competence, for they keep the complex body-machine running with remarkable success, although the knowledge of how this is done never rises into the individual's field of awareness. These are the levels of instinctual urges and drives, of the will-to-live, the instinct of self-preservation, of sexual desire, and the gregarious tendencies which we share in common with all life. Upon these the individual builds the levels of his own desire-mind. " My pleasure ", " my comfort ", " my power ", " my welfare "—this web of egocentric concern fortifies him and differentiates him from the amorphous base of Life. It is upon this crude base that the aspiring crown of higher Mind, with all its enormous potentiality, has to be slowly built. The higher Mind has its intellectual aspect, through which it comes to

* Gerald Heard : Op. cit., p. 73, etc.

study and interpret the world without, and it has its buddhic aspect, by which it is linked to the creative, inspirational, intuitive world of wisdom or values. It is from this latter that all originality springs, whether it is expressed by the mind in the symbolism of mathematics, poetry or prose, music or art, or in the insights of true religion. It is only a very small percentage of homo sapiens of whom it can be said that they have contributed creatively to the culture of humanity. This is because a new idea can only be formulated by the mind which is sufficiently evolved to recognise it and prepared by a discipline to express it. The most exquisite melodies will remain unexpressed unless they are clothed by a mind which can appreciate them and has studied the technique of recording them. The most visionary beauty will delight no other beholder unless it comes to the mind of an artist who, through his equipment and training, can hold it and express it in form and colour.

In one of his most charming books * Æ, the Irish poet, artist and mystic, has analysed, so far as he could, the sources of his own poetic inspiration. In one passage he says :

> " There was always an element of the unexpected in the poetry itself, for it broke in upon and deflected the normal current of consciousness. I would be as surprised at the arising within me of words which in their combination seemed beautiful to me as I would have been if a water-lily had blossomed suddenly from the bottom of a tarn to make a shining on its dark surface. The words often would rush swiftly from hidden depths of consciousness and be fashioned by an art with which the working brain had but little to do."

Henri Poincaré,† writing on the genesis of mathematical discovery, has described how many of his own discoveries came in moments of illumination, perhaps as he was crossing the street or engaged in some other task, but always after he had first exercised his conscious mind on the problem to the limit of its power :

> " These sudden inspirations are never produced . . . except after some days of voluntary efforts which appeared absolutely fruitless, in which one thought one had accomplished nothing and seemed to be on a totally wrong track. These efforts however were not as barren as one thought ; they set the unconscious machine in motion, and without them it would not have worked at all."

Creative thought or originality in any of the arts is comparatively rare. What passes as " thought ", even on intelligent levels, among the generality of men, is the restatement of old ideas, the reiteration

* Æ : *Song and its Fountains*, p. 24 (Macmillan & Co., 1932).
† Henri Poincaré : *Science and Method*, Chapter 3 (Thos. Nelson & Sons).

of commonplace views with contemporary illustrations or in new settings—in short, it is largely a game of permutation and combination with old shibboleths.

Sometimes we claim that the processes of thought are leading us to objective judgments on a subject, but it is very doubtful if, outside the fields of mathematical thought, and to some limited extent scientific and philosophical thought, anything approaching complete objectivity is possible. The stratum of desire throws up its influences on to the level of judgment, even though with delicacy and restraint. It is doubtful, for example, if in forming a philosophy of life one could ever "sum up against one's dearest wishes or condemn one's hopes to death". There is nothing deplorable or necessarily undesirable about this : it is a fallacy to suppose that by a strict adherence to logic and the processes of reason we can hope to discover the whole truth about the things which matter most to us. At the same time, it is important that we should recognise what is the true nature of our thinking, and not delude ourselves that it is objective, when it cannot be so.

What passes for " thought " in the outpourings of the daily press, in almost all speeches, lectures and sermons, and in the banalities of conversation, is but an endless circulation of the currency of a limited number of ideas : a process perpetuated by the suggestibility of the human mind. What is not, I think, at all generally appreciated is the telepathic inter-linkage of minds, so that a sufficiently powerful idea will pass below the level of consciousness to other minds, which may then re-echo it. In terms of our imagery of the islands and the submarine continent, we may picture an explosion on one island communicating itself by earth-tremors through the submerged land-mass, so that it is felt far and wide on other islands. In this reside the possibilities of leadership for good or ill.

The phenomenon of suggestibility, of the laws and nature of which we really know very little, must, I surmise, be associated with the degree of conductivity of thought through the island base—as though there might be a stratum at the sea-level either highly conducting or in varying degrees isolating the individual mind from the collective level. The behaviour of crowds is well known to psychologists ; the characteristics of irrationality, capacity for violence, passion and panic are well recognised.* In other words, the crowd-mind is a collective mind swayed by the animal and primitive in Man. It is created apparently by the breakdown of the individual insulating strata and by the temporary submergence

---

* An interesting study is found in W. Trotter : *Instincts of the Herd in Peace and War* (T. Fisher Unwin, Ltd., 1916).

of the personal in the collective. It is highly suggestive : currents of fear, hatred, or any of the emotions can be set moving in it by a strong individual who retains his awareness. All this is made use of not infrequently by unscrupulous persons for their own ends. We have seen examples in the huge rallies of Nazism and Fascism, in the oratory of the demagogue and the emotional fervour of the evangelist. The techniques of induction of the group-mind are comparatively simple : the crowd must be doing the same thing, and their minds engaged on the emotional level. This, of course, is the level below the intellectual. Hence the use of massed marching and of massed bands playing rhythmic martial music. Hence the arts of the demagogue in building up, in order to exploit, the sense of grievance, injustice, and hatred of an oppressor. Hence the sentimental choruses of evangelists and the fervid " Hallelujahs " and " Amens " of the emotional group-mind.

The formation of the group-mind is, we must remember, predominantly moved by emotion and profoundly suggestible. Hence the sexual excesses of such groups, the crowd's passion for revenge, as in lynching, and the extraordinary psychical epidemics which occur from time to time. We have the historical examples of the Crusades, the dancing manias in Germany and Holland in the late fourteenth and early fifteenth centuries, the processions of pilgrims which moved about Europe, engaged in violent self-flagellation, in 1348–49 (the time of the Black Death), and the hysterical witchcraft-hunting of the fifteenth century. The history of medieval religion contains innumerable examples of this sort, and there can be found modern equivalents in our day. There is no doubt that certain techniques are deliberately used by tribal and other groups to achieve this common collective mind, in order to enter into the powerful sensuous intoxication of those primitive volcanic forces found in the deeper levels. The shamanistic dancing of many African tribes,* the corroboree of Australian aboriginals, the frenzy of the dancing dervishes, are all examples of the use of rhythm combined with religious emotion, to submerge the individual mind through a " participation mystique " in the group-mind. It seems probable that certain forms of drug-addiction lead to the same end. On a " higher " level—higher because it does not involve a submergence in the primitive—there is built up a temporary group-mind in theatres and picture-houses. The focusing on a common interest and the emotional identification with the fortunes of the hero or heroine create conditions favourable to this.

In primitive peoples conscious contact with the primitive group-

* Geoffrey Gorer : *Africa Dances* (Penguin Books).

mind is apparently achieved without difficulty—if indeed it is not constantly present. Dr. John Layard tells of " primitive peoples who quite suddenly will all act of one accord with no visible or audible cause ".*

" I instanced the other day the case of the anthropologist accompanied by a native in the depths of the African bush when distant drums were suddenly heard, whereon the native fell on his face saying ' The Chief of so-and-so is dead '. The anthropologist thought, ' Now, I shall be able to solve the riddle of drum-signals ', and asked his companion just what drum rhythm it was that had given this very precise information. The native looked wonderingly at him. The anthropologist insisted, but met with an uncomprehending gaze. It finally transpired that the drum-signal was a perfectly common-or-garden one simply telling the native to internalise his attention, whereupon the native had seen the image of the chief's dead face conveyed not through the cerebro-spinal system, but, as I believe, through the sympathetic nervous system through which as with the insects, this form of communication occurs."

We have looked at these phenomena in some detail so that we may justly estimate Man as a thinker. Creative thought is rare : it flashes into the higher minds of the few who are capable of appreciating it from the buddhic level. All that these can reasonably take pride in is the prepared vessel : the precious water of truth and beauty flows into it from beyond.

Poor homo sapiens (a description, we may hope, anticipatory and prophetic) has feet of clay. As a " thinker " he has for the large part not mounted far above the level of desire, prejudice and self-interest. The veneer of his civilisation is very thin, and just below the surface is a primitive being. In the paper on my table today I read :

" London, July 9th, 1950.
" A wedding was going on in Kena Province, Upper Egypt, at the week-end, when two dogs started fighting nearby. This roused the passions of wedding guests, who started a fight themselves. Firearms, clubs and other weapons were whipped out. Three people were killed and seven injured."

> . . . Man, proud man,
> Drest in a little brief authority,
> Most ignorant of what he's most assured,
> His glassy essence, like an angry ape,
> Plays such fantastic tricks before high heaven
> As make the angels weep.

* *Proceedings of London Society for Psychical Research*, Part 168, p. 239, July 1944.

3. MAN THE ENGINEER

The engineer I take as the type of the man of action, the extravert, the inventor, the technician, the moulder of the natural environment to suit better the needs of Man. One of his earliest discoveries was probably that of fire—a discovery celebrated in the myth of Prometheus. An early offshoot of this must have been artificial light by making use of torches or animal fats and wicks, for some of the drawings in the far recesses of caves are beyond the penetration of daylight. His earliest instruments and weapons were made from stone and bone. Stanley Casson in his fascinating book * says :

> " Actually the making of the first stone implement the eolith, was the greatest *psychological* advance in the history of man at any age. The Paleolithic axe was a vast *technical* advance in that it had a specific and fixed shape. That meant that in the mind of man the first *general idea* had taken shape."

Between these two inventions it is suggested that a period of 180,000 years may have elapsed : a reminder of the enormously accelerated rate of the modern scientific era. The making of tools definitely marked Man off from all other creatures, who, like him, roamed and hunted to collect their food.

The oldest experiment in civilisation of which we know through archæological work is that of Sumer. These people came from mountainous highlands farther north into the valley of the Tigris and Euphrates in the fourth millennium B.C., and created city-states ruled over by kings. They appear to have had organised military forces to protect their civilisation. They applied irrigation and were skilled in agriculture, which was carried on around their cities. The working of metals was performed by them, and their architecture was massive and rectangular. To them goes the credit of inventing a cuneiform script, usually dated about 3000 B.C., and using it to record their laws. It would be difficult to overestimate the invention of writing as a factor contributory to civilisation, for through this in later centuries the knowledge of men in all fields of thought and action has been preserved for succeeding generations.

The Egyptian civilisation which developed later in a land truly described as " the gift of the Nile " has left singularly little by way of legacy to our modern world. Their craftsmanship with stone is the one great achievement at which we wonder today. Almost all else has vanished, leaving only the tradition of an advanced priestcraft skilled in magical and occult lore.

* Stanley Casson : *Progress and Catastrophe* (Hamish Hamilton, 1937).

It is not proposed here even to attempt a summary of the rise and fall of civilisations. This has been done by many competent historians.* I should like to draw attention to two things only. First, the enormously accelerating rate of technical achievement in modern times, and secondly the grave dangers resulting therefrom. Professor Haldane † has said :

> " Between 3000 B.C. and A.D. 1400 there were probably only four really important inventions, namely, the general use of iron, paved roads, voting, and religious intolerance. Perhaps I should have added coinage and long-distance water-supply."

Two hundred years ago life in Great Britain was scarcely more advanced in the technique of civilisation than it had been for the previous 1,500 years. Travel was slow and not without hazard, on foot, on horseback, or in horse-drawn vehicles. News travelled only at the same speed. Houses were lit by oil-lamps or candles, as they had been for millennia, and the life of the country was still predominantly agricultural and urban. Education was rudimentary, and reading and writing were the accomplishments of a minority.

Then began the awakening, and a machine age came into being. James Watt filed the famous patent for his steam engine in 1769, and from then onwards progress in mechanisation has developed at an increasing rate. The steam-propelled engine gave us locomotives not dependent on horses, and ships not dependent on sail. Almost a century later the internal-combustion engine in its varied forms placed a source of power in the hands of the small manufacturer and farmer, and made possible the later development of the motor-car and aeroplane. Up to the end of last century power could be transmitted economically only as far as gears, shafts and belts could convey it : now the electrical transmission of power has made possible its centralised manufacture and widespread distribution, like any other commodity. It has made possible the electrification of railways, the existence of underground railways, radiators and refrigerators and the dentist's drill.

Few things have contributed more to the rapid acceleration of modern civilisation than methods of communication. So long as the leading creative minds of humanity were isolated from each other, progress was inevitably slow. The propagation of ideas through printing must therefore be reckoned as one of fundamental advance. When we contrast the system of bonfires on hill-tops which sig-

---

* Stanley Casson's book is recommended to the general reader. A fuller account is in H. G. Wells' *Outline of History*, and for the specialist student Toynbee's *Study of History* is of course unrivalled.
† J. B. S. Haldane : *The Inequality of Man* (Chatto & Windus, 1932).

nalled to England the appearance of the Spanish Armada with the radar-detection which located the German air-fleets while they were many miles distant from her shores, we have a symbolic picture of the change between then and now. In the mid-nineteenth century the electric telegraph was invented, followed shortly by submarine cables and the invention of the telephone, which has increased the tempo of modern business. Finally in our century came wireless telegraphy and telephony, with their offshoots, the photo-radiogram and tele-vision. With these it is now possible for a person to see the original of any photograph, finger-print or document in any part of the world. The development of broadcasting on a large scale is a force today for good or ill in the life of modern communities.

It is now common knowledge that planes have been built to travel faster than the speed of sound. The technical knowledge which has gone to this achievement is remarkable, when it is remembered that the first flight in a heavier-than-air machine was made only in the early years of the present century. It would be possible to expand an account of modern invention almost indefinitely, but it will suffice to mention in conclusion the recent discovery of a method of transforming a limited amount of nuclear mass into energy, thus ushering in the " Atomic Age ". On December 2nd, 1942, the first self-sustaining chain-reaction pile was set going : the prototype of those forms in which it can be of inestimable value to humanity. On July 16th, 1945, the first bomb releasing nuclear energy was ex-ploded : the precursor of those forms in which it can bring unparal-leled devastation upon the world. It is a melancholy reflection that the culmination of this remarkable co-operative effort by the most brilliant team of mathematicians, physicists, chemists and engineers ever brought together to solve one problem, should have been first applied to the destruction of human life in a large city.

No one surveying the last half-century can fail to be impressed by the enormously accelerated rate of scientific advance, especially in its applied aspects. This rate has resulted in the possession by civilised man of enormous material powers, while no appreciable advance in moral and spiritual achievement has been made. This state of disbalance is full of menace for our time. Man the doer has outstripped spiritual man, and ever and anon arise from the vast deep of his primitive mind those horrific shapes of fear and greed which rule there. The fact is that Man has not yet, for the large part, formed any conception of Life's meaning and purpose in terms beyond the world of sense. He has attached weight to the things he could see and handle, and has neglected as a chimera of imagina-tion or a pious aspiration a world of reality lying behind and inter-penetrating the world of appearance. With this limited outlook he has concentrated on what *he* called reality. He has sought power over Nature. If he has had a slogan to guide him, it has been " the greatest good for the greatest number "—but his concept of this " good " has been economic security, material comfort, pleasurable entertainment and the exercise of power. These have been ends in themselves, and to achieve these ends within the framework of the national state we have seen the fierce competitions of commerce, the pathetic bickerings of politicians and the exploitation of man by man. It should not be a matter for surprise that these primitive emotional drives found in most individuals of every community are reflected on a larger scale in the attitudes of the nations to each other. But whereas too flagrant a disregard for the welfare of others is restrained within the community by law and authority, there is no super-state to exercise a corresponding control of nations. Hence we are looking into the abyss.

In a very charming volume of Rabindranath Tagore's letters*
which we owe to C. F. Andrews, there are many letters which were written during the poet's visit to America in 1920. It is very revealing to note the impact which the life of the West made upon the sensitive mind of the poet. Page after page tells of his craving for the simpler life of his Indian retreat, and of his sense, amid its alien immensities, that the West had lost its way.

> " These Western people have made their money and killed their poetry of life. Here life is like a river, that has heaped up gravel and sand and choked the perennial current of water that flows from an eternal source on the snowy height of an ancient hill. I have learnt since I came here to prize more than ever the infinite worth of the frugal life and simple faith. These Western people believe in their wealth which can only multiply itself and attain nothing. How to convince them of the utter vanity of their pursuits! They do not have the time to realise that they are not happy. They try to smother their leisure with rubbish or dissipation, lest they discover that they are the unhappiest of mortals. They deceive their souls with counterfeits, and then, in order to hide that fact from themselves, they artificially keep up the value of those false coins by an unceasing series of self-deceptions.
>
> " What makes me feel so sad in this country is the fact that people here do not know that they are not happy. They are proud, like the sandy desert, which is proud of its glitter. This Sahara is mightily big; but my mind turns its back upon it and sings:
>
> I will arise and go now, and go to Innisfree,
> And a small cabin build there, of clay and wattles made;

* C. F. Andrews: *Letters to a Friend* (George Allen & Unwin, 1929).

Nine bean rows will I have there, a hive for the honey bee,
And live alone in the bee-loud glade.

In the modern age, with all its facilities of communication, the access to Innisfree has become most difficult."

Allow that much of Tagore's prose is poetry, and compels assent by the beauty of its expression, it is nevertheless true that for real insight, few either of the East or West can be regarded as his equal. What he saw clearly was that our type of civilisation offers men that which is not in itself spiritually satisfying. Its offerings are fundamentally material wealth and the things such wealth can procure.

What our best Western thinkers realise, and have told us again and again, is that we must determine what really constitutes the good life, and then our actions may become a means to this end. It does not mean that we shall fail to pursue to its utmost limits knowledge of the physical world, or cease to build upon such knowledge further technological achievements. It would mean, however, that we should not be enslaved by these achievements, and that they would be seen in correct perspective as a part—and only a small part—of a vast universe.

4. MAN THE ESCAPIST

The West is apt to forget, in its interpretation of life, that one third of mankind has never shared its enthusiasm for action and achievement, but has regarded this world as a place to be endured, and whenever possible escaped from. This attitude has been, at least in the popular mind, associated with Buddhism, and to a lesser degree with Hinduism, but it has in some measure a place also in Christianity. The attitude of escapism, therefore, has religious sanctions, based upon an estimate of the relative importance of this life to a larger whole, and as such it has both its eloquent defenders and its violent critics. We here only remark that both groups have commonly misunderstood the real inwardness of religious teaching on this matter. We shall let a distinguished Indian philosopher speak : *

"The question is not, What shall I do to be saved ? but, In what *spirit* shall I do ? Detachment of spirit and not renunciation of the world is what is demanded from us . . . what matters is not the possession or non-possession of things, but our attitude towards them. The

* S. Radhakrishnan : *Eastern Religions and Western Thought* (O.U.P.), pp. 101, 131.

question relates to the desires and the appetites, not to the things to which they are directed. It is what a man *is*, not what he *has*, his frame of mind that matters."

There are so many forms of escape, that some analysis is called for. If a man can persuade himself that the work he is doing is valuable—and success is one of the subtlest persuasives—his outlook is likely to be one of extraverted full participation in life. He will be a believer in action. If, on the other hand, a man cannot persuade himself that his work is worth while, whether because others have not so regarded it or because it is in its nature unsatisfying to the creative urge, his outlook becomes one of escape. Many ordinary people are involved in work of which much is dreary and monotonous. They are, in Joad's phrase, "persons of no distinction performing actions of no importance". The nature of modern civilised life is such that many are required to perform tasks in which any sense of service to the community is comparatively remote, in which the varied exercise of judgment is little called for, and in which there remains but little æsthetic or creative satisfaction. The natural result is that people are concerned to acquire the maximum of leisure from this work and the maximum means to enjoy their leisure.

Associated with modern industry and business is the growth of the big industrial city—an obnoxious and cancerous growth. Compounded of streets from which even the sunshine is half excluded by miscellaneous and ugly buildings, sprayed by the smoke of a myriad chimneys, polluted by the fumes of cars and motor-buses, a place of constant noise, exhibiting all the sordidness of slums and all the tawdriness of cheap wares and advertisements, the modern industrial city is the very antithesis of the things with which the human spirit has its real affinity. We are not as yet many generations removed from a simpler life in contact with the Earth, and a common nostalgia for this is shown by the widespread desire to escape from the city whenever possible, and the marked reluctance to return to it.

Some forty years ago A. C. Benson, Master of Magdalene College, Cambridge, a writer and essayist, tried an interesting experiment in escape. He tells us that he decided to choose a life which was "wholesome, temperate and simple, in exchange for one which was complicated, restless and mechanical". It was not, he disclaims, an attempt to shirk his share of the natural human burden, but that he felt he had carried the burden long enough without having the curiosity to see what it contained. He went to live in a little house in the Cambridge Fen country, and called it the Silent Isle because of the spacious sense of remoteness and unapproachability which the scene conveyed. He describes *

> " the vast space of sky everywhere, the enormous perspective of rolling cloud bank and fleecy cumulus. . . . The morning comes up more sedately ; the orange-skirted twilight is more lingeringly withdrawn. The sun burns lower, down to the very verge of the world. . . . Nothing but a little tide of homely life ebbs and flows in these elm-girt villages about the fen. Of course the anxious and expectant heart carries its own restlessness everywhere ; but to read of the rush and stress of life in these grassy solitudes seems like the telling of an idle tale."

Here Benson tried his experiment :

> " to live simply and honestly, without indolence or haste, neither wasting time nor devouring it, not refusing due burdens but not inventing useless ones, not secluding myself in a secret cell of solitude, but not multiplying dull and futile relations."

The fruit of this time is given to us in two of the author's books. It must suffice to say that the opportunity to order his life exactly as he desired did not yield to him that secret key of understanding for which he was searching. He wrote afterwards :

> " The fact is that one is purloining experience instead of paying the natural price of it, estimating things by the outside instead of from the inside, and growing thus to care more for the strangeness, the contrast, the picturesqueness of it all, than for the love and hope and the elemental forces, of which the world is but the garb and scene."

Benson thus expressed his discovery that there is no ultimate satisfaction or happiness for men in substituting for an aspect of the external world for which they do not care, another aspect of it for which they think they would care more. The true escape is within, from a level of lesser significance to one of greater significance. It is here we must look for the key to life's meaning. As Milton said :

> The mind is its own place and in itself
> Can make a heaven of hell, a hell of heaven.

In their attitude to life people seem to fall in five groups :

(a) The extraverts, the men of action, the full participants. " Life here and now is all we know," they say. " This alone matters, all else is speculation. Live it intensely, drink deep of all experience, that the full potentialities of your personality may be realised ! " Here are the generals and soldiers of fortune, the politicians and the pirates, the merchant princes, the pleasure-seekers, the adventurers and

* A. C. Benson: *The Silent Isle*, pp. 2, 13, 389 (John Murray).

explorers, the conquerors of sea, land and air, the builders and destroyers of empires, the Churchills and Alexanders—all who have shown courage and lent colour to the world.

(*b*) There are the ethical participants, benevolent, human, compassionate, idealistic : often, though not necessarily, religious-minded men. They see life as an opportunity for service. The ideal order of society—Utopia, or whatever it may be called—is to be built on earth through devoted work and self-sacrifice.

> I will not cease from mental fight,
> 　　Nor shall my sword sleep in my hand,
> Till we have built Jerusalem
> 　　In England's green and pleasant land.

Action is not for its own sake, not for the exhilaration or the plaudits which it brings to the doer : it is for a great and noble purpose, a social end far beyond the self. They accept the world as a rather mysterious battle-ground of the opposites, and throw themselves into the fight on the side of the good. Here are to be found many of the noblest men and women—philanthropists, reformers, teachers, healers, and many others who have placed mankind immeasurably in their debt.

(*c*) The third group are the hedonist-escapists. Their environment is confining or their work is unsatisfying, and thus they seek diversion or forgetfulness in sex, sport, speed, and in other ways. It is not a true, or in the long run a satisfactory escape ; for it is an attempt to change the environment, instead of the self. In our day and in our Western form of civilisation this constitutes a very large group.

(*d*) The fourth group are the religious-escapists. They believe there is real happiness to be found, but that it is independent of external circumstance. They see change, futility and suffering as the main characteristics of the outer world. The efforts of the good and the doings of the bad are alike swept away by the stream of time. The wise man therefore abandons the world, with its insensate strife and barren activity, for an attitude and a quest in which true joys are to be found. In our modern day many of those in this group find escape into music, art, literature and philosophy. The religious man who believes the supreme good is in union with God turns to meditation, contemplation and mysticism. This famous attitude to life of world-negation or renunciation is traditionally Indian, and, on the whole, alien to the Western temper. But in Greece it found a flowering in Stoicism, and through this contributed to almost all later philosophies. It was a tenet of Gnosticism, and markedly influenced Christian thought in its first two centuries. Indeed, it took historic forms in eremitism, monasticism and puritanism.

(e) To these we must in justice add a fifth group whose philosophy of life requires a *via media* between the second and fourth groups. They would balance both contemplation and action, the worship of God and the service of Man, believing that here and now both elements must contribute to the best living. This philosophy of life can be more effectively presented later.* Here we shall merely recognise the truth in the view of Plotinus that we live simultaneously in two worlds (possibly in more than two). From this arise the tensions of Man's life, and in this are enshrined the interest and the greatness of his destiny.

* See Part IV.

Chapter

5

TOWARDS A PHILOSOPHY OF SCIENCE

" Matter is an abstraction ; we shall never be able to realise what
it is, for our world of reality does not acknowledge it. Even the
giant forces of the world, centripetal and centrifugal, are kept out
of our recognition. They are the day-labourers not admitted into
the audience-hall of creation. But light and sound come to us in
their gay dresses as troubadours singing serenades before the
windows of the senses. What is constantly before us, claiming
our attention, is not the kitchen but the feast ; not the anatomy of
the world, but its countenance."

RABINDRANATH TAGORE (*Creative Unity*).

" There is no more fundamental way in which reality inheres in
anything finite than as an *aspect* of something which lies a step
nearer to the absolutely real."

G. N. M. TYRRELL (*Grades of Significance*).

AFTER a survey of the data which natural science has accumulated,
and the theories which it has advanced to correlate and understand
them, the enquiring mind is always haunted by the questions " Why
should these things be ? What sort of a universe is it in which
these data arise ? Can they tell us anything of its nature, or what is
our own relationship to it ? " As soon as we try to answer these
questions we enter the realm of philosophy. The humble scientist
who approaches this territory seems to see the warning notice,
" Enter these enchanted woods, you who dare ", and with something of the trepidation of the adventurous little boy who fears to
meet a gamekeeper, he must tread softly and circumspectly.

That which can be said at the present stage of our enquiry is, in
my view, very limited ; for it will be the purpose of this book to show
that the data of psychic research and mystical experience also demand
consideration in any satisfactory philosophy of life.

I. THE WORLD OF PHYSICS AND THE WORLD OF
COMMON SENSE

The plain man has no doubt that there is a real world outside him :
a world of objects such as chairs and tables, rocks and trees and
people, and a world of events such as cause him to hear a sound or

see a flash of light. If he is asked whether his thoughts and feelings are also real, he will probably say, " Yes, but not in the same way, because they cannot be seen or heard or handled by people." If the convenient distinction between objective and subjective were explained to him, he would probably be quite happy to accept a " real " world containing these two classes of objects : some of which existed outside himself, which everyone could verify, and of which he was not the creator, and others which existed within himself for which he was responsible. If we proceeded to ask him about his dreams or imaginations, he would probably become rather worried and wish to sub-divide the subjective realm into some things which were real and some which were not. Probably we should not elicit his views any further.

The ordinary non-philosophically-minded physicist or chemist considers that there is a real world outside himself composed of matter and energy. These two things he probably regards as different forms of one and the same thing ; for he is aware that matter can be transformed into energy and that there is a quantitative relationship between them. Matter, he says, is constructed from ninety-two different kinds of atoms, and these in turn are constructed from protons and electrons—arranged in different ways. All things, he would say, are built up from these positive and negative charges in rapid motion and the radiation-energy they emit and absorb. If he is asked how he reconciles this picture with the plain man's world of colours, smells, tastes, etc. (which certainly electrons and protons do not themselves possess), he probably says these qualities are created and bestowed upon the outside world by the observer's mind. He regards the objective reality as the scientist's world, and when this impinges through the special senses upon the observer's mind, he derives the plain man's world of colours, tastes, smells, temperatures, etc.—which he would say is obviously subjective.

The more critically-minded scientist is, I think, in a state of be-wilderment. Sometimes he is disposed to regard the plain man's world of colours, tastes, smells, etc., as subjective, created by the Mind, and thus a world of appearance only. In this case he reason-ably asks why the minds of men make that particular choice of qualities which in fact they do, with which to endow the world. The range of creative choice is very wide : why these particular qualities ? Moreover, once postulate that the Mind creates and endows the world of appearance and we must naturally feel anxious to know the limits of this kind of activity, and the governing con-ditions—if we are ever to find Truth. Sometimes, on the other hand, he is disposed to regard the observer's mind as selective, not creative. This view seems persuasive when we reflect upon the extent to which the world of appearance changes with the power and range of the instruments (including the special senses) used to survey it. We amplified this in Chapter 2 (4). On this view, then, there must be a background which is more comprehensive than the world of appearance, the latter being derived from this background by the selectivity of the special senses. We used earlier the simile of Mind as a prisoner in a round tower only able to view the outside through five slits. On such a view we have to decide what is the nature of this background from which all these properties of colour, taste, touch and smell are selected. Obviously it is not material in the form of protons, electrons and energy : presumably it is of the nature of mind.

When we ask the more critically-minded scientist what status and significance he attaches to the physicist's world-picture of protons and electrons, we shall find, I think, that he is equally uncertain. If he takes the first of the above views—that the mind is *creative* of the plain man's world, which is thus subjective—he naturally regards the physicist's world as the objective basis of it and in some sense real. There then arise to haunt him the strange discoveries of recent physics referred to in the Appendix. The " objective " bricks of the physicist's world have not turned out to be the straightforward *particles* they were once pictured. They sometimes appear to behave like waves. They seem elusive in space and time, and leading physicists like Heisenberg long ago abandoned objective mechanical models of atoms, electrons, protons, etc. They are content to take the metrical data of the world and correlate them mathematically. The terms " electron ", " proton ", etc., are thus regarded as symbols only—perhaps reflections of something which exists in a more real background. Thus we have left behind the objectivity of the physicist's world. It looks as though it, too, is *selected* from a background by the mind and is to this extent another subjective world. We seem, then, to have two worlds of appearance : the plain man's world, and the physicist's world, both derived from some more comprehensive background by the *selectivity* of the special senses and mind. The qualitative selection gives the plain man's world, and the quantitative selection gives the physicist's world.

Such a view leaves unanswered some fundamental questions :

What is the nature and status of this background ?

What is its relation to the world of values ?

What determines the particular selectivity of Mind, both qualitative and quantitative ?

Before we attempt to answer such questions, let us ask the philosopher what he has to say about the physicist's world and the plain man's world. This question, in fact, is a particular form of one of his major problems : the nature of knowledge. If he understood fully what was involved in the statement " I see a table ", half his problems would be solved. Most philosophers, I think, agree that what we experience every day through the use of our senses are not so-called physical objects, such as chairs and tables, but are sense-data. They are such things as patches of contrasting colour, sounds, smells, sensations of resistance to touch, etc. Such sense-data may lead us to infer something which we call a physical object as the source of them, but it seems quite clear that we must not regard our collection of sense-data as *identical* with this external " something ". Joad,* for example, says, " The notion of a persistent physical object is logically no more than a hypothesis to explain the fact that the objects of a number of perceptual situations can be correlated ". Joad is not apparently able to go farther than to say, " The direct apprehension of a sense-datum causes the apprehender to *think* of a physical object ". As an algebraic expression is deduced from, and is a summary of, a large number of numerical data, so the object postulated is a deduction from, and a summary of, the sense-data which are all that we really know. This object, supposed to be in the outside world, might quite conceivably be of the nature of mind, and not crudely physical at all. I think we must admit logically we cannot directly know anything of its inherent properties. All we really perceive are the sense-data, and because other people in the same neighbourhood, as far as we can determine, have approximately similar sense-data, it seems reasonable to postulate some object of common reference, apart from the individual observers.

Similarly, scientific objects such as electrons and protons are not directly apprehended as parts of the physical world ; our supposition as to their existence is an inference wholly based on a selection of sense-data (Eddington's " pointer-readings "). They have, in other words, the same relation to sense-data and the same status as the supposed " physical objects ". Joad definitely holds that gathering knowledge is a process of revelation and not of construction; that the mind's function is in this respect like a searchlight's, which is to reveal what is there. He does not consider that either the so-called " physical " objects or scientific objects are mental *constructions*, but considers them as elements in a " subsistent world " which the mind

* C. E. M. Joad : *Philosophical Aspects of Modern Science*, pp. 137, 140 (George Allen & Unwin, 1932).

D

is able to apprehend directly just as it is able to apprehend sense-data directly. It is the world of sense-data alone which Joad considers should be called the *physical* world. The subsistent world is considered to be composed of the objects which we know otherwise than in sensory experience. It is the world which the mind apprehends in thinking, whether in judging or imagining. It is the world of " objects of thought ", a world of which minds become aware when they reach a certain stage of evolutionary development. Thus animals and babies may be supposed aware of sense-data only ; men and perhaps some higher animals become aware of this " subsistent " world. More advanced types of men, such as artists, become aware, beyond this subsistent world, of objects of value.

With apologies to the reader who prefers the symbols of language to those of geometry, the appended diagram may convey a hint of

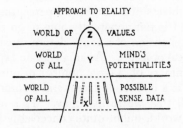

these relationships. The conical round tower is the individual mind, which, as it evolves, is pictured as rising through three orders of existence. The lowest stratum is that of all conceivable sense-data : the physical world such as it might appear to a creature with an infinite range of senses. The worlds of actual appearance are selected by the five slits symbolising the special senses.

If it be asked what determines the particular selectivity which is in fact made—why, for example, there are five senses, instead of four or six ; why the eye only responds to a certain narrow range of colours ; why of all possible values for the velocity of light it should be 300,000 kilometres a second, and of all possible values for Planck's constant it should be just 6.55×10^{-27} erg-sec. and not otherwise, no answer seems within reach. I am not sure that they are wholly reasonable questions. If one plays a game, it is reasonable enough to ask what is its aim and purpose ; but not why the rules are just as they are, and not otherwise. It is only within *these* rules that *this* game can be played, and only within the framework of *some* rules that *any* game can be played. So it is only within the framework of some limitation that the individual can arise : this at least is clear.

Moreover, we have seen that the whole evolutionary trend is towards increasing awareness—an awareness of objects of increasing significance. This is important and satisfying knowledge, though its full import lies far beyond the confines of the world which science has explored.

2. LIMITATIONS OF THE SCIENTIFIC METHOD

A most remarkable change of outlook has marked the thought of leaders of science in the last half-century. Up to the end of the nineteenth century science was prepared to describe itself as " organised common sense ". The plain man and the physicist both accepted their environment substantially at its face value as real, substantial and mechanical, nor were they troubled by the speculations of philosophers, which they regarded as belonging to a world apart from theirs. Then came a period of intense study of the atom, and the architecture of atoms and molecules was built up on the newly discovered fundamental particles—electrons, protons and neutrons. Up to this point, science had taken pride in its objectivity : its truths had been rooted in the external world, and were not dependent on any observer. From then onwards the first doubts began to arise, for manifestly the plain man's world contained data of colour, smell, hardness, etc., which the fundamental particles could not be supposed to possess. Moreover, relativity had found it necessary to bring the observer into the picture, to account for large-scale phenomena. It was still, however, supposed that mechanism, in terms of which large-scale phenomena were understood, was also the basis of the atomic order. The difference was presumed to be one of scale only. Then at last came the shattering blow to mechanism The fundamental " particles " proved not to be particles at all in any ordinary sense : sometimes, in fact, they behaved like waves. Space and Time—valuable and useful concepts in the plain man's world—became elusive concepts in the microcosm. The very objectivity of the fundamental " particles " became open to question, and they were spoken of as " shadows " or " symbols " : reality was elsewhere. No change of outlook could be more complete, and Joad * in surveying this speaks of the " all-fours " attitude to various forms of human experience which it is now proper to adopt.

" Conscious experience takes many forms. Of these one is the consciousness of the scientist. . . . If this is in essence revelatory, and introduces us to an external reality of objective things, a similar

* Joad : loc. cit., p. 191.

claim must be conceded in respect of the religious and æsthetic consciousness. . . . If the worlds of art and religion are subjective, mere externalisations of our minds and projections of our wishes, so too, may be the world of science. The claims of each to reveal to us an objective world must in fact be treated on merits."

Eddington * expresses the same idea in the following sentence :

> " Physical Science has limited its scope so as to leave a background which we are at liberty to, or even invited to, fill with a reality of spiritual import."

Apart from its now-recognised limitation of scope, there is another limitation inherent in scientific method, which it is important not to overlook. This limitation arises from the fact that the method of science is essentially analytical : finding out more and more about less and less. It has been expressed by different thinkers in different terms. J. C. Smuts expresses it in his philosophy of Holism, and G. N. M. Tyrrell in his book *Grades of Significance*.

Consider our scientific methods of studying anything—say, a piece of country. The surveyor using *his* instruments could prepare an accurate map of surface relationships and heights. The agricultural expert could give us a map of cultivation and soil-properties. The geologist with a different technique could give us another map with quite different information. An artist using very different methods might present to us pictures of the country which stirred our emotions. Each method gives us its own aspect of the truth about the country. It is reliable *as far as it goes*, but it is an abstraction from the reality itself. If you went to live in this countryside you would realise its essential nature far more vividly and completely than from a study of all the maps, pictures and guide-books. Yet you could never know it fully ; for the reality is more than the sum of all the knowledge which can be gathered about it. No abstract knowledge, nor the sum of all such knowledge, can ever convey the fullness of immediate experience. It is probable that the measure of sympathetic identification achieved by a poet † when he can write, " It is I who bloom in flowers, spread in the grass, flow in the water, scintillate in the stars, live in the lives of men of all ages ", is as profound an understanding as can be achieved.

Every science is analytical in its character, and according to its type of technique and its instruments of analysis it sifts out knowledge. Thus in the study of Man, anatomy studies his bodily structures ; histology studies these tissues under the microscope ; physiology studies the modes of functioning ; biochemistry studies

---

* Eddington : *The Nature of the Physical World*, p. 339 (C.U.P.).
† Tagore : *Letters to a Friend*, p. 70 ; by C. F. Andrews.

the chemical processes involved; psychology studies his mental processes, and so forth. Each of these methods of study presents doubtless an accurate, but certainly only a very partial, aspect of Man. When you have made a complete study of all the sciences of Man, there is still something of the utmost significance missing. It is that which constitutes individuality—which makes one man different from another—and makes for the richness of human friendship. The experience of being man gives you something which the sum of all scientific study could never provide.

The method of scientific study is to abstract from the whole a certain type of data. As someone has said: " Each science is like a net which catches a certain type of fish and allows other kinds to slip through." In thus isolating data, and making an increasingly minute study of smaller parts, we need to realise that we may be progressively leaving something out : something which depends on the relationship of the parts and may be of great significance. A work of art is an example of this. You could remove from a canvas all the red pigment, then the blue, then the yellow, the green, and so on, and by chemical analysis you might come to learn a lot about pigments—but that which gave æsthetic pleasure has vanished with the disturbed relationship of the pigments. The picture was much more than the sum of the pigments : they were all there on the palette beforehand, but the significant relationship was then absent.

Take a simple example from chemistry. We know that the ninety-two different chemical elements are constructed from various arrangements of the three fundamental particles, electrons, protons and neutrons. The number and relationships of these determine all the variety of properties known in the chemical elements : a fact so familiar that we do not find it surprising. We know the properties of sodium, a soft, shiny-looking metal which tarnishes easily and reacts violently with water. We know the properties of chlorine, a faint greenish-yellow gas with a pungent odour. No one could have predicted from this the properties of a molecule of sodium chloride—common salt. These two atoms placed in a close relationship form a new whole, with properties that do not inhere in either of the individual atoms. Millions of cells may form organs, and a complex of organs may form an organism. As larger wholes are formed, some new properties emerge because of the new *relationships* involved. These new properties are not deducible as the sum of the properties of the component parts. This is the essence of J. C. Smuts' philosophy of " Holism "—a philosophy of " wholes ".

It is important to keep in mind, when we are studying some part or aspect of a large whole, that we may have no inkling from our study of the parts of the potentialities of the whole. Some of the surprising faculties of Man as a functioning being are very unlike anything which might be guessed or predicted from these partial studies. They may derive, in fact, from the relationships between different parts of his very complex structure (see Chapter 12).

The study of selected aspects, and the analytical methods which characterise the sciences, are very reminiscent of our own self's selective relationship, which we depicted in the diagram of the round tower. It is as though within it there are miniature round towers— the scientific techniques—each selecting its own type of sense-data for study. The limitations of the knowledge which each of these isolates bears to the greater whole something of the relationship of our restricted world of sense-data to the vast world of which we regarded it as a selected part. In studying Man as a functioning whole, those of us who are trained in the partial disciplines of science should bear in mind the unpredictable properties of wholes. We should be prepared to expect the unexpected—and we shall not be disappointed.

3. GRADES OF SIGNIFICANCE

In a book with this title,* G. N. M. Tyrrell has made a different approach to the same theme. These ideas are so important (being, indeed, a key to understanding in all fields of enquiry), and Tyrrell's method of approach is so persuasive, that we shall here present a very brief summary of them. He points out that all things and all events can be regarded as existing on various grades of significance, and the measure of significance which they possess for the apprehending mind depends on the latter's development. To an animal a book would be a coloured shape; to a savage it might be, in addition, a collection of a lot of black marks curiously arranged on the paper. An intelligent savage who did not know anything of writing might investigate the symbols and discover by patient classification and analysis the external laws of ordering and using these symbols. To an educated man the book conveys meanings and ideas, a concept which our analytically-minded savage would find difficult to grasp. His facts belong to a lower significant grade, and from that level of significance the higher man's view that the book expressed meanings would seem fanciful and mystical.

A human being may be a collection of interesting physico-chemical processes to a physiologist, a complex assembly of behaviour patterns

---

* G. N. M. Tyrrell: *Grades of Significance* (1st ed., 1930; 2nd ed. 1947). The reader is strongly urged to study this book. (Rider & Co.)

to a psychologist, a useful servant to an employer, a lovable person to a friend, a focus of infinite spiritual possibilities to the sage. He is what the observer has the capacity to see in him. What he is seen to be is a measure of the observer's degree of development. A poet has truly said, " Who worships greatness passing by, himself is great ". Understanding or true knowledge is always a function of being.

This general principle is relevant to the philosophical questions we have been discussing. When the plain man and the physicist look at the world, they see different aspects, because they occupy different observation points. It is not that one view is truer or profounder than the other : both views are partial and alike abstracted from reality. They are both apprehensions of the world on approximately the same level of significance—the intellectual level, which is only one level among many. As Tyrrell says : *

> " Understanding is knowing on one definite grade of significance, and it is on this account that intellectual concepts are all abstractions. This is also the reason why knowledge intellectually gained is so clear and precise—so satisfactory to the tidy mind; so unsatisfactory to the mind that hungers for meanings."

The plain man's world and the physicist's world (X in our diagram of the round tower) are not regarded as illusions, but as having a degree of reality arising from the fact that they are aspects of something which is more real. It is on this deeper level (Y in our diagram) that the more real essences of things are supposed to exist, and that all perception really takes place. Perception of physical objects does not take place on the physical level by means of physical organs such as eye, ear, nose and touch. The human body and its sense-organs are themselves *aspects* of something else—of the more real person lying beneath. Objects, events, processes—all that we project on to an external world are conceived as shadows or aspects of underlying realities, and the more real activities and relationships are located there. The more fundamental phenomena take place on level Y, but we, as incarnate beings, project them on to the level of greater separateness X, which we call the physical world.

The common sense picture of the world is adequate for the ordinary business of living, but as soon as we want to know meanings, we have got to approach on a higher level of significance, and then we discover a world very unlike the familiar one—a world of which the latter is only a partial aspect. As we have seen, X is a shadow or an aspect of Y; likewise we may assume Y is a shadow

* Loc. cit., p. 52.

or an aspect of Z, and so on.   We may regard existence as stratified —i.e., as realisable on different grades of significance.   It is the recognition of this which gave rise to the Eastern doctrine of Maya, often glibly interpreted by the West as " All is illusion ".   From the viewpoint of a higher grade of significance, a lower grade of inter-pretation is seen to be so inadequate and partial and lacking in knowledge of the larger whole, that although it is undesirable to do so, it scarcely seems an injustice to call it " illusion ".   From the viewpoint of a lower grade of significance, the very existence of any higher grade may be unrecognised, and even to postulate it may seem imaginative or mystical.

This general standpoint indicates the inherent limitations present in any type of enquiry.   Natural Science has ordered and classified and correlated data on one level of significance : the physical level or level of sense-data.   For long its leaders believed that they were studying a self-contained objective field, with no direct connection with the observing minds ; now they recognise this is not so.   They have not, however, yet come to recognise, what from our standpoint is apparent, that the continuous pursuit of physical data, their further ordering and correlation, cannot ever hope to provide answers to the profounder questions of " Why " and " Wherefore ".   To answer these, and so fully to understand the physical world, we must penetrate into and interpret from a higher significant grade.   The next higher significant grade is found, we venture to think, in the field of psychical research.   This complex field, which we may find it necessary to subdivide, ranges between the physical on the one hand, and the mental on the other.   It holds, we believe—although our knowledge of it is only elementary as yet—the clues to a full understanding of the physical world, and it becomes therefore our immediate field of enquiry in the following section of this book.

PART II
THE DATA OF PSYCHICAL RESEARCH

Chapter

6

TELEPATHY AND CLAIRVOYANCE

" The limits of our spectrum do not inhere in the sun that shines,
but in the eye that marks his shining. Beyond each end of that
prismatic ribbon are ether waves of which our retina takes no
cognisance. . . . Even thus, I venture to affirm, beyond each end
of our conscious spectrum extends a range of faculty and perception, exceeding the known range but as yet indistinctly guessed.
. . . Beyond the *red* end, of course, we know . . . that organic
processes are constantly taking place within us, which are not
subject to our control, but which make the very foundation of our
physical being. . . . The faculties that lie beyond the violet end
of our psychological spectrum will need more delicate exhibition,
and will command a less ready belief . . . yet it is *that* prolongation
of our spectrum upon which our gaze will need to be most
strenuously fixed. It is *there* that we shall find our enquiry
opening upon a cosmic prospect, and inciting us upon an endless
way."

F. W. H. MYERS (written before 1896).

" It is hardly necessary for me to reiterate my often expressed
conviction of the extreme importance for philosophy and psychology
of the well-established results of psychical research, and my regret
that most philosophers and psychologists are content to remain in
ignorance of them. Telepathy, both simultaneous and precognitive, is now an experimentally established fact."

PROFESSOR C. D. BROAD (written recently).

I. INTRODUCTION

IT is astonishing to reflect upon the indirectness and complexity of
the means by which one mind communicates its thoughts and
feelings to another mind. If A wishes to communicate with B he is
obliged to use some mutually understood code. The most commonly used codes are black marks on paper (writing) and sounds in
air (speaking). Where neither of these is possible, gestures with
the fingers may be used, or in the case of the blind, the Braille code.
Communication by any of these means is then possible between
two persons who know the same language, but the extent and precision of communication are clearly limited by the degree to which
they share in common words and associations which convey to each
of them the same subtleties of feeling and delicacies of meaning.
Consider further the complexity of one of these processes—e.g., that
by which A speaks to B. The idea in A's mind, in some wholly

mysterious way, produces electrical excitation in several related parts of his cerebral cortex. From one part of the cortex impulses pass along nerves to the intercostal muscles and the diaphragm to control the rate of expulsion of air through the larynx. From another part of the cortex nerve-impulses pass to the muscles of the lips, cheeks and tongue to dispose them correctly as regards volume and shape. At the same time nerve-impulses from another part of the cortex operate muscles which control, as regards tension and position, the vocal cords in the larynx. As a result of this co-ordinated action, sound-waves of a very complex character are emitted into the air. Some of them—a very small fraction only—impinge on the tympanic membrane of B's ear. A chain of three small bones conveys vibrations to a small oval window, passing through which they are carried by fluid to the delicate basilar membrane. Minute fibres in this are caused to vibrate sympathetically, and delicate hairs are thus subject to varying tensions. Nerve-impulses pass away from these hair-cells and are conveyed by the auditory nerve to a part of the brain of B, where some wholly mysterious interaction with the mind of B leads him to believe that he has the same idea as A formerly had.

Reflection upon the complexity and indirectness of this process, by which communication between the minds of A and B takes place through the intermediate activity of their physical bodies and of physical energy in the space between them, naturally leads to the question whether some more direct form of communication does not exist. The word " telepathy " was devised by F. W. H. Myers to denote the communication of ideas from one mind to another, independently of the recognised channels of sense. Whether in fact there is such a thing was one of the first major questions which the Society for Psychical Research, founded in 1882 in London, set out to determine. Throughout human history, from the earliest records, we gather that there has been a persistent popular belief that some people have possessed a power or faculty of gathering knowledge other than through sensory means or rational inference. Such beliefs have included not only telepathy (one aspect of which is sometimes called thought-reading), but also clairvoyance (often called second-sight), dreams that are prophetic, oracles that proclaim future events, hauntings and apparitions and many such para-normal phenomena. The attitude of orthodox science to these popular beliefs has generally been one of indifference : it has regarded them as superstitious or " old wives' tales ". Occasionally it has been one of hostility to those who have spent time in investigating them. Although these attitudes are strictly incompatible with the scientific temper and outlook, there are adequate psychological reasons for them. It must be remembered how much fraud, charlatanry and sensation-mongering have gathered round these subjects, creating for the scientific mind associations of antipathy and mistrust. It must be remembered also that the scientist has fought a long fight, successfully, against popular superstition and medieval theological dogmatism, and is naturally vigilant to see that such things are not readmitted to the world of knowledge in respectable disguise. Moreover, the measure of success which scientists have had in interpreting the natural world has led them to believe that certain types of alleged events, which cannot be explained by any known laws, are for that reason highly improbable. To give but one illustration : science has always regarded it as axiomatic that causes precede effects in the time-series. If it be supposed that a future event can become foreknown, all processes of deduction or rational inference being ruled out as accounting for this, then it looks at first sight as though a future event must be the cause of a present mental state. The utter strangeness of some of the alleged facts gives them an aura of improbability, and at least calls for a very high and unimpeachable quality of evidence if they are to be considered seriously. A little thought shows that if even one such phenomenon as telepathy is established, the basis of any materialistic philosophy is destroyed, and we are introduced to a new order of things existing in its own right, and not just as an epiphenomenon of matter. If such paranormal phenomena as telepathy, clairvoyance and precognition are established, it is not too much to say that the bounds of Man's universe are widened without known limit, and he himself is a star of the first magnitude. The issues involved are therefore of the utmost importance.

A number of factors in the mid-nineteenth century conspired to produce the first serious critical investigations of the para-normal. On the one hand, the phenomena of hypnotism had been subject to study and scrutiny by a number of medical men. In this unusual state of consciousness not only was it found possible to suggest anæsthesia under which major operations could be performed, but several investigators had noticed at times a mental rapport between the agent and the subject which appeared to be telepathic in character. Cases were reported where the agent placed various substances in his mouth, unknown to the patient, who correctly described the taste as though experienced by himself. Pain produced by pinching various parts of the agent's body was felt and localised by the hypnotised subject in another room. Janet, the distinguished French psychotherapist, is said to have succeeded in inducing hypnotic trance *telepathically*, in eighteen out of twenty-five of his patients at times when they had no reason to expect it. Such ostensible examples of telepathy were a stimulus to further examination.

About the middle of the nineteenth century were also to be found the first beginnings of spiritualism in New York. Despite all the welter of credulity and fraud which came to be associated with its rapid growth, there were notable examples of mediums such as D. D. Home * and W. Stainton Moses,† in whose presence paranormal phenomena of both a mental and physical type had been witnessed by numerous responsible observers. These, together with the nature of mediumship and the validity of claims based upon it, challenged responsible and impartial scientific enquiry. Fortunately a group of men in Cambridge of outstanding scholarship and integrity were willing to undertake this task, and in February 1882 the Society for Psychical Research was founded. Its first President was Henry Sidgwick, Knightbridge Professor of Moral Philosophy in Cambridge. Other foundation members were F. W. H. Myers, a distinguished classical scholar and educationalist; Edmund Gurney, also a classicist with an aptitude for psychological experiment; Frank Podmore, a brilliant and sceptical thinker, and William Barrett, Professor of Physics in Dublin. During its history the Society has had the support in its Presidential Chair of such men as Professor Balfour-Stewart, F.R.S., the Earl of Balfour, O.M., Professor William James, Sir William Crookes, O.M., F.R.S., F. W. H. Myers, Sir Oliver Lodge, F.R.S., Professor Charles Richet, Bishop Boyd Carpenter, Professor Henri Bergson, Dr. F. C. S. Schiller, Professor Gilbert Murray, Dr. L. P. Jacks, Lord Rayleigh, O.M., F.R.S., Professor William McDougall, Professor Hans Driesch, Dr. W. F. Prince and others. The *Proceedings* of the Society, which now cover about seventy years of research and investigation, have maintained a critical standard comparable with the best publications of learned scientific societies. It can now be claimed that there is a mass of well-attested and carefully sifted evidence, as well as of experimental research, upon which reliable conclusions may be based. Every competent student of this field is aware that our knowledge is as yet infinitesimal compared with the field of the unknown—but this is true also in the domain of the natural sciences. It is, however, a matter of the most profound and far-reaching implications to be able now to claim that telepathy, clairvoyance and precognition are indubitable hard facts; that the

---

* *Proc. S.P.R.*, Vol. 35, Part 93, pp. 1–284.
† *Spirit Teachings*; or *Proc. S.P.R.*, Vols. IX and XI.

evidence for them is as well-founded and reliable as for the basic facts of physics and chemistry. The second section of this book is designed to outline the sort of evidence upon which this statement is founded, to point towards some of the laws governing para-normal phenomena—or, at least, towards helpful theories of their nature —and finally to consider the implications. What sort of a universe is it in which these things are facts ? What do they tell us of the nature of Man himself ?

It is not proposed here to attempt even an outline of the work and history of the Society for Psychical Research.* We shall instead take the salient fields of enquiry : those phenomena which, if established, are deemed to be of the greatest significance in relation to these profound questions. The present chapter deals with tele- pathy and clairvoyance alone. Telepathy we have already defined. By clairvoyance we mean awareness of some approximately con- temporary event or some object in the *material* world without the use of sense-organs or rational inference based on sense-data. Such would include knowledge of an event in a distant place or of the order of cards in a shuffled pack—where such knowledge was not known to any living person, and could not therefore be acquired telepathically.

It is convenient for study to consider separately the spontaneous data and the experimental work. The relative importance of the contribution which these have made to our knowledge of the subject will be discussed later.

2. SPONTANEOUS PHENOMENA

In the field of the natural sciences experimental research based upon some theory or hypothesis is the normal method of progress. In the field of psychical phenomena this method is more limited in its application, for we do not know enough to be able to produce the phenomena, at least in their more striking and dramatic forms, at will. The recording of such things as and when they happen, in the fullest detail, is important as evidence which can later be critically examined. From time to time the huge mass of collected accounts has been critically examined by the Society for Psychical Research. One of the most recent surveys made by D. J. West,† which deals largely with precognitive dreams and reports of apparitions and

* W. H. Salter : *The Society for Psychical Research : An Outline of its History* (London, 1948).
† D. J. West : " The Investigation of Spontaneous Cases ", *Proc. S.P.R.*, Vol. 48, Part 175, p. 264.

hallucinations, indicates in general how difficult it is to form a balanced judgment in some of these fields of enquiry. Such matters as fraud, chance, coincidence, delusion, and all the possibilities of explanation along " normal " lines have to be weighed as carefully as possible. The problem of assessment in all records of spontaneous cases is not unlike that of the historian or lawyer who is called on to evaluate the testimony of witnesses or reliability of documents. We give below a few representative cases to illustrate the type of evidence which has to be assessed.

Case 1 (quoted by Mrs. Salter in *Evidence for Telepathy*, Sidgwick & Jackson, 1934):

> " I had a telepathic impression from my brother two years ago. He was taken suddenly ill and sent to a nursing home. He had some great domestic trouble and his nerves gave way. I seemed to feel all he did. . . . I was so unstrung that my husband . . . was at a loss what to do for me. I said I knew something was very wrong and wrote to enquire at once. . . . The date was October 23rd, 1931. Before there was time to receive a reply, a cable came telling of his death, November 13th, after exactly three weeks' illness. The subsequent letter confirmed everything. He was calling me all the time and thought the night nurse was I."

Here the telepathic link between brother and sister was such that the latter, as percipient, experienced acute anxiety and knew that its source was her brother.

Case 2—Miss Margaret Jones : *

> " I have to go into details to explain the circumstances : I was on night duty (as a professional nurse), which explains why I was asleep in the day-time. One evening, May 19th, 1931, I was startled out of my sleep by a voice, which called out my name distinctly, ' Margaret, Margaret '. I felt positive that someone had been in my room by my bed and rushed out again. I was never called by my Christian name at the hospital ; however, I did not pay much attention to that, as I was asleep. I thought it must have been the maid calling the night nurses, and she had not switched my light on. I got out of bed and looked down the corridor. I did not hear or see anybody. I looked at my clock ; *it was* 5.30 *p.m.* This was quite early, as we were not called until 7.30 p.m. I sat up in bed thinking over the strangeness of the situation. However, I dropped off to sleep again.
> " At breakfast that night I told some of my colleagues about my strange experience, and they just joked about it. I went on duty at 10.30 p.m. The night sister came to me, called me to one side, and asked me did I know anyone living at ——. I said ' Yes, my sister lives there '. ' Well, nurse,' she said, ' I am afraid there is bad news

* From *Jour. S.P.R.*, Vol. 28, p. 253.

for you.' She handed me a telegram, which said: ' Darling Peggy passed away at 5.30 p.m.' The telegram had been opened by Sister, as there were five Nurse Joneses in that particular hospital. Peggy was my little niece, aged eight years. We were great friends. She was taken suddenly ill and an immediate operation was performed, but she lived only a few hours. When I met my sister I told her what I had experienced, and she told me that the child called out, ' Margaret,' and she remarked to her husband, ' Is she calling herself or Auntie Margaret ? ' It is a strange fact that the stated time of the child's death on the wire was 5.30 p.m., just about the time that I was disturbed from my sleep. I did not know the child was ill; it was very sudden. I cannot describe my feelings as I read the telegram, which reminded me of my strange experience at 5.30 p.m."

There were corroborative statements from the child's mother and a nursing colleague who was present when the dream was related. Here we note the telepathic impulse emerged into the percipient's consciousness as an apparent voice.

Case 3—Mrs. Bettany : *

" When I was a child I had many remarkable experiences of a psychical nature, which I remember to have looked upon as ordinary and natural at the time.

" On one occasion (I am unable to fix the date, but I must have been about ten years old) I was walking in a country lane at A, the place where my parents then resided. I was reading geometry as I walked along . . . when in a moment I saw a bedroom known as the White Room in my home, and upon the floor lay my mother, to all appearance dead. The vision must have remained some minutes, during which time my real surroundings appeared to pale and die out; but as the vision faded, actual surroundings came back, at first dimly, and then clearly. I could not doubt that what I had seen was real, so instead of going home, I went at once to the house of our medical man and found him at home. He at once set out with me for my home, on the way putting questions I could not answer, as my mother was to all appearance well when I left home. I led the doctor straight to the White Room, where we found my mother actually lying as in my vision. This was true even to minute details. She had been seized suddenly by an attack of the heart, and would soon have breathed her last but for the doctor's timely advent. I shall get my father and mother to read and sign this."

In answer to questions, Mrs. Bettany added :

1. I was in no anxiety about my mother at the time of the vision.
2. I found a handkerchief with a lace border beside her on the floor. This I had distinctly noticed in my vision.
3. This was the only occasion, I believe, on which I saw a scene transported apparently into the actual field of vision, to the exclusion

* From *Phantasms of the Living*, Vol. I, p. 194: Gurney, Myers and Podmore (S.P.R., London, 1886).

of objects and surroundings actually present. I have had other visions in which I have seen events happening as they *really* were in another place, but I have been also conscious of real [i.e., immediate] surroundings.

Her father, Mr. S. G. Gwynne, interviewed, said :

" I distinctly remember being surprised by seeing my daughter in company with the family doctor outside the door of my residence ; and I asked ' Who is ill ? ' She replied, ' Mamma '. She led the way at once to the White Room, where we found my wife lying in a swoon on the floor. It was when I asked when she had been taken ill that I found it must have been *after* my daughter had left the house."

Here the mind of the mother was the agent, and the telepathic impulse presented itself to the child's awareness as a vivid picture or visual presentation of the desperate situation.

Case 4 (told by Mrs. S., " Margaret " of the narrative) : *

" A and B are two villages in Norfolk, distant about five miles from each other. At the time of the occurrence about to be related, the clergymen of these parishes both bore the same name, though there was no relationship between them ; at the same time there was a great friendship between the two families. On 20th February, 1870, a daughter, Constance, about fourteen years old, of the clergyman of A, was staying with the other family—a daughter, Margaret, in that family, being her great friend. Edward W., the eldest son of the Rector of A, was at that time lying dangerously ill at home with inflammation of the lungs, and was frequently delirious. On the day mentioned, at about noon, Margaret and Constance were in the garden of B Rectory, running down a path which was separated by a hedge from an orchard adjoining ; they distinctly heard themselves called twice, apparently from the orchard, thus : ' Connie—Margaret ; Connie—Margaret.' They stopped, but could see no one, and so went to the house, a distance of about forty yards, concluding that one of Margaret's brothers had called them from there. But to their surprise they found that this was not the case ; and Mrs. W., Margaret's mother, assured the girls no one had called them from the house, and they therefore concluded that they must have been mistaken in supposing they heard their names repeated. This appeared to be the only explanation of the matter, and nothing more was thought of it.

" That evening Constance returned to her home at A. On the following day Mrs. W. drove over to enquire for the sick boy Edward. In the course of conversation, his mother said that the day before he had been delirious, and had spoken of Constance and Margaret, that he called to them in his delirium, and had then said, ' Now I see them running along the hedge, but directly I call them they run towards

* From *Phantasms of the Living*, Vol. II, p. 164.

the house '. Mrs. W., of B, at once called to mind the mystery of the previous day, and asked, ' Do you know at what time that happened ? ' Edward's mother replied that it was a few minutes past twelve, for she had just given the invalid his medicine, twelve being his hour for taking it."

Interest here is associated with the fact of collective percipience : both girls apparently " heard " the voice. Also the sick boy ostensibly showed clairvoyant perception of their reaction.

It would be possible to fill a large volume with such cases. The best early collection is to be found in *Phantasms of the Living* (published 1886), and the best later collection of 190 cases was classified by Mrs. Henry Sidgwick * in 1922. To get the cumulative effect of spontaneous cases a report such as Mrs. Sidgwick's should be studied. It may be asked whether anything can be regarded as " proved " by such collections. Admittedly the perfect case is rare : this implies fraud has been ruled out, and that there were adequate witnesses to check all the significant points. Even so, there remains the hypothesis of chance—coincidence. That this is a probable explanation of so many cases, even imperfect in the sense of not being adequately witnessed at every point, is one which it is difficult to accept.

It will be noted that in the above cases, selected to illustrate various methods by which the percipient becomes para-normally aware of a distant event, the agent was in each case ill or in distress. A strong emotional factor was operative, and this obviously is not one which can be assumed or introduced into experimental work. Where it exists, however, it seems to create the possibility of vivid and dramatic effects in the percipient's mind.

The most convincing examples of telepathy, to those who constantly experience them in the family circle † or with particular friends, are not, of course, such as would ever be recorded, nor could they be evidential except to the persons concerned. I have frequently remarked, when listening to a friend of mine expounding his views on some difficult philosophical subject, an illumination and understanding at the time which seemed largely to have vanished when a later attempt was made to recollect it. It seems to me likely that the experience may be due to a temporary telepathic rapport to which his conversation was merely auxiliary, and that the part which could be recalled later was only those meanings absorbed through the auditory cerebral mechanism. To this feature may be due the

* *Proc. S.P.R.*, Vol. 33, Part 86, pp. 23–437.
† E.g. " Family Telepathy," by G. N. M. Tyrrell, in *Jour. S.P.R.* Vol. 34, p. 196 (1948).

enormous superiority of personal tuition over book-learning, given by the right kind of teacher. It may also account for the importance attached in the East to the *guru*-disciple relationship in the latter's advancement.

3. EXPERIMENTAL WORK (QUALITATIVE)

In experimental work attempts are made by two or more people to convey ideas or impressions from one to the other. The term " agent " is used for the active person who attempts to transmit, and the term " subject " or " percipient " for the one who attempts to receive. If the ideas transmitted are symbols on playing-cards, numbers, words, letters, colours, or correspondingly simple ideas, the determination of a " hit " or a " miss " is comparatively easy, and if an agreed limited number of such ideas were to be used, it is clear that the results could be quantitatively assessed. On the other hand, if drawings or patterns or sentences or events or any such complex ideas are used, there may be resemblances which would be judged " partially correct ", but where a clear-cut hit or miss cannot be assigned. A vast amount of experimental work of this sort has been recorded. Some of it is very impressive, and can leave little doubt in the mind of the student that a factor of extra-sensory perception is at work—in other words, that chance coincidence is inadequate to account for such results. For an exact assessment of what are the odds against chance as an explanation, we have to turn to the quantitative work which will be discussed at length in the next section. Some of the qualitative work will be here described briefly. Early volumes of the *Proceedings of the Society for Psychical Research* contain many records of work done under satisfactory experimental conditions.

Professor Gilbert Murray of Oxford carried out two long series of experiments in telepathy, with his daughter, Mrs. Arnold Toynbee, usually acting as the agent.* Generally other persons were present with Mrs. Toynbee, who announced to them what she proposed to think of. The first series, conducted between 1910 and 1915, comprised 505 experiments, of which 33% were judged successful, 28% partially successful and 39% failures. The second series of 295 experiments between 1916 and 1924 comprised 36% successes, 23% partial successes and 41% failures. The procedure described by Professor Murray himself is as follows :

> " I go out of the room and of course out of earshot. Someone in the room, generally my eldest daughter, thinks of a scene or an

* *Proc. S.P.R.*, Vol. 29, p. 46 ; Vol. 34, p. 212.

incident or anything she likes, and says it aloud. It is written down, and I am called. I come in, usually take my daughter's hand, and then, if I have luck, describe in detail what she has thought of. The least disturbance of our customary method, change of time or place, presence of strangers, controversy and especially noise, is apt to make things go wrong. I become myself somewhat over-sensitive and irritable, though not, I believe, to a noticeable degree. . . . When I am getting at the thing which I wish to discover, the only effort I make is a sort of effort of attention of a quite general kind. The thing may come through practically any sense channel, or it may discover a road of its own, a chain of reasoning or of association, which, as far as I remember, never coincides with any similar chain in the mind of anyone present, but is invented, for the purpose of the moment."

Here are a few examples taken from a series of experiments made on one particular evening.

(*Mrs. Toynbee* as agent): " I think of Helena Cornford and Tony grown up, walking beside the river at Cambridge."
Professor Murray: " This is not a book. It's got a sort of Cambridge feel in it. It's the Cornfords somehow. No—it's a girl walking beside the river, but it isn't Frances [Mrs. Cornford]. Oh! is it baby Cornford grown up? Ought I to know what she is doing? ("Who is she with?") " No, I don't get who she is with—No, I should only be guessing." (Everyone: " Go on.") " No, I should only think of another baby grown up—Tony " [a small grandchild].

(*Miss Agnes Murray* as agent): " Terence [a nephew of Professor Murray] and Napoleon standing on a hill above the Marne and watching the artillery down below."
Professor Murray: " This is a war scene—I don't get the persons clearly, but I think on the hill looking down on the artillery. It is not Saumarez. They may be Oxford people. I get the bursting of shells. I should think it was Terence and somebody else—I don't think I know the other person. I don't think I know him. No, I can't get him."

(*Miss Agnes Murray* as agent): " I think of *Diana of the Crossways*. Diana walking up the road in the rain, and crouching down in front of the empty grate in the house."
Professor Murray: " This is a book. Oh, it's Meredith. It's Diana walking. I don't remember the scene properly. Diana walking in the rain. I feel as if she was revisiting her house, but I can't remember when it happens." (" A little more.") " No—can't oblige."

(*Mrs. Toynbee* as agent): " I'll think of Rupert [Brooke] meeting Natascha in *War and Peace*. Running in a yellow dress—running through a wood."
Professor Murray: " Well, I thought when I came into the room it was about Rupert. Yes, it's fantastic. He's meeting somebody

out of a book. He's meeting Natascha in *War and Peace*. I don't
know what he is saying—perhaps 'Will you run away with me ? '"
(" Can't you get the scene ? ")   " I should say it was in a wood."
(" Colour of the dress ? ")   " No, I can't get it."

These successful examples will suffice to show how remarkable
was the degree of success.   One of the fundamental questions to
be answered is whether there was any possibility whatever of
hyperæsthesia—in this case hyper-acute hearing—accounting for
the results.   Mr. Gerald Balfour, who was present at the sitting
from which these examples are selected, " came away from it with a
conviction that hyperæsthesia, to whatever length it might be
stretched, could not be made to cover every case ".   Needless to
say, tests were made by the experimenters to see if any fragments
of ordinary conversation could be heard at the place to which Professor Murray retired, and that they were satisfied they could not.
Professor Murray's ordinary hearing is said to be normal, not unusually acute ; but he considers that when experimenting he may
pass into a state of slight hyperæsthesia, since noises of all kinds
become intolerable to him.   Mrs. Sidgwick discusses at length
several instances of experiments in which possibly this explanation
might appear to have some cogency, as for example where the rhythm
of a sentence or verse is caught, but not the complete idea.   But
against this as a general explanation are many examples in which
Professor Murray has correct impressions of things not mentioned
by the agent when announcing the idea to be communicated.   Here,
for example, is one case :

(*Mrs. Arnold Toynbee* as agent): " Greenmantle [by John Buchan]
where the German peasant woman takes them in in a snowstorm."
   Professor Murray: "This is something out of a book. I don't
think I've read it. It's not Russian. It's got no particular [national]
character. It's a snowstorm. It's somebody—I think it's a peasant
woman giving shelter to a spy. I think it's a German peasant woman.
I'm not sure. I think it's a German woman."   (" What sort of a
spy ? ")   " I think he is English. I think it is a book of adventure."

The character in the book was a spy and an Englishman, but the
agent had neither stated nor hinted at this.
   Another type of case which does not fit into the auditory hyperæsthesia theory is that in which Professor Murray fails to recognise
a person or a book named by the agent but states something true
(not mentioned by the agent) about that person or book which would,
however, have been a natural inference if he had grasped the name.
Here is one example :

(*Mrs. Toynbee* as agent): " I'll think of Margaret K—— at a particular restaurant in Munich where I used to have lunch."

Professor Murray: " It's some girl I don't know—a Cambridge girl, I think—I can't get it clear—is she standing in a restaurant or something like that ? "

It is difficult to see how this correct information would be obtained other than telepathically if the name had not been grasped.

The mode of " approach " to a subject through a description of impressions also suggests the telepathic cause, since we may rule out any intention to mislead. For example :

(*Mr. Arnold Toynbee* as agent): " I'll do Rip Van Winkle coming down the mountain."

Professor Murray: " Oh, I've got this. It's an old sort of gnome-like person with a matted beard coming down—very funny feeling expecting to be known and find things—Oh, it's Rip Van Winkle."

Or again :

(*Mr. Patrick Murray* as agent): " The lion in the Zoo trying to reach a large piece of meat just outside the cage."

Professor Murray: " A sort of smell of wild animals—carnivorous animals. Something grabbing through bars at a piece of meat at a Zoo. Don't know the animal."

Another mode of approach by Professor Murray to the idea of the agent, through first bringing forward an associated idea in his mind, is also of interest :

(*Lady Mary Murray* as agent): " I have had in my mind for some time George Trevelyan with his ambulance falling back in the rout from the Bainsizza plateau."

Professor Murray: " I get Geoffrey Young with his leg off, having to retreat with George Trevelyan in the Italian retreat." [Mr. Young did retreat under these circumstances.]

Another type of criticism against these experiments might be that Professor Murray in some cases held the agent's hand, hoping to increase rapport. Approval or disapproval might have been unconsciously communicated to him by slight muscular responses. Apart from the fact that the withdrawal or contradiction by Professor Murray of a statement already made is infrequent, Mrs. Sidgwick has pointed out in her report that there were a sufficiently large number of successful experiments in which the agent's hand was not held, to eliminate this as a necessary condition.

These experiments, in which a group of people all know the selected idea, raise interesting questions as to the part played by the principal agent. Analysis of the results showed that the principal agent played the predominant part, since with the same group of persons in the room, certain persons acting as principal agent were much more successful than others.   It would seem that the rapport is substantially between the percipient and the principal agent. There were, however, interesting cases of failure attributed by Professor Murray to " interference " from certain of the other persons present.   He often noticed he could not receive messages from Mrs. Arnold Toynbee if X or Y were present, whereas if she went away and one of them was the agent, the results were good, or if they went away and left her as agent, the results were good.   He attributed the disturbance to a sort of restless desire on their part to be the principal agent, though not a desire amounting to any anger or keen irritation. This, Professor Murray says, would have incapacitated him.

Speaking in 1924, Mrs. Henry Sidgwick referred to this whole group of experiments as " the most important ever brought to the notice of the Society, both on account of their frequently brilliant success and on account of the eminence of the experimenter ". Certainly if hyperæsthesia be ruled out—and in the opinion of competent persons who participated it could be ruled out—they demonstrate in Professor Gilbert Murray a most remarkably developed degree of telepathic sensitivity.   Chance as an explanation is completely out of the question.

We turn now to an interesting record of experiments published in 1930 by Upton Sinclair,* a responsible and well-known American writer on public affairs.   His wife, Mrs. Craig Sinclair, was in all cases the percipient.   In the majority of experiments Mr. Sinclair was the agent, but in a few others his brother-in-law, R. L. Irwin. The material used for transmission was a drawing constructed by the agent.   The experiments with R. L. Irwin as agent (who was forty miles away) took this form.   He would choose an object at random, draw it, and concentrate on the drawing for some minutes at an agreed time.   Mrs. Sinclair, with eyes closed, would desire to obtain what was in her brother-in-law's mind, and, having obtained a persistent or recurring image, would take paper and pencil and also draw it.   These two drawings were later compared with each other.

The great majority of experiments between Mr. and Mrs. Sinclair were made with minor variations upon the following simple technique.   He would make a set of drawings, usually of fairly simple things—a bird's nest with eggs, a helmet, a tree, a flower, a pattern, etc.—and enclose each in an opaque envelope.   Then, or later, Mrs. Sinclair would relax on a couch, take them one at a time, and after she considered she " knew " its contents, would draw them.

* Upton Sinclair : *Mental Radio* (T. W. Laurie, 1930).

The book which contains the record of this work includes numerous examples of pairs of drawings. Of these, Professor William McDougall writes :

> " The degree of success and the conditions of experiment were such that we can reject them as conclusive evidence of some mode of communication not at present explicable in accepted scientific terms, only by assuming that Mr. and Mrs. Sinclair either are grossly stupid, incompetent, and careless persons, or have deliberately entered upon a conspiracy to deceive the public."

Both suppositions are of course untenable.

Interest attaches to Mrs. Sinclair's description of her state of mind and mental processes while acting as percipient. She had previously acquired by practice the ability to attain a certain poised state of mind, well known to students of yoga, and gives an interesting description of the technique.* The ability to hold in consciousness (without any sense of strain) a single idea, such as a coloured image or flower, must be first acquired. No association trains must be allowed to develop, no thinking *about* the idea must take place, and a complete sense of relaxation of body and mind must be achieved.

The state of sleep can be avoided by holding on to the single idea. When success in this has been achieved, the necessity for the single idea has passed and a poised state of blankness of mind can be held equally well, again without any effort or strain. It is possible while retaining this state to give an order to the deeper mind to present on this blank screen of awareness the knowledge required (perhaps of a drawing in an opaque envelope). The possibility of doing this at all is an indication of the complexity of our mental structure—of different levels of mental functioning. Everyone, of course, recognises that in dreams one level is the creator of dramatic incident and action, while another level is a surprised and interested spectator of it. In Mrs. Sinclair's experiences only fragments usually appeared at first, delicately sketched, and swift in their coming and going. Other levels of mind were prone to present their " guesses " and confuse the authentic information. Mrs. Sinclair's subjective sense included at least three levels : the conscious screen, a region of rich association-trains prone to guessing, and a deep level of authentic knowledge.

To attempt to assess the measure of success with drawings is difficult, but the reader will gain an impression from the figures of Mr. Sinclair. Out of 290 drawings, sixty-five were judged successes, 155 partial successes, and seventy were failures.

* Loc. cit., Chapter XXI.

Many other investigations of a qualitative kind have been made.* A book by René Warcollier, entitled *Experiments in Telepathy* (George Allen & Unwin, 1939), includes a great deal of qualitative data, throwing light on the conditions of working. It is time, however, to look at the important and enormously expanding field of quantitative experimental work, for it is this which offers coercive proof to the scientific and sceptical mind of the fact of extra-sensory perception.

4. EXPERIMENTAL WORK (QUANTITATIVE) †

Although some of the early experimenters, such as Richet and the Sidgwicks, had done quantitative work, the era of its systematic development began in 1930, through the work of Professor J. B. Rhine and his collaborators at Duke University, U.S.A. This was sponsored by Professor William McDougall, who had a distinguished name in psychology, and the work of Rhine and his colleagues has been given to the world in the *Journal of Para-psychology* and a number of books.‡

Before giving an account of this, the present place may be appropriate to discuss some of the terms used. Telepathy and clairvoyance are the old descriptive terms. Thus, if a card was drawn from a shuffled pack and named correctly by a distant percipient (the knowledge of which card it was being in no person's mind), this would be described as pure clairvoyance (P.C.). If an agent thought of a card and a percipient named it correctly, this would be called pure telepathy (P.T.). If, however, an agent drew a card out of a pack and looked at it, the percipient's information might ostensibly be acquired either from the card or the agent's mind, or both, and Rhine's term for this is general extra-sensory perception (G.E.S.P.). There are some, however, who criticise the term " extra-sensory perception " on the ground that the phenomena may not be a kind of *perception* at all. For one thing, the percipient does not know when he is guessing right. Some have used the alternative term " para-normal cognition ", but this also may be criticised on the ground that it is scarcely *cognition* if the percipient does not know if the knowledge is right or wrong. Moreover, it is possible that the adjective para-normal may some day be regarded

* *Proc. S.P.R.*, Vol. 6, p. 128; Vol. 7, p. 199; Vol. 8, p. 422; Vol. 11, p. 174; Vol. 21, p. 60, etc.
† Some general readers without mathematical training may find this section of little interest. They should omit it and pass on to the next section.
‡ E.g., J. B. Rhine : *The Reach of the Mind* (Faber & Faber, 1948).

as a misnomer. For this reason some investigators use the non-committal term " psi " (ψ), following a proposal of Wiesner. The term ψ is used to include all of the individual terms, telepathy, clairvoyance, precognition of the sensory type, and phenomena like psycho-kinesis (P.-K.) of the motor type. As long as it is understood that we are not committing ourselves to any theory of its nature, we may continue to speak of E.S.P., as the term has had wide currency.

Rhine's Work. The bulk of the early work was directed to establish clairvoyance (P.C.) and G.E.S.P. Geometrical symbols were commonly used, and special packs of twenty-five playing-cards were made, containing five stars, five rectangles, five crosses, five circles and five wavy lines. These are sometimes called Zener cards. The procedure to test clairvoyance was as follows : The pack was shuffled and placed face downwards by the experimenter. The percipient, placed so that no sensory clues were possible, was asked to " guess " the nature of the top card. This was recorded by the experimenter, and the card removed from the pack (but not looked at). At the conclusion the recorded guesses were compared with the actual order. It is obvious that the chance of a correct guess is one in five, or five out of twenty-five ; for there were five different symbols in the pack. If some clairvoyant factor assisted the guessing, then a deviation from the chance score may be found. The question that then arises is : how likely is it that chance alone might account for the observed deviation ? This can be answered definitely by mathematics. For example, if a person ran four times through the pack, thus making 100 guesses, and in the course of this obtained thirty correct instead of the chance expectation of twenty correct, mathematical statistics allows us to calculate that such a deviation of + 10 should occur once in 150 times.

It is necessary, of course, that the reader shall make up his mind what odds against chance as an explanation of a deviation he will be prepared to accept as " significant ". Certainly in ordinary scientific work, if odds were 150 to 1 against chance accounting for a result, scientists would assume that some other factor was operative and would start to look for it. What sort of results were in fact obtained ?

One of his first percipients—A. J. Linzmayer—was tested under G.E.S.P. conditions (telepathy and clairvoyance both possible) and P.C. conditions. His high rate of scoring (viz., 49·5% correct in both cases) showed that the faculty was essentially a clairvoyant one. He made altogether 4,505 guesses, and his average was 33·6% correct. The odds against chance as an explanation are astronomical. In the course of time Linzmayer's faculty declined, and was close to the chance level two years later. C. E. Stuart, a graduate assistant, made 7,500 guesses under P.C. conditions and scored 24·2%. Herbert Pearce made 10,300 guesses under P.C. conditions, with an average scoring rate of 36·4%.

Even on the data of his first three years of work, taking *all* his subjects into account, Rhine was able to report about 85,000 guesses with an average scoring rate of nearly 28%. The odds against chance as an explanation are so large that we can say categorically that a para-normal factor is involved.

In the years that followed his early work, as might have been expected, these researches were subject to criticism of every kind. All conceivable sources of error in the experimental conditions were considered, and experiments subsequently successfully devised to meet these criticisms. The experiments were loaded with precautions and checked by witnesses to an extent probably unequalled in any other field of research. On the mathematical side the following authoritative statement was issued by the American Institute of Mathematical Statistics in 1937 :

> " On the statistical side, recent mathematical work has established the fact that, assuming that the experiments have been properly performed, the statistical analysis is essentially valid. If the Rhine investigation is to be fairly attacked, it must be on other than mathematical grounds."

Rhine's proof of clairvoyance has been supported by the results of other investigators. As one noteworthy example we cite work done by Miss Dorothy Martin and Miss Frances Stribic at the University of Colorado over a period of three years with one outstanding individual, Mr. C. J. He was selected by preliminary tests from 332 volunteers. Between the percipient and experimenter was a wooden screen, and the pack of cards, after shuffling, was placed in a pile face downwards on the table. The percipient made his guesses down through the pack—i.e., as he believed the order to be, from top to bottom. No fewer than 91,475 guesses were made by C. J., and his average score over the whole was 27·4% correct. The odds in favour of chance as an explanation of this are absolutely negligible.

G. N. M. Tyrrell's Work. Mr. Tyrrell has for over thirty years been engaged actively in the field of psychical research. He was President of the London Society for Psychical Research in 1945, has written two excellent books * on the subject, and made valuable

---

* *Science and Psychical Phenomena* (Methuen, 1938) ; *The Personality of Man* (Pelican Books, 1946).

research contributions.   He worked principally with one percipient, Miss Gertrude Johnson, who had shown a flair for finding lost objects when not consciously looking for them.   Tyrrell's experiments were designed to use this particular form of E.S.P.   Five small boxes were placed side by side on a table, and a screen fitted closely over the top of them, thus hiding a person sitting on one side of the table from a person sitting on the other.   On the side on which the experimenter sat the boxes were open; on the side on which the percipient (Miss G. J.) sat they had sloping, overhanging lids.   The boxes were well padded and lined with soft flannel.   Tyrrell placed a polished wooden pointer into the boxes at random, saying " In " as he did so.   G. J. opened the lid of the box in which she believed the pointer to be, and Tyrrell could score a success or failure by the light which came through.   Needless to say, the boxes were carefully tested to see if any sound arising from the introduction of the pointer was discernible.   His results from 30,000 trials, which on a chance basis should have been 6,000 successes (since there were five boxes), gave 9,364 successes (30·2%).   The odds against chance as an explanation of this deviation are billions to one.   In further experiments six different operators worked with G. J., and in 8,500 trials scored 2,126 or 25% successes, in which again the odds against chance as an explanation are billions to one.   In another series of 37,100 trials, with twenty-nine different persons (other than G. J.) the successes were 7,756, or 20·9%: the odds against chance explaining this comparatively small deviation from 20% are about 100,000 to 1.   The deviation was mainly due to one of the twenty-nine who showed some appreciable E.S.P.

It might be urged in criticism of G. J.'s high scoring with Tyrrell that perhaps it arose from certain habitual preferences for particular boxes coinciding in the two people.   But it must be noted that G. J. also scored highly with six out of seven other operators who were tried.   On this view, then, these six operators must have had habitual preferences coinciding with G. J.'s—which seems improbable.   Moreover, two of the six successful operators were among the twenty-nine persons who worked with Tyrrell as operator, and they then failed to score above the chance level.   This is surprising if their habitual preferences were supposed to be similar.   It is far more plausible that the high scoring was on account of a faculty peculiar to G. J.

The other line of criticism might be that G. J. had a faculty of auditory hyperæsthesia.   Tyrrell says that there was no independent evidence of this and he points out further, that, even so, accuracy of *locating* a faint sound is different from accuracy of perception of it.

The electrical form of the apparatus which Tyrrell later devised was designed, however, to eliminate this possible explanation. Instead of using a pointer, each box was fitted with a small electric pea-lamp, and had a silent key permitting it to be lit. The boxes were thoroughly tested for light-tightness, the lids were revetted, the boxes lined with red velvet, and the lamps run dimly.

Tyrrell also devised a commutator which could be put into action by pressing a button. Its function was to take the wires from the keys, and on the way to the lamps transpose them, so that on pressing any particular key the experimenter did not know which lamp he was lighting (the boxes being completely closed). Such a device broke up any possibility of habitual preferences affecting the results —the commutator being reset at intervals. Moreover, when the commutator was in action, since the operator did not know which lamp he was lighting, telepathy was also eliminated. The recording of the results was now done mechanically. A strip of moving paper was driven mechanically and could be marked by two ink-wheels placed side by side. Raising any lid caused one of the ink-wheels to mark the paper. If this box contained the lighted lamp, the second ink-wheel also marked the paper. As a precaution against fraud, the ink-wheel operated with very little movement of the lid, and if by chance two lids were lifted, the whole record was mechanically cut out. In later experiments Tyrrell introduced a purely mechanical selector of the keys based upon a rotating arm moving over contacts. This was tested carefully and found to give a truly random selection (eliminating any possibility of number-habit preferences entering in). In one long series using this device there were 7,809 trials, of which 1,841 or 23·5% were correct, instead of the chance number of 1,562. The odds against chance explaining this are a hundred billions to one.

Tyrrell demonstrated that G. J. scored approximately the same when telepathy was eliminated as when it was possible. He also showed that there were occasionally runs of from six to ten correct scores superimposed on a chance-background. This strongly suggests a special faculty temporarily in action, and G. J. had a subjective awareness of these periods—of " almost losing consciousness of her surroundings " and " a peculiar exalted feeling . . . making her feel that it is almost impossible to fail ". New conditions or the presence of visitors were usually found to send the rate of scoring down, but gradual recovery followed.

We shall refer in the next chapter to further work of Tyrrell with this apparatus. We shall only make very brief reference to its character here, but it is the strongest possible evidence that a leakage of light from the box could not account for the results. He introduced a relay into the lighting circuit of the lamps which in effect placed a gap in the circuit, so that although a lamp was selected, it did not actually light. As soon as any box lid was raised, however, this operated the relay and lit the lamp. It suffices to say here that G. J. scored without much change under these conditions also. The reader will of course recognise the implications of this—that the extra-sensory faculty is apparently not one of clairvoyance of *contemporary* events only, but of *future* events. G. J. showed a knowledge far beyond chance, of the box in which a lamp would *in the future* be lit. Tyrrell remarks, " It is indeed one of the most extraordinary things, that it did not appear to matter as far as scoring was concerned whether the lamp was lit before the box was opened or afterwards ! "

S. G. Soal's Work. Dr. Soal is a mathematician of the University of London. For many years he worked in this field, organising many group experiments and attempting to repeat Rhine's work. He met with virtually nothing significantly above chance in tests for extra-sensory perception conducted with 160 different people and involving about 128,350 guesses in the period (1934–39). Fortunately Mr. Whately Carington had just discovered the precognitive or " displacement " effect, by researches we shall describe in the next chapter, and he persuaded Dr. Soal to re-examine his own results to see if a displacement effect would be found. In this way Dr. Soal discovered that two subjects of the 160 had been scoring substantially above chance, but in a remarkable way. Mrs. Stewart had been scoring high on the +1 and −1 cards—that is, the cards respectively one ahead and one behind that at which the agent was looking ! Mr. Shackleton scored substantially, particularly on the +1 card (the precognitive effect).

In 1945 Dr. Soal was able to begin a series of significant experiments with Mrs. Stewart, and we shall describe these briefly here. It was then found, nine years after the first experiments, that the displacement effect had gone, and she was now scoring higher than previously, but on the target card. The average for about 17,000 guesses under G.E.S.P. conditions was nearly 28%. The odds against chance as an explanation are of astronomical magnitude. The type of experiment was as follows : The ideas used for " transmission " were five animals (zebra, pelican, giraffe, elephant and lion), which were each depicted on a playing-card. The percipient sat in one room with a scoring sheet and recorded the initial Z, P, G, E or L of the animal card at which he guessed the agent to be looking. The agent, together with an experimenter, sat at a table in an adjacent room with the door ajar, so that voice signals could be used to synchronise the guessing. They were separated by a screen across the middle of the table, the screen having a small square aperture in it. The experimenter had a table of random numbers from 1 to 5, and his duty was to call the trial and show a card numbered 1, 2, 3, 4 or 5 at the aperture, according to his column of random numbers. The agent sitting on the other side of the screen had previously shuffled the five animal-cards and laid them down in a row faces downwards. Upon seeing a number (say 4) presented at the aperture, he turned up the fourth card from the left, looked at it and let it fall back again. After fifty guesses the experimenter walked round the screen, turned over the cards, and recorded the code—i.e., the animal which corresponded with each number. Another run of fifty guesses could then be made with a new shuffling of the five animal-cards. The percipient's score-sheets were later decoded into numbers and compared with the random-number tables. As the percipient recorded his guess he said " Right " as a signal to the experimenter that he was ready for the next trial. The advantages of this procedure are at least two : (a) the table of random numbers eliminates any criticism of imperfect shuffling of a pack, and (b) the experimenter who calls the trials does not know which animal-card the agent is looking at, and therefore the pitch or inflexion of the voice in calling cannot be regarded as offering any clue to the percipient. To test pure clairvoyance the agent, instead of turning up an animal-card to look at it, may merely touch it on the back. Such blocks of fifty guesses under G.E.S.P. conditions could be alternated with blocks of fifty guesses under P.C. conditions, either with or without the percipient's knowledge that it was being done.

What results were obtained ? Unlike the majority of Rhine's percipients, both Mr. Shackleton and Mrs. Stewart failed to score above chance under *clairvoyant* conditions. In other words, for both of them an agent was necessary. While Mr. Shackleton scored with only three out of about a dozen agents tried, Mrs. Stewart scored above chance with eight out of twelve. Since, as we previously mentioned, Mr. Shackleton's scoring was principally on the $+1$ card, we might describe his faculty as precognitive telepathy— i.e., knowledge of future content of the agent's mind (about $2\frac{1}{2}$ seconds ahead). Many variations of the main type of experiment made with Mrs. Stewart throw considerable light on the conditions for successful E.S.P.

In one variation the agent was instructed at the beginning of a run of fifty trials to turn over the five animal-cards, look at them for half a minute and then turn them face downwards. He was not asked to make any effort to remember their order; but by looking at them, presumably this knowledge was conveyed to his subconscious mind. In the subsequent experiment he was merely asked to touch the backs of the cards indicated by the presentation of successive numbers by the experimenter. This procedure worked quite as well as the normal one, even when the agent's preliminary observation of the cards was reduced to 5 seconds. We may infer that it is by no means necessary for the agent to be *consciously* thinking of the image when he transmits it. The supposition that intense conscious concentration is involved as a condition of successful telepathy is apparently without foundation.

In another variation two agents were used. The first agent sat as usual behind the screen, and touched the back of the appropriate card when the experimenter presented a number. But the five cards in front of him in a row were *blank* cards. The second agent took five animal-cards with him into a room adjoining the other two and was asked at the beginning of an experiment to shuffle, lay them in a row and look at them for half a minute. Under these conditions, the success in which was very little less than with only one agent, it is clear that Mrs. Stewart had to acquire two pieces of information : the number presented, and the order of the five cards, and these were respectively in the minds of two different persons.

In an experiment similar to this, where the essential information was divided between two agents, a run of 200 trials was made in which Mrs. Stewart was given the impression that only one agent was involved. For 200 following trials she was informed that two agents were involved. In the first run Mrs. Stewart's score was a little *below* chance expectation; in the second case there was a significant score of sixty correct. This indicates the necessity of a conscious orientation towards the persons necessarily involved.

In another variation of the original form of experiment two agents were used, each seated where they could see the number presented by the experimenter, and each having a set of the five animal-cards. Each was informed of a specific number of arrangements of the five animal-cards which they might use, and was asked to select one. The arrangements permitted to one agent differed from those permitted to the other, so that no animal-card would ever be placed in the same position by the two agents. The effect is most simply stated by regarding the agents as working in opposition, or at least in conflict with each other. Mrs. Stewart knew two agents were acting, but was given the impression that they were working " together ". Later she was told that a particular one was the agent,

E

although both still acted as before. In the first case 400 trials were made showing scores with the two agents of eighty-four and ninety-six only, compared with the chance level of eighty—obviously but little difference from chance. In the second case 400 trials gave seventy-four and 113 correct with these agents, the latter, needless to say, applying to the agent to whom she was directed. The odds are 10,000 to 1 against chance as an explanation of the 113/400 score. The importance of conscious orientation in the right direction is again apparent.

5. THE ROLES OF EXPERIMENT AND SPONTANEOUS DATA

The kind of experimental work we have outlined is clearly capable of enormous extension and elaboration, and should throw increasing light on the nature of E.S.P., the conditions under which it can operate and the laws governing it. The development and testing of theoretical views leading to the formulation of laws are essentially the important function which experimental work will have to perform in coming years. It may be said to have fulfilled its first major task of demonstrating to the scientifically-minded sceptic the hopelessness of any attempt to explain away the data of E.S.P. on the basis of chance or coincidence.

The continuous accumulation of records of spontaneous phenomena is, however, still of great importance. There are some fields of psychical research into which the experimental method has not yet penetrated: apparitions, hauntings, poltergeist phenomena, levitations, etc. Here the only available method of progress at present is through the collection of well-attested data with as much detail of conditions as possible. We must remember that there are some branches of scientific enquiry in which the collection of facts and their classification is the sole method of progress—e.g. in astronomy and geology. Even in those branches of psychical research where the experimental method is possible, the study of spontaneous occurrences is still important, for several reasons. The most dramatic and informative phenomena occur under these conditions where emotional factors are probably operative, or where consciousness is partially relaxed, as in trance states or automatic writing and drawing. In experimental conditions where the material has no emotional content, and where quasi-normal states of consciousness are the rule, the effects are comparatively small, even though they have the advantage of statistical evaluation. Tyrrell * has repeatedly drawn attention to the question as to whether it is justifiable

---

* *Proc. S.P.R.*, Vol. 47, Part 171, p. 312.

to extrapolate conclusions arrived at by the experimental study of such " marginal " phenomena. At deeper levels of the mind wholly different phenomena may be brought to light. We cannot answer this question, and it is the more important that the phenomena which arise from deeper levels shall continue to be collected and studied carefully, even though no control of them appears to be possible. Tyrrell commends the attitude of Columbus " eagerly scanning the water for every scrap of floating weed and wrack, noting the changing colour of the sea and the flight of birds, grasping at every hint of the proximity of land. If Columbus had possessed the former [statistical] type of mind, he would have rejected these hints as being below evidential standard, and have refused to admit the proximity of land." The fact is, of course, that the two types of enquiry— qualitative and spontaneous on the one hand, and quantitative on the other—are complementary and both needed. The most useful directions for future experimental work are likely to be found through careful classification and analysis of spontaneous data, and this is now being undertaken on a large scale.*

6. THEORIES OF TELEPATHY

It is desirable that we should consider what general views are held by responsible persons about the nature of telepathy. Let us clear the ground by considering first the type of theory which is impossible. All theories of the "wireless" or "mental-radio" type which suppose that some kind of wave-motion or physical radiation passes from one brain to another brain are quite untenable, for several reasons. (a) All physical types of energy fall off in their intensity inversely as the square of the distance from the source. There is no evidence that distance affects telepathy at all. (b) The transmission and reception of physical radiation or energy implies the existence of material organs for this purpose. There is no evidence of such existing. (c) Ideas can be conveyed from one mind to another by the intermediate activity of physical energy only if there is a mutually understood code. Language, both spoken and written, is of course a code. If telepathy is physical, then an idea in A's mind must be encoded, and when it reaches B's mind it must be decoded. Where and what is this code in the subconscious minds of all people, which no one has ever learned, and of which no one seems to know anything? All authorities agree that we can completely rule out physical theories of telepathy.

We are left, then, with two classes of theory. One assumes it is a type of mind–brain relationship. Thus the mind of A, as we know, controls A's brain : may not the mind of A achieve under certain conditions a similar relation to B's brain ? Or may not A's brain be similarly linked under certain conditions with B's mind ? This, briefly, is a view presented by Thouless and Wiesner : clearly an attempt to regard the para-normal phenomena as an extension of a normal relationship. The other class of theory is of a mind-to-mind relationship : this places the phenomena on a wholly mental level. Whately Carington's views are a noteworthy example of this latter class, and we shall shortly discuss them.

Tyrrell's Views. G. N. M. Tyrrell has laid stress on the importance of weighing carefully the less restricted type of para-normal event—the spontaneous type—in formulating any theory. One of the significant facts to be weighed is that a percipient is never aware of a telepathic, clairvoyant or precognitive *process* at work within him. He is only aware of the *product* of the process. This product is not para-normal ; it is the *process* which takes place in the subconscious or subliminal self which is mysterious and which we call para-normal. There is a wide range of sensory hallucinations which psychology recognises as " normal ", although they are not very common. The hallucinations may affect sight, hearing or touch. To these we may add a strong impulse to take a certain course of action in spite of reason. In all cases through some such means a message or direction makes its way from the deeper or subliminal mind into the conscious level. The deeper mind constructs the hallucination or impulse as a mediating vehicle to effect this. Such mediating vehicles may range from vague subjective feelings, dreams or impulses to full-blown externalised visual, auditory or tactile hallucinations. Where the motive or originating source is in someone else's mind, we usually say the phenomena are para-normal, but we should note that the same use of mediating vehicles is made in both cases (" normal " and " para-normal ").

The case is reported,* for example, of a person who awoke to " see " a piece of paper bearing a written message, that her friend living in another place had died during the night. The paper and message were hallucinatory, but the information was true.

In another case † there is related a dream by Mrs. B., who has a son H. in the army in West Africa. In the dream a sergeant said to her (in reply to a question about her son's whereabouts), " Don't be alarmed ; they are carrying him along all right. He has broken his leg. You cannot see him yet, but you will by-and-by." The facts were that H. was seriously ill and was being carried : he died

* *Jour. S.P.R.*, Vol. 27, p. 326.   † Ibid., Vol. 10, p. 162.

in the following month. But he had not broken his leg : this accident had taken place about the age of five. Here we see one and the same mediating vehicle conveying para-normal knowledge (of the illness) and a piece of normal knowledge (the broken leg) linked up in her memory with H.

Tyrrell suggests that telepathic experiments might well be planned to study the conditions of formation of the mediating vehicle, which is so obviously a device created by a deeper level of the mind to convey knowledge to consciousness.

We use labels such as telepathy, clairvoyance and precognition, but what do these mean ? Are they aspects of one comprehensive faculty of apprehension which Mind possesses by reason of its own nature ?

In Case 3, cited on p. 113, we may suppose the mother's subliminal mind was the agent responsible for the powerful telepathic impression on the child's mind. The situation was desperate, and a strong motive was present. The child was afterwards impressed by the accuracy of the detail of her vision—even down to the lace-bordered handkerchief. The " mediating vehicle " here appears to be a vivid picture of the scene itself. The accuracy of detail may be accounted for either as due to clairvoyant perception by the mother's *subliminal* mind (the collapsed physical state being presumably no barrier to this) or clairvoyant perception by the child's subliminal mind, " attracted " to the situation telepathically. As soon as we try to separate that which is telepathic from that which is clairvoyant in these cases, we are attempting an impossible task. It may, in fact, be impossible, because the distinction we make between them may be artificial (a result suggested by Tyrrell's experimental work with G. J.). The full use of the mind's " para-normal " powers might result in a complete grasp of any situation, including all the mental, emotional and physical data. Even the imperfect use of the mind's powers may give some data of each type. It is only in the simple, uncomplicated card-type of experiment that the effecting of an artificial separation of " telepathy " from " clairvoyance " is possible—and we suggest that this *is* artificial.

Carington's Association Theory. This is based upon the general idea that individual minds are not altogether separate or isolated, but that there are associational links between them. Some persons would go so far as to say that at a certain depth there is a common subconscious. Now, the normal and familiar principle of asso-ciation of ideas in a single mind is this. If an idea O has become associated with an idea K, the subsequent presentation of K to consciousness makes it more likely that O will be drawn up from the subconscious. Carington's theory is very simple—viz., that the presentation of K to *another* mind makes it then more likely that O will appear in that mind also. Where an experiment is taking place between two persons, or between one person and a group of others, the common K-idea will simply be " the idea-of-the-experiment ". Carington carried out many interesting series of experiments with drawings (some of which are described in Chapter 7) and claims that a study of these supports the Association Theory of Telepathy.

On this theory we should expect telepathy to take place more freely or effectively between persons who have a large number of ideas or experiences in common. Carington would explain Case 3 of p. 113 by saying that the mother's collapse on the floor in the White Room was the cause of a powerful complex of ideas in the mother's mind charged with fear and concern. The mother's associated thought of her child would be a K-idea : Carington would conceive the child's sense of herself linked with this, and capable of bringing up to her consciousness the first group of ideas. Alternatively, if the child suddenly had even a fleeting thought of her mother, this might be the effective K-idea bringing all the mother's group into consciousness.

Of course, if pure clairvoyance is admitted as a fact, Carington's Association Theory cannot explain it—see Section 7 later—for it is a theory wholly of mental relationship.

Thouless and Wiesner * prefer to use the Greek letter ψ (psi) for all the so-called " para-normal " faculties of Mind. The terms " telepathy ", " clairvoyance ", " precognition " are regarded only as distinguishing the conditions of the situation under which this one faculty is operative. We must here anticipate the material of Chapter 11 to say that the mind not only has " para-normal " faculty for reception of knowledge, but also " para-normal " motor faculty—e.g., for the movement of detached objects. This is now believed to be another aspect of ψ and to distinguish these, Thouless and Wiesner use ψ_y (psi-gamma) for the cognitive aspect of the faculty, and ψ_κ (psi-kappa) for the motor aspect of the faculty. These Greek letters do not commit us to any theory of the nature of the faculty— e.g., we can avoid the use of the term " para-normal ". Their view of clairvoyance is very simple, and is illustrated by the

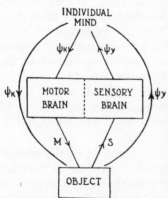

INDIVIDUAL MIND

ψ_κ ψ_y

ψ_κ MOTOR BRAIN   SENSORY BRAIN ψ_y

M   S

OBJECT

* *Proc. S.P.R.*, Vol. 48, Part 174, p. 177 (1947).

right-hand side of the diagram. The mind of a clairvoyant is regarded as being in the same relationship to an external object as in ordinary sense-perception the mind is to the sensory part of its own brain. This has the advantage of reducing two mysterious relations (perception and extra-sensory perception) to one. At first sight this theory may seem improbable, for it may be said that a clairvoyant knows directly the external event or object, while a person in normal perception does not know the physiological process in his brain. The latter is certainly true; but is the former? What actually happens is that he makes some response, such as writing, speaking or doing, which we say is caused by the external event. But the external event may not be, indeed it seems not to be, the immediate causal ancestor of the response. There is no reason for supposing that a cognition must necessarily have the character of " seeing ", " hearing " or any other of the sensory modes. We know, in fact, that cognition is sometimes received as a symbol which has to be interpreted. The mind may have a vast number of ways of experiencing knowledge. One of these ways may certainly be the presentation of a visual and accurate *picture* of the scene, as in Case 3 on page 113. But we need not assume that actual visual perception is necessarily taking place. The symbolic character of the presented knowledge is of course obscured in card-guessing experiments, where the guess and the object must coincide for success, but in spontaneous phenomena the symbolism is frequently evident.

Thouless and Wiesner suggest that the para-normal phenomena of temporal displacement which we shall consider in Chapter 7 (precognition and post-cognition of events) may be paralleled in the mind's relationship to " intentions " and " memories " which are regarded as future and past *brain* states. At this point I am compelled to differ. There may possibly be a precognitive relationship to future brain states, perhaps accounting for such phenomena as " déjà vu " (the feeling that one has seen it before, which one knows is physically impossible), but that such a relationship is the nature of intentions and purposes seems most unlikely. Intentions may never be realised—i.e., may never correspond to brain states. Moreover, some distant memories may be recalled with a vividness and detail which suggest as very unlikely a retrocognitive relationship to brain states of perhaps fifty years ago.

The difference between " para-normal " ψ of an object or event and " normal " sensory perception is therefore something imposed upon the latter by the character of the brain processes and special senses. Experiment has shown that conscious effort by a person is unfavourable to ψ, the faculty being apparently then canalised or concentrated through the brain. This is wholly consistent with Bergson's conception of the brain-function as one of limitation, its purpose being to focus attention on everyday life. Although we do not know what are the limits of ψ so far as space and time are concerned, there must be some kind of limitation, for if a card experiment is being performed, the faculty obviously distinguishes this pack from thousands of other packs in the world. In spontaneous phenomena the directing of ψ may be effected by the agent's telepathic impulse.

This leads us to Thouless and Wiesner's conception of telepathy, which is a psycho-physical one. They consider that the mind of a

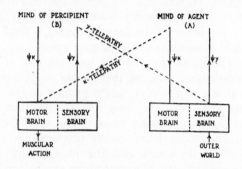

percipient B may achieve the same relationship to the sensory brain of A as it normally has to its own sensory brain. This might be called γ-telepathy. It means that sense-data in the brain of A are alike accessible to the minds of A and B. Another kind of telepathy, which might be called κ-telepathy, would be possible through volitions or motor impulses from the mind of A controlling the motor brain of both A and B. The two broken lines in the diagram illustrate these possibilities. It might be supposed that " thought-reading " is a case of γ-telepathy and that the percipient B could tap latent memories of A. Certainly on a " brain-trace " theory of memory such a process would seem quite plausible. The present writer does not, however, hold such a theory of memory (which he believes to be essentially mental or at least psychic in character). An attempt to account for a spontaneous occurrence such as Case 3 on p. 113 along the lines of γ-telepathy also leads to difficulties. If the child's mind was related through ψ_γ to the sensory brain of her mother, would she not be expected to have viewed the scene as her mother saw it before collapsing, and not as though from another position in the room ? Moreover, what caused the child's mind to single out the mother's brain from all others ? Was it a telepathic impulse of the ψ_κ type from the mother ? It does not seem likely, for it was not a motor activity that was induced, but a vision. Most of the " crisis type " of telepathy conveys a visual or auditory impression to the percipient, and not a motor impulse, and as it must be initiated by the agent who is passing through the crisis, it is difficult to see that Thouless and Wiesner's theory is likely to apply to it. (The broken lines of the diagram illustrate this.) On the other hand, it is quite possible that Tyrrell's early experimental work with G. J., in which the agent knew which box the pointer or light was in, operated through ψ_κ on the percipient's motor brain. Bearing in mind, then, later work which showed that whether the knowledge was in the agent's mind or not made no difference to G. J.'s rate of scoring, clairvoyance seems the more likely process.

It has been suggested that possibly the induction of hypnosis without any sensory suggestions, such as words spoken or signals given, is an example of ψ_κ telepathy, but it may equally well, of course, be a mind-to-mind relationship. This might be represented in the previous diagram by arrows horizontally between Mind A and Mind B in place of the diagonal broken lines.

Thouless and Wiesner's views are interesting and stimulating, and have the merit of attempting to assimilate the less familiar to the more familiar. My own view, held of course tentatively in the present state of our knowledge, is that the diagonal linkage probably is the mechanism of *some* phenomena, possibly of a certain class of mediumistic trance, but that it is not likely to be the mechanism of telepathy as it commonly occurs. On the other hand, the interpretation of clairvoyance appears to me to be sound as far as it goes, but it leaves the nature of ψ just as mysterious as ever. At the end of a philosophical discourse Professor C. D. Broad said, " We must consider seriously the possibility that each person's experiences initiate more or less permanent modifications of structure or process in something which is neither his mind nor his brain," * and this substratum, described later as a psychic æther, seems to me a useful, if not a necessary, hypothesis to explain some of the phenomena of the psychic field.

7. THE PROBLEM OF CLAIRVOYANCE

In my view, the phenomena of " psychometry " or " object-reading " (see Chapter 8) render almost inevitable some such hypothesis. I postulate a psychic æther or " substance " which

* *Proc. S.P.R.*, Vol. 43, p. 437 (1935).

partakes of some of the qualities of matter (such as localisation in space and retention of form), and which is yet capable of sustaining thought-images and emotions : something, in short, which is a bridge between matter and mind.   This psychic æther, I postulate, is organised into specific form in the presence of ordinary matter : to put it crudely, there is an ætheric duplicate of every material object.   It is this duplicate, I believe, which the mind apprehends by ψ_y in clairvoyance and which it controls by ψ_κ in psycho-kinesis (see Chapter 11).   An ætheric world of this sort, with its own phenomena and laws, seems to me something we may be driven to recognise. Professor H. H. Price postulates it to account for hauntings and apparitions (Chapter 9).   I believe it is also involved in poltergeist phenomena and is of special interest and great importance in the structure of Man himself.   We shall therefore introduce the idea here. It may, of course, ultimately go the way of the physicist's æther as knowledge develops, but it probably takes us just a step nearer to the ultimately real from the ordinary matter of physics and chemistry.

There are numerous recorded instances of " transposition of the senses ", of which clearly the right explanation is in terms of clair-voyance or, better, let us say ψ_y.   Professor Boirac * has described cases of hypnotised (and carefully blindfolded) subjects who could " read " newspapers either by running the fingers over the print, or placing the latter against the forehead or the pit of the stomach. Photographs could be " seen " and described, the time could be " read " from a watch, etc.   Telepathy was eliminated in some experiments by the random choice of a book and page, the contents of which were known to no one present.   It seems possible that many strange phenomena, such as exteriorised tactile sensibility reported by Boirac, will finally be understood in terms of ψ_y and ψ_κ acting on ætheric structures, when we know more about the laws governing this inter-action.

8. FACTORS AFFECTING ψ_y

In attempting to discover the conditions under which telepathy, clairvoyance, etc., work, many important observations have been made.   These are in some cases well confirmed, in others fragmentary and isolated ; but all indicate the vastness of the field in which further research must continue if we are to discover the nature of, and laws governing ψ-cognition.

* Émile Boirac : *Our Hidden Forces* (trs. W. de Kerlor, F. A. Stokes Co., 1917).

Distance. There is no evidence that distance between agent and percipient has any effect on telepathy, or the distance between object and percipient any effect on clairvoyance. Most spontaneous examples involve considerable distances : in some cases thousands of miles. Experimental work has specifically shown that no falling-off of the ψ-faculty with distance occurs. In the Pearce–Pratt clairvoyance experiments with cards, Pearce averaged eight correct guesses per run of twenty-five (for 900 calls) at a yard's distance, nine correct guesses per run (for 750 calls) at 100 yards distance, and nearly seven correct guesses per run (for 1,100 calls) at 250 yards distance. In experiments using telepathy, Miss Turner (percipient) and Miss Ownbey (agent) made eight correct guesses per run (275 calls) in the same room, and at 250 miles distance made ten correct guesses per run (for 200 calls). In a recent series of G.E.S.P. experiments conducted by Dr. Soal, with Mrs. Stewart as percipient in Antwerp, and two agents in London well known to Mrs. Stewart, the results showed beyond any doubt that the same order of scoring was maintained as was customary between these collaborators. Nor did change of location of the agents by a distance of several miles (unknown to the percipient) affect the rate of scoring significantly. Dr. Soal remarks :

" In telepathic communication it is personality, or the linkage of personalities which counts, and not spatial separation of bodies. This is what we might expect on the assumption that brains have spatial location and spatial extension, but that minds are not spatial entities at all. If this is true then there is no sense in talking about the distance between two minds, and we must consider brains as focal points in space at which Mind produces physical manifestations in its inter-action with matter."

Decline Effects. Most of the experimental records examined by Rhine and his colleagues show that successful scoring declines through a run. If runs (say of twenty-five trials) are set out in successive horizontal rows, the scoring rate on the right half of the page proves invariably less than that of the left half. Moreover, vertical decline effects are also quite marked. As only a few runs will be carried out at a sitting, the vertical decline effect shows what may be considered a long-period decline of the faculty. ψ has been shown by many experimenters to vary with the percipient's attitude and mood, and it seems possible that the horizontal decline may be a type of fatigue effect, and the general long-period decline may be one arising from lack of stimulus due to the novelty " wearing off ". Similar decline effects are found in psycho-kinesis experiments (see Chapter 11) which test ψ_κ.

Percipient's Mood and Attitude. There seems to be general agreement that a cheerful, friendly, informal, playful atmosphere favours the operation of ψ. In the case of children, a friendly, competitive atmosphere seems also to assist. An agent capable of creating this atmosphere may succeed with a group, while another person with the same group cannot obtain scores above chance. The rate of guessing consciously preferred by the percipient was also found to be the most favourable one. One of the most striking correlations of attitude towards ψ with scoring ability was demonstrated by Dr. Schmeidler of New York, who showed that those persons who, before they began their tests, had some sort of belief in it or favourable attitude towards it scored consistently higher than those who had not.

Personality Type and Mentality. No evidence has been found that psychopathic types suffering from delusions of telepathic rapport with people have in fact any unusual ψ-ability. In general, ψ seems rare among people of sub-normal intelligence, and Dr. Humphrey has demonstrated a positive correlation between intelligence rating and ψ-scoring in a group of students. It may perhaps not be wholly chance that a famous high-scoring subject investigated by Dr. Riess (who scored eighteen correct guesses per twenty-five through seventy-four runs) suffered from hyperthyroidism, and that her ψ-faculty sank to normal after medical treatment for this condition. Psychological testing should do much to indicate how ψ is correlated with personality traits. It has already been found that the " expansive " rather than the " constricted " type favours ψ-cognition.

Drugs. Knowledge of the effect of drugs on the ψ-faculty is at present very limited. A small amount of alcohol appears to assist the scoring rate, but a large amount (when it acts as a narcotic) depresses it to chance level. Sodium amytal, a narcotic, depresses it also. On the other hand, a stimulant such as caffeine, given to counteract the administration of a narcotic, assists to restore ψ-scoring to its normal value. The same effects have been noticed in psychokinesis experiments (vide Chapter 11). Rhine expresses the interesting opinion that the favourable conditions for ψ are closely similar to those involved in " delicately original and creative work in the arts ". A recent paper by Dr. A. J. C. Wilson * discusses the effects of three drugs—ayahuasca, peyotl and yagé.

Group Effects. Attempts have been made to use large groups of percipients working with one agent; the idea being that possibly weak ψ-faculty might be widespread, and reveal itself in the group-

* *Proc. S.P.R.*, Vol. 48, p. 353 (1949).

results. With the exception of Whately Carington's group experiments (see Chapter 7), no measure of success has been achieved. Warcollier * has described some interesting results obtained with a group of a dozen personal friends. He remarks that with the simultaneous employment of a number of agents their influence was less. He also gives many examples of telepathy between the percipients themselves, who induced a certain type of mental passivity as a preliminary to their experiments. Successful " transmission " seems to Warcollier to arise not directly through conscious concentration on an idea, but rather through its activation by associated ideas after it has sunk into the subconscious.

Sex. It is interesting to note that from a total of 383 spontaneous recorded cases analysed by Warcollier, the distribution of the respective roles of agent and percipient was as follows : male to female, 35% ; male to male, 28% ; female to male, 18% ; female to female, 19%. It indicates that the male is on the whole more effective as agent and the female as percipient.

9. BIOLOGICAL IMPLICATIONS OF ψ

We know as yet very little of ψ and its laws, but the little we do know which indicates the enormous potentialities of Mind both cognitive and psycho-motor, points the way to a future understanding of biological phenomena.

The " fields " of Smuts are obviously related to ψ, and in its two forms—ψ_γ and ψ_κ—it is presumably the mechanism by which mind is informed of and controls the complexity of individual development and the evolutionary process. A. C. Hardy, Professor of Zoology at Oxford, has recently made a beginning with a theory of this kind.† He has said : " The discovery that individual organisms are somehow in psychical connection one with another across space is of course one of the most revolutionary biological discoveries ever made." When we reflect upon the fact that no two cells occupy the same space, and that their processes of growth and change are co-ordinated with that of their neighbours and with the needs of the whole organism, is it not probable that a psychic connection links them also ? The difference between two cells and two organisms in this respect is primarily one of the *degree* of separation, and we have already seen that ψ is apparently unaffected by distance.

It is for the future also to determine how far a ψ-relationship

* Warcollier : *Experiments in Telepathy* (Chapter 2).
† *Jour. S.P.R.*, Vol. 35, p. 225, May 1950.

(telepathic) may exist between Man and lower animals. It is tempting to speculate that the understanding between a shepherd and his sheep-dog is closer than can be accounted for on the basis of sensory clues. P. H. Plasch makes the interesting suggestion that the apparent commands and whistles are perhaps only κ-objects in the Whately Carington sense. Similarly, the reports which persist of holy men and others who have apparently a remarkable power over wild animals may not be without foundation.

Most observers of Nature have at one time or another wondered at the unanimity of behaviour of flocks of birds and shoals of minnows. That *sensory* clues originating in a " leader ", and heard or seen by all the others, can account for the swiftness and similarity of response seems well-nigh impossible. Perhaps it will be possible to test this : it may well prove necessary to postulate in such cases a group-mind, controlling through ψ the whole aggregate of physical organisms. Carington and others have drawn attention to the possibility that such a group-mind does control insect communities, such as ants, bees and termites, in much the same way as the mind of a higher animal may control through ψ the cells of its body. He suggests, with great cogency, that the extraordinary instinctive patterns of behaviour which Natural History is constantly unfolding for our admiration must arise from a group-mind (perhaps of the species) and be conserved and controlled by ψ. Certainly when we reflect upon the intricacy of behaviour of, say, the web-spinning spider, doing something in a novel situation which it has not practised or seen done, or of creatures of the garden or the field preparing a food supply essential to the welfare of future progeny which they will never see, we may find in our knowledge of ψ something far more equal to accounting for these things than inheritable " brain tracks ".

The problem of bird navigation and migration is one that has always intrigued observers. In a recent paper * surveying the various physical theories, A. J. C. Wilson concludes that " the mechanism of bird navigation is still unexplained "—a conclusion which at least leaves open the possibility of ψ-control from a bird group-mind.

10. BERGSON'S VIEW OF THE FUNCTIONS OF MIND AND BRAIN

It is impossible to theorise about the nature of ψ without constantly making reference to the relative functions of mind and brain,

* *Jour. S.P.R.*, Vol. 35, p. 30 (March 1949).

and since the views propounded by Bergson seem to the present writer to illuminate the whole subject, a very brief account is here presented. Henri Bergson died in 1941, although the period of his most fruitful work was 1890–1914. His presidential address * to the Society for Psychical Research dealt with this theme, and his views are summarised by Professor H. H. Price † in a brief account of which we shall make use here.

Bergson considers intellect a practical tool of the Self, and gives to intuition a more profound place in the apprehension of truth. He conceives the physical brain as primarily an organ of action. So far as perception goes, he considers its function is selective; that is to say, it shuts out from our consciousness the great mass of impressions, and only permits us to become aware of a part of the whole, this part being the possible material for action. Perception he regards as serving the practical end of action, and not primarily existing as a means of knowledge which could be gathered otherwise. The brain limits perception : it focuses the mind's awareness on to " life ". It is when the closeness of the link is temporarily loosened that the mind's wider awareness is made manifest, as in telepathy, clairvoyance, etc.

Bergson distinguishes between habit-memory and memory proper. In reciting a verse of poetry there is no real recall of a past memory : it is an habitual type of action impressed on the brain and capable of repetition. Memory proper, which is the storage of past experiences, is a purely psychical function, and is not to be supposed related to " brain-traces ". The brain is in this respect also an organ of limitation, generally shutting out from recall all the past except that which is relevant to the present practical situation. In illness, mental derangement and some dreams, it is noticeable that this control goes, and a disorderly jumble of apparently useless memories floods in.

Certain brain injuries which result in " loss of memory ", word-blindness or loss of the faculty of speech are not regarded as a destruction of memory through destruction of " brain-traces ", but as indicating that the connection between memory and the expression of memory has been severed. The damage has prevented a certain class of *actions* from occurring. Bergson's view of the nature of thinking is quite different from the orthodox one, which postulates that there is a specific brain state corresponding to each mental state —a one-to-one correspondence. Apart from its sensory functions, which we have seen are selective and limiting, the brain's function

* *Proc. S.P.R.*, Vol. 27, pp. 157–75.
† Ibid., Vol. 46, Part 164, pp. 271–7 (1941).

in the process of thinking is solely to express in action (muscular movements and postures) what the mind thinks.   It is, so to speak, an organ of pantomime or dumb-show.   A super-physiologist who, examining the brain, could infer the results, would only be able to deduce the laryngeal movements, facial muscular contractions, etc. ; of words—which are encoded thoughts—he could know nothing.   The brain, then, merely mimes the mental life, but a little reflection makes clear that this is an important function without which we could not insert ourselves into, or respond to, our physical environment.   Bergson says :

> " Though consciousness is not a function of the brain, at any rate the brain keeps our consciousness fixed upon the world in which we live ; it is the organ of attention to life. . . . To orientate our thought towards action, to induce it to prepare the act which circumstances require, that is the task for which our brain was made."

To sum up : the brain is primarily the organ of action of the thinker in the material world.   It is an organ of limitation : it canalises ψ_κ by limiting action to muscular processes, and it canalises ψ_γ by limiting awareness to sensory processes.   It is only in states of relative inattention to life that the wider activity or knowledge is possible : this, we have seen, accords with empirical evidence.   Thouless suggests that ψ-faculty was probably the primitive way in which organisms managed to orientate themselves to their environment, and that the evolution of sense-organs was a subsequent evolutionary development of greater biological utility.   This was precisely because it canalised awareness to the immediate neighbourhood and the present moment.   Thouless points out that a deer would not know whether the tiger of which it became aware was near or distant, or whether it was a tiger which had been there yesterday or would be there tomorrow.   Of course, the corresponding disadvantages would also apply to the tiger !   It is clear that it is only through sensory limitation in space and time that a world of effective action could come into being.   If we imagine the case of human beings, sensitive without the power of discrimination or selectivity to thought from their fellow beings, it would be a less tolerable and less valuable state of affairs than that which obtains with auditory limitations. These considerations support the view that ψ-function was perhaps the primitive means of communication, gradually overlaid and superseded—though not destroyed—by the development of special sense which had greater biological utility.   It might be more accurate to say ψ_γ was canalised or focused through the special senses, and ψ_κ through the muscles (see diagram, p. 134).

Once the possibility of consciously directed or precisely orientated ψ is available, as in the Soal–Goldney experiments with Mrs. Stewart, we have the beginning of an enormous extension of our powers. The view which regards ψ as primitive function, superseded in evolution by sensory faculty, is not held by F. W. H. Myers and others, who rather see in it something which is evolving and capable of bringing Man into touch with higher ranges of truth.

The present writer inclines to the view that what we have hitherto collectively called ψ may require differentiation into at least two levels of faculty. There is one level of phenomena on the " infra-red side of the spectrum of consciousness " (to use Myers' metaphor) which is our animal inheritance. It is the level of ψ involving all the inter-relations of mind with matter (possibly through the medium of a psychic æther) and some of the relations of mind with mind, and it is perhaps this level which has been involved in all the examples used in this chapter. But there is probably another level of ψ-faculty corresponding, in Myers' phrase, to the " ultra-violet extension of the spectrum of consciousness ". It is this level which is involved in the inter-relations of higher minds, the level of creative inspiration leading to insights, to great art, poetry, music and sculpture. This ψ-cognition lacks the vagueness and the uncertainty of the lower type : it possesses clarity and precision of form, and carries inspiration with it to the percipient mind. This kind of ψ links the centre of consciousness (which in most of us is on the mental level) * to a higher world, just as the other more primitive kind of ψ links it to the physical-etheric world. It is obviously much rarer and far less developed, and with Myers and modern writers like Heard † we believe it is the hopeful direction of man's future evolution. The similarity of conditions favouring " lower-ψ " to those which Rhine describes as involved in " delicately original and creative work in the arts " (and which we have suggested are due to the operation of " higher-ψ ") arises from the fact that in them both a displacement of consciousness takes place. There is in both cases a measure of withdrawal of mind from its close gearing with the physical brain, but in one case it sinks towards the collective unconscious, and in the other rises towards the buddhic level.

II. ATTITUDE TOWARDS FACTS

In 1935 Professor C. D. Broad wrote :

> " For my own part I have no doubt that telepathy among normal human beings happens. . . . But we know quite well that most scientists

* See Chapter 12, p. 266.
† E.g., Gerald Heard : *Pain, Sex and Time* and *The Third Morality*.

and the bulk of the general public would not admit this for an instant. And we know that this is not because they have looked into the evidence and found it faulty or have suggested plausible alternative explanations. They would no more think of looking into the evidence for telepathy than a pious Christian thinks of looking into the evidence for Mahometanism or a pious Mahometan of looking into the evidence for Christianity."

The position today is that ψ, in which we include telepathy, clairvoyance and precognition, must be regarded as a fact established by as great a weight of observation and experiment as that which supports the basic facts in other sciences. While individual scientists, philosophers and psychologists have recognised this, it still remains true that the majority are either apathetic or mildly hostile to the subject. The hostility probably arises from the recognition that if these things are true they have to face data which cannot fit into the well-established system of law which governs the material world. In other words, materialist philosophies are undermined. The apathy, in view of the importance of the issues involved, is difficult to account for on logical grounds. Tyrrell, who has written frequently on this prevalent attitude, has expressed his conviction of its psychological origin. He follows Bergson's line of thought in supposing that the brain keeps the mind tied down very closely to the world of action, and that whenever knowledge or beliefs arise which would draw interest away from the world of action, this factor operates to discount them. He cites, for example, the report of a committee of three most competent and trusted observers who, with the utmost vigilance, and taking adequate precautions, nevertheless witnessed para-normal physical phenomena in the case of a medium they were investigating. In their report they wrote " These things seemed to roll off our minds and . . . we lapsed back into scepticism again ". Tyrrell * says :

" It is because the constitution of our minds, as a result of biological evolution, causes us to reject whatever is entirely foreign to the world of common experience. If we succeed in resisting this psychological tendency even for a moment, we can see quite clearly that there is no reason why our bodily senses should reveal the length and breadth of all existence. There is no reason why nature should terminate at the point where our senses cease to register it, and no reason why, beyond this point, it should not be governed by unfamiliar laws—no reason, but so strong is the sense-centredness of our minds that we find ourselves smiling at the idea that anything important can exist in the universe which we cannot either directly perceive or grasp with our existing mental equipment. It is the sense of the ante-

* G. N. M. Tyrrell (Presidential Address), *Proc. S.P.R.*, Vol. 47, p. 301.

cedent improbability of things which are quite strange which dominates the subject of psychical research and accounts for the negative treatment it receives. And this sense of improbability is prompted by a factor in our minds which is non-rational."

The essential point could not, I think, have been put more clearly, and we should do well to keep it in mind as we plunge deeper into this strange world behind the façade of matter and common sense.

Chapter

7

PRECOGNITION AND RETROCOGNITION

" In any attempt to bridge the domains of experience belonging to the spiritual and physical sides of our nature, Time occupies the key position."

A. S. EDDINGTON

" It is impossible to meditate on Time and the mystery of the creative passage of Nature without an overwhelming emotion at the limitations of human intelligence."

A. N. WHITEHEAD.

" Indeed, life's development, the evolution of awareness, may best be rendered into three attitudes towards Time. Then we see successively the Time-unaware animal, the Time-haunted man, and the Time-understanding mind."

GERALD HEARD.

" I suspect that it is not by wider purview, wiser inference alone, that finite minds, in the body or out of it have attained to knowledge of what yet must be. I imagine that the continuity of the universe is complete; and that therefore the hierarchy of intelligences between our minds and the World-Soul is infinite; and that somewhere in that ascent a point is reached where our conception of time loses its accustomed meaning."

F. W. H. MYERS.

I. INTRODUCTION

CAN the future be foreknown and predicted? History is full of stories of oracles and prophets, soothsayers and fortune-tellers. Is there any basis for the suggestion that some persons in some circumstances have any para-normal faculty enabling them to do this? There are, of course, certain forms of prediction which are commonplace and arouse no surprise : predictions of eclipses of the sun and moon, of the times of sunset, of high tides, etc. All this is prediction based upon knowledge of the past, upon the observation of Nature's regularities and of their complete reliability. There are also predictions which can be made with a fair measure of reliability based upon human intention. Because a person follows a certain business routine with regularity, and because the railway company intends to run certain trains, it may be possible to predict with some confidence that he will arrive home at a certain time. All this is, however, based on past observations. By precognition we mean knowledge of the future not based upon knowledge of the past or present, howsoever acquired. Does this occur? It is important to have an answer to this question, and we may anticipate the conclusion of this chapter to say that the answer is " yes ". This, then, raises for us all some of the profoundest questions. Does this imply that the future is fixed and unalterable? Where does free will come in? How can something which doesn't exist, because it is in the future, be the present cause of knowledge about it? And before we realise it, we are plunged into the metaphysical depths of the most baffling problem which has ever perplexed the mind of Man : the nature of Time.

Our first task is to consider the evidence for precognition. We shall, for convenience, look first at the spontaneous evidence where the phenomenon appears in its most interesting and dramatic forms, then afterwards at the experimental work which shows its existence beyond any shadow of doubt, such as is implied in the words " chance ", " accident " or " coincidence "

2. SPONTANEOUS EVIDENCE

Those who desire to know the real weight of evidence should at this stage be willing to read at least one of the books * devoted exclusively to it. In 1934 H. F. Saltmarsh reported to the London Society for Psychical Research the result of a critical study which he had made of 349 cases of ostensible precognition which the Society had published. To be wholly satisfactory, a case should satisfy the following conditions :

(*a*) It should have been recorded in writing or told to a witness, or acted upon in some significant manner *before* the subsequent incident verifies it.

(*b*) It should contain a sufficient amount of detail verified by the event, to make chance coincidence unlikely.

(*c*) Conditions should be such that we can definitely rule out the following as explanations : telepathy and contemporary clairvoyance, auto-suggestion, inference from subliminally acquired knowledge and hyperæsthesia.

It may be helpful to give illustrations of cases which could be ruled out on each of these grounds. Suppose, for example, a person dreams that a certain telegram or letter bearing a particular message is on its way, and that this is subsequently verified. In such cases

* E.g., H. F. Saltmarsh : *Foreknowledge* (G. Bell & Sons, 1938) or Hon. Mrs. Alfred Lyttelton : *Some Cases of Prediction* (G. Bell & Sons, 1937).

telepathy from the sender, or clairvoyance by the percipient of a message already in existence is quite a possible explanation. Again, X may have a vivid dream of a certain landscape which he has never seen before, and a few days later may actually see it. Contemporary clairvoyance might be a reasonable explanation of this dream. Below is a case which might be accounted for by telepathic awareness of an intention in another person's mind—although the percipient does not recognise at the time that it is of this origin.

> *Case of Mrs. F. C. Alpine.** " Being at length tired, I sat down to rest upon a rock at the edge of the water. My attention was quite taken up with the extreme beauty of the scene before me. There was not a sound or movement except the soft ripple of water on the sand at my feet. Presently I felt a cold chill creep through me, and a curious stiffness of my limbs, as if I could not move though wishing to do so. I felt frightened, yet chained to the spot, and as if impelled to stare at the water straight in front of me. Gradually a black cloud seemed to rise, and in the midst of it I saw a tall man, in a suit of tweed, jump into the water and sink.
>
> " In a moment the darkness was gone, and I again became sensible of the heat and sunshine, but I was awed and felt eerie—it was then about four o'clock or so—I cannot remember either the exact time or date. On my sister's arrival I told her of the occurrence ; she was surprised, but inclined to laugh at it. When we got home I told my brother ; he treated the subject much in the same manner. However, about a week afterwards a Mr. Espie, a bank clerk (unknown to me), committed suicide by drowning in that very spot. He left a letter for his wife, indicating that he had for some time contemplated his death. My sister's memory of the event is the only evidence I can give. I did not see the account of the inquest at the time, and did not mention my strange experience to anyone saving my sister and brother."

In a case such as this it still remains mysterious why, of all possible minds, it should be that of Mrs. Alpine which received subliminal knowledge of the bank clerk's intention. I incline to another explanation of this case (see Section 8).

Then, again, there are some cases in which a person gets a fixed idea that he is going to have a particular illness or die at a certain time : here the possibility that autosuggestion has been operative in bringing the event about is quite plausible. Again, a person may have a vision or dream of the death of a friend who on conscious levels he believes to be in good health. The event may be fulfilled shortly afterwards, but clearly there is a possibility that the person has acquired knowledge by clairvoyance or telepathy of the serious internal condition of his friend. Consider another case :

* *Proc. S.P.R.*, Vol. 10, p. 332.

*Case.** A lady sitting in the porch of her wooden house had a hallucinatory vision of a distant fire. After watching it for about ten minutes she heard a faint crackling sound and upon getting up to investigate found her own house on fire and was only just in time to save her child.

We might here suggest auditory hyperæsthesia, or even clairvoyance, as a possible cause of the hallucinatory vision.

By this type of critical examination Saltmarsh reduced the 349 cases to a resistent core of 183. Below are given a few examples of precognition which cannot easily be explained on the grounds discussed above.

Case of Mrs. Calder.† In 1928 Mr. Calder, who resided in Middlesex, was appointed headmaster of Holmfirth Secondary School in Yorkshire. Mrs. Calder, who had not been to Yorkshire, dreamed of an old greystone house, set in a lovely valley through which ran a stream of clear but black-looking water. In their house-hunting near Holmfirth they came across the very house which Mrs. Calder had seen in her dream; they took it, or rather one half of it, and moved in in August 1928. They found that the water of the stream was frequently discoloured by indigo from a nearby dye-works. In her dream Mrs. Calder had seen that only one half of the house was occupied and that outside the door of that half was a barrel which was used as a dog-kennel. When they went to live there, though the other half was occupied, there was no barrel. A year or so later, there was a change of tenants of the other half of the house. When the new people arrived they brought with them a dog and placed a barrel outside the door for its kennel.

The Marmontal Case.‡ This case is remarkable for its detail. The foreknowledge was obtained by Mrs. Verrall through automatic writing, and the substance of the first script was in another person's possession before the date of verification. On December 11th the following was written.

" Nothing too mean; the trivial helps, gives confidence. Hence this. Frost and candle in the dim light. Marmontal he was reading on a sofa or in bed—there was only a candle's light. She will remember this. The book was lent, not his own—he talked about it." This writing was followed by a reference to another incident and a recognisable attempt at the name Sidgwick. As the writing had no meaning for Mrs. Verrall she communicated with Mrs. Sidgwick (one of the founders of the S.P.R.), who wrote back on December 17th that she could make nothing of it. On the evening of the day Mrs. Verrall felt a strong impulse to write again and obtained the following:

" I wanted to write, Marmontal is right. It was a French book,

---

* *Proc. S.P.R.,* Vol. 11, p. 418.
† *Some Cases of Prediction,* p. 106, quoted in *Foreknowledge,* pp. 64–5.
‡ *Proc. S.P.R.,* Vol. 20, p. 331.

a Memoir I think.   Passy may help.   Souvenirs de Passy or Fleury. Marmon al was not on the cover—the book was bound and was lent— two volumes in old-fashioned binding and print.   It is not in any papers—it is an attempt to make someone remember—an incident."

After returning to Cambridge on December 25th, chancing to look through a list of books, Mrs. Verrall saw advertised " Marmontal, *Moral Tales*, Selected and translated by G. Saintsbury ". This was her first conscious knowledge of Marmontal as a French writer.   In January a friend, Mr. Marsh, was invited to come for a week-end visit, and March 1st was fixed.   On this evening at dinner Mr. Marsh mentioned he had been reading Marmontal.   Mrs. Verrall asked if he had read the *Moral Tales*, and he replied it was the *Memoirs*.   In response to questions he said that he had got the book from the London Library and took the first volume only to Paris. He read it by the light of a candle, on the evening of February 20th, lying on his bed, and on the evening of February 21st lying on two chairs.   He talked about the book to the friends with whom he was staying in Paris.   The weather was cold but not frosty.   The Library copy was not in modern binding but scarcely old-fashioned.   The name Marmontal was on the back of the book though not on the face of the cover.   The edition was in three volumes : Mr. Marsh had one only in Paris but had read the second before this visit to the Verralls. On returning to town Mr. Marsh verified that he had on February 21st been reading a chapter in the Memoirs describing the finding at Passy of a panel etc. connected with a story in which Fleury plays an important part.

In spite of the minor discrepancies it is clearly a remarkably detailed description (in the past tense) of something which took place seventy-two days later.

Case of the Derailed Engine.*   The account was given by Mrs. W., wife of the Rev. Dr. W., and related to the Sunday afternoon of July 15th, 1860, when she was staying with her little daughter A. and a servant in lodgings at Trinity, near Edinburgh.   The account below is abbreviated and is interesting as showing a strong apprehension of danger (although its nature was not known), and action was based upon it which as far as can be judged saved her daughter's life.

" Between three and four o'clock I told A. to go out and take a short walk, and as she was quite alone I advised her to go into the railway garden (a name she gave to a strip of ground between the sea-wall and the railway embankment, which was closed by a gate at either end).   A few minutes after her departure I distinctly heard a voice, as it were, within me say, ' Send for her back or something dreadful will happen to her '.   At the same time I was seized with violent trembling and a feeling of great terror took possession of me.   I rose

* *Jour. S.P.R.*, Vol. 8, p. 45 (March 1897).

THE DATA OF PSYCHICAL RESEARCH

hastily, rang the bell, and ordered the servant to go immediately and bring Miss A. home. . . . During her absence the terror which so unaccountably possessed me seemed to increase, and I feared that I should never see my child again alive." In about a quarter of an hour the servant returned with her safe and well. The child was asked to promise her mother that she would not go to the place she had intended, but told she might play anywhere else, and on her leaving the house the mother records that all anxiety on the child's account passed away. Later that afternoon an engine and tender jumped the rails, broke through the protecting wall and crashed on the rocks where A. had been intending to sit. Three men out of five who were there were killed. A. and her brother visited the scene of the accident and saw the shattered engine on the spot to which she had been going, and where she had spent two hours with her brother the previous Sunday.

In his book *An Experiment with Time*, J. W. Dunne gives many examples of his dreams, of which he kept careful records over many years. They contain numerous cases of precognitions, mostly fulfilled in the near future, but in one or two instances referring to unusual events years ahead.

A book published in 1948 by Dr. W. H. C. Tenhaeff * contains a large number of dreams and visions containing precognitive elements which had to do with the war in Holland. Thus, for example, Mrs. R. of E. over a period of forty years had recurrent dreams that the part of Rotterdam largely between the River Maas and the Exchange would be reduced to a barren plain, with here and there heaps of rubble. These dreams became comparatively frequent in 1938, 1939 and early 1940, but after the bombing of Rotterdam did not return. The dream-images were very clear, and, after waking, a feeling of depression lingered for some hours. Although it may be, as Dunne suggests, that fragments of trivial and largely unnoticed futuristic material intrude into ordinary dreams, there seems good reason to think that the genuine precognitive dream is in a class by itself and that it is realised to be such by the dreamer. Thus Miss V. de W., who from 1935 onwards had numerous dreams of this type, says :

"The visions always occur during my sleep (they are therefore dream-images). Afterwards I always wake up and then the images stand out clearly in my mind. It is curious that usually the day after I have had such a dream, I am dead tired. This tiredness occurred in particular after those dreams which were related to the war. The tiredness always went gradually and did not disappear until several days later."

* Vide *Jour. S.P.R.*, Vol. 35, p. 47 (March 1949).

In a paper called " Forecasts in Scripts concerning the War ",
Mr. J. G. Piddington * has made a critical study of the automatic
writings and kindred activities of a number of ladies closely identified
with the Society for Psychical Research. The reader who studies
these for precognitive material will, I think, remark on their general
vagueness—on the fewness of the grains of wheat and the large
amount of chaff. Possibly we should not be surprised at this. If
precognitive knowledge emanates from the transcendental self, it may
find but few occasions when it can emerge into consciousness without
dragging with it a whole association network which obscures and
corrupts it. There do, however, occur fragments which are most
surprising. Thus on May 24th, 1915, in a script of the Hon. Mrs.
Alfred Lyttelton, appear the words,† " The hand stretched out
to stay Berchtesgaden ", and in a script on January 31st, 1915, the
words, " The Munich bond, remember that. You will see strange
things." Such phrases had no significant meaning until twenty-
three years later.

C. Drayton Thomas ‡ has made a recent study of forecasts and
precognition based upon material obtained through the mediumship
of Mrs. Osborne Leonard. For the present we shall merely remark
that the techniques of bringing precognitive knowledge to consciousness are very varied, and that our knowledge of their mechanisms is very limited indeed, but of the fact of precognition we can
entertain little doubt.

3. EXPERIMENTAL EVIDENCE

Work of Rhine. Professor Rhine and his co-workers recognised
that since the telepathic and clairvoyant faculty had shown that
mental function transcended spatial limitations, it was at least
probable that it would be in some degree " time-free " also, for time
is inferred as a result of changes in spatial position. Experiments
were therefore undertaken with subjects of proved clairvoyant ability
using the method of guessing the order of a pack of cards " down
through "—i.e., from top to bottom. Instead, however, of shuffling
the pack and then asking the percipient to record his guesses, as in
tests for clairvoyance, the percipient was now asked to record his
guesses for a pack which he was told would be shuffled at a fixed time
later. With some 4,500 runs through a pack under these conditions
the score averaged between five and six correct out of twenty-five, for

* *Proc. S.P.R.*, Vol. 33, p. 439 (1923).
† *Proc. S.P.R.*, Vol. 48, Part 176, p. 335.
‡ Ibid., Vol. 48, Part 175, p. 306.

which result the odds against chance as an explanation are 400,000 to 1. A criticism of this, as evidence for precognition, might be that the use of contemporary clairvoyance, when the pack was being shuffled, might lead to the experimenter stopping the shuffling so as to give an above-chance score. Independent groups of experiments with a mechanical type of shuffler, however, confirmed the ostensible explanation of precognition. By still other critics it was suggested that the experimenter might be using his mind psycho-kinetically (see Chapter 11) so as to influence the cards even in the machine-shuffling. This objection was met by cutting the pack of cards in a predetermined way after machine-shuffling. This method of cutting was made to depend on daily temperature records in a given newspaper—this being taken as an unpredictable chance factor. But scoring still remained significantly above chance !

Work of Tyrrell. In the previous chapter it was explained that Tyrrell could introduce a relay into his apparatus, by pressing a switch unknown to the percipient. The effect of this was that although the lamp to be lit was selected in the usual way, it did not actually light until one of the box lids was lifted by the percipient. Lifting the lid worked the relay which lit the lamp. In 1,845 trials without the relay 28·6% correct were scored; in 1,855 trials with the relay 26·2% correct were scored. The odds against chance as an explanation are in both cases enormous, and it is, of course, clear that in the second series of trials a precognitive faculty is involved. The lamp was not lit at the time the choice was made.

Tyrrell could, apart from this device, adapt his apparatus to test for precognition. All that it was necessary to do was to give the signal to the percipient to open a box *before* pressing the key to light a lamp (the particular lamp to be lit being unknown to the agent because of the commutator). In 2,255 trials of this kind 23·9% successes were obtained—a result for which the odds are millions to one against chance as an explanation.

In still another arrangement a mechanical selector was set running, and the act of opening a lid cut off power from the selector and lit a lamp depending on the contact on which it stopped. This pre-cognitive device could be put in action or out of action by a switch, and Tyrrell remarks that Miss G. J. frequently failed if she knew it was being used, otherwise it made no appreciable difference.

The Soal–Goldney Experiments. Reference has been made in the preceding chapter to the work of Dr. Soal and Mrs. Goldney with two high-scoring subjects, Mrs. Stewart and Mr. Shackleton. The reader should refresh his memory with this. Mr. Shackleton's notable feature was his ability to score consistently above chance on the $+1$ card—i.e., the card one place ahead in the pack, and therefore not yet in the mind of the agent. It was found that when the interval between successive calls, which was usually about $2\frac{1}{2}$ seconds, was reduced to about $1\frac{1}{2}$ seconds by faster calling, he now scored above chance on the card $+2$. If the rate of calling was slowed down to give 5-second intervals, the scoring fell to chance level. This suggests that he had a displacement of $2\frac{1}{2}$ to 3 seconds forward in time so far as his ψ-faculty was concerned : a natural precognitive effect.

It might, however, be urged against this conclusion that the two pieces of information necessary to score in this way were both accessible to clairvoyance—viz., the *next* random number on the list and the order of the five animal-cards. To meet this criticism, experiments were carried out in which the agent had before him a bag containing equal numbers of counters in five different colours. By deciding at the beginning that each colour should correspond to one of the five cards (e.g., green ; second from left, etc.), a random choice could be made by drawing out a coloured counter. This method eliminated the objection mentioned above and established precognition of the future content of the agent's mind. It will be remembered that Shackleton, like Mrs. Stewart, appeared to require the knowledge to be in someone's mind—i.e., their faculty was what we call telepathic, not clairvoyant.

In the case of Mrs. Stewart, whose percipient faculty was on the contemporary card, an interesting effect was observed to develop in the course of the research. While she continued to score successfully on the contemporary target card, a negative deviation—i.e., a steady scoring rate *below* the chance value—began to appear on the $+1$ card. It is scarcely necessary to say that scoring *below* the chance level is quite as remarkable as scoring above it, and is evidence of some para-normal cognition as to what this card actually is. It was conjectured that this phenomenon may have been an unconscious protest against any intention of playing second fiddle to Mr. Shackleton, whose noteworthy achievement was to score above chance on the $+1$ card !

Whately Carington's Experiments. This monumental piece of work reflects the extraordinary patience of its late author. He conducted these experiments with drawings over many years, and altogether about 20,000 drawings were collected.* A large number of collaborators (percipients) in different parts of the country were each provided with ten forms, and the experiment was as follows. Carington selected an object by using mathematical tables opened at

---

* His last paper is in *Proc. S.P.R.*, Vol. 47, Part 168 (1944).

random and opening a dictionary at the page indicated. He then drew the first concrete object and pinned this in his study from 7 p.m. to 9.30 a.m. A similar procedure took place on ten successive nights. Each percipient forwarded the ten drawings he had made, purporting to be guesses at these ten originals. A run of ten such trials constituted an "experiment", and Carington conducted eleven experiments, in several of which about 250 persons participated. In comparing drawings with originals, the problem of a hit or a miss is always one of personal judgment. For this reason, all the experimental data were judged by a third party, and a method was devised by which either too much rigour or laxity of judgment would cancel itself out in the end. We shall not add to the length of this chapter by going into this method. His conclusions, however, are very important.

The most interesting conclusion he was able to draw from all this work was that as the occasion of display of a target is approached the proportion of ostensible hits on that target gradually rises, reaches a maximum on or about that occasion, and then gradually declines again to the chance level. Will the reader pause to consider this conclusion: that forty-eight hours before the target-picture was chosen by a random method there was an appreciably greater likelihood of drawing it than, say, a week earlier. At twenty-four hours before the choice of target-picture this likelihood was greater still. It rose to a maximum on the night of its actual choice—and following this, the likelihood of drawing it declined gradually. The rate of incline and decline (precognition and retrocognition) appeared to be related more to the rate of experimentation than to clock time. Carington's impression was that it was the "idea" or "content" or "meaning" of the original that was perceived more often than the exact form. He also regarded the drawing as merely efficacious in impressing the idea on the experimenter's mind, and says that it was not essential that the object should be drawn to get the effect. (There is no need to go into further detail, except to say that the odds against chance as an explanation of his results were extremely high.)

4. EFFECT OF PRECOGNITION ON STATUS OF TELEPATHY AND CLAIRVOYANCE

Professor Rhine has aptly remarked that the implications raised by the existence of precognition are about as formidable as those which would confront a chemist who had discovered a universal solvent and did not know how to contain it. One of the first issues which Rhine himself raised is this : assuming clairvoyance is factual, would not precognitive clairvoyance account for all the data previously assumed to be evidence for telepathy ?   Consider, for example, the supposed " pure telepathy " experiment in which the agent thinks of five cards in succession, and does not record these until *after* the percipient has recorded his guesses.   If we admit precognitive clairvoyance, it would be possible for the percipient to precognise the agent's record.   Suppose we imagine an experiment of the Soal–Goldney type, in which the experimenter uses random numbers which he presents at the screen aperture, but in which the agent has five blank cards in a row.   He *mentally* decides on the order of the animal-pictures which he will ascribe to each of the cards.   He must never write this down or tell it to anyone, otherwise precognitive clairvoyance or clairaudience might discover it.   He must simply check up mentally on the correctness or otherwise of the percipient's record.

In a thousand trials Mrs. Stewart scored 293 correct, compared with the chance level of 200—a result of which the odds are millions to one against chance as an explanation.   Such an experiment, and others like it, eliminate the suggestion made, that telepathy might not really exist, but that precognitive clairvoyance might account for the facts.   Such a suggestion might, however, have been regarded as not worth consideration when all the evidence of a spontaneous type and all the accumulated evidence of " thought-reading " in trance experiments are weighed.

There might, on the other hand, be some who are disposed to rule out *clairvoyance* as factual, on the ground that precognitive telepathy could account for the same facts.   Thus they would say : suppose a percipient has guessed the order of a shuffled pack of cards, then someone (say the agent) must subsequently compare these guesses with the actual order.   The percipient might have precognised this future state of the agent's mind, not the designs on the cards.   In so simple an experiment as this it may be so ; but there are numerous other experiments where precognitive telepathy as an explanation is ruled out.   Tyrrell's electrical apparatus, it will be recalled, made recordings on a tape.   A single mark indicated a trial and a double mark a successful trial.   While by subsequent examination of this tape the experimenter could count successes, he could not know which box was on each occasion the correct one.   Hence precognitive telepathy is ruled out.   There are many kinds of experiments for which this can also be claimed.

We can sum up by saying that the evidence is strongly in favour of the view that clairvoyance, telepathy and precognition are all established facts to be reckoned with.   The Tyrrell experiments demonstrate both clairvoyance and precognitive clairvoyance: the Soal–Goldney experiments with Shackleton and Mrs. Stewart established that telepathy was essential to secure both the contemporary and the precognitive results. We shall in future assume that the symbol ψ includes all three types of para-normal functioning.

5. RETROCOGNITION

By retrocognition we mean knowledge acquired of some past event or state other than through the senses or inference based on sense data. Precognition has always attracted far more attention than retrocognition. It is perhaps natural that this should be so, for at first sight retrocognition does not seem to involve the same difficulty with causation, nor does it suggest any limitation on our present freedom. Yet, a little consideration suggests that the backward view in time is probably not less mysterious than the forward one.

Petit Trianon Case. This extraordinary example of retrocognition has been frequently quoted because of the detailed character of the experience and the prestige of its narrators.* Miss Moberly was Principal of St. Hugh's College, Oxford, and Miss Jourdain at that time Vice-Principal. In August 1901 they were visitors to the Petit Trianon at Versailles, and had certain experiences which subsequently led them to believe that they had seen it as it was in the time of Marie Antoinette (more than a century before). It was a " live " scene in which several persons figured and much information was gathered which was afterwards confirmed by documents in the French National Archives. The written accounts of the two ladies were substantially the same, though not in every detail. The weight of evidence must be studied in their book if it is to be assessed properly, and a recent criticism by W. H. Salter † is of value in this connection.

Miss L. M. Bazett,‡ a person to whom para-normal faculty appears accessible almost at will, has given an interesting description of similar experiences in the Palace and Gardens of Versailles. She describes several experiences associated with the sites of abbeys and old buildings, and remarks: " This psychic perception of the past appears to be of the nature of real experience, in varying degrees of vividness."

The Avebury Case. Miss Edith Olivier § has described a very

* Anne Moberly and Eleanor Jourdain: *An Adventure* (1911).
† *Jour. S.P.R.*, Vol. 35, p. 178 (Jan. 1950).
‡ L. Margery Bazett: *Beyond the Five Senses* (Blackwell, 1946).
§ Edith Olivier: *Without Knowing Mr. Walkley* (Chapter XVI) (Faber & Faber, 1939).

interesting experience, where some years elapsed before she realised
it contained a para-normal element. On a wet, dreary October
evening between 5 p.m. and 6 p.m., during 1916, she was driving
a small car from Devizes to Swindon in Wiltshire. She left
the main road and found herself passing along a strange avenue
" through a succession of huge grey megaliths, which stood on either
hand, looming like vast immovable shadows within a curtain of
softly falling rain ". She assumed she must be approaching Avebury,
which she had not visited before, but of which she had seen pictures
in archæological books. (Avebury was originally a circular mega-
lithic temple approached by long stone avenues.) Arriving at the
end of the avenue, she climbed on to the bank of the great earthwork
which surrounds the temple and saw the huge megaliths standing
or fallen irregularly, with cottages here and there interspersed among
them. On this particular night a village fair appeared to be in
progress, although rain was falling. She saw flares and torches from
the booths and shows, primitive swing-boats, coconut shies and
strolling groups of villagers. Then the rain becoming unpleasantly
heavy, Miss Olivier got into her car and drove away. Nine years
later, visiting Avebury with a friend, she was surprised to discover
from the guide-book that a fair had formerly been held every year
in Avebury, but that it had been abolished in 1850! The next
year, when visiting Avebury again as a member of a learned society
studying the monument, she discovered to her surprise that the
avenue of megaliths up which she believed she had come in her
first visit had disappeared before 1800. It looked as though she
must substantially have viewed the scene as it was in the eighteenth
century or earlier.

This type of experience suggests a kind of persistent memory in
the psychic æther associated with a place, to which in a certain
receptive state of mind a sensitive person may tune-in. Alternatively,
the observer's mind may have been invaded telepathically by the
surviving mind of someone who saw it thus. Towards the end of
the next chapter we shall again refer to this type of effect. Some
places and localities undoubtedly have strange " atmospheres " to
which persons may be more or less sensitive. The subjective effects
may range from vague discomfort and a sense of weirdness to the
full-blown retrocognitive experience when the sensitive appears to
participate in the living past.

We do not know what our own memory is : we know only that
it is something on a non-material level to which we respond uniquely
as individuals. Bergson's distinction between habit-memory (a sort
of habitual type of activity impressed on the brain) and memory

proper, which is a psychical function, may be a true pointer to an extended view of memory. We tend to assume, because of our familiarity with our own mental functioning, that the mind alone has memory. In fact, we may have to admit that something akin to memory (i.e., some kind of record) exists on every level (physical and mental); that even inanimate matter may have its own memory akin to that passive habit-type associated with our brains. The psychic æther which we have postulated may be the vehicle of such a record or memory. This seems to be a plausible hypothesis when we consider later the extraordinary phenomenon of object-reading (sometimes called psychometry). That which we have described as habit-memory cognised by our mind in relation to our brain, is " object-reading " when cognised by our mind in relation to a separate material object. And if objects have this type of cognisable memory, so have places and buildings, and given the right ψ-relationship, this memory can apparently be tapped. It is necessary to note that the recorded cases of " retrocognition " have this character—i.e., they appear to have been stimulated by a particular locality or historic building. If it seems a fantastic idea that inanimate objects should possess a cognisable memory-record, this is probably because we are not accustomed to distinguish clearly between the memory (i.e., the record) and the act of remembering, which we believe is a function of the instrument Mind. Rocks cannot remember—but they may hold a memory (in their associated psychic æther *), which the mind of a man in favourable circumstances can cognise. The common assumption that what we call " our " memory is " in " our mind (whatever this means) should probably be replaced by the idea that our mind is the instrument of apprehending all memory. The uniqueness which leads us to call a certain part of memory " ours " may be in the capacity of response of the individual instrument. To some parts of memory one individual alone may have a capacity of response—i.e., he alone can " remember " it.

I venture to quote from the rather remarkable automatic script of Geraldine Cummins † purporting to come from the late F. W. H. Myers, which expresses what I now believe to be the same idea.

' Now memory may be likened to the sea. It is all about you ; and as elusive as the water of the ocean. When we are alive we come to it like children with our small buckets and fill them with the salt fluid. How little we carry away up the sands. How easily and

* See Chapter 6 (7).
† Geraldine Cummins : *The Road to Immortality* (L.S.A. Publications Ltd.).

F

swiftly we spill it upon the ground yet behind us is that vast area of water booming endlessly upon the shore. The sound of memory is now to me like the sound of the tide, as when in the olden days I listened to it through the summer evenings. . . . One [mind] mentally draws to it a greater share of the collective memory than another. It is changed when filtered through the brain of man; it takes upon itself his colour, his personality, and eventually it comes up to his consciousness as original thought, but horribly dull and unoriginal at times. For the average man draws through him mostly the recent memories ejected by many living brains. The thinker has a greater capacity for drawing to him the memories that lie in the depths of human nature. . . . What is rapidly cast off does not continue to live for any length of time. It is only the emotional memories or the memories created by a fine vehemence that permanently endure."

It is clear, however, that Myers is referring to the " memory proper " of Bergson (i.e., the " record " on the level of mind) and not to the memory-record of inanimate Nature.

6. J. W. DUNNE'S " EXPERIMENT WITH TIME "

Some years ago J. W. Dunne wrote a book which provoked a great deal of interest and discussion, and based upon his experimental results a philosophy of " Serialism ". Although the conclusions at which he arrived—i.e., his theory and his philosophy—are not acceptable to most thinkers, they merit consideration in any discussion of precognition. Dunne was a very careful and systematic observer of his dreams, of which he kept records for long periods. Many of these furnish excellent examples of precognition, but we shall not add to the length of this chapter by further illustrations. In addition to some unusually vivid precognitive dreams, Dunne came to the conclusion that many dreams had " futuristic " material in them (as well as past material) though often unrecognised as such. To explain this he adopted the view of experience which for brevity we may call that of the " Eternal Now ". Expressed simply, this means that all the events which ever have been, are now, or will be, are eternally in existence, and that we as individuals move among these events. The events in an individual's experience are spread like beads on the string of time. A moving slit, which we may call the present moment, limits the view of the individual to one bead at a time (the present event); but as the slit moves along, one bead after another comes into view. This seems at first sight a deterministic view of events, not one which allows the individual any real freedom —but we shall say more of this later. In an ordinary waking state the slit is a narrow one and the observer peering through the slit is

aware only of the present event, not of the past or future ones.   The
diagram will illustrate these ideas.   Now, a little consideration
shows that we have already split the observer himself into two parts.
One part, which we have called Observer$_{(1)}$ is really stretched out in
Time$_{(1)}$.   He *is* the beads on the string.   The other part of him,
which we will call Observer$_{(2)}$, looks through the slit of the present
moment and sees Observer$_{(1)}$'s *present* experience.   A little further
consideration shows that we have also introduced a second kind of
Time.   Time$_{(1)}$ is the ordinary familiar time in which all events are
spread out (i.e., the string of our diagram) in which the birth and
death of Observer$_{(1)}$ are shown marked.   When we pictured the slit
as *moving* from left to right, we automatically assumed another sort
of time : Time$_{(2)}$ to measure the speed of movement of the slit in
Time$_{(1)}$.   Similarly we could go on logically to infer that since there
is movement or change in Time$_{(2)}$, there must be another sort of time

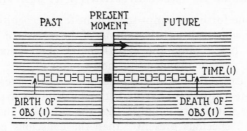

—Time$_{(3)}$—to account for this.   Incidentally we then require an
Observer$_{(3)}$, and so forth.   This is a strange situation : we tried to
understand how events happened to an ordinary observer in our
familiar time, and unwittingly we find the ordinary observer seems
to change into an infinite series of observers (who are all aspects of
himself), and ordinary time is replaced by an infinite series of times.
When this strange situation, which is called an " infinite regress ",
is found, philosophers usually return to see what is wrong with their
original assumptions, and start again with new ones.   Mr. Dunne
was made of sterner stuff : he accepted these regresses and built a
philosophy of serialism upon them !   Since we differ from Dunne
here, let us say where, in our opinion, he went wrong at the beginning.
He went wrong in treating time as though it were another dimension
of space : whatever else time is, we cannot believe it is that.   If
we persist in regarding it as such, the real nature of time will continue
to elude us.   For any of the observers all the preceding " times "
have simply turned into additional spatial dimensions.

   If we were prepared to accept Dunne's theory, what merit has it by way of interpretation of facts? Primarily it has this merit: that precognition is not fundamentally mysterious if future events are already in existence. The problem of precognition then relates only to the *means* by which these events can be cognised in advance. Dunne's view is that in certain states of consciousness, where thinking wholly of the past is arrested, the slit temporarily widens and Observer$_{(2)}$ can see glimpses of Observer$_{(1)}$'s future. Particularly in sleep is this supposed to be the case, and thus Observer$_{(2)}$ can observe what is both past and future for Observer$_{(1)}$. We have necessarily done less than justice to the ingenuity of Dunne's theory, since to do so would involve mathematical treatment, but I think there can be no doubt that Broad's * detailed criticism of this theory is unanswerable.

7. THEORY OF PRECOGNITION (H. F. SALTMARSH)

There is one further attempt to account for precognition by H. F. Saltmarsh, † who made a critical survey of the records of spontaneous cases. It is based upon the experimental observation that what we call " the present moment " is not a point of time, but a small time interval called the " specious present ". This corresponds to the small but finite width of the narrow slit in the diagram on p. 163. The theory can be stated very simply: that the subconscious mind has a much larger " specious present " than the conscious part. In the diagram this would be equivalent to a much wider slit for the deeper mind. On this view, events which would all be " present " for the deeper mind would comprise events which were past, present and future for the conscious mind. If some of this knowledge rose up into conscious awareness, it would thus be interpreted as pre-cognitional or post-cognitional.

To explain some relatively small time displacements, such as those involved in scoring on $+1$ and -1 cards, such a theory seems quite plausible. We are faced, however, with some precognitions and retrocognitions which cover a span of many months and years. A " specious present " which enlarges to this extent begins to approach the basic conception of an " Eternal Now ". Rightly understood, so that this basic idea is realised as not incompatible with freedom of choice, I think there is here a possible way through our difficulties.

---

* The detailed views of Professor C. D. Broad about precognition will be found in *Proc. Aristotelian Soc.*, Supp. Vol. XVI, pp. 177–245 (1937).

† H. F. Saltmarsh: *Foreknowledge* (G. Bell & Sons, 1938), pp. 94–9.

8. THEORY OF PRECOGNITION (CONCLUSION)

Let us endeavour to clarify our ideas, and decide if so far we have found any theory of precognition which will account for all the facts. The problem, stated as simply as possible, is this. There is an event E, and at an earlier point of time there is a veridical precognition P of this event: how are they causally related? Few, if any, would suggest that P is the cause of E, so let us dismiss this. We are then left with only two alternatives: (*a*) that E is the cause of P or (*b*) that P and E have a common cause which precedes them both in time: that P is one of the earlier effects and E one of the later effects of this common cause. We shall consider this latter alternative first.

It was this alternative which we considered in Section 2, where we said that a subconscious inference from observed data, or a subconscious intention to bring E about, were possible explanations of *some* cases; for these inferences or intentions might be the common causal ancestor of both P and E. Likewise a subconscious inference or intention in another human mind (or a discarnate mind) conveyed to the person having the precognition may be the common causal ancestor of both P and E. Now, the question is, do all our cases of precognition fit naturally into this type of explanation?

The case of Mrs. Alpine (p. 150) might perhaps be regarded as one of subconscious intention in another human mind picked up telepathically. The hallucinatory vision of a fire (p. 151) might be a case of subconscious inference from sense-data which did not receive conscious attention. The case of Mrs. Calder (p. 151) might be explained by supposing that using contemporary clairvoyance, she had gone house-hunting in her sleep and that then a subconscious intention was formed to realise her precognition. This explanation does not, however, account for the critical incident of the barrel. No explanation along these lines seems to account for the Marmontal case (p. 151), or for the case of the derailed engine (p. 152), or for the war references in Mrs. Alfred Lyttelton's scripts which had no significant meaning until twenty-three years later. Is it going to be seriously claimed that subconscious inference or intention had any part in bringing about such cases as these?

We could multiply examples of cases which do not fit into this hypothesis—some momentous and others trifling in character. What, for example, is the common causal ancestor of the dream given below and the subsequent experience which fulfilled it? *

" Mrs. C. related to her husband and family at breakfast that she had a most unpleasant dream of being followed by a monkey. After

* *Proc. S.P.R.*, Vol. 11, p. 488.

breakfast she took the unusual course of going out for a walk with her children to try and throw off the depressing atmosphere of her dream. While walking in the streets of London, she was to her horror followed by a monkey which she described as ' the very monkey of her dream '."

It is when the inadequacy of the " common causal ancestor " line of explanation becomes so apparent, that a tendency arises to fall back upon what (for simplicity) may be called the " spiritualist " explanation.* This is, that discarnate minds have far wider powers of inference than incarnate ones, and may telepathically convey such information to us in the form of precognitions. I should not wish to deny this possibility; but clearly a new assumption is here introduced. In any case, this " explanation " is not really giving us an understanding of precognition: it is simply removing the problem on to a level where investigation is fraught with still greater difficulties. Why and how do the discarnate minds precognise events?

It is also clear that the hypothesis of a common causal ancestor to both P and E offers no clue whatever to the experimental precognitions of Section 3. How can subconscious inference or intention in any human mind (incarnate or discarnate) be considered an explanation of the increased probability of hitting Whately Carington's target pictures twenty-four or forty-eight hours before they were chosen by a completely chance process? The more we survey the problem of precognition, the clearer it becomes that the hypothesis of a common causal ancestor to P and E will only account for a certain type of case, and that innumerable experiments and spontaneous cases remain unexplained.

We now turn to consider the alternative line of explanation—viz., that E is the cause of P: that the event which lies in the future relative to P is nevertheless a cause of P. The natural tendency of the mind is to reject this proposition immediately, for we say to ourselves that causes must *precede* effects on the time-scale. It is because of our experience on the *material* plane—experience on which the edifice of all our science has been built—that we have not thought of questioning for a moment that the causes of events must lie in the past (or present). But a precognition is not a material event, it is a psychical one, and we are going to affirm that *on the psychical or mental level, future events as well as past events may be causative of a present state.*

In developing this view we adopt the basic idea of an " Eternal Now ": that all events, past, present and future, exist for the deep

* See C. Drayton Thomas on " Forecasts and Precognitions," *Proc. S.P.R.*, Vol. 48, p. 306 (1948).

transcendental self of each individual. They are " Now ". For this deep self the time-series does not stand divided arbitrarily into that which was and that which will be : it *is* now. The first thing to recognise clearly is that the fact that the transcendental self (or spirit) *knows* the future, does not mean that the superficial self (the body–mind complex) has *no* freedom of choice. The future which is, and which the transcendental self knows, is the future-which-results-from-the-exercise-of-its-freedom. It is not a future created by some power external to ourselves ; it is a future created largely by this transcendental self, which deliberately leaves a very limited but important area of choice to the superficial self. The foreknowledge of the future which the transcendental self possesses, and which it sometimes throws up as a precognition into the consciousness of the superficial self, is based on its knowledge of how the latter will use its limited freedom of choice. It is the so-called future event which conditions the knowing of the transcendental self, not the present knowing of the latter, which conditions the event. To ask whether the future can be altered has no meaning. The future which " will be " for the superficial self, and becomes for it in due course the " past ", exists " now and always " for the transcendental self or spirit. When the superficial self looks back on the past it does not believe the past was all completely " determined " and that it had no freedom of choice. Yet there was a point in time when this " past " was once in the future. Why, then, should a person at *that* point of time assume the future determined ? To take an example : Cæsar once crossed the Rubicon. We, looking back, do not doubt he was free, within limits, to make this choice. Why should a person X living prior to this event be justified in assuming that Cæsar was not free to make this choice ? Suppose X had been a sensitive, and precognised Cæsar's crossing of the Rubicon, it would be because the sensitive's mind acquired this information from Cæsar's transcendental self for which the crossing was a present fact. A sensitive therefore does not " see " possibilities, but actualities.

I hope the reader is satisfied that the whole series of events constituting the experience of a life can be pictured as existing like beads on the string of time (see p. 163) without this precluding freedom of choice at each stage (within limits which we shall discuss later). So far as this basic concept is concerned we agree with Dunne, but in most other matters we diverge from him. Thus in one development of his theory he conceives it possible that as a result of a precognition of the future a person might intervene prior to the foreseen event so as to change it or eliminate it. This conception of a plastic or changeable future has for us no meaning. If it can be changed, it is not the future. The future is that which will *in fact* be—and for the deep self it *is* already. This is therefore a good stage to consider cases which are sometimes cited as indicating that the future foreseen can be changed by intervention. Consider the following : *Case of Lady Z and the Coachman* * (abbreviated account).

" One day I determined that on the morrow I would drive to Woolwich in our brougham taking my little child and nurse. During the night I had a painfully clear dream of the brougham turning up one of the streets north of Piccadilly, and then of myself standing on the pavement and holding my child, our old coachman falling on his head on the road—his hat smashed in. This so much discomposed me that when in the morning I sent for the coachman to give him his orders, I almost hoped that some obstacle to the drive might arise, so that I might have an excuse for going by train. The coachman was an old and valued servant. I asked him if he would have the carriage ready to drive to Woolwich at ten. He was not given to making difficulties ; but he hesitated, and when I suggested eleven instead he said that he would prefer that hour.

" All went well until we reached Piccadilly on the return journey . . . and looking through the glass front of the brougham I saw that the coachman was leaning back in his seat as though the horses were pulling violently, of which however I felt no sign. We turned up Down Street. He retained his attitude. My dream flashed back upon me. I called to him to stop, jumped out, caught hold of my child, and called to a policeman to catch the coachman. Just as he did so the coachman swayed and fell off the box. If I had been in the least less prompt, he would have fallen just as I saw him in my dream. I found afterwards that the poor man had been suffering from a serious attack of diarrhœa on the previous day, and had gradually fainted from exhaustion on the drive home. . . . My premonitory dream differed from the reality in two points. In my dream we approached Down Street from the west ; in reality we came from the east. In my dream the coachman fell on his head, the crushing of his hat on the road being the most vivid point of the dream ; in reality this was just averted by the prompt action which my anxious memory of the dream inspired."

The first thing to remark is that this dream may have been caused by the future event, leaving only the important difference in the actual ending and the dream ending to be accounted for. For the transcendental self of Lady Z the catching of the coachman by the policeman was a present fact. It was a present fact because the transcendental self knew how the superficial self of Lady Z would act in the critical situation if given a warning. It intended to give that warning to the superficial self, and did so in the form of a precognitive dream, attaching to it a tragic ending to stimulate the

* *Proc. S.P.R.*, Vol. II, p. 497.

action. It is, of course, notorious that distortion is liable to occur in dreams. We have one example of this in the direction of travel in Down Street, which was the opposite in the dream and in the event. (Dunne several times records distortions and exaggerations of this sort.) My view would be that the factual ending (i.e., of the coach-man being caught by a policeman while falling) was distorted by the transcendental self for the reasons given already. We are liable to make considerable mistakes if we assume that dreams which usually contain precognitive material among much else are pure and undistorted pre-presentations of the future event.

As an example of a case of pre-sentience where the future appears to be the sole causative agent, I take the following. The lady— Mrs. X—whose account is given below is well known to me, and her integrity is unquestionable. Reports of the plane crash on November 8th, 1948, are found in the Melbourne Press of the next day. Un-fortunately, a letter which Mrs. X wrote to Miss Y, the children's governess, prior to the plane crash, telling of her strange experience, has been destroyed, but I have personally received Miss Y's assurance that she did receive such a letter prior to the event, and that its content was consistent with the account given below.

> " Late in October I was having a few days' holiday on Mount Macedon by myself. One morning I walked through the forest to the Cross, but once there I did not stay long to admire the view because I noticed some smoke curling up the Mount on the Woodend side, and come blowing towards me. Not wishing to be involved in a bush fire, I decided to take the path leading directly to my home. I discovered that it crossed a firebreak, and once past that I entered the forest again and sat down under a tree to eat my lunch and to read Wordsworth. But for some reason I felt uneasy and was unable to concentrate. Was it fear of the fire, I wondered, or could there be some woodcutter of evil intent nearby, or was it merely the soughing of the wind in the tree-tops, which by now was making rather an eerie, lonely sound? I stood up and listened. There seemed nothing of which to be afraid. It was barely one o'clock and still sunny. Telling myself not to be foolish, I found a hollow, where I crouched down so as to be hidden from the view of anyone approach-ing the firebreak, and waited.
>
> " Then suddenly it happened. Over me flowed a wave of acute terror, loneliness and pain, amounting almost to an agony. After a moment of paralysing suspense, I turned and ran through the forest. Nor did I stop until I reached home, panting. The feeling slowly subsided, but I decided not to venture out again that day. Instead I sat down and wrote a brief account of it in a letter to my friend, Miss Y, but unfortunately this has been lost. How-ever, she remembers the description and my efforts to explain it.
>
> " I faced all the physical possibilities that could have induced fear,

but decided that the overwhelming character of the sensation was not justified by any known physical cause.   I rather tended to think that, having had similar experiences twice in my life before, it was associated with some event that had occurred in that place in the past, as were the other two experiences.

"A week *later* a Douglas DC3 air-liner crashed in the firebreak close to the very spot where I had been sitting and both pilots were killed, one immediately, one dying after an hour's agony of mind and body."

The part played by the locality itself is puzzling.   That a locality should hold the memories of the past has been illustrated in Section 5.   Perhaps here we have a complementary phenomenon : it may hold the record of the future ! Alternatively, and perhaps more plausibly, the experience might be regarded as precognitive telepathy —i.e., a rapport with the states of mind a week hence of passengers in the plane.   But why were the pre-sentient effects felt in that spot ? Perhaps the answer is, that given the appropriate mental state, they would have been felt anywhere.

Many of the interesting cases of J. W. Dunne are obvious examples of the causation of a present mental state by a future mental event. He has described, for example, how he took a new book, which he proposed subsequently to read, and recorded all the odds and ends of images which came into his mind.   After rejecting those derived by association with the past, he occasionally found notable examples of images which were coming from a future mental state—viz., that of reading the book.   From a number of such experiments Dunne drew the conclusion that there was no insuperable barrier between past and future, but that when thinking about the past was arrested, the future might appear in present thought in disconnected flashes. In other words, fragments of the present knowledge of the transcendental self arose into the conscious focus of the superficial self under favouring circumstances.

The barrel in the case of Mrs. Calder (p. 151), the whole Marmontal case (p. 151), the case of the derailed engine, the case of Mrs. C.'s dream of a monkey, and many other examples which might be cited, all find a natural explanation if the future mental event can cause a present mental state.

Dunne has one particular case which offers strong support for this view.   In a precognitive dream of a volcanic eruption in Martinique, he dreamed that the number of lives lost was 4,000.   It was in fact 40,000, or was stated to be so in the newspaper account which Dunne later read.   The important feature is, however, that when Dunne looked at the newspaper account he misread the figure as 4,000, and did not actually discover his original misreading until going through the files some years afterwards.   It is clear that it was Dunne's *mental state* in the near future that caused his earlier precognitive dream—not the future *material* event.

Since an overwhelming proportion of our dreams is not remembered afterwards, it is quite probable, as Dunne has suggested, that the curious feeling which people occasionally have of " I've been here before " or " This situation is strangely familiar ; I know what will happen next ", is accounted for by the partial stimulation of a forgotten precognitive dream.

If the reader will turn back to Section 6, where a condensed summary of Dunne's views is to be found, he will recall that we criticised Dunne's way of treating time as though it were another dimension of space.   One obvious difference between space and time is that we can move through a spatial dimension in either direction, or we may remain stationary, but we cannot do this in time.   Time is, I think, a concept inferred from change, but Dunne is treating $\text{Time}_{(2)}$, $\text{Time}_{(3)}$, etc., as percepts.   In fact, no one has ever measured any time-interval in these times.   Apart from this, I fail to see the necessity for an *infinite* number of observers and times.   Suppose we were to postulate that for $\text{Observer}_{(3)}$ the moving slit vanishes by becoming infinitely wide.   The " specious present " of $\text{Observer}_{(3)}$ thus comprises *all* $\text{Time}_{(2)}$.   There is now no point in introducing $\text{Time}_{(3)}$, for there is nothing moving through $\text{Time}_{(2)}$.   The $\text{Observer}_{(3)}$ would then be, on such a view, the transcendental Self—for which there is only an Eternal " Now ".   This kind of view would probably interpret $\text{Observers}_{(1), (2), (3)}$, etc., as strata, or significant levels of that hierarchy which we call the Self.   Although this standpoint avoids an infinite regress, and necessitates only a few time-dimensions, I hesitate to suppose that it represents the truth about time.

We infer the passage of time in the external world because of our succession of varying mental states which are consequent upon varying sense-data.   Do not let us forget that this flow of ordinary commonplace time is only a supposition of the same status and validity as that there is an external spatial world of objects outside us. Doubtless there must be something corresponding to Time as long as there is something corresponding to Space.   But just as individuality is not rooted, I think, in a spatial concept, but in a unique quality of consciousness, so I cannot think it is rooted in Time. Nevertheless, we always come back to the recognition that the order of succession of different states of consciousness, even at a deep level of the self, must involve something which is the prototype of Time as we ordinarily experience it.

The mystery of Time remains (along with the mystery of Space)

after we have made all our analysis.   One is inclined to the view that
thinking cannot illuminate either mystery, and that only in certain
higher mystical states where intellectual processes are transcended
is insight into their nature possible.*

9. FREEDOM AND THE PATTERN OF LIFE

As a consequence of examining precognition we have already
touched upon some of the profoundest questions—viz., of the purpose
of human life, Man's measure of freedom and his destiny.   These
questions will be looked at more closely in Part IV of this book.
We shall, however, comment at this point on the implications of the
many recorded cases of future events in a person's life being " read "
by a medium or sensitive.   There are too many well-authenticated
cases to leave any doubt of the possibility of this : nor does it introduce us to any new principle.   If to the transcendental self the distinction of past from future is not fundamental, if events are all
present in an Eternal Now, and if sometimes in dreams, visions and
moments of insight, knowledge emerges from this level up to the
conscious level, there is nothing new involved in the acquisition of
such knowledge through the telepathic rapport of a sensitive with
this deep level.

An interesting illustration has been given by Mrs. L. J. Bendit in a
recent book.†

" The swarthy, black-eyed woman asked me in the usual way to
cross her palm with silver, then she lightly touched my finger-tips
for a moment, shut her eyes and poured out a torrent of speech.
Her character-reading was astonishing; and she mentioned without
hesitation a number of incidents in my past life.   She was particularly clever in her analysis of my psychic abilities, seeing both their
weaknesses and their strength.

" Eventually she began to foretell the future.   It sounded incredible,
not to say impossible.   She sketched correctly the kind of professional
life I was then living and said that it would change radically.   ' You
will marry a man who is either a doctor, or who is in a profession
associated with sharp, bright instruments.'   She went on adding
various details about him.   ' You will work together and write books
together.   You will travel together and neither of you will work
alone in the future.'   She then foretold a number of events which
would lead up to this.   Then, guessing my doubts, she said, ' You
don't believe me, so I am going to tell you three important things
which will come true within the next seven days.   When they do,

* E.g., see Rupert Brooke's poem, "Dining-room Tea ".
† Payne and Bendit : *This World and That*, pp. 159-60 (Faber &
Faber, 1950).

you'll remember what the gypsy said, and you'll see that in the next few years the big things will happen too.'

" She then told me that I should very shortly receive a gift of stones; that I would also be given a ring; and that, on some very stony ground, I should find two sprays of white heather where no other white heather grew.

" I said nothing of all this to my hostess, but that evening while I was dressing for dinner she came into my room, bringing a box of unset cairngorm stones, beautifully cut. She said, ' I got these for you for last Christmas. But you will remember that I had 'flu and was too ill to send them off. So here they are.' Three days later a registered parcel arrived from London. It contained an old ring and a note from a friend who said, ' I meant to leave you this ring in my will, but I don't see why you should not have it now, so I am sending it at once.' Then, on the fifth day, we were out for a picnic, and on the way home, as we went through a desolate pass in the hills, my hostess said, ' There's rather a fine cairn just at the top of this hill. Let's climb up and have a look at it.' I had nearly reached the top of the rough and stony track when I saw, growing in solitary beauty, two sprays of white heather. There was not another scrap in sight."

One of the most impressive source-books of similar data is that of Dr. Eugene Osty,* who gave many years of research to the study of such sensitives. As a result of this he came to the conclusion that at a deep level of every human being there is a transcendental stratum or principle which " shows that it is aware of the general course of the individual life and is capable of foreknowing its circumstantial development ".

It looks as if the transcendental self (of each individual) manifesting through bodily form in space and time lays down for itself a plan or pattern to which the life-span of its physical representative must substantially conform. It cannot, of course, be a pattern or " blue-print " in isolation : it is interlinked with and interpenetrates the pattern of a larger whole in which other selves are manifesting. There are doubtless Karmic laws of Cause and Effect working on this deep level, for we must suppose Law (of which, except on the physical level, we know very little) is operative throughout the universe. As we proceed outwards from the deep levels of the self to the more superficial levels, we are doubtless passing from levels primarily of causes to levels increasingly of effects. The area of real freedom which remains to the superficial self—that self which manifests in space and time—is, I believe, vitally real, and the use made of it is of the greatest importance. It is, however, a much smaller area than most people suppose. At this stage of our book it is too early to state and

* Eugene Osty : *Supernormal Faculties in Man* (Methuen).

defend a philosophy. I shall therefore content myself by saying that freedom is not something easily available to the superficial self : it has to be won. All men *think* they are free. At the lowest level of self-development *Man* is completely slave, but does not know it : at the highest level of his self-development, when he becomes sage and saint, then only is he completely free and knows it. Most men are found between these two extremes, and according to the use made by the surface self of the little area of freedom it possesses, it achieves more.

Chapter

8

OBJECT READING OR PSYCHOMETRY

All things, by immortal power,
Near or far,
Hiddenly
To each other linked are,
That thou canst not stir a flower
Without troubling of a star.

FRANCIS THOMPSON.

I. NATURE OF THE PHENOMENON

THERE are some sensitives who, when handed an object, are able to proffer information about the person or persons who have previously touched the object. This faculty was first called " psychometry " by Buchanan, an anthropologist, and although the name is an unfortunate one, it has been so widely used that we shall continue to use it here. It seems to the writer a key-phenomenon which, when more fully understood, should throw much light on the mysterious territory ranging between mind and matter. Experimental work, notably that done by Hettinger, has not only established the phenomenon with a very high degree of probability, but has also revealed some of the conditions under which it takes place. One of the most interesting and significant of these is that it is not essential for the sensitive to handle the object (which may be in a sealed envelope). It is sufficient for the sensitive to establish some kind of mental rapport or relationship to it. In ordinary speech it is sufficient for the sensitive to " concentrate " on the object, though it is no more a state of concentrated attention than is the state of mind which is favourable to telepathy.

The phenomenon has been established when the experimenter (who presents the object in a sealed envelope to the sensitive) has no knowledge of the subject from which it has come. Otherwise the simplest explanation would be that the sensitive acquires his information telepathically from the experimenter's mind. As it is, the simplest statement of the observational data seems to be, that contact of a person with an object appears to communicate something of a permanent nature to that object, and this is so characteristic and peculiar that it permits a sensitive to identify and achieve telepathic rapport with that person's mind. Just as a finger-print on an object is a physical characteristic of a particular person, so by the mere act of contact there is associated with an object some psychic quality—mento-emotional, perhaps—which is a unique means of identification. It is scarcely necessary to add that nothing which we know of the physics or chemistry of matter throws any light on how this can be.

The hypothesis of a psychic æther, a medium which provides a bridge between the material and the mental, which is plastic and influenced by matter on the one hand and modified by mind on the other to be a conveyor of thought-images—such an hypothesis seems indicated strongly by the facts of psychometry. Just as clairvoyance (for example of the unknown order of cards in a pack) may be regarded as a perception of the modified *form* of the associated psychic æther, so object-reading may be regarded as a perception of the modified mental characteristics of the æther. The former faculty, so to say, operates near the material end of the ætheric bridge, the latter operates near the mental end.

2. EXPERIMENTS AND VIEWS OF DR. EUGENE OSTY

Dr. Osty was a French physician with a deep interest in, and a scientific approach to, the problems of psychical research. He became Director of the Institut Métapsychique International in Paris, and made investigations covering many years of a group of talented French sensitives. The results of this work are available in an important book translated in 1923.* Some of the sensitives exercised their faculty under hypnosis, others in the waking state. An object which had been in contact with a person—perhaps a few lines of writing—was a sufficient directive of the faculty towards the right subject. All devices and procedures, such as sorting playing-cards, looking in a crystal ball or a bowl of water, at tea-leaves in a cup or pins thrown on a carpet, are merely conventional means of assisting the mind to enter that state in which telepathic rapport becomes possible.

It is impossible by brief extracts or a few examples to do justice to the wide range and accuracy of the ψ-faculty of some of these sensitives : Mme. Morel, Mme. Peyroutet, Mlle. de Berly and others. Sometimes the faculty was one of clairvoyant diagnosis of an obscure physical condition in the subject, sometimes a description of the mental, emotional and moral characteristics of the subject, sometimes it was as though the sensitive achieved rapport with some deep level

* *Supernormal Faculties in Man* (Methuen, 1923 ; trs. by Stanley de Brath).

of the subject and could reproduce not only the detailed life-history of the past, but could also predict with accuracy leading events in the future of that person. To avoid loading this chapter with data, I shall give below only one illustration of the sort of possibility. M. Émile Boirac, Rector of the Academy of Dijon, asked Dr. Osty to give him an example of Mme. Morel's faculty. Dr. Osty thought the most convincing evidence would be an experiment, and asked M. Boirac if he chanced to have in his possession any article belonging to another person. After hesitation he left a small manual of Esperanto with Dr. Osty, and the account Dr. Osty gives is as follows :

> " In absolute ignorance of the person whose book this might be I put it into the hands of Mme. Morel, hypnotised, asking her to speak of the life of the person to whom it belonged.
> " She said, ' A young man appears to me tall and rather slight. There is nothing very characteristic in his appearance but his eyes, which are not like those of other people. There is nothing wrong with them, but their form is peculiar. . . . I see this young man for a long while in a place where there is no danger. . . . He was there with many other men. . . . Then one day, one morning, he departs with others . . . a long march . . . he then goes in a train. I see him a little later with others in a kind of hole. . . . He is standing up with shining eyes . . . I hear much noise . . . I see fury in his brain ; he goes up. . . . What a noise I hear ! He feels a blow and falls . . . gets up . . . receives another blow, and falls afresh with others on a road . . . on one side I see grass and cultivated land, on the other side grey mud. He is wounded in the throat and head by a piece of iron.' [Then follows description of his being carried away, dying, and the place where his body was laid. Two days later this account was sent to M. Boirac, who replied as follows] :

> " The little manual of Esperanto that I gave you was taken from the civilian clothing left at my house by the son of one of my friends. The young man was afterwards a second lieutenant in the 27th Regiment, killed or missing on December 12th in a trench attack at the Bois-Brule. G. M. was aged twenty-five or twenty-six, tall, slight, face rather long, and his eyelids had a slight fold like the Chinese, serious and quiet expression. . . . As far as is known he was wounded leading the attack, but continued at the head of his men, then fell at the edge of the German trench which is still in the hands of the enemy. The first wound seems to have been in the shoulder, the second in the head. The body is supposed to have been taken up by the Germans and buried by them, but there is no certainty. He was returned as ' missing '. The vision is therefore correct, with some particulars that cannot be ascertained. I can state that the little book was touched by G. M. some months before the scene to which it gave rise." [It had remained with M. Boirac while the young man passed through the last stages of his life.]

Some of the general conclusions, based upon his years of observation, at which Dr. Osty arrived, are these :

1. Each human individual who has touched the object may be cognised. The experimenter cannot know in advance which will first be spoken of.

2. Each such person is cognised distinctly : there is no transposition or confusion of events or characteristics between these persons.

3. Once rapport with a personality has been established, the object is no longer necessary, and may be destroyed or removed.

4. The moment in life at which the contact with the object was made is unimportant. If it was made twenty years ago, the sensitive can establish rapport with the person and cognise the life as a whole, including of course the present time.

5. The physical and chemical nature of the object does not seem significant.

6. Contact between various objects does not in any way modify their distinctive properties : they do not communicate their properties to each other.

7. The degree of reaction to a given object touched by a person appears to differ with different sensitives : also, a sensitive will always be more successful with some subjects than with others. The degree of telepathic affinity of percipient and subject is clearly important.

In an example such as that detailed above (which can be matched with many others given by Osty), it seems evident that the rapport must have been with the discarnate mind of the young lieutenant, unless we assume that the sensitive derived the verifiable part from M. Boirac's mind and manufactured the remainder. This seems unlikely, but if it is seriously advanced, other cases can be cited where knowledge in no living mind was proffered by the sensitive, and was subsequently verified. Osty categorically says that his accumulated experiments showed that " sensitives deal with a ' dead ' personality in the same way as with a living one. . . . The information they receive and express is of the same kind, and refers to the same matters." The importance of this conclusion—from so experienced an observer as Osty—need not be emphasised.

There will, I think, be no hesitation on the part of anyone who surveys all Osty's evidence, to accept his conclusion that the paranormal knowledge offered by the sensitive is derived from the subject —i.e., the person who once touched the object. The mechanism being what we have called telepathic, all the previous conclusions about the latter should be verifiable here. It must be recognised that the sensitive's statements may contain errors from many sources. It is obvious that the subject's fears, hopes and desires, both conscious and subconscious, may be drawn out by the percipient and represented as facts or predictions. Dr. Osty clearly recognises the different levels of a subject's personality with which a sensitive may achieve rapport, and be unable at the same time to differentiate between them. He says: "The ideal percipient would be one sensitive only to the transcendental plane of all personalities." In addition to this source, other errors may arise in the information provided by the percipient due to the defective functioning of his own faculty, due to wrong interpretations of the emerging data, and due to " interference "—i.e., temporary and partial telepathic rapport with other subjects (e.g., the experimenter who is generally present).

A remarkable feature of the functioning of Osty's sensitives was the extent to which some of them were able to establish rapport with the deeper or " transcendental plane " of the subject's being, and the detail and accuracy of delineation of the subject's life. At this level of contact, knowledge of the future appears to be accessible, and Osty, who had some remarkable experience in this direction, has expressed important views. He is definite that foreknowledge of the future does not imply determinism. On the contrary, he says :

" Foreknowledge is variable knowledge constantly and progressively elaborated ; like life, it is evolutionary and living—as if the transcendental mode of thought of each man, aware of the general direction and outstanding events of existence, were progressively informed of the events circumstantial to its foreknowledge as the human personality takes its way through the current of surrounding lives."

The sensitive is able to be most accurate and detailed when dealing with matters in actual course of realisation—although unknowable by inference as to the outcome. Prediction is less detailed where the conclusions are distant in time, just as a traveller moving through new country sees on the far horizon only vague general masses of colour, while in the middle distance he can distinguish villages and woods, and close at hand trees, houses, and people. Osty gives an example * in relation to his own life. Two years before the event a percipient said to him, " Oh ! peril of death after a while . . . perhaps an accident . . . but you will be saved, your life continues." Four months before the event Mlle. de Berly said to him, " Take care, you will soon have a serious accident. I hear a violent shock . . . a loud noise . . . you will be very near death . . . What luck ! You will take

* *Supernormal Faculties in Man*, p. 175.

no hurt ! I see a man bleeding on the ground ; he is moaning, and all round him some things are strewn, I can't say what." Dr. Osty's account of the event itself is :

> " I was going at an easy pace in my car when a drunken baker, driving furiously, pulled the wrong rein and collided. The shock was such that the shafts which struck the frame of the front glass were shivered to pieces, and one wheel mounted the bonnet and crushed it in. My friend ——, who was with me, and I also, were stricken with amaze at the suddenness of the accident and our good fortune in being unhurt. Turning round we saw the horse galloping off, the cart in the ditch, wheels uppermost, and the baker stretched moaning and bleeding in the middle of the road with a number of loaves scattered round him."

Osty rightly rejects as too naïve the concept that all events exist already in an ideal world and are foreseen by para-normal faculty. It is clear, on the contrary, that they are in process of becoming, as a series of successive precognitions reveals. The clearest evidence that sensitives are not perceiving existent events outside human individuals is found if the faculty is exercised on each of a group of persons affected by common events in their lives. Osty remarks that he has never found any case of an event being derived by the sensitive from a subject not involved in it. The common event is precognised only in its relation to each person : as Osty puts it, " The field of cognition only covers what a human being will become, rather than any perception of an impersonal future ".

3. EXPERIMENTS OF DR. HETTINGER

Dr. J. Hettinger in or about the years 1930–40 carried out a pioneering piece of experimental work in the field of psychometry. His conclusions were embodied in a book *The Ultra Perceptive Faculty.** The importance of the work lies in its being the first attempt to assess quantitatively the probability of existence of this faculty. The work was done with the aid of two professional sensitives, and the procedure was as follows. He took with him to each sitting, of about an hour's duration, from four to six different articles in sealed envelopes, obtained from different persons. Each envelope would be handed in turn to the sensitive, who would make on an average about a dozen statements relative to the person from whom the article had come. These were written down at the time. In a preliminary series of tests about 172 articles were submitted and

* Rider & Co. (1940).

2,000 statements made. There were statements about feelings and emotions such as :

" Fidgety about clothes : I see this person touching them constantly."
" When this letter was written the writer was suffering from an attack of giddiness."

There were statements about events such as :

" Presentation of a silver-mounted walking-stick."
" Giving up present position to someone else and does not like the idea."

There were actions such as :

" A lot to do with books in paper covers."
" Impressed with the rising sun and watching the dawn."

And so on.

The objects were of all kinds—wallets, pencils, fountain-pens, watches, rings, locks of hair, gloves, letters, or blank sheets of paper which had been carried on the person. The nature of the object seemed irrelevant. It was also found that significant results were obtained whether the experimenter who presented the objects to the sensitive knew the subjects to whom the articles belonged, or not, so that telepathy between the sensitive and the experimenter does not explain the observations.

One of the important questions, of course, is how the statements of the sensitive were checked up. The most obvious method of presenting a list of these to the owner of the article and asking for " yes " or " no " to each statement, allows very little to be inferred. Thus, for example, one or two correct statements out of twelve might be impressive if they were very specific or unusual in character. Moreover, persons differ widely in the rigour of their judgment as to what constitutes a hit or a miss. Methods of control were therefore devised to make statistical evaluation possible. For example, one method used was to intersperse the twelve statements given by a sensitive with twelve spurious statements. The latter were drawn from a box containing a large number of statements previously made by the sensitive about other subjects. The list presented to the subject for checking thus contained equal numbers of genuine and spurious statements, the subject being unaware which were which. If R is the number claimed as correct from among the genuine items, and W the number claimed as correct from among the control items, then if the ratio R: W is greater than one, the sensitive is scoring above the chance value, while if the ratio R : W is equal to, or less than one, the sensitive is not scoring above chance. To illustrate this, we have a series of seventy-six objects which yielded 948 genuine items. These were mixed with 948 control items. Of the genuine items, 328 or 34·5% were claimed as correct; of the control items 222, or 23·5%, were claimed as correct. A variety of control methods was used. Thus in one series of experiments each subject was handed two lists of statements, one of which applied to himself and the other applied to another person, and he was asked to check them both for accuracy in relation to himself. It is unnecessary here to go into the detail of all these methods, but the final totals are impressive. The experiments with two sensitives occupied 623 hours. The total number of statements made by the sensitive was 6,631. The percentage of these accepted as correct was 38·75%. The proportion of control items accepted as correct was 28·85%. From these figures we observe that the sensitive scored 34% higher than the control. The deviation from the chance score was evaluated as 14·6 times the probable error—a result which makes it possible to affirm that the " ultra-perceptive " faculty is *very* highly probable.

Some of the observations made by Hettinger are important and interesting.

(*a*) The nature of the objects, and the sentimental or emotional associations they may possess are not significant factors.

(*b*) Handling of the object by a sensitive is not essential to the exercise of the faculty.

(*c*) The degree of the sensitive's response differs from subject to subject, attaining a high value in the case of some subjects and being negligible for others. Where some twenty or thirty objects had been provided by one subject, it was noticed that for some subjects the whole twenty or thirty values of R–W would be positive. With others the R–W values would be about as often negative as positive, showing thus only a " chance " score.

(*d*) Many of the correct statements concern experiences of the subject between the time he had parted with the article and that of the sensitive's interpretation.

(*e*) The correct statements represent para-normal cognition of the subject not only at the actual time of the test, but cover a period in the past of the subject, and occasionally a little of the future. An approximate survey using 147 objects and yielding 1,658 items showed an approximate distribution of applicability to the subjects as follows : 33% true from fourteen days to five days before the experiment, 25% true from five days to one day before the experiment, 32% true on the day of the experiment, with a further 10% applicable at the precise time of the experiment.

(*f*) The sensitive cannot always be clear whether a given statement concerns the owner of the article or someone associated with the owner.

These are all significant observations with which any theory of psychometry must be consistent.

As regards the many statements made by the sensitive but not accepted as correct by the subject, Hettinger's views are strikingly similar to Osty's. Some may be just guesses; others may be items arising through processes of association in the sensitive's mind; others may be items wrongly interpreted or distorted by the sensitive; others may be items arising through temporary rapport with the minds of the experimenter or other persons who have touched the articles. Finally, a number of items may not be identified as correct through a lapse of memory on the part of the subject when checking. Saltmarsh,* commenting on his results with Mrs. Warren Elliott as the sensitive, expresses generally similar views.

In a second book published in 1941, *Exploring the Ultra-Perceptive Faculty*, Hettinger gives an account of a different type of experiment. The subject—in some distant place—is at the prearranged time of the test asked to co-operate by reading or looking at pictures in an illustrated magazine. As he does so he is asked to mark on each page the time at which the page was read or the picture viewed. Simultaneously the sensitive, who had been handed an object belonging to the subject, is asked to make statements in the usual way, and the experimenter records these and the time when they were made. An item given by the sensitive may properly be compared with any picture or article on the two pages being viewed by the subject—possibly a considerable number of things. Many striking resemblances were found which in themselves are impressive, but of course *how* impressive is a matter of personal judgment as to the chance possibilities of such statements being made. This method could doubtless be developed to apply statistical methods to it, but Hettinger regarded his earlier work as providing statistical proof and regarded this later work as providing convincing direct evidence.

The whole of Hettinger's work has been subject to very searching criticism by Christopher Scott,† and from this I think most readers

---

* *Proc. S.P.R.*, Vol. 39, p. 135 (1930).
† *Proc. S.P.R.*, Vol. 49, pp. 16–50 (1949).

will recognise the necessity for a great deal more research to which statistical methods are applicable, so as to place this faculty of object reading on the same absolutely unquestionable basis as telepathy and clairvoyance. That it does exist there is, I consider, already quite impressive evidence, but in the strange field of psychical research every position must be made invulnerable.

4. EVIDENCE FROM OTHER INVESTIGATORS

Here is an example given by M. Maeterlinck : *

> " I received from England a request for my autograph. Unlike most of those which assail an author of any celebrity, it was charming and unaffected ; but it told me nothing about the writer. Without even noticing from what town it was sent to me, after showing it to my wife I replaced it in its envelope and took it to Mme. M——. She began by describing us, my wife and myself, who both of us had touched the paper and consequently impregnated it with our respective ' fluids '. I asked her to pass beyond us and come to the writer of the note. She then saw a girl of fifteen or sixteen, almost a child, who had been in rather indifferent health, but who was now very well indeed. The girl was in a beautiful garden, in front of a large and luxurious house standing in the midst of a rather hilly country. She was playing with a big, curly-haired, long-eared dog. Through the branches of the trees one caught a glimpse of the sea. On inquiry, all the details were found to be astonishingly accurate ; but, as usual, there was a mistake in the time, that is to say, the girl and her dog were not in the garden at the instant when the medium saw them there."

In the *Proceedings of the American Society for Psychical Research* (Vols. XV and XVI) the faculty of a Mexican lady, Señora Maria Reyes de Z., is described at length. This lady was a patient of Dr. Pagenstecher, a leading physician, and moreover, Dr. Walter Franklin Prince investigated her faculty independently. One particularly notable example of Señora Z.'s exercise of the faculty may be cited.†

A friend of Dr. Pagenstecher sent to him a letter containing two sealed envelopes. He was informed that one contained a letter, and the other a description of the writer of the letter. He was asked to submit the first sealed envelope to a sensitive for psychometry, and not to open either envelope until after the sitting. Señora Z., presented with the first envelope, proceeded to describe a large liner sinking, the frightened people putting on life-preservers, and then in some detail a particular man with a pronounced scar over the left eyebrow

---

* *The Unknown Guest*, p. 56 (Methuen, 1914).
† See *Jour. S.P.R.*, Vol. 21, pp. 218–19.

writing a message on a leaf torn out of a pocket-book which he put into a corked bottle and threw into the sea. When the seals of the first envelope were broken in the presence of Dr. Pagenstecher and Dr. Prince there was found a slip of paper apparently torn from a pocket-book with the following message written in Spanish. " The ship is sinking. Farewell, my Luisa : see that my children do not forget me. Your Ramon. Havana. May God care for you and me also. Farewell." The second envelope contained the information that the above note had been found in a bottle washed up in the Azores. Enquiries in Havana showed that a gentleman who passed under the name of Ramon B. disappeared from New York about the time of sailing of the *Lusitania* on her ill-fated voyage and it was concluded he was lost on that ship. His physical appearance, including the detail of the scar, resembled that given. He had a wife Luisa and children, and his hand-writing closely resembled that of the note in the bottle.

It would be possible to add further illustrations, but we shall assume that the reader will consider that a good case for the faculty has been made, and proceed to theorise about it.

5. THEORY AND SPECULATION

What is the function of the object involved in psychometry ? All the experimental data presented are most simply understood if the function of the object is merely directive—i.e., if it enables the sensitive to discover and establish rapport with the mind of the subject to whom the article belonged. The data cognised then come under the category of information passing telepathically between mind and mind. If the reader will look again at the observations of Osty and Hettinger he will see that this view is quite consistent with them. The naïve suggestion that in some obscure way the article itself is the *source* of the information is inconsistent with the facts that the article can be destroyed once the process has been started, and that many of the statements relate only to the period after the article has left the possession of the subject. Clearly the object's function is only that of an intermediary.

As we stated at the beginning of this chapter, the hypothesis of a psychic æther appears to have in psychometry one of the best illustrations of its usefulness. The bridge between mind and brain, we conceive, must be via a complex " ætheric " structure—for the psychic æther which fulfils this function is modified into an effective instrument of both. The modification of the psychic æther which the mind of an individual subject creates within himself may similarly be conveyed in some degree to the psychic æther of an object (see diagram). The mind of a sensitive can become aware of this characteristic modification of the ætheric object, and is enabled thereby to identify the originating mind, following which a greater or lesser degree of telepathic rapport is possible. The appended diagram is of course no more than a crude attempt to express these relationships. It was remarked by Hettinger that it was not essential for the sensitive to touch the object; it was sufficient to " concentrate " the mind upon it. I am not aware that the following suggestion has been tested by experiment, but I would venture to predict that an object need not be physically touched by the subject, but could be made an effective vehicle if the latter " concentrated " his mind upon it. Sensitives frequently speak of the characteristic " vibrations " or " vital fluid " of a person—modes of speech which tend rather to offend the scientific mind, but which are presumably

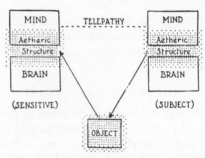

picturesque ways of trying to convey the feeling of distinctive mento-emotional qualities in different personalities. I do not think it is surprising that individuals have a unique and identifiable psychical quality, any more than that they have unique faces or finger-prints. Here, for example, is a description of his sensations given to Dr. Osty by M. de Fleuriere.*

"When I am in proximity to an unknown person, and especially when a light touch places us in contact, I feel as though I were permeated by an indefinable fluid that radiates from his whole person. This physical and psychic fluid seems to me to be composed of several elements in which there is light and heat, vibration, electric or magnetic currents, and sometimes even odoriferous effluvia. But these elements never present themselves equally, so to say; their proportions vary enormously with different persons—usually one or two, or rarely three predominate, the others being faint or barely perceptible.

"The impression of light is localised in the eyes, the forehead and the brain; the impression of warmth in the breast, the heart and the

* *Supernormal Faculties in Man*, p. 170.

large arteries; the impression of vibratory movement in the arms, the nervous system, and finally the sensation of a kind of electric or magnetic current in the cerebellum, the solar plexus and especially in the papillæ of the finger-tips.

"Just as one cannot find two faces exactly alike, I think that I have never found two fluids that have given me exactly the same impressions; there are those that seem to me gentle, agreeable, sympathetic . . . endowed with calming and beneficent power. On the other hand, there are some that are keen, sharp, violent and repelling . . . like an antipathetic and discomforting principle. . . . I do not remember any fluid, however, that has been to me purely negative : the most disturbing always clears up a little by harmonising with and reacting on my own more or less, and in the end with time and patience gives some interesting indications."

The sensitive is clearly struggling with the limitations of language designed to be appropriate and precise on the material level, to express perceptions on another level of significance. His description of the apparent localisation of different sensations is quite in harmony with occult traditions which maintain that there is an ætheric body or "double" which interpenetrates the physical body in every part, which is itself highly organised, and extends a little beyond the outline of the physical structure giving rise to a fringe or aura. I had a close friend, who died a few years ago—a man of outstanding ability and intelligence, who claimed that so far back as he could remember into childhood he had always been able to discern this aura around the human form. He told me it appeared to be modified by the conditions of physical health and disease, and that having correlated certain known physical conditions with this "appearance" he could diagnose such conditions reliably. On the other hand, he had observed marked changes in the aura with emotional and mental states of individuals—all of which seem not inconsistent with our own postulated properties of a psychic æther which we should expect to be modified to an exceptional degree in the human organism. There is clearly a need for systematic work under carefully controlled conditions to place our knowledge of such matters upon an unchallengeable and scientifically acceptable basis. The exploration of this field will involve collaboration * between sensitives or clairvoyants and medical men (physicians and pathologists).

The observation of Hettinger that physical contact of the object with the sensitive was not necessary led me to predict that similarly physical contact of a subject with the object would also be found unnecessary. A concentration of thought upon the object should be

* Payne and Bendit : *The Psychic Sense* (Faber & Faber, 1943), a good piece of pioneering work.

sufficient to modify its associated psychic æther.   Speculating further this would suggest that the veneration or prayer offered over centuries to certain relics and images, and in certain places, may create a permanent modification of the associated psychic æther, so that other minds subsequently " concentrated " on them may be seized with the same emotion or veneration.   The data of psychometry suggest that the supposed virtues of amulets, charms or talismans may not necessarily be based wholly on suggestion.   They may serve to give a sufficiently sensitive person a telepathic link with the person who first touched or blessed them.   Likewise it may be that certain jewels described as ill-omened, or treasures from Egyptian tombs which seem to have proved fatal to their possessors, have had an associated psychic field of an undesirable kind communicated to them by their former owners.

What may be true of small objects is true also of some localities which appear to have a peculiar psychic atmosphere about them which can affect a sensitive very markedly.   A friend of mine who visited the Isle of Iona some years ago told me of a strange experience which much impressed him.   He was visiting it for the first time, and walking around to see what he could.   Standing on a little hillock and contemplating the scene, he found himself unaccountably affected, as though by an atmosphere of strange and alien things.   The experience passed away as he left the spot. The next day, walking round with a friend, he told him of this strange feeling, and was surprised to learn that the hillock, according to tradition, was the very site of ancient pagan worship.   Such experiences could doubtless be matched by many others where sensitive people are concerned.*   There is no very clear line to be drawn between them and the phenomena of haunting (see Chapter 9) :   there appears to be a range of experiences varying from vague feelings to apparently objective sense-data.

In the phenomenon of object-reading as studied by Osty, Hettinger and others, the instructions to the sensitive were to acquire information about the person or persons who had touched the object.   For reasons that we have stated, the function of the object was solely to permit rapport between the minds of the sensitive and subject to be established.   This being achieved, the object could be dispensed with.   There may, however, be another form of psychometry in which, through the intermediary of the object, rapport is not established with a person in the present, but with a past time-series of events in the ætheric world in which the æther associated with the object has had a part.   The relation between the two aspects of

*E.g., see A. C. Benson : *The House of Quiet*, Chapter 23 (John Murray).

psychometry may be perhaps something like that between " perception " and " recollection " on ordinary mental levels—but this I do not press. I have already suggested that this second aspect of psychometry is probably the basis of retrocognition (see Chapter 7 (5)). Here a whole locality may virtually be the object psychometrised, and the rapport established by the sensitive is with the ætheric memory of that locality.

This aspect of psychometry appears to have been the one largely investigated by Professor William Denton,* his wife and son. He was a geologist by professional training, and frequently experimented with geological specimens, with interesting and sometimes remarkable results. Unfortunately, instead of applying his undoubted faculty under conditions permitting of control and verification—which would have given his work scientific value—he applied it in directions incapable of verification.

I shall conclude this speculative chapter by stressing the vastness of this whole field, in which research is urgently needed, and by quoting Professor H. H. Price, who said in his Presidential Lecture : " We may safely predict that it will be the timidity of our hypotheses, and not their extravagance, which will provoke the derision of posterity."

* W. Denton : *The Soul of Things* (Denton Pub. Co., 1863).

Chapter

9

APPARITIONS AND HAUNTINGS

" In the collection of facts, one cannot be over-cautious. But in the invention of theories, especially in a field so peculiar as ours, where analogies drawn from the existing sciences are almost useless, a canny and sober circumspection would be the greatest mistake. If people accuse us of being speculative and even ' metaphysical ' we must refuse to be frightened. . . . The phenomena with which we are concerned are so peculiar, and so unlike those visible and tangible facts which ordinary language is designed to deal with, that the right theory of them is bound to seem nonsense when first propounded."

PROFESSOR H. H. PRICE
(in his Presidential address to the S.P.R., 1939).

" Telepathy demands a revolution in current ideas about human personality; and precognition demands a revolution in current ideas about time. In general, the entire outlook necessitated by the findings of psychical research breaks up the naïve realism in which the human mind is steeped and shows it to be largely illusory; and I suggest that the distaste for psychical phenomena is mainly due to a half-conscious instinct which prompts people to rally in defence of commonsense realism. It is, in a sense, a reaction to defend a creed. . . . Before we can realise that psychical facts fit naturally in the complete scheme of things, we must realise also that this psychologically ingrained view does not tell us the ultimate truth about the world, but is a peculiar system of appearances got up to serve a practical end."

G. N. M. TYRRELL
(in the F. W. H. Myers Memorial Lecture, 1942).

1. INTRODUCTION

STORIES of apparitions and ghosts are as old as humanity. It may be a matter of surprise to the student of science who is unacquainted with the literature of psychical research, that a subject which seems so obviously the product of popular credulity and superstition and a happy hunting-ground for the short-story writer, merits our careful consideration. It has been the business of psychical research to attempt to sift truth from error, and the interested student can today study the records of many hundreds of reports which have been checked and counter-checked so far as this was possible. One of the earliest collections of this kind was the book *Phantasms of the Living* by Gurney, Myers and Podmore, published in 1886. A further collection of 200 cases is given by Mrs. Henry Sidgwick,* covering the period 1886–1920. H. and E. B. Hart made a shorter study of selected cases in 1933.† Sir Ernest Bennett published fifty new cases in 1939 in a book entitled *Apparitions and Haunted Houses*. Various representative selections from these sources have been published, of which that by A. T. Baird ‡ is a good example. The student of these will possibly feel like the sceptical Professor Richet, who said that although he doubted almost every case individually, he was nevertheless impressed, probably quite illogically, by the massed evidence.

In 1890 an attempt was made to discover by a census how widespread was personal experience of this para-normal kind. The question circulated was " Have you ever, when believing yourself to be completely awake, had a vivid impression of seeing or being touched by a living being or inanimate object, or of hearing a voice ; which impression, so far as you could discover, was not due to any external physical cause ? " The question was framed to exclude dreams. Of 17,000 persons questioned, 1,684 or 9·9% answered " yes ". A similar census in 1948 which elicited 1,519 replies showed that 217 or 14·3% answered " yes ". The data were analysed from many different standpoints. The 1890 census showed, for example, that 32% of the hallucinations were of living persons, 14·3% of dead persons and 33·2% of unidentified persons ; the comparable figures for the later survey were 40·5%, 9·0% and 27·5%. Contrary to popular ideas, apparitions of the living substantially outnumber those of the dead. Analysis of the senses affected showed : § visual, 54·8% ; visual combined with auditory or tactile, 11·6% ; auditory, 25·6% ; tactile, 7·1% ; auditory and tactile, 0·9%.

The most outstanding contribution made to the subject, apart from the labours of those who collected and checked the original records, seems to me that of G. N. M. Tyrrell,‖ who in 1942 delivered the F. W. H. Myers Memorial Lecture on " Apparitions ". To this valuable survey, classification and analysis, the present chapter is greatly indebted. For purposes of illustration I shall give a number of examples of apparitions in each of the four classes which Tyrrell found it convenient to recognise : (*a*) Experimentally produced apparitions, (*b*) Crisis cases, (*c*) Post-mortem cases and (*d*) Hauntings.

* *Proc. S.P.R.*, Vol. 33, Part 86, pp. 23–429 (1923).
† Ibid., Vol. 41, Part 130, pp. 205–49 (1933).
‡ *One Hundred Cases for Survival after Death* (T. W. Werner Laurie, 1943).
§ *Jour. S.P.R.*, Vol. 34, p. 187, March 1948.
‖ Published by S.P.R., 31 Tavistock Square, London.

2. EXPERIMENTAL CASES

It may be a matter of some surprise to the reader that there should be cases of apparitions initiated consciously by a living agent. While these are relatively few in number, they may be of considerable importance for an understanding of their nature and origin. Tyrrell's views, stated very simply, are that apparitions are telepathically caused by an agent, but are constructed jointly with certain mental levels of the percipient. We do in fact find innumerable stages between vague feelings and fully fledged apparitions affecting several senses. The accounts given below as examples are abbreviated, but references will allow the student to go back to the sources for detail.

*Case 1. Mr. S. H. Beard.** S. H. Beard was known to Sir William Barrett and friends of W. T. Stead as a man of high character. He strongly willed to make his presence felt in a certain bedroom three miles away, where two sisters, Miss L. S. Verity (aged 25) and Miss E. C. Verity (aged 11), slept. The older was terrified to see S. H. B. standing at her bedside in evening dress, and woke her sister, who also saw the apparition at the time when S. H. B. was experimenting. The older sister spoke of her experience to S. H. B. spontaneously some four days later.

About a year later another similar experiment was successful. S. H. B. strongly concentrated about 9.30 p.m. on the interior of the house at Kew in which Miss V. and her two sisters then lived. He says :

"During this experiment I must have fallen into a mesmeric sleep, for although I was conscious I could not move my limbs. I did not seem to have lost the power of moving them, but I could not make the effort to do so. . . . At 10 p.m. I regained my normal state by an effort of will. . . . When I went to bed on this same night, I determined that I would be in the front bedroom of the above-mentioned house at 12 p.m. and remain there until I had made my spiritual presence perceptible to the inmates."

He continues :

"On the next day I went to Kew to spend the evening, and met there a married sister of Miss V. [This was Mrs. L., whom he had only met once two years previously and for a short time.] In the course of conversation, although I did not think for a moment of asking her any questions on the subject, she told me that on the previous night she had seen me distinctly on two occasions. At about half-past nine she had seen me in the passage going from one room to another, and at 12 p.m., when she was wide awake, she had seen me enter the bedroom and walk round to where she was lying and take her hair (which is very long) into my hand. She also told

* *Phantasms of the Living*, Vol. 1, pp. 104–8.

me that the apparition took hold of her hand, and gazed intently into it, whereupon she spoke saying, ' You need not look at the lines, for I have never had any trouble '. She then awoke her sister, Miss V., who was sleeping with her, and told her about it. After hearing this account, I took the statement which I had written down on the previous evening, from my pocket, and showed it to some of the persons present, who were much astonished, although incredulous. I asked Mrs. L. if she was not dreaming at the time of the latter experience, but this she stoutly denied, and stated that she had forgotten what I was like, but seeing me so distinctly she recognised me at once."

Several points may be noted. The agent's apparition appeared to Mrs. L., whom he did not know to be there, the mutual association being slight. Moreover, the apparition behaved in a way the agent had not purposed or imagined (walking in the passage, holding her hair and her hand and speaking). Such details may be of importance in formulating any theory of the nature of apparitions. Mr. B. made another experiment on March 22nd, 1884, informing Mr. E. Gurney by letter of his intention to try to appear and touch Miss V.'s hair. On April 2nd, calling upon Miss V., she informed him that on March 22nd, while wide awake, she had seen a most vivid and unmistakable apparition of him coming towards her and stroking her hair. Miss V.'s sister signed a statement that she had been told about this before Mr. B. called.

The two following cases are abbreviated from F. W. H. Myers.*

Case 2. Mr. Kirk. Each night from June 10th to June 20th, between 11 p.m. and 1 a.m., without giving any indication to his friend Miss G. of the experiment, Mr. Kirk endeavoured to make himself visible to her by an act of concentration. He was particularly careful to drop no hint of these experiments, and remarks that each time Miss G. called at his house during this period she complained of being sleepless and restless from an uneasy feeling which she was unable to describe or account for. On June 23rd he heard he had succeeded on an occasion when he might not have expected to. The experiment was made at his office on the spur of the moment, on the afternoon of June 11th.

" I had been rather closely engaged on some auditing work, which had tired me, and as near as I can remember, the time was between 3.30 and 4 p.m. that I laid down my pencil, stretched myself, and in the act of doing the latter I was seized with the impulse to make a trial on Miss G. I did not of course know where she was at the moment, but with a flash, as it were, I transferred myself to her bedroom. I cannot say why I thought of that spot, unless it was that

* F. W. H. Myers : *Human Personality*, Vol. I, pp. 690–700 (Longmans, Green & Co., 1903); or *Proc. S.P.R.*, Vol. X, p. 270.

I did so because my first experiment had been made there. As it happened, it was what I must call a 'lucky shot', for I caught her at the moment she was lightly sleeping in her chair, a condition which seems to be peculiarly favourable to receiving and externalising telepathic messages."

Mr. Kirk was impressed by the fact that Miss G. described him as wearing a dark-reddish check suit, which he was in fact wearing at the office, although it was unusual for him to do so. Miss G.'s account is :

" A peculiar occurrence happened to me on the Wednesday of the week before last. In the afternoon (being tired by a morning walk), while sitting in an easy-chair near the window of my own room, I fell asleep. At any time I happen to sleep during the day (which is but seldom) I invariably awake with tired uncomfortable sensations, which take some little time to pass off; but that afternoon, on the contrary, I was suddenly quite wide awake, seeing Mr. Kirk standing near my chair, dressed in a dark-brown coat, which I had frequently seen him wear. His back was towards the window, his right hand towards me; he passed across the room towards the door, which is opposite the window, the space between being 15 feet, the furniture so arranged as to leave just that centre clear; but when he got about 4 feet from the door which was closed, he disappeared. . . . I then thought, knowing he must be at the office at the time I saw him (which was quite as distinctly as if he had been really in the room), that in this instance, at least, it must be purely imaginary, and feeling so sure it was only fancy, resolved not to mention it, and did not do so until this week when, almost involuntarily, I told him about it. Much to my astonishment, Mr. Kirk was very pleased with the account, and asked me to write it, telling me that on that afternoon, feeling rather tired, he put down his pen for a few moments, and, to use his own words, 'threw himself into this room'. He also told me he had purposely avoided this subject in my presence lately, that he might not influence me, but was anxiously hoping I would introduce it. I feel sure I had not been dreaming of him, and cannot remember that anything had happened to cause me even to think of him that afternoon before falling asleep."

Mrs. Sidgwick interviewed Miss G., who was confident she was awake : it was as if she had wakened up to see the apparition, but had not been dreaming of Mr. Kirk. The apparition did not look towards her or appear to take any interest in her.

Case 3. Wesermann's Experiments. H. M. Wesermann had made numerous attempts to transfer mental images to sleeping friends— i.e., to impress dreams upon them. He had been successful in four previous cases. The experiment described below resulted in an apparition. The intention in Wesermann's mind was that in a dream, a lady who had been dead five years should appear to Lieut. ——n and incite him to good deeds. Contrary to expectation, Lieut. ——n had not gone to bed at the time of the experiment, but was discussing

the French campaign with his friend Lieut. S—— in an ante-room.
Lieut. ——n said that suddenly the door of the room opened, the lady
entered, dressed in white with a black kerchief and uncovered head,
greeted S—— with her hand three times in a friendly manner, then
turned to ——n, nodded to him and returned through the doorway.
Lieut. S—— gave the following written account of the incident :

> " Herr ——n came to pay me a visit at my lodgings about a league
> from A——. He stayed the night with me. After supper, and when
> we were both undressed, I was sitting on my bed and Herr ——n was
> standing by the door of the next room on the point also of going to
> bed. This was about half-past ten. We were speaking partly about
> indifferent subjects and partly about the events of the French cam-
> paign. Suddenly the door opened without a sound, and a lady
> entered, very pale, taller than Herr ——n, about five feet four inches
> in height, strong and broad of figure, dressed in white, but with a
> large black kerchief which reached to below the waist. She entered
> with bare head, greeted me with the hand three times in compli-
> mentary fashion, turned round to the left towards Herr ——n, and
> waved her hand to him three times ; after which the figure quietly,
> and again without any creaking of the door, went out. We followed
> at once in order to discover whether there was any deception, but
> found nothing. The strangest thing was this, that our night-watch
> of two men, whom I had shortly before found on the watch, were now
> asleep, though at my first call they were on the alert, and that the door
> of the room, which always opens with a good deal of noise, did not
> make the slightest sound when opened by the figure." *

It is scarcely necessary to say that the dead woman had nothing
to do with the apparition. Wesermann describes it as a " dream in
the waking state ", but this is not very helpful so long as we remain
ignorant of the mechanism of dream production. Tyrrell regards
the case as on a par with other apparitional cases, except that the
agent's own apparition was replaced by another figure. He points
out that Wesermann did not know there were two possible percipients, and would naturally have assumed that Lieut. ——n was
at home in his own bedroom. The whole drama was thus inevitably
a joint creation or production in which certain levels of the three
minds were acting together.

3. CRISIS CASES

Here a living agent is the involuntary cause of the apparition.
Case 4. Hon. Miss K. Ward.†

> " Two years ago, on awaking one morning at 8 o'clock, I saw a
> distinct appearance of my sister Emily, seated at the foot of my bed

---

* F. W. H. Myers, loc. cit., p. 699.
† *Proc. S.P.R.*, Vol. 33, p. 255. Mrs. Sidgwick's paper.

in her night-gown.   She was rocking herself backwards and forwards as if in pain.   Putting out my hand to touch her, the phantasm vanished.   Going into my sister's room half an hour later, I related to her my experience, and she (being still in much pain) informed me that at 8 o'clock she had actually been in the position above described *on her own bed* and had meditated coming into my room, but had not liked to disturb me.   (She had been perfectly well the night before.) My sister's room is at some distance from mine, being divided therefrom by a corridor and cross-door."

Case 5.   Mr. Kearne.*   Mr. Kearne, who was the percipient, had lived for some years with two intimate friends, Alfred Hobday and Arthur Bent.   He was expecting them back about 10 p.m. from a musical tour of the provinces and was sitting reading about 10.50 p.m.

" I had read some twenty minutes or so, was thoroughly absorbed in the book, my mind was perfectly quiet, and for the time being my friends were quite forgotten, when suddenly, without a moment's warning, my whole being seemed roused to the highest state of tension or aliveness, and I was aware, with an intenseness not easily imagined by those who have never experienced it, that another being or presence was not only in the room but close to me.   I put my book down, and although my excitement was great, I felt quite collected and not conscious of any sense of fear.   Without changing my position, and looking straight at the fire, I knew somehow that my friend A. H. was standing at my left elbow, but so far behind me as to be hidden by the arm-chair in which I was leaning back.   Moving my eyes round slightly without otherwise changing my position, the lower portion of one leg became visible, and I instantly recognised the grey-blue material of trousers he often wore, but the stuff appeared semi-transparent, reminding me of tobacco smoke in consistency.†   I could have touched it with my hand without moving more than my left arm.   With that curious instinctive wish not to see more of such a ' figure ', I did no more than glance once or twice at the apparition and then directed my gaze steadily at the fire in front of me.   An appreciable space of time passed—probably several seconds in all, but seeming in reality much longer—when the most curious thing happened.   Standing upright between me and the window on my left, and at a distance of about four feet from me and almost immediately behind my chair, I saw perfectly distinctly the figure of my friend—the face very pale, the head slightly thrown back, the eyes shut, and on one side of the throat, just under the jaw, a wound with blood on it.   The figure remained motionless with the arms close to the sides, and for some time, how long I cannot say, I looked steadily at it ;   then all at once roused myself, turned deliberately round, the figure vanished, and I realised instantly that I had seen the figure behind me without moving from my first position,

* F. W. H. Myers : loc. cit., Vol. I, p. 672 ; or *Jour. S.P.R.*, Vol. 7, p. 25.
† The trousers of grey-blue stuff proved to be what A. H. wore the evening the vision was seen.

—an impossible feat physically. I am perfectly certain I never moved my position from the first appearance of the figure as seen physically, until it disappeared on my turning round."

Mr. Kearne described his anxiety for the following forty-five minutes, until at 11.35 p.m. a hansom cab drew up. A. B. came upstairs and said, " Come and see A. H. ; what a state he is in ! " They found him in the bathroom with collar and shirt torn open, bathing a wound under his jaw which was bleeding. It appeared that they had been to a restaurant after arriving in London, that A. H. had complained of feeling faint from the heat of the place, and going out into the fresh air had fainted and fallen forward, striking his jaw on the edge of the kerb. Mr. Kearne calculated, from the distance and average speed of a cab, that this incident must have been within about three minutes of the time of appearance of the apparition. He refers to the curious mental sympathy between A. H. and himself by which they were often aware of each other's thoughts, and often each aware of the proximity of the other prior to seeing him.

*Case 6. M. J. and J. Pedley.** This is a collective case, the apparition of the dying mother being seen ten hours before her death and again three months later, on the night before her baby's death.

" A friend of mine named Mrs. J. died in November 1877 ; she had been confined just over a week. A few days before she died she said to me, ' I am going to die ', and asked me to take care of her baby, which I did until it died three months after. The night before she died we were awakened between twelve and one o'clock by a noise like tapping at the window twice. My husband got up and went downstairs but could see nothing. So we tried to settle to sleep again, when all of a sudden we were alarmed by our little boy, who was not quite two years old, calling out ' Auntie ', by which name he used to call her, and pointing towards the foot of the bed, and there I saw her, standing all in white. She died the next morning between nine and ten. She appeared again a second time about three months later : it would be about midnight. My husband saw her standing by the fire. At first he thought it was I, until he turned round and saw I was in bed. We were very much frightened for a long time after. The baby died the next day about three o'clock in the afternoon."

4. POST-MORTEM CASES

Here the simplest hypothesis, though not the only one, is that a discarnate agent is responsible for the apparition in the same way that an incarnate or living person was responsible for those previously recorded. Of the *modus operandi*, we have not as yet said anything.

* Sir Ernest Bennett : *Apparitions and Haunted Houses*, p. 26 (Faber & Faber, 1939).

Case 7. *Lord Brougham.** Lord Brougham, aged twenty-one, was travelling in Sweden with friends.

" We set out for Gothenburg, determining to make for Norway. About one o'clock in the morning, arriving at a decent inn, we decided to stop for the night. Tired with the cold of yesterday, I was glad to take advantage of a hot bath before I turned in, and here a most remarkable thing happened to me—so remarkable that I must tell the story from the beginning.

" After I left the High School, I went with G., my most intimate friend, to attend the classes in the University. There was no divinity class, but we frequently in our walks discussed and speculated upon many grave subjects—among others, on the immortality of the Soul, and on a future state. This question, and the possibility, I will not say of ghosts walking, but of the dead appearing to the living, were subjects of much speculation ; and we actually committed the folly of drawing up an agreement, written in our blood, to the effect that whichever of us died first should appear to the other, and thus solve any doubts we had entertained of the life after death. After we had finished our classes at the college, G. went to India, having got an appointment there in the Civil Service. He seldom wrote to me, and after a lapse of a few years I had almost forgotten him ; moreover, his family having little connection with Edinburgh, I seldom saw or heard anything of them, or of him through them, so that all this schoolboy intimacy died out, and I had nearly forgotten his existence. I had taken, as I have said, a warm bath, and while lying in it and enjoying the comfort of the heat, after the late freezing I had undergone, I turned my head round, looking toward the chair on which I had deposited my clothes, as I was about to get out of the bath. On the chair sat G., looking calmly at me. How I got out of the bath I know not, but on recovering my senses I found myself sprawling on the floor. The apparition, or whatever it was, that had taken the likeness of G., had disappeared.

" The vision produced such a shock that I had no inclination to talk about it even to Stuart ; but the impression it made upon me was too vivid to be easily forgotten ; and so strongly was I affected by it that I have here written down the whole story, with *the date*, 19*th December*, and all the particulars as they are now before me. No doubt I had fallen asleep ; and that the appearance presented so distinctly to my eyes was a dream, I cannot for a moment doubt ; yet for years I had had no communication with G., nor had there been anything to recall him to my recollection ; nothing had taken place during our Swedish travels either connected with G. or with India or with anything relating to him or to any member of his family. I recollected quickly enough our old discussion and the bargain we had made. I could not discharge from my mind the impression that G. must have died, and that his appearance to me was to be received by me as a proof of a future state, yet all the while I felt convinced that the whole was a dream ; and so painfully vivid, so unfading was

* Wm., Lord Brougham : *Life and Times of Henry, Lord Brougham* (1871).

the impression, that I could not bring myself to talk of it, or to make the slightest allusion to it."

Lord Brougham afterwards wrote :

" Soon after my return to Edinburgh, there arrived a letter from India, announcing G.'s death, and stating that he had died on the 19th of December."

Case 8. Rev. Arthur Bellamy.

" When a girl at school my wife made an agreement with a fellow pupil, Miss W., that the one of them who died first should, if divinely permitted, appear after her decease to the survivor. In 1874 my wife, who had not seen or heard anything of her former school-friend for some years, casually heard of her death. The news reminded her of her former agreement, and then, becoming nervous, she told me of it. I knew of my wife's compact, but I had never seen a photograph of her friend or heard any description of her. [Mr. Bellamy told Gurney in conversation that his mind had not been in the least dwelling on the compact.]

" A night or two afterwards as I was sleeping with my wife, a fire brightly burning in the room and a candle alight, I suddenly awoke and saw a lady sitting by the side of the bed where my wife was sleeping soundly. At once I sat up in the bed, and gazed so intently that even now I can recall her form and features. Had I the pencil and the brush of a Millais, I could transfer to canvas an exact likeness of the ghostly visitant. I remember that I was much struck, as I looked intently at her, with the careful arrangement of her coiffure, every single hair being most carefully brushed down. How long I sat and gazed I cannot say, but directly the apparition ceased to be, I got out of bed to see if any of my wife's garments had by any means optically deluded me. I found nothing in the line of vision but a bare wall. Hallucination on my part I rejected as out of the question, and I doubted not that I had really seen an apparition. Returning to bed, I lay till my wife some hours after awoke, and then I gave her an account of her friend's appearance. I described her colour, form, &c., all of which exactly tallied with my wife's recollection of Miss W. Finally I asked, ' But was there any special point to strike one in her appearance ? ' ' Yes,' my wife promptly replied ; ' we girls used to tease her at school for devoting so much time to the arrangement of her hair.' This was the very thing which I have said so much struck me. Such are the simple facts.

" I will only add that till 1874 I had never seen an apparition, and that I have not seen one since." *

Case 9. Captain Eldred Bowyer-Bower.† Captain Bower, aged twenty-two, was shot down in his plane in France on March 19th,

---

* F. W. H. Myers : loc. cit., Vol. II, p. 350.
† Proc. S.P.R., Vol. 33, pp. 167–76 (1923); or Jour. S.P.R., Vol. IX, pp. 39–46.

1917.   The case is remarkable in that a number of " appearances "
to different people took place, three approximately at the time of
death and the other two in December 1917.   The most remarkable
was to his half-sister, Mrs. Dorothy Spearman, who was at the time
staying in a hotel in Calcutta.   She did not, of course, know of
Eldred's death, or even that he was out in France again, as he had
been home several months and had only returned there three weeks
before he was killed.   Her baby was baptised on the day of Captain
Bower's death, and he was to have been the child's godfather.   The
following extract is from a letter to Captain Bower's mother (January
1918) :

> " Eldred was greatly on my mind when baby was born and I could
> only think of him.   On March 19th, in the late part of the morning,
> I was sewing and talking to baby ; Joan was in the sitting-room and
> did not see anything.   I had a great feeling I must turn round and
> did, to see Eldred ; he looked so happy and had that dear mischievous
> look.   I was so glad to see him, and told him I would just put baby
> in a safer place, then we could talk.   ' Fancy coming out here,' I said,
> turning round again, and was just putting my hands out to give him a
> hug and a kiss, but Eldred had gone.   I called and looked for him.
> I never saw him again.   At first I thought it was simply my brain.
> Then I did think for a second something must have happened to him
> and a terrible fear came over me.   Then again I thought how stupid
> I was, and it must be my brain playing tricks.   But now I know it
> was Eldred, and all the time in Church at baby's christening he was
> there, because I felt he was, and know he was, only I could not see
> him.   All the time I thought why do I feel like this when Eldred is
> safe. . . . ?"

About the time of his death a little niece of his, not quite three
years old, appears to have had some visual impression of him.   On
the morning of his death she came up to her mother's room about
9.15 a.m. (the latter being still in bed), and said, " Uncle Alley Boy
is downstairs ".   Although her mother told her he was in France,
she insisted she had seen him.   The third contemporary impression
was received by Mrs. Watson, an elderly friend of Captain Bower's
mother, who had not written to Mrs. Bower for eighteen months
but felt impelled to write a letter to her on March 19th : ". . . Something tells me you are having great anxiety about Eldred.   Will you
let me know ? "

5. HAUNTINGS

There is a class of apparition which differs from the preceding
classes in that it seems to be associated with a particular locality.   It
makes recurrent appearances at such a place, and in general appears

to pay little attention to human beings. This type, the so-called ghost, gives the impression to percipients of " somnambulistic " or automatic behaviour.

Case 10. *The Morton Case.** The six percipients in this case were all interviewed by F. W. H. Myers. The principal percipient, Miss R. C. Morton, was a young medical student, and the testimony was very consistent. The phenomena covered a period of years 1882–89, and the full account is an impressive and straightforward one, giving an account of the large number of occasions when it was seen and the number of witnesses to it. There was substantial agreement in the descriptions of the figure.

> " The figure was that of a tall lady, dressed in black of a soft woollen material, judging from the slight sound in moving. The face was hidden in a handkerchief held in the right hand. . . . I saw the upper part of the left side of the forehead, and a little of the hair above. Her left hand was nearly hidden by her sleeve and a fold of her dress. As she held it down, a portion of a widow's cuff was visible on both wrists, so that the whole impression was that of a lady in widow's weeds. There was no cap on the head, but a general effect of blackness suggests a bonnet, with long veil or a hood."

During the two years 1882–84 Miss Morton saw the figure about half a dozen times, and on three separate occasions it was seen by her sister, Mrs. K., by a housemaid and by her young brother and another little boy. The appearances reached a maximum in July and August 1884, thereafter gradually diminishing in frequency to 1889. From then on the appearances ceased. The light, muffled footsteps associated with the figure persisted a little longer, but they also eventually ceased. For the first two years Miss Morton describes it as appearing to be so solid and life-like that it was often mistaken for a real person. It intercepted the light, but Miss M. was not able to determine if the figure cast a shadow. Its appearance later became less distinct. Twice Miss M. reported having seen the figure pass through fine strings, and says, " It was not that there was nothing there to touch, but that she always seemed to be *beyond* me, and if followed into a corner simply disappeared." An extract from Miss Morton's account will illustrate the type of experience.

> " On the evening of August 11th we were sitting in the drawing-room with the gas lit but the shutters not shut, the light outside getting dusk, my brother and a friend had just given up tennis, finding it dark ; my eldest sister, Mrs. K., and myself both saw the figure on the balcony outside, looking in at the window. She stood there for some minutes, then walked to the end and back again, after which

* *Proc. S.P.R.*, Vol. 8, pp. 311–32.

she seemed to disappear. She soon after came into the drawing-room, when I saw her but my sister did not. The same evening my sister E. saw her on the stairs as she came out of a room on the upper landing.

"The following evening, 12th August, while coming up the garden, I walked towards the orchard, when I saw the figure cross the orchard, go along the carriage drive in front of the house, and in at the open side door, across the hall and into the drawing-room, I following. She crossed the drawing-room and took up her usual position behind the couch in the bow window. My father came in soon after and I told him she was there. He could not see the figure, but went up to where I showed him she was. She then went swiftly round behind him, across the room, out of the door and along the hall, disappearing as usual near the garden door, we both following her. We looked out into the garden, having first to unlock the garden door, which my father had locked as he came through, but saw nothing of her.

"On 12th August, about 8 p.m. and still quite light, my sister E. was singing in the back drawing-room. I heard her stop abruptly, come out into the hall and call me. She said she had seen the figure in the drawing-room close behind her as she sat at the piano. I went back into the room with her and saw the figure in the bow window at her usual place. I spoke to her several times, but had no answer. She stood there for ten minutes or a quarter of an hour; then went across the room to the door and along the passage, disappearing in the same place by the garden door.

"My sister M. then came in from the garden, saying she had seen her coming up the kitchen steps outside. We all three then went into the garden, when Mrs. K. called out from the window on the first storey that she had just seen her pass across the lawn in front and along the carriage drive towards the orchard. This evening, then, altogether four people saw her. My father was then away and my youngest brother was out."

Miss Morton remarks that the figure was not called up by a desire to see it, and says that on all those occasions when parties of them had sat up at night hoping to see it, they had always been disappointed. The figure was believed to be connected with a lady who had lived in the house (the second Mrs. S.) and who had died in September 1878. Mr. S., an Anglo-Indian, had lived in the house from 1860 to 1876. His first wife, to whom he was deeply attached, died, and he became an intemperate drinker. His second wife had hoped to cure him, but instead took to drinking herself, and their life was embittered and quarrelsome. The grounds for identifying the figure with the second Mrs. S. were (a) the widow's garb—Mr. S. had died two years before she did; (b) several people who had known her identified her from the description, and Miss Morton picked out the sister of Mrs. S. from a number of portraits as being most like the figure.

Miss Morton gives grounds for believing that the apparition was on two occasions seen by dogs. She also makes the interesting observation that when familiarity with the apparition had eliminated her feelings of awe, so that she could be analytical and observe more closely, she was " conscious of a feeling of *loss*, as if I had lost power to the figure ".

Case 11. *Borley Rectory.** The two books which Harry Price wrote on this case are extremely readable, and include the records of ten years' observations in which about 100 people participated. They make this probably one of the best-attested cases of haunting. The rectory, built in 1863 and destroyed by fire in 1939, was built on the site of a much older building, of which the foundations were traced, and probably others preceded it. It is impossible to do justice in a few extracts to the variety and number of the phenomena. The apparition of a nun was seen by as many as seventeen people, singly or collectively, between 1885 and 1943. The most amazing and sensational phenomena were of the " poltergeist " type, and Price estimates that during the period October 1930 to October 1935, during which the Rev. Lionel A. Foyster, M.A., and his family resided there, more than 2,000 poltergeist phenomena were experienced. Mr. Price says :

> " I visited the Rectory several times in 1929 and witnessed many phenomena *under perfect conditions of control.* In addition to the incessant para-normal bell-ringing I saw showers of pebbles and keys coming from nowhere, and on one occasion a Roman Catholic medallion, and a badge struck during the French Revolution came tumbling down the stairs in good light. Also, we managed to obtain phenomena *at request.* We asked the ' entities ' to ring one of the house-bells for us, and it was rung—under perfect control. . . . As we reached the study an empty claret bottle was hurled down the staircase well, smashing at our feet. At the same moment one of the bells rang violently. We rushed upstairs again but could not account for the phenomena. Then a further outbreak of bell-ringing, and small pebbles rattled downstairs."

Mr. Price himself secured a lease of the rectory for a year from May 17th, 1937. During this period he organised constant surveillance of the house, with the assistance of some forty men of standing in various walks of life. He reports :

> " I will say at once that most of the major phenomena were experienced under scientific conditions. The nun was seen again : many footsteps and similar sounds were heard ; raps, taps and knockings were frequent ; there were many para-normal movements

* Harry Price : *The Most Haunted House in England* (Longmans, Green & Co., 1940) and *The End of Borley Rectory* (Harrap, 1946).

of objects, and appearances, disappearances and reappearances of strange articles ; a luminous phenomenon, pleasant and unpleasant odours, sensation of coldness, tactual phenomena, etc."

What are we to make of experiences such as these :

> " On another occasion Mr. Mark Kerr-Pearse (a British pro-consul at Geneva) was alone in the Rectory and was having his evening meal in the Base Room with the door closed.   He heard the key in the lock turn.   Something had locked him in.   The extraordinary thing was that the key was on the inside of the door.   Consequently whatever locked him in remained in the room. . . . On May 7th, 1938, Mr. M. Savage, a B.B.C. television engineer, and a friend named Bowden reported new pencillings which ' appeared ' *while they actually watched the walls.*"

The full account should be studied by those who desire to feel the accumulated weight of evidence in which 200 witnesses are involved. Mr. Price says :

> " In view of the legal opinions printed above, plus the evidence of two hundred witnesses, and what I have seen with my own eyes, there is only one conclusion at which I can arrive : the Borley phenomena (or most of them) occurred in the way they were said to occur ; they were of para-normal origin ; they have been scientifically proved ; and as Sir Albion Richardson emphasises, the evidence for their para-normality is as conclusive as human testimony can ever be."

Of the nature of poltergeist phenomena we shall have something to say in Chapter 11.   If this type of phenomenon is to be accepted— and it is all a question of evidence, which in the above case is con- sidered by competent jurists adequate and incontrovertible—we shall have to take into account an order of existence, inter-acting with the material one, but involving forces, energies and purposes of a kind quite outside that orderly scheme of material things which science has studied so successfully.   We are not concerned at present with the motor phenomena but with the sensory phenomena only. As a preliminary to considering a theory of these, we must look at the nature of sense perception.

6. SENSE PERCEPTION, HALLUCINATION AND ILLUSION

Philosophers have considered at great length the nature of sense perception : it is very important to know its real nature, for the world of science and the plain man's world are both the results of using our senses.   When a person says, " I see an apple ", this is called an act of perception, and it is, in fact, rather a complex act. What he really *experiences* are sense-data.   He senses a nearly circular, green, shiny patch of colour in contrast with a background. When he makes the act of perception he makes an intuitive jump beyond these sense-data. (He does not *infer* that an apple is there, for inference is a logical process based on premises and deduction.) As a consequence of this " jump " he believes without any doubt that there exists out in space an object, and that the greenness, roundness and shininess are properties of the surface of this object. This, we say, is common sense, and all sane persons agree about it. Now, " common sense " is the interpretation of things which is adequate for all practical purposes, but when we are trying to understand the mysterious character of the world in which we live and our knowledge of it, we find common sense does not take us very far. We saw nowhere more clearly than in the biological field (Chapter 3) how completely inadequate it is to explain growth or the act of seeing. We must therefore be prepared to examine without prejudice many of the things we take for granted, and which we say are just common sense, if we want really to understand the world.

To return, then, to our analysis of perceiving an apple, we have to admit that " seeing " does not give us the *direct* acquaintance with things which common sense imagines. We are *directly* acquainted only with our own sense-data, not with " things " outside. The following considerations, if carefully weighed, should convince us of this. (*a*) We never see things as they are, but only as they were. In practice this distinction does not usually matter, because of the enormous speed of light, but in the case of distant stars or nebulæ, whose light may take 100,000 years to reach us, the " thing " which we say we see will have changed, and may even no longer exist.

(*b*) The " direct-acquaintance " or common-sense view says that the greenness, roundness and shininess are properties of the thing's surface. But are they? One person (who is colour blind) thinks it is grey, another sees no shine upon it, another sees it rather flattened. As a person moves around, his own sense-data may change, the size and shape of the colour patch, its shine and its tint. Have the properties of the surface changed? And where several observers differ, who is right? (Consider again the discussion in Chapter 5, Section 1.)

Reflection shows that sense-data, which we are prone to project on to an external object, are really private and personal. That they have much in common with other people's sense-data is no doubt true. That there is a " subsistent object " which corresponds to an impenetrable region of space outside ourselves *may* also be true. All we want to be clear about is that the sense-data are what the mind is immediately acquainted with, and that they are not a part or property of the subsistent object, but are the mind's contribution to the art of perceiving. We might put it in the form of an equation :

$$\text{Material Object} = \text{Subsistent Object} + \text{Sense-Data}$$
$$\text{for a person} \qquad\qquad \text{for that person.}$$

Of the nature of the subsistent world we can know nothing through our senses. Since this is so, it is open to us to speculate that it may be of the nature of a permanent mental field to which our own minds are related or in which they are immersed. The assumption that because the subsistent object has the quality of impenetrability it has the sort of concrete materiality which common sense pictures, has no foundation in observation or experiment. Indeed, modern physics reminds us, what common sense is always making us forget, that the quality of impenetrability is due to electromagnetic fields of force, and even the supposedly " concrete " particles often behave

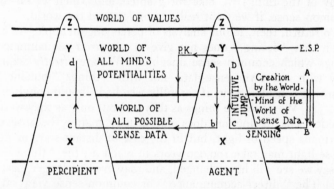

in a way quite inconsistent with such a view of their nature. We know so little of the real nature of both the electromagnetic fields and the so-called " particles ", that to claim them as being of the nature of mind is quite plausible. When we go on to consider the biological world (vide Chapter 3) with the indubitable evidence of purpose and the necessary inference of mental fields or patterns to which " matter " must conform, I think we may feel that there are indeed strong indications that the subsistent world is of the nature of Mind. We may regard the subsistent world as the ever-present dominant background of a World Mind to which our own individual minds are related in a selective manner (as we have tried to suggest in the round-tower diagram of Chapter 5). One hesitates to use diagrams to illustrate ideas of this kind, for diagrams are more precise and clear-cut than words. Both of course are symbols, and both very inade-quate to the task of clearly portraying ideas of this kind. The diagram shown is an attempt to convey just a suggestion of these ideas. The round tower is an individual mind. Five slits (not shown) corresponding to the special senses can be imagined as penetrating the thick walls of the tower in the zone X and permitting a limited selection of sense-data to pass to the prisoner within. The act of perception is portrayed on the right-hand side (sensing + an intuitive jump). The three downward-pointing arrows on the right symbolise the creation of the whole lower stratum of sense-data by the operation of a World-Mind in the stratum next above. Physicists interpret this activity in terms of electromagnetic fields— but this is a label for an " unknown ". This higher stratum, with which zone Y of the individual mind is in touch through the ψ-faculty, must be very complex. It includes, among much else, the subsistent world of which we have spoken. The left-hand tower represents a percipient mind. While higher-ψ would presumably be symbolised by a horizontal arrow (not shown) from zone Y of the agent to zone Y of the percipient, the common mechanism of apparitions may perhaps be portrayed by the arrows $abcd$, a functioning of lower-ψ. With the risk of pressing the diagram too far, we might say ab represents the concentration and visualisation of the agent, bc is the inter-personal mental field, and cd is the intuitive jump of the percipient to the conclusion that there is an apparition outside himself —i.e., objective. The whole process $abcd$ is similar to that portrayed on the right-hand side of the diagram. The arrow ab is a feeble mimicry, without permanence in Time, by an individual mind, of the creation of the whole world of sense-data maintained by the World-Mind. The arrows bcd are the process of normal perception.

Hallucinations (or apparitions) would thus be regarded as perceptions similar to those of everyday life, except that they lack permanence and impenetrability, due to the evanescent character of the subsistent object created at a. Presumably this mechanism is similar to, if not identical with, that by which a hypnotised person can be made to " see " what to others is a non-existent object. Alternatively, the mechanism may sometimes be the direct higher-ψ linkage in the zones $Y-Y$.

Illusions are different from hallucinations. In hallucinations (of which apparitions are a special type) the sense-data are genuine enough, but the subsistent object is evanescent. In illusions the interpretation of the sense-data is mistaken. In our diagram the upward-pointing arrow (labelled " intuitive jump ") would have a fault in it. Thus a person who sees a piece of coiled rope and believes he sees a snake, suffers an illusion, but a person who sees a piece of rope which other observers cannot see, suffers an hallucination.

7. THEORIES OF APPARITIONS

We are now in a position to look at the theories advanced about apparitions. There seems no good reason to distinguish between phantasms of the living and the " dead " ; a satisfactory theory may be expected to account for both. The early workers in the Society for Psychical Research all appeared to hold a telepathic theory of apparitions which, stated very simply, is that an agent telepathically impresses a percipient who embodies the message in this visual dramatic form. On this view apparitions are simply an objectified and vivid form of vehicle for a telepathic message or impulse. If we revert to Chapter 6, we have there numerous examples of different vehicles. In Mrs. Upton Sinclair's case it was visual imagery (though subjective) ; in Professor Gilbert Murray's case it was verbal-visual imagery of remarkable accuracy : in Case 1 on p. 112 feelings of acute anxiety were the vehicle ; in Case 2 we have an hallucination of the auditory sense as a vehicle, as also in Case 4 ; in Case 3 we have an experience originating telepathically, but of great clairvoyant vividness. In this last case, if the child had seen her mother in front of her on the road, appealing for help, it would have been described as an apparition ; but as the child " saw " the scene as it actually was at home, we call it clairvoyance. We do not know enough to say what are the precise conditions of the two minds which favour the one form of communication rather than the other. It seems, however, quite plausible that hallucinations of the visual sense may at times be the vehicle of a telepathic message or impulse : whether *all* apparitions are in this category is quite another question, and I personally do not think so.

One of the impressive features to be taken into account in any theory is that there is plenty of evidence for collective percipience— i.e., perception by two or more persons at once. This feature, of course, immediately suggests to us that an apparition *does* consist of something physically present in space external to both observers. This is just the point at which our immediate commonsense reaction must be examined critically, as we did in the preceding section. We saw there that in ordinary perception sense-data are in some measure private to each individual person. Each member of a crowd round a table might say " I see a green apple ", establishing thereby, so far as possible, a large measure of common agreement in their sense-data—even though each one's sense-data have their peculiarities. Because they all make the intuitive jump involved in their acts of perception we postulate a subsistent object as the common cause of their agreement. (We also find the " subsistent object " useful to explain why, if the crowd go to sleep, as a result of which all their sense-data vanish, the apple does not cease to exist, and there is no necessity for a miraculous new creation of similar sense-data the next morning.) We have postulated that a World-Mind creates and sustains this subsistent world, with which, as it were, individual minds are in mental rapport. The end result of the act of perception is a belief in the common-sense world of space, a convenient conventional fiction so far as philosophers are concerned, equally convenient for, but not regarded as a fiction by, the ordinary man.

Because apparitions can be collectively perceived, it means no more and no less than the fact that apples can be collectively perceived. I infer a " subsistent apparition ", if for brevity I may write in this inexact way, as well as a " subsistent apple ". The former has its origin in an individual mind, and is often the cause of incompletely developed sense-data. It is also evanescent. The latter is a part of the pattern sustained by the World-Mind. From our standpoint we see that Edmund Gurney's denial that apparitions are present in space has the same validity only as a denial that chairs and tables are present in space. Gurney conceived the telepathic process to operate by a kind of " infection " where more than one percipient was involved, but such analogies are little more than picturesque modes of presenting observational data. Myers was obviously oscillating between ideas of the non-material character of apparitions and their localisation in space. He used the term " metetherial " for an order which would combine these characteristics, and was, I believe, thinking along the lines of the psychic-æther hypothesis, to which I have referred on several occasions. To this theory Professor H. H. Price has given the most satisfactory form.

The most important contribution to the theory of apparitions has been made by G. N. M. Tyrrell.* I shall here present an outline of his views, indicating the points at which I venture to differ. Tyrrell regards the perfect apparition as a " material thing without a physical occupant ". He uses the term " physical object " where we have used " subsistent object ". Considering the simple equation we wrote down previously—Material Object for a person = Subsistent Object + Sense-Data for that person—this would mean that an apparition is the aggregate of sense-data without a subsistent object. The sense-data are quite real, but are not physically caused—i.e., no light-waves impinge from without on the retina, no sound-waves on the ear-drum, no pressures on the hand. The sense-data are caused

* *Apparitions*: the F. W. H. Myers Memorial Lecture (1942) (pub. S.P.R., London).

inwardly or centrally—not peripherally or externally. Tyrrell's view is that the whole apparatus of sense-perception can be put into operation in either of these ways : one way is that of normal sense-perception, under stimulus from " without "; the other way is under the stimulus of an implanted idea, in which case certain mid-levels of both the agent's and percipient's minds collaborate closely. Tyrrell then makes the bold suggestion that perhaps this dual control of the mind is more apparent than real, and propounds the startling hypothesis that there is really only one control—viz., the psychological or centrally caused one. All that the brain-processes do when stimulated by lights, sounds and pressures from without is to act in a guiding or advisory manner to these mid-levels of mind which are the causative agent of the sense-data. These mid-levels do in practice create sense-data with remarkable fidelity to the advisory stimuli received from the brain ; but it is not inevitable or obligatory that they should do so. They do so, Tyrrell suggests, to secure the survival of the physical organism, much as car-drivers obey the traffic lights, and for similar reasons. In the course of evolution these mind-levels causing sense-data have come to follow the stimuli of the special senses and brain, semi-automatically. When these levels do occasionally start to work without such advisory stimuli from the brain, the result is hallucination—often a little imperfect or amateurish compared with normal sense-data, as we have observed from recorded cases. The agent who is responsible for causing an apparition is acting on the mid-levels of the percipient's mind with the stimulus of an idea conveyed telepathically, much as a hypnotist is acting on these levels with a verbal stimulus. In so far as there are collective hallucinations of the Indian rope-trick variety, these would seem to depend on the ability of an agent to create telepathically a common mental field with a dominant idea, operating on the mid-levels of the minds of all observers.

Tyrrell considers some of the characteristics of apparitions and what can be inferred from these about the conditions of their production. Where an apparition of the agent himself appears, the latter certainly does not visualise himself in other than the most general way, yet he appears in perfection of detail. Moreover, apparitions adapt themselves to the percipient's surroundings in behaviour and action—apparently open doors, walk round furniture, etc., in a way which suggests that the production is a joint effort of both the agent's and percipient's minds. It is recognised that there must be various levels in the human mind : possibly one which supplies the motif or general idea with the necessary driving force, and other executant levels, like the producer of a play and the stage carpenter. These mid-levels of the two or more personalities involved must operate together in a close relationship in the production of any apparition. Tyrrell points out that the product usually in some degree suggests consciousness is operative, and in some degree that mechanism is operative, and coins the term " idea-pattern " for it.

There can be little doubt, I think, of the co-operative nature of the process leading to apparitions, and of the fact that the human mind has many complex levels of functioning. We are all aware how in dreams one level throws up the theme or motif, another disguises and dramatises it, and still another level of the self is a surprised spectator of the drama which it observes. Tyrrell's theory, however, introduces the concepts of peripheral and central excitation, with the latter the immediate cause of sense-data, as explained above. I venture to suggest that this distinction is without meaning : that there is only one mode of excitation of sense-data which is identical for both normal " objects " and apparitions. In both cases the fact of collective percipience leads naturally to the view that there is a subsistent object. This world of subsistent objects is a stratum of the " World of all Mind's potentialities " in the diagram. A and a are subsistent objects in this stratum, only A has permanence—i.e., of substance, not necessarily of form—because of the World-Mind which sustains it, while a is evanescent, being created by an individual mind through a transient act of thought. D is the state of mind of a person who perceives an ordinary object (whose subsistent is A) and d is the precisely analogous state of mind of an observer who perceives what we call an apparition (whose temporary subsistent was a).

I cannot find that any of the characteristics of apparitions which Tyrrell carefully listed and considered in his Myers Lecture are inconsistent with the views I have expressed above. That apparitions should appear and disappear in locked rooms and vanish while being watched, that they *may* pass through physical objects (though they do not always do so), and that they leave no traces behind, are all consistent with the transient character and difference in degree of development of the subsistent object. There is nothing remarkable about different degrees of materialisation (or different densities—as the physicist might put it). We may recall that the Borley Rectory case suggested some extraordinary materialisations, and so do certain séance-room phenomena—of which more in a later chapter. The fact that apparitions are seen or heard by some, but not by all, of those persons present, is again not surprising. We have agreed that the sense-data constituting the apparition are a joint construct of the agent and one or more percipient minds. It is not to be expected that a mind not participating in the common idea-pattern would perceive the data. These are two ways of saying the same thing. If this seems strange at first, let us recall that there are many different states of consciousness—e.g., absorption in a problem, or day-dreaming, in which a conversation or an action is not noticed—though everyone else may have been aware of it. There is an appropriateness of mental state required for even normal perception, and there is no more reason why an apparition should be perceived by everyone in a locality than there is for everyone in a percipient's locality to be in similar telepathic rapport with an agent.

The manner in which apparitions simulate in behaviour their more common counterparts, which borders on the miraculous if the former are regarded as " non-physical ", requires no explanation in our view. The process of perception is the same in both cases. When the percipient shuts his eyes or when he turns his head he no longer sees the apparition ; if a mirror is appropriately placed he sees it in the mirror—all of which are normal because some degree of light reflection *is* involved in these cases too. In a case such as 5 on p. 196, where Mr. Kearne maintains he could see the apparition as though through the back of his head, we may postulate clairvoyant perception on his part. It does not seem unreasonable that in the state of *telepathic* rapport with his friend this kindred faculty may also be exercised if necessary with equal facility. It probably *is* exercised in support of normal perception of the apparition in many such cases, where it is afterwards realised that details have been observed beyond the power of normal seeing at that distance. It is a fact that in collective percipience, each one sees the apparition from a position appropriate to his spatial relations, one seeing the profile and another the full face, etc. This is almost incredible on a non-physical theory, but is to be expected if there is no difference in existential status between commonplace objects and apparitions except that inhering in the transient and possibly weak or imperfectly developed character of the subsistent object.

The question may be raised whether there is, then, no difference in existential status between a well-developed apparition capable of stimulating all the senses of a human being, and a living person. Our answer would be " None "—so far as sense-data are concerned—but this is, of course, a correspondence only on the lowest of the significant levels in our diagram. On the next higher level of mental qualities there is a most marked difference. The apparitional behaviour is usually confined to a semi-automatic type. Anything beyond this is generally of a single idea or purpose—e.g., to stroke hair, to wave the hand, to exhibit a wound, to frequent a neighbourhood or to demonstrate continued existence; having done which the sustaining subsistent thought (or object) has expended the impulse which gave it birth and it fades away. Such mono-ideaism is far removed from the wealth and complexity of mental structure of the normal living person. We may also add, though we shall not enlarge upon it at this stage, that those higher levels of significance, beyond the mental, which are represented in the human being by structures constituting the essential self and its sustaining self-consciousness, have, as far as can be seen, no representative in apparitions. In other words, an apparition of a human being is not a centre of consciousness : it is, so to speak, a psychical marionette given temporary life by some quite separate centre of consciousness. This is doubtless true both of apparitions of the living and the " dead " (with reservations made in regard to another type of apparition to be discussed in the next chapter).

8. CONCEPTION OF A PSYCHIC ÆTHER AND ITS RELATION TO HAUNTING

We have postulated on several occasions the conception of a medium intermediate between mind and matter as a key to the *modus operandi* of object-reading (Chapter 8), clairvoyance (p. 137), psycho-kinesis (Chapter 11), and retrocognition (p. 159). Such a concept may finally have to go the way of the physicist's æther; in the meantime it is a helpful hypothesis. It provides a bridge—to use everyday terms—between mind and matter, and it must be supposed malleable and plastic to the action of mind, on the one hand, while it interpenetrates matter and is modified and moulded by it, on the other. Using the terminology of the preceding section, it is a medium structurally modified by those mid-mind levels described as the " stage-carpenter " by Tyrrell. It is an æther of " images " in which certain types of thought achieve an objectivity or form of existence. It may well be the vehicle or medium of those fields of force of Smuts, or those mental " blue-prints " of which we saw clear evidence in the biological world (Chapter 3). Professor H. H. Price, in his Presidential Address to the Society for Psychical Research * in 1939, has given perhaps the best exposition of the psychic æther and its necessary properties, especially applying it to a theory of hauntings. He conceives that when a certain level (or function) of mind creates a mental image, this image has a degree of persistence in the psychic æther, and moreover is no longer private to the mind

* *Proc. S.P.R.*, Vol. 45, pp. 307-43.

which originated it.   Every image may be endowed with a kind of telepathic charge in virtue of which it persists and can affect other minds or mental contents ;   when this charge finally fades out with lapse of time, the image may disappear.   Such an æther of images may be regarded as one stratum of the collective mind—a more primitive stratum than that of verbal constructs, which is obviously a much later evolutionary development necessary to abstract thinking. While abstract thinking is the type developed by our educational system because it is necessary in science, technology and philosophy, the stream of image-thinking proceeds continually in a lower stratum of mind, and breaks through into consciousness at times of relaxation, fatigue, fever and in the approach to, and emergence from, the sleep state (where it is called hypnogogic and hypnopompic imagery). Price suggests that the cultivation of lower-ψ is tantamount to overcoming the barrier which cuts off this level from normal consciousness, and that this is in fact facilitated by such mental techniques as crystal-gazing or such physiological techniques as fasting, hatha-yoga and the employment of certain drugs.   My own view is that every significant level of the self has its own type of communication with the corresponding levels of other selves, through the " world stuff " or " world-structure " of that level.   For this reason I have used rather loosely the term " lower-ψ " to connote communication through a psychic æther (possibly the bc level of the previous diagram).

Returning to Price's conception of the properties of the ætheric images, it is considered that they may have " greater or lesser degrees of telepathic affinity ".   Between the images formed by two persons A and B there might be little or no telepathic affinity, even though their bodily organisms are close together, while between the images of A and C there may be considerable telepathic rapport, although their bodies are widely separate in space.   The ætheric world has an air of strangeness about it embodying something of the material and something of the mental order in its make-up.

The theory of haunting to which this leads is quite naturally called the psychometric theory, for it considers the mechanism as being similar to that of " psychometry " or object reading, where, however, a house or locality takes the place of the small object.   In Chapter 7 (5) we spoke of the " memory " of places and assimilated the phenomena of retrocognition to this view.   The main question in this case is why the memory of one particular time should be accessible in preference to any other.   It may be supposed that the emotions and thought-images of some person who once occupied the house have intensely modified the psychic æther associated with it, and that, given a suitable percipient-mind in the locality, an apparition is constructed as a consequence. The production is similar to that of those apparitions previously discussed where the mid-levels of the minds of agent and percipient co-operate to produce the idea-pattern. In haunting, however, the original agent has (on this theory) no direct part in it : he may possibly have no consciousness of the surviving phenomena. The " charged " psychic æther of the locality becomes as it were the proximate " agent ", and, together with the normal ætheric memory of the place, co-operates with the appropriate levels of the percipient's mind. (In this connection the sense of " loss " of energy to the apparition remarked by Miss Morton in Case 10 is of interest.) It is obvious that by a simple extension of this psychometric theory we may pass over to a " spiritistic " one. For example, it might be maintained that the " charged " psychic æther in the locality was maintained in this condition by persistent activity of the surviving mind of the original agent. On the psycho-metric theory the psychic æther in the locality retains a persistent dynamic memory—the telepathic charge possibly corresponding in degree to the emotional intensity of the original cause. When a person comes into the locality, if there is some small measure of telepathic affinity between his mental content and the localised imagery, he may feel a vague emotional malaise or a sense of depression or of a " presence ". In cases of marked telepathic affinity there may be actual generation of a phantasm. Possibly there is a joint contribution of energy to its production : it may be that in time the telepathic charge leaks away, corresponding to the gradual expenditure of its imprisoned energy and the fading of the haunting phenomena (as in the Morton case).

In terms of the previous diagram, haunting would be interpreted somewhat as follows. The original and probably intensely emotional acts of thought (a) create a semi-permanent subsistent image-structure stored in the psychic æther somewhere near b. The originating mind may no longer operate " there "—i.e., at a. If, however, a percipient having the appropriate telepathic affinity approaches the locality of b, the process bcd is then generated. Price expresses this idea by saying that " haunting is a kind of deferred telepathy resulting in a post-dated telepathic phantasm ". It will be a telepathic transaction between Smith as he was ten years ago when he lived in this room, and I who am in it now. It is interesting to observe that the psychometric theory of haunting, in postulating the persistence of thought-images independently of a brain and nervous system, indicates as at least likely, the continued survival of the complex mind which gave it origin. Professor Bozzano considered that many cases of haunting can in fact only be explained satisfactorily on the hypothesis of activity by a surviving discarnate mind.

Professor Price recognises and considers carefully the difficulties of a purely telepathic theory of ghosts, assuming they are non-physical in character. The most obvious difficulty is, that in being highly localised, as hauntings are, we are placing a restriction on telepathy for which we have no other warrant at all. I am of the opinion (as is Tyrrell) that there is no essential difference between apparition and ghost, but I differ from him in regarding both as being physical. Many of the characteristics of apparitions, as we have seen, are extraordinarily difficult to understand on a non-physical theory, and are immediately intelligible if a physical theory is accepted. I would maintain that they *do* reflect in a limited degree ordinary light-waves. Because of their transience and unheralded appearance, the possibilities of photography are obviously quite small, but there is one noteworthy instance where a photograph was obtained,* and this has been published.

Captain Provand, Art Director, and Mr. Indre Shira, Court Photographer of London, were photographing Raynham Hall, Norfolk, seat of the Marquess of Townshend. It was a routine commission. Neither of these experienced photographers were interested in Psychical Research. About 4 p.m. on September 19th, 1936, they were ready to photograph the oak staircase. Mr. Shira, observing what he described as " an ethereal veiled form " moving slowly down the staircase, shouted out excitedly, and Captain Provand, whose head was under the cover, removed the cap of the lens, while Mr. Shira pressed the flashlight pistol. Captain Provand was sceptical and not in a position to have seen the apparition; Mr. Shira stoutly maintained that he had seen it. When the negatives were being developed Captain Provand suddenly exclaimed, " Good Lord, there's something on the staircase negative after all." Mr. Shira took a glance at the negative and then hurried off to bring in Mr. Jones, Manager of Blake, Sandford and Blake, chemists, as a witness. He arrived in time to see the negative being taken from the developer and placed in the hypo bath. Mr. Harry Price examined the negative, which he pronounced innocent of any faking, and was unable to shake the witnesses' story.

Expressed in the simplest terms, I regard the telepathic thought-form as the animating principle or transient " mind " which clothes itself in an ætheric body. This may condense enough chemical matter around it to reflect light. The extent to which it does this seems to differ greatly : sometimes the figure is transparent and the background can be seen through it ; at other times it has a solidity indistinguishable from an ordinary figure.

* *Country Life*, Dec. 16th, 1936 (Country Life, Ltd.).

Professor H. H. Price raises the interesting question why, on this psychometric view of haunting, so few places are haunted ? Even if it be supposed that emotions of great intensity are a necessary condition, it is surprising that all old houses, law-courts, hospitals, railway stations, etc., are not haunted. The suggestion he makes is that every such long-inhabited place is saturated and overlaid with a multitude of persistent and localised images, the mass of which does give to the sensitive percipient a characteristic feeling or " psychic atmosphere ". But because of the massed effect, nothing individual can, however, be perceived, just as a large number of finger-prints does not permit the identification of any one. To be perceptible, an ætheric image must stand out in intensity and also be of the quality or " telepathic affinity " to which a percipient can respond.

Our study of apparitions has perhaps shown us that ranging between mind and body are complex levels of personality with many different functions and not the least remarkable of these are creative potentialities, which, though transient, are reminiscent of those more permanent sublime forms which are created and sustained in such rich profusion by the World-Mind.

Chapter

10

EXPERIENCE OUTSIDE THE BODY

" We must hold fast to the fundamental insight that through
the medium of illusion we can relate ourselves to Truth."

LAWRENCE HYDE : *The Nameless Faith*, p. 55.

" There are seas to be explored, and I can only sail a little way out
and come back with a report that the sea stretches infinitely vast
beyond them."

EDMUND GURNEY (in the Willett scripts).

. . . from this wave-washed mound,
Into the furthest flood-brim look with me ;
Then reach on with thy thought till it be drown'd ;
Miles and miles distant though the last line be,
And though thy soul sail leagues and leagues beyond—
Still, leagues beyond those leagues there is more sea.

D. G. ROSSETTI : *The Choice.*

I. SOME QUESTIONS AND DEFINITIONS

IN the study of apparitions in the preceding chapter we saw that the
phantasm was a joint product of certain mental levels of the agent
and percipient, and that its behaviour was generally suggestive of
automatism or the expression only of one or two animating ideas.
No one supposes that apparitions are vehicles of consciousness, but
rather that they bear the same kind of relation to the agent's self
as a thought-image does to the mind that gives it birth. The
question that arises in the speculative mind is this : May we not
expect to find sometimes apparitions which embody a real mental
structure, and possibly a centre of consciousness ? Expressing it
from the agent's standpoint, is it possible for the agent to transfer
his consciousness in some greater or lesser degree into a vehicle
which may or may not be visible to others, leaving his physical body
without consciousness or with only a residium of it ? The appeal
must be to experience : mere speculation has no merit in the field
of enquiry or experiment. In this chapter we shall consider some
cases which support this possibility.

A few words may be appropriate at this point about the use of
certain terms. Is there any meaning in talking of consciousness
being in one point of space as distinct from another ? Is not consciousness extra-spatial ? Where is consciousness ? There is no

doubt that the term is used ambiguously, and we shall therefore state the sense in which for the future we shall use it. Consciousness is a fundamental idea which cannot be defined—yet without it nothing else can be defined. It is unlike all else in that it is at once subject and object. It is, and it knows that it is. To talk of perceptions, feelings, thoughts, memories, etc., as the stream of consciousness, is wrong : they are a stream of experience. Consciousness, or the " I ", is conscious only of itself, but it is *aware* of that which constitutes the not-self. Perceptions, feelings, thoughts and memories are parts of " I's " experience ; they are an intimate part of it, for they constitute his empirical self or personality or Ego. His central, unchanging, transcendental self or essence is what we have called " I " or the true Self. The " I ", then, is conscious of itself and aware of the not-Self. (The term self-consciousness might have been used for the first, and " consciousness of " for the second, but we shall strictly avoid doing this.) " Consciousness belongs to the order of the ' One ' and awareness to the order of the ' Many '," says Warner Allen.* To sum up, then, we shall use the following terms as equivalent : Consciousness, " I ", the true Self. On the other hand, the sum of memories, thoughts and experiences will be designated by such terms as the Ego, the empirical self, the personality. The relations of the true Self and the Ego are discussed in a later chapter (17 (1)).

An answer to our questions can now be attempted. Consciousness by its very nature is not *in* space at all. It is true, if properly understood, to say rather that all space is contained *in it* ; for space is only a concept of great practical convenience in our everyday life. Because of the increasing degree of limitation placed upon an aspect of consciousness as it enwraps itself in the many structures of the self— the mind, the psychic æther, and finally organic matter—it does become aware of that which is other than itself at a particular point of space and time. This limitation, indeed, seems to me the only process by which the Self could initially become aware of the not-Self at all. Such awareness can be moved about in space by movement of the physical organism, as we do when we travel : it also appears that it can be transferred from one place to another by a process which seems to be a temporary withdrawal from the physical organism. We shall look at the evidence for this now.

* I am indebted to Warner Allen's book *The Timeless Moment*, Chapter I (Faber & Faber, 1946) for much clarification of these terms. It is important, however, to note that my own use of " Ego " as equivalent to the empirical self is quite different from his. I have made this use of it because of the association of Ego with Egotism which has to be outgrown on the spiritual path.

2. INVOLUNTARY TRANSFER OF FULL AWARENESS

Case 1. *Sir Auckland Geddes.** In an address to the Royal Society of Medicine on February 26th, 1927, entitled " A Voice from the Grandstand ", Sir Auckland Geddes gave the experience of a man for whom he vouches. Tyrrell's abridged version is here given :

" On Saturday 9th November, a few minutes after midnight, I began to feel very ill, and by two o'clock was definitely suffering from acute gastro-enteritis, which kept me vomiting and purging until about eight o'clock. . . . By ten o'clock I had developed all the symptoms of acute poisoning ; intense gastro-intestinal pain, diarrhœa ; pulse and respirations became quite impossible to count, I wanted to ring for assistance, but found I could not, and so quite placidly gave up the attempt. I realised I was very ill and very quickly reviewed my whole financial position. Thereafter at no time did my consciousness appear to me to be in any way dimmed, but I suddenly realised that *my* consciousness was separating from another consciousness which was also me. These, for purposes of description, we could call the A- and B-consciousnesses, and throughout what follows the ego attached itself to the A-consciousness. The B-personality I recognised as belonging to the body, and as my physical condition grew worse and the heart was fibrillating rather than beating, I realised that the B-consciousness belonging to the body was beginning to show signs of being composite—that is, built up of ' consciousness ' from the head, the heart and the viscera. These components became more individual and the B-consciousness began to disintegrate, while the A-consciousness, which was now me, seemed to be altogether outside my body, which it could see. Gradually I realised that I could see, not only my body and the bed in which it was, but everything in the whole house and garden, and then realised that I was seeing, not only ' things ' at home but in London and in Scotland, in fact wherever my attention was directed, it seemed to me ; and the explanation which I received, from what source I do not know, but which I found myself calling to myself my mentor, was that I was free in a time-dimension of space, wherein ' now ' was in some way equivalent to ' here ' in the ordinary three-dimensional space of everyday life."

The narrator then says that his further experiences can only be described metaphorically, for, although he seemed to have two-eyed vision, he " appreciated " rather than " saw " things. He began to recognise people he knew, and they seemed to be characterised by coloured condensations around them.

" Just as I began to grasp all these," he continues, " I saw ' A ' enter my bedroom ; I realised she got a terrible shock and I saw her hurry to the telephone. I saw my doctor leave his patients and come very quickly, and heard him say, or saw him think, ' He is nearly gone.' I heard him quite clearly speaking to me on the bed, but I was not in touch with my body and could not answer him.

* Tyrrell : *The Personality of Man*, pp. 197-8 (Pelican Books).

I was really cross when he took a syringe and rapidly injected my body with something which I afterwards learned was camphor. As the heart began to beat more strongly, I was drawn back, and I was intensely annoyed, because I was so interested and just beginning to understand where I was and what I was 'seeing'. I came back into the body really angry at being pulled back, and once I was back, all the clarity of vision of anything and everything disappeared and I was just possessed of a glimmer of consciousness, which was suffused with pain."

*Case 2. F. S. Smythe.** This is abbreviated from an account of his own experience. The late Mr. Smythe was a distinguished mountaineer, and his books will be known to many readers. He was climbing in the Dolomites with a friend E. E. Roberts.

" It was a perfect morning, a morning on which to enjoy the beauty of creation, a morning on which to realise to the full the supreme joy of health and life. . . . A sudden startled shout, a frightful crash of falling rocks, a convulsive leap and jerk of every nerve and muscle, an instinctive bracing of every bone of my whole body to receive a shock.

" A few instants before, the rope had lain idly against the rock or slid gently upwards as I took it in. Now, like a sleeping snake stirred by a stick, it sprang into furious activity. It whipped, as though alive, across the rocks to the right, and I realised in the fraction of a second that it took to do so that Roberts was not directly beneath me and that the strain would come sideways as well as downwards; it tightened in my hands and tore cruelly through them, it tugged at my shoulder and body, tugged irresistibly, and snatched me from my holds as casually and easily as a man brushes an insect from his cheek. In another moment I was sliding down the slabs, at first on my side, then on my back, driving my heels, elbows, forearms and palms of my hands against the rocks in an endeavour to stop myself. For 10 or 12 feet I slid thus, then shot over the edge of the precipice.

" I remember no jerk, but I found myself hanging on the rope a few feet below the crest of the ridge. I turned, snatched at the rocks and clawed my way back to the ridge. I had fallen altogether about 20 feet, and the rope, which was a comparatively new one, had held.

" I had scarcely regained the ridge when I heard Roberts's voice. He was safe and sound. . . .

" So much for events. I will now describe in detail my feelings from the moment when danger intervened to the moment when I found myself oscillating on the rope against the face of the precipice.

" When I heard Roberts's shout and the crash of falling rocks, my body, as already described, instinctively braced itself to receive a shock. The shock came; I was unable to resist it, and found myself on my back sliding and bumping helplessly down the slabs of the ridge. Now, one half of my brain must have known subconsciously

* F. S. Smythe : *The Spirit of the Hills*, pp. 277–8 (Hodder & Stoughton, 1937).

that 20 feet of slack rope separated me from the belay, but if it did know this, it was singularly reticent on the subject, and it was the other half that took charge, and this told me that I had been secured close to the belay, that the rope had come off and that I was certain to be killed. In view of my subsequent sensations, the certainty which existed in my mind that nothing could stop me falling and that I was to be killed, is interesting and important. Nevertheless, even though I had assumed thus early that I was as good as dead, I made desperate attempts to stop myself, as I have already described. During the time that I was doing this, a curious rigidity or tension gripped my whole mental and physical being. So great was this tension that it swamped all pain and fear, and rendered me insensible to bumps and blows. It was an overwhelming sensation, and quite outside my experience. It was as though all life's forces were in process of undergoing some fundamental evolutionary change, the change called death, which is normally beyond imagination and outside the range of ordinary human force or power. Think of the force required to knit an atom, and the equal and opposite force required to split that atom. What an experience for that atom to have such vast forces concentrated on its evolution—the supreme power of the universe concentrated to one end. I was the atom on the Gröhmannspitze, and I felt that power which alone can separate spirit from body—death. I know now that death is not to be feared, it is a supreme experience, the climax, not the anti-climax, of life.

" For how long I experienced this crescendo of power I cannot say. Time no longer existed as time; it was replaced by a sequence of events from which time as a quantity or quality in terms of human consciousness no longer existed. Then, suddenly, this feeling was superseded by a feeling of complete indifference and detachment, indifference to what happened to my body, detachment from what was happening or likely to happen to that body. I seemed to stand aside from my body. I was not falling, for the reason that I was not in a dimension where it was possible to fall. I, that is my consciousness, was apart from my body, and not in the least concerned with what was befalling it. My body was in the process of being injured, crushed and pulped, and my consciousness was not associated with these physical injuries, and was completely uninterested in them. Had the tenant already departed in anticipation of the wreck that was to follow ? Had the assumption of death—when my slide was not checked by the rope I assumed death as certain—resulted in a partial dissolution of the spiritual and physical ? Was it merely a mental effect due to a sudden and intense nervous strain ? It is not within my province to discuss that which only death can prove; yet to me this experience was a convincing one; it convinced me that consciousness survives beyond the grave."

Case 3. This is one of several similar cases given in the *Journal of the Society for Psychical Research* recently.

" I was stationed in Aden in 1913 and was seriously ill with dysentery. I got to the stage of having to be lifted from side to side,

as I was too weak to move myself in bed.   From the instructions I
heard the M.O. give the orderlies (we had no nurses in Aden then)
I gathered that a collapse was expected and that in the event of the
occurrence I was to be given a saline injection via the rectum.

" Shortly afterwards, I found myself lying parallel to the bed, about
three or four feet above it and face downwards.   Below me I saw my
body and witnessed the giving of the rectal injection.   I listened to
all the conversation of the two orderlies and of a strange M.O. who
was directing affairs and was indeed a very interested spectator of the
whole business.   I remember well that the saline came from an
enamel kind of vessel which was connected to a rubber tube—the
vessel being held up at arm's length by an orderly.

" I found myself next back in bed, feeling much better.   I told my
story to the orderlies, who were quite sceptical.   I particularly
enquired about the strange M.O.   I found there had been one ;
he was en route for Bombay, I think, and had called at the hospital in
time to help.   I never saw him again.

" I have always been convinced that my spirit (or soul if you will)
had actually left my body but returned as a result of the injection.
When kindred subjects have cropped up I have told friends of my
experience.   They have listened in a tolerant fashion, but I have
always felt that my story was really being received ' with nods and
becks and wreathed smiles '.   You may imagine then how delighted
I was to hear you narrate an almost similar experience—and I sat
down immediately and wrote to you. . . .

" On reading the above I find I have omitted to mention that the
orderlies said I couldn't possibly have any knowledge of the matter,
as I was quite unconscious before and after the operation."

Case 4 * is related by an army Colonel.

" Six years ago I had pneumonia and pleurisy combined, and I
remember the doctor saying (whilst in my room) that he could do no
more and I must fight it out myself.   I cannot think I was supposed
to hear this aside.   With what strength I had, I pinched myself and said,
' You *shall* get better '.   Now this was the crisis.   I feel quite certain
that I left my body.   I felt it getting heavier and heavier and sinking
into the bed.   I was sitting on top of a high wardrobe near the door
looking down on my bed at myself, and the nurse sitting by me.
I was disgusted at my unshaven appearance.   I saw everything in the
room—the mirror on the dressing-table and all small details.   Fear
was absent entirely.   The next thing I remember was my nurse
holding my hand and shortly afterwards heard her say, ' The crisis
has passed.'

" Some time after all this, I told the nurse what had happened to
me, described what she was doing at the time and the details of the
room.   She said I was given up and that it was because I was
delirious.

" No, I was dead for that time, but made myself go back."

* *Jour. S.P.R.*, Vol. 34, pp. 206–11 (1948).

Case 5.* *Wilmot.* This frequently quoted case was checked as far as possible. Here is Mr. Wilmot's account.

" On October 3rd, 1863, I sailed from Liverpool for New York, on the steamer ' City of Limerick ', of the Inman line, Captain Jones commanding. On the evening of the second day out, soon after leaving Kinsale Head, a severe storm began, which lasted for nine days. During this time we saw neither sun nor stars nor any vessel ; the bulwarks on the weather bow were carried away, one of the anchors broke loose from its lashings, and did considerable damage before it could be secured, and several stout storm sails, though closely reefed, were carried away, and the booms broken.

" Upon the night following the eighth day of the storm the tempest moderated a little, and for the first time since leaving port I enjoyed refreshing sleep. Toward morning I dreamed that I saw my wife, whom I had left in the United States, come to the door of my state-room, clad in her night-dress. At the door she seemed to discover that I was not the only occupant of the room, hesitated a little, then advanced to my side, stooped down and kissed me, and after gently caressing me for a few moments, quietly withdrew.

" Upon waking I was surprised to see my fellow-passenger, whose berth was above mine—but not directly over it, owing to the fact that our room was at the stern of the vessel—leaning upon his elbow, and looking fixedly at me. ' You're a pretty fellow ', said he at length, ' to have a lady come and visit you in this way.' I pressed him for an explanation, which he at first declined to give, but at length related what he had seen while wide awake, lying in his berth. It exactly corresponded with my dream.

" This gentleman's name was William J. Tait, and he had been my room-mate in the passage out, in the preceding July, on the Cunard steamer ' Olympus '. A native of England, and son of a clergyman of the Established Church, he had for a number of years lived in Cleveland, in the State of Ohio, where he held the position of librarian of the Associated Library. He was at this time perhaps fifty years of age, by no means in the habit of practical joking, but a sedate and very religious man, whose testimony upon any subject could be taken unhesitatingly.

" The incident seemed so strange to me that I questioned him about it, and upon three separate occasions, the last one shortly before reaching port, Mr. Tait repeated to me the same account of what he had witnessed. On reaching New York we parted, and I never saw him afterward, but I understand that he died a number of years ago in Cleveland.

" The day after landing I went by rail to Watertown, Conn., where my children and my wife had been for some time, visiting her parents. Almost her first question when we were alone together was, ' Did you receive a visit from me a week ago Tuesday ? ' ' A visit from you ? ' said I, ' we were more than a thousand miles at sea.' ' I know it,' she replied, ' but it seemed to me that I visited you.' ' It would be impossible,' said I. ' Tell me what makes you think so.'

* *Proc. S.P.R.*, Vol. 7, p. 41 ; or *Human Personality*, Vol. I, pp. 682–5.

" My wife then told me that on account of the severity of the weather and the reported loss of the ' Africa ', which sailed for Boston on the same day that we left Liverpool for New York, and had gone ashore at Cape Race, she had been extremely anxious about me. On the night previous, the same night when, as mentioned above, the storm had just begun to abate, she had lain awake for a long time thinking of me, and about four o'clock in the morning it seemed to her that she went out to seek me. Crossing the wide and stormy sea, she came at length to a low, black steamship, whose side she went up, and then descending into the cabin, passed through it to the stern until she came to my stateroom. ' Tell me,' said she, ' do they ever have staterooms like the one I saw, where the upper berth extends further back than the under one ? A man was in the upper berth, looking right at me, and for a moment I was afraid to go in, but soon I went up to the side of your berth, bent down and kissed you, and embraced you, and then went away.'

" The description given by my wife of the steamship was correct in all particulars, though she had never seen it."

Mrs. Wilmot in reply to a question said " I know that I had a very vivid sense all the day of having visited my husband ; the impression was so strong that I felt unusually happy and refreshed to my surprise."

The shipping information was checked with the files of the *New York Herald*, and Mr. Hodgson got into touch with both Mr. and Mrs. Wilmot and Mr. Wilmot's sister, who was on the ship with him. Miss Wilmot remembered Mr. Tait asking her if she had been to see her brother—and on her replying in the negative, told her what he had seen.

The cases 1, 3 and 4 were all produced by extreme illness, fever or weakness of the body. Case 2 was provoked by the intense shock and anticipation of immediate death. Case 5 differs in several interesting points. The originating cause seems to have been the extreme anxiety in Mrs. Wilmot's mind, and the projection was accompanied by a sense of travelling with full consciousness. The most interesting point, however, is that she was visible to her husband in a dream and to his companion, Mr. Tait, who was wide awake. We shall postpone discussion of the implications of this until we have surveyed all the typical cases.

I give below one more case out of a wide range of choice. It is one of Prof. E. Bozzano's cases and was experienced by Guiseppe Costa, a distinguished engineer.

Case 6. " It was an airless torrid night of June, when I was working hard for my examinations. . . . I had been obliged to yield, completely exhausted, to an imperative need for repose, and had thrown myself on the bed, fainting rather than asleep, without extinguishing the paraffin lamp. An unconscious movement of my arm probably overturned the lamp between the table and the bed,

H

and instead of going out it gave off a dense smoke which filled the room with a black cloud of heavy, acrid gas. . . . I had the clear and precise sensation of finding myself, with only my thinking personality, in the middle of the room, completely separated from my body, which continued to lie on the bed.   I saw—if I may call by that name the sensation I experienced—the objects around me as though a visual radiation penetrated the molecules of the objects on which my attention rested, as if matter dissolved at the contact of thought.   I saw my body perfectly recognisable in all details, the profile, the figure, but with the clusters of veins and nerves vibrating like a swarm of luminous living atoms. . . . I saw the objects, or rather their almost phosphorescent outlines, melt together with the walls, under the concentration of my attention, allowing me to see in the same manner the objects in the neighbouring rooms.   My thinking self was without weight, or rather without the impression of the forces of gravity or the notion of volume or mass.   I was no longer in the body, since my body lay inert on the bed; I was like the tangible expression of a thought, an abstraction, capable of transferring itself to any part of the earth, sea or sky more swiftly than lightning, in the same instant that I formulated the wish, and therefore without any notion of time and space.

" If I were to say I felt free, light, ethereal, I should not express at all adequately the sensation I experienced in that moment of boundless liberation.   But it was not a pleasant sensation : I was seized with an inexpressible anguish from which I felt instinctively that I could only free myself by freeing my material body from that oppressive situation.   I wanted therefore to pick up the lamp and open the window, but it was a material act that I could not accomplish, as I could not move the limbs of my body, which I felt should move with the breath of my spiritual will.

" Then I thought of my mother, who was sleeping in the next room.   I saw her clearly through the dividing partition, quietly asleep in her bed ; but her body, unlike mine, seemed to emanate a luminosity, a radiant phosphorescence.   It seemed to me that no effort of any kind was needed to cause her to approach my body.   I saw her get hurriedly out of bed, run to the window and open it, as if carrying out my last thought before calling her ; then leave her room, walk along the corridor, enter my room and approach my body gropingly and with staring eyes.   It seemed as though her contact possessed the faculty of causing my spiritual self to re-enter my body ; and I found myself awake with parched throat, throbbing temples, and difficult breathing, while my heart seemed to be bursting in my chest."   The narrator rules out any possibility of suggestion as responsible for the experience, and continues, " Neither could it have been a dream . . . because never have I had so vivid a sensation of existing in reality as in the moment when I felt myself separated from the body.   My mother questioned by me soon after the event, confirmed the fact that she had first opened the window, as if she felt herself suffocating, before coming to my aid.   Now the fact of my having seen this act of hers through the wall while lying inanimate on the bed entirely excludes the hypothesis of hallucination and nightmare during sleep."

The detail of these observations by a careful observer with a scientific training makes this account particularly interesting and valuable. William Gerhardi in his book *Resurrection* and Arnold Bennett in *The Glimpse* give experiences of their own which all have a remarkable degree of consistency about them.

3. INVOLUNTARY DIVIDED AWARENESS

Below are given two cases which do not differ in principle from the previous group, but where it appears from the account that some slight measure of control of the bodily structure was still retained.

*Case 7.** " I was an armoured-car officer engaged in medium- and long-range reconnaissance work with the 21st Army Group. At about 2.30 p.m. on August 3rd, 1944, I was in a small armoured scout car which received a direct hit from a German anti-tank gun. Our car, which was full of various explosives, grenades, phosphorus bombs, etc., blew up. I might mention that it was stationary at the time, having just halted. The force of the explosion threw me about twenty feet away from the car and over a five-foot hedge. My clothes, etc., were on fire, and there were various pieces of phosphorus sticking to me which were also burning. Now my immediate reaction to the explosion, which appeared to me from the middle of it like a great white cold sheet, with a strong smell of cordite, was (naturally enough) fear. I imagined for a split second that I had gone to hell, and I quickly tried to recollect some particular vice which might have been my qualification. It is interesting to notice that I did not see any rapid ' trailer ' of my past life as, I believe, drowning persons report. All this took a fraction of a second, and the next experience was definitely unusual. I was conscious of being two persons—one, lying on the ground in a field where I had fallen from the blast, my clothes, etc., on fire, and waving my limbs about wildly, at the same time uttering moans and gibbering with fear—I was quite conscious of both making these sounds, and at the same time hearing them as though coming from another person. The other ' me ' was floating up in the air, about twenty feet from the ground, from which position I could see not only my other self on the ground, but also the hedge, the road, and the car which was surrounded by smoke and burning fiercely. I remember quite distinctly telling myself, ' It's no use gibbering like that—roll over and over to put the flames out.' This my ground body eventually did, rolling over into a ditch under the hedge where there was a slight amount of water. The flames went out, and at this stage I suddenly became one person again.

" Of course, the aerial viewpoint can be explained up to a point as a ' photograph ' taken subconsciously as I was passing over the hedge as a result of the blast. This, however, does not explain the fact that I saw ' myself ' on the ground quite clearly and for what

* Loc. cit., *Jour. S.P.R.*, Vol. 34, p. 207, 1948.

seemed a long time, though it could not have been more than a minute or so.

" Naturally there can be no witnesses as to this, and the fact that I have told the occurrence to a number of people since, might have led me to exaggeration of those details—though I do not think this is the case. I can still remember all the details quite clearly as they happened at the time."

Case 8. *N. F. Ellison.**   Mr. Ellison sent this account of his personal experience to Sir Oliver Lodge.

" The worst trenches we had ever been in. No repairs had been done to them for months and months. At worst, they had collapsed inwards and did not give head-shelter ; at best they were a trough of liquid muck. H. and I in the same traverse and straight away on sentry duty. We were both too utterly fed up even to curse. Bodily exhausted, sodden and chilled to the bone with icy sleet, hungry and without rations or the means of lighting a fire to boil a dixey of water ; not a dry square inch to sit upon, let alone a square foot of shelter beneath which to have the solace of a pipe, we agreed that this was the worst night of concentrated physical discomfort we had come across hitherto—and neither of us were strangers to discomfort.

" Several hours of this misery passed and then an amazing change came over me. I became conscious, acutely conscious, that I was outside myself ; that the real ' me '—the ego, spirit or what you like—was entirely separate and outside my fleshly body. I was look-ing in a wholly detached and impersonal way, upon the discomforts of a khaki-clad body, which, whilst I realised that it was my own, might easily have belonged to somebody else for all the direct con-nection I seemed to have with it. I knew that my body must be feeling acutely cold and miserable, but I, my spirit part, felt nothing.

" At the time it seemed a very natural happening—as the impossi-bilities of a dream seem right and natural to the dreamer—and it was only afterwards that I came to the realisation that I had been through one of the most wonderful experiences of my life.

" In the morning H. remarked to me upon my behaviour during the night. For a long time I had been grimly silent and then suddenly changed. My wit and humour under such trying circumstances, had amazed him. I had chatted away as unconcernedly as if we had been warm and comfortable before a roaring fire—' as if there was no war on ' were his exact words I remember.

" I never mentioned a word to H. or to anybody else about my spiritual adventure that night. He would not have understood and would have laughed at it all, but nothing will shake my inward belief and knowledge that on this particular night my soul and body were entirely separated from each other."

In Case 7 the projected self retained enough control over the separated body to cause it to roll over into the ditch. In Case 8 the projected self was able to maintain the body presumably in its normal attitudes and use it as the vehicle of speech.

* *Jour. S.P.R.*, Vol. 25, p. 126.

Case 9. Miss M. A. B.* This lady had to undergo a slight operation, and ether was being administered. Her brother had recently died, and she says :

" Almost at once I had the strong idea, ' This is what brother felt like when he died. I won't die. I won't.' I struggled violently so that two nurses and the specialist were unable to hold me, and were obliged to hurry for chloroform and try that. . . . The next thing I knew was some piercing screaming going on, that I was up in the air and looking down upon the bed over which the nurses and doctor were bending.

" What specially struck me, and remains particularly in my mind, were the white crosses on the nurses' backs, where the bands of their white uniforms cross at the back. I was aware that they were trying in vain to stop the screaming, in fact I heard them say : ' Miss B., Miss B., don't scream like this. You are frightening the other patients.' At the same time I knew very well that I was quite apart from my screaming body, which I could do nothing to stop. I said to myself, ' Those silly idiots ! if they had but enough sense to send for E. (a great friend of mine waiting below in the hospital), I know she could stop it.'

" And just then the strangest thing happened. At my thought that was exactly what they did ! One of the nurses rushed downstairs and begged her to come up. She touched my physical body, spoke to me, and immediately the screaming ceased. . . . In a short time I was physically conscious again."

It is as well to admit that we do not know enough to attempt an explanation of such a group of facts. The increased facility for using telepathy, and the immediate effectiveness of it in the projected state will be noted, however. Many other cases demonstrate this feature. There are also quite a number of recorded cases where the administration of anæsthetics was the cause of projected awareness. The particular anæsthetic used, and some peculiarity of the person anæsthetised, appear, however, to give rise to very varying results. Thus William James † has recorded instances where consciousness has been liberated from the enfolding structures resulting in a definite *mystical* experience ; a mode of separation quite different from those we have described above.

4. VOLUNTARY PROJECTION : MULDOON'S WORK

One of the most interesting of circumstantial accounts of out-of-the-body experience is that of Sylvan J. Muldoon, given in his books *The Projection of the Astral Body* (1929) and *The Case for Astral*

* From H. F. P. Battersby : *Man outside Himself*, p. 56 (Rider & Co.).
† William James : *Varieties of Religious Experience*, p. 389 (Longmans, Green & Co., 1943).

Projection.*   It is a record of many years of experimenting, and bears the stamp of being a true and simple account of personal experience. Dr. Hereward Carrington wrote an introduction to the first book. The account given is very detailed, but some attempt must be made to give an impression of Muldoon's work.   Among other things, he claims to be able, at will, to leave his physical body, which then lies inert upon the bed, and to retain full consciousness in a subtler vehicle.   He claims to become aware of events and things while in this subtle body of which he had previously no knowledge, and later to be able to verify the facts.   On some occasions he claims that while in this subtle body he has moved physical objects.   He gives, moreover, details about the mechanism of projection which should enable others who desire to experiment in this field to attempt the same thing.   The literature of the subject, such as it is, is given in Dr. Carrington's introduction to Muldoon's book—and I shall not attempt to review it here.

Muldoon says that in sleep it is normal for the " astral body " to be displaced slightly out of coincidence with the physical body—since by so doing the former can charge itself with vital energy more freely. He remarks that many people must occasionally have had the experience, when waking up, of coming to consciousness, but finding themselves cataleptic—that is, temporarily paralysed—and unable to move their physical body.

Most people get fearful at this, and a conscious desire soon passes down to what Muldoon calls the " subconscious will " and produces normal alignment of the " astral " and physical bodies.   If, instead, the emotion of fear or alarm is controlled, and the person thinks of rising slowly upwards towards the ceiling, Muldoon says that the exteriorising process may continue.   The process he describes is slow ; the phantom or astral body is rigid, and remains so during the process.   It rises to from 3 to 6 feet above the body—in a horizontal position, then moves feet forward, and finally begins to take the vertical position with a swaying motion.   He says that there is an astral cable or cord linking together the heads of the physical and astral body—of great elasticity.   This exerts a considerable pull or control up to a variable range of about 8 to 15 feet.   Once outside this range there is a feeling of freedom, but the cord is always present, even though quite thin, and it retains the same thickness indefinitely. This " astral body ", he maintains is the exact duplicate of the physical.   While within cord-activity range, a deep breath in the astral body will produce an identical breath in the physical.   If the

* Muldoon and Carrington : *The Projection of the Astral Body* (Rider, 1929) ; Muldoon : *The Case for Astral Projection* (Aries Press, 1936).

person is conscious at *this stage*, considerable control of all emotion and effort of will is necessary to get outside the cord-activity range. Fear, or a noise, or any emotion will bring back the astral body into the physical with great rapidity, and a rather violent shock may result which he calls repercussion.

Dreams of falling and of flying through the air are, in Muldoon's view, occasioned by the sensations of interiorisation of the projected astral body, and I shall mention shortly the technique which Muldoon suggests for causing projection. Once the astral body gets to the limit of cord-activity range, the deeper mind apparently frees the astral body from the catalepsy characteristic within this range. If it is released from catalepsy within this range, it finds itself staggering or swaying badly.

The sense of touch, so far as material objects are concerned, is not felt by the astral body, which can pass through solid objects, but Muldoon says that within cord-activity range any movement of, or thing touching the physical body is felt as if experienced by the astral body. He cites an occasion when his dog jumped up on the bed while he was exteriorised within cord-activity range. This resulted in oscillations of the astral body, which were then followed by the sense of pressure against the side of the astral body.

Muldoon says that it is possible to " dream " of moving an object and actually to do so, such movement being delayed some two seconds after the dream action. He is disposed to think that some type of energy can be externalised and used as a rod. Clearly we are here coming to the field of psycho-kinetic or poltergeist phenomena, about which we shall speak later.

Once the astral body has moved beyond cord-activity range it is free, and no longer liable to eccentricity of the senses, instability of the body, etc. The cable then diminishes to a fine, thread-like structure and, as might be expected, the flow of energy from the astral to the physical body is greatly reduced.

Muldoon says that where projection is distant and prolonged the physical body may almost have the appearance of being dead, and may undergo a substantial temperature fall—a phenomenon closely resembling hibernation in animals. If the projector tries to stay away too long, he finds that he cannot retain consciousness in the astral body. The deeper mind is obviously in control of the situation, with a greater wisdom than the superficial mind. Muldoon says he has noticed himself brought back at intervals to within cord-activity, when, of course, the larger cable permits stronger respiration of the physical body. If we are to believe the accounts of yogis and fakirs, being buried alive for periods of up to thirty days, and being resuscitated by their friends at the end of such periods, it is to be presumed that it is achieved by some such projection of the astral body.

Death of the physical body is presumably caused by the severance of the astral cord.

It appears that in the majority of cases of astral projection, whether there is consciousness associated with the vehicle or not, is a matter of chance. It seems that where consciousness appears in the astral state, a good deal of energy is used up, and the projector feels very tired after the experience. On the other hand, astral projection without awareness is said to be very refreshing. While Muldoon found it sometimes possible to have full awareness from the beginning of exteriorisation, more commonly the earlier part was achieved in sleep, and awareness emerged only outside cord-activity range as the result of a special sort of dream. When dreaming, says Muldoon, we are partially conscious on the astral plane. The body in sleep is always to some extent out of coincidence with the astral body, and we are in some degree of correspondence with both the physical and astral planes. It is through the reception of impressions from both these planes that many dreams originate. The dream-state lies between complete consciousness and complete unconsciousness on the astral level. If you dream, therefore, while projected, it is only a question of the right step to secure consciousness there.

Muldoon says, on the basis of his experience, that when the action of the dream corresponds to the action of the astral body, the dream causes the latter to exteriorise. The clue to projection is, then, what might be called " dreaming true ". Presumably the semi-conscious mind of the dreamer uses the dream to convey a " suggestion " to the subconscious will, which then displaces the astral body. If, however, the physical body is not already sufficiently incapacitated by being slightly displaced from the " astral body ", then somnambulism will result instead of projection. This, then, is the technique :

1. For some nights practise watching yourself during going to sleep. Try to keep a state of awareness right up to the last minute.

2. Construct now a dream, and hold this in mind while going to sleep. The dream constructed must be one in which you are active, and moreover one in which the action gone through corresponds to the route taken by the astral body when first projected. (It should consist of movement upwards and forwards.) It should be as pleasant and enjoyable as possible ; for example, the dream might be of lying on your back—in an elevator, which starts to rise slowly. At the top you are going to get to your feet, walk out of the elevator, look out and walk

around—enjoying everything; then reverse the procedure. The same dream must be used over and over again. The idea is that you should begin to dream this just as the transition to sleep comes over you. It is important to plan a pleasant dream.

3. To bring about consciousness in the projected phantom it is necessary to use suggestion and to pre-determine that in a particular place in the dream, you will wake up. Muldoon says that especially with the nervous, temperamental person, many dreams of a vivid kind in which we seem to be active are astral somnambulistic dreams, and by identifying these and planning in advance to wake up at a given place in the dream, consciousness may arise.

Muldoon goes into a great deal of detail on the precise conditions which favour success. The fundamental law of projection he states thus: " When the subconscious will becomes possessed of the idea to move the body [i.e., the coinciding bodies], and the physical body is incapacitated, the subconscious will moves the astral body out of the physical." Habit, Desire and Dream, says Muldoon, are the three factors which can, in certain circumstances, produce enough stress to bring about astral projection—just as they may give rise to physical somnambulism if the physical body is insufficiently incapacitated. The incapacitation—as Muldoon calls it—of the physical body is facilitated by slowing down the heart rate, which can be done by auto-suggestion. I suggest that anyone proposing to experiment in this field would do well to study the detailed experience of Muldoon set out at length in several chapters.

The impression left on the reader's mind will, I think, be that we are in fact dealing with genuine experiences—of a kind which many others have described. But whereas the majority were uncontrolled experiences associated with shock or extreme weakness of the body, Muldoon's were controlled and experimental, and they are, I think, worthy of study for the light they throw on the structure of the human individual.

We have used the term " astral body " without comment: we shall consider its significance later.

5. VOLUNTARY PROJECTION: WORK OF OTHERS

We shall conclude in this section a survey of a few typical experiences of others, before we ask ourselves how the facts are to be interpreted. Oliver Fox * has written a book which is worthy of study.

* Oliver Fox: *Astral rojection* (Rider & Co., 1939).

His first projection was associated with a dream at the age of sixteen. He dreamed he was standing outside his home, and noticed that the paving-stones were not set as he remembered them. In his dream he then *realised* he was dreaming, and with this realisation the quality of the dream changed to one of intense awareness. He says :

> " Instantly the vividness of life increased a hundredfold. Never had the sea and sky and trees shone with such glamorous beauty, even the commonplace houses seemed alive and mystically beautiful. Never had I felt so absolutely well, so clear-brained, so divinely powerful, so inexpressibly *free !* The sensation was exquisite beyond words, but it lasted only a few minutes and I awoke. . . ."

He came to realise that one method of projection was to make the discovery in a dream that he was dreaming, by keeping a measure of the critical faculty awake to detect some incongruity. He discovered that he was unable to stay out of his body very long without the gradual development of a pain in the head. He observed in the last phase of prolonging the experience, when the pain was considerable, that he had dual consciousness. " I could feel myself standing in the dream and see the scenery ; but at the same time I could feel myself lying in bed and see my bedroom."

About a year later, with considerable courage, he tried the experiment of enduring the pain and willing to remain out. A point was reached where he seemed to hear a " click ", the pain vanished and he was free from the pull of his body. He found himself walking on the sea-shore half a mile from his home ; people were walking past him, and he tried to stop one man to ask him the time, but could not attract his attention. He found, to his alarm, that willing to return to his body had at first no effect, and it was only after great effort that he seemed to hear again a " click " and found himself in his body—but paralysed. This cataleptic state alarmed him, and only by further intense effort was he able to get his muscles working again. He later found that when awaking in the cataleptic state, he had only to doze off again to find himself normal on waking.

On one occasion, experimenting with chloroform, he noticed clearly the silver thread which appeared to link him with his physical body, and he had a sense of dual consciousness. He remarks, " When I spoke, it seemed to me that my words travelled down the thread and were then spoken by my physical self—but the process was instantaneous." Mr. Fox subsequently found two other methods of projection which he calls the use of the " Pineal Door " and " Instantaneous Projection ". These different methods appeared to provide him with slightly different kinds of experience, into the detail of which it is unnecessary to go here. In some circumstances he was at the mercy of " currents " which would sweep him away to places he did not know; at other times this was rare. Sometimes he was visible to persons he met and could converse with them; at other times he was invisible! On some occasions he could stay away from his body for a longer time than at others.

Yram,* a French investigator, appears to have had considerable natural facility for projection, and remarks on the possibility of projecting a " double " of very varying density, so that under some conditions physical objects (such as a wall) could not be penetrated, while under others there was no difficulty. His experience appears to have taken him to levels remote from the material world, but he confirms the general views of Muldoon and Fox about the less remote levels.

" After having roamed about in space, I came back close to my physical body, and without completely reincorporating myself, I found myself at the exact point of balance where the anatomical sensitivity passes into the next body or plane. By a mere act of will I found myself able to incline the balance towards one point or the other. . . . As soon as I brought my mind back to my physical body the intensity of the projection diminished. My body was as heavy as lead and my breathing slowed down. . . . I could hear noises from the street. Taking my mind back towards the idea of projection, the equilibrium immediately went the other way. All these physical sensations disappeared with lightning-like speed. I once more found myself in the state I had just left, and began to enjoy the peace, the cool sweetness and the inexpressible sense of well-being of this state. The phenomenon is not therefore a state of sleep natural or induced. It has a clarity far superior to that of terrestrial life."

I propose to include only one further witness of this type of phenomenon. The extract below is from a book of Miss L. Margery Bazett.†

" There is another type of this clairvoyance which I shall call travelling clairvoyance; because when entirely quiescent one seems to move out of this physical body; in my experience, it felt like moving through and out of a tunnel, as a train does. I have undertaken this experiment only under the direction of an expert in these matters; it is not advisable to do so otherwise. As I experienced it, I found it most exhilarating; and I appeared to visit various parts of the globe in a surprisingly short time. I set forth on these visitations to other parts of the globe from a room that was dimly lighted, and at the time of the year when the weather was dull and over-clouded. Projecting myself to a distance in space, I was deeply interested to find myself in bright sunshine over the Mediterranean, looking down from a

* Yram: *Practical Astral Projection* (Rider & Co., 1935).
† L. Margery Bazett: *Beyond the Five Senses* (Blackwell, 1946).

considerable height on a beautiful city. I particularly noticed a magnificent church, which I could see in detail. I knew I was over the Mediterranean, though how I knew, I could not say; neither was I aware of other places en route; actual movement was my only sensation. . . . I was not moving in any ordinary way but rather felt as if I were floating. The keenest sense of adventure I experienced on another occasion, when after passing through the ' tunnel ' I arrived, so to speak, in the East; here again I knew that I was in Tibet. I mounted higher and higher until rocky landscape was observable everywhere. It was very dark, yet I noticed a few stars; and later, as I neared the summit, there was a clear sky, evidently at dawn. I came upon certain temples. . . . Deep meditation was taking place within; and I was exceedingly interested to see that according to the depth and quality of the meditation, so the figure created and radiated light of a rare character; with some, this was very marked. The darkened temple was lit by no lighting save the self-created lighting of each individual person. I remember, too, hearing the deep-toned bells that I believe are used in these temples; they, too, varied in depth and fineness of tone according to the quality of the meditation. Someone who knew Tibet was greatly interested in all that I had seen of it, and could corroborate the visions."

6. DISCUSSION OF THE DATA

When we were dealing with apparitions we had to rely on the evidence of human testimony and decide whether there was a sufficiently coherent body of facts. These " facts " were in the case of apparitions, sense-data—visual, auditory, tactile, etc. In the present chapter we have to consider another mass of human testimony and decide whether it is coherent and trustworthy. The data in this case are subjective; we are called to assess what people say they have experienced. We have, in fact, to determine two things : (1) Are the narrators telling the truth or telling lies ? and (2) If telling the truth, are they suffering from illusions ? (in the technical sense, of wrongly interpreting their experience). We are assisted to determine this by assessing the quality and variety of the narrators and the relative consistency of their descriptions. The latter is quite remarkable. In Cases 1, 3, 4, 6, 7, and 8, some fever, weakness or shock to the body preceded the experience, in Case 2, mental shock, and in Case 5 acute anxiety. The observations made independently and in common were that the physical body could be seen from outside, that while thus separated, persons were insensitive to pain in the latter, and that the experience out of the body was one of intense vividness and pleasantness. (Only in Case 6 was there an element of unpleasantness, arising, we may suppose, from the will-to-live and the danger of asphyxiation.) All convey a novel sense of freedom in space, and several of them demonstrate the immediate accessibility and effectiveness of telepathy and clairvoyance in the state of projection. Cases 1 and 6, as well as the accounts of Gerhardi and Arnold Bennett and most of the experimental projectors, refer to a quality of " vision " or apprehension which is sustained and vivid to a degree which impressed them when contrasted with normal vision in the body, but which might naturally be supposed to occur when the observing mind is not restricted by the organs of sense.

It might be urged that the knowledge of Mrs. Wilmot and Miss Bazett might be accessible to a well-developed clairvoyant faculty without there being any question of actual projection from their physical bodies. It *may* be so, but if others' testimony is convincing in the matter of out-of-the-body experiences, there seems no very good reason to deny the correctness of these two observers' sensations. The lines of explanation of Case 5, by Tyrrell's theory, would be as follows.* Mr. Wilmot was really the agent. He had the knowledge of the cabin shape, disposition of berths, presence of Mr. Tait, etc., and by an elaborate piece of constructional work between the mid-levels of the minds of Mr. and Mrs. Wilmot, this information was presented to her with hallucinatory vividness. A *different* hallucinatory percept by the same two minds, to which the mind of Mr. Tait was related, created the apparition of Mrs. Wilmot in the cabin. But Mrs. Wilmot was mistaken in believing she was present in the cabin in the proper sense, while Mr. Tait (and Mr. Wilmot) were mistaken in supposing she was in the proper sense " there ".

I find this explanation far-fetched; it requires the postulate that the *different* hallucinatory percepts were created simultaneously by the minds of Mr. and Mrs. Wilmot and each saw one of these. I would suggest rather that Mrs. Wilmot was the agent and that it was a case of projection such as others have described. This accords with her feeling of conviction, not that she had " seen " her husband merely, but that she had visited him. The rather unusual feature of the projection was that she was visible to Mr. Tait, who did not know what she looked like (although Mr. Wilmot did, with whose mind Mr. Tait's may have been *en rapport*). I do not deny to a " projected mind " the same facility for constructing apparitions in co-operation with another mind, as it might normally possess. I cannot, however, find any good reason for not supposing that the vehicle of Mrs. Wilmot's consciousness was itself made visible to the perception of Mr. Tait, in just the same way as created apparitions have been regarded hitherto as being made perceptible.

Looking at the whole evidential picture of this and the preceding

* Vide *Apparitions*: Myers Memorial Lecture, pp. 84-5.

chapter, it is obvious that they include data of profound significance for an understanding of the structure of the human self. In the present state of our knowledge (or ignorance), theorising must necessarily be tentative and speculative. Muldoon and other experimenters use the term "astral body", others use the term "ætheric double". There is a definite Hindu teaching of a subtle body which is the duplicate of the physical one, in some "finer substance". Those who have studied Theosophical ideas will be aware that Theosophists believe in several bodies, vehicles or principles of which a complete synthesis gives the human self. There is an almost inevitable scientific prejudice against beliefs held on any other grounds than that they constitute the minimum hypothesis necessary to explain the data of observation. We must, however, be courageous enough to accept suggestions from any quarter, as long as they keep this scientific principle firmly in mind, and offer us clues to the unification of so complex a field of enquiry.

It is difficult to formulate any hypothesis which does not look too definite, precise and material; we are faced with the use of words or diagrams which are only symbols, after all; and which are not particularly fitted to convey the ideas and concepts of those orders of reality which pertain to the non-physical self. Every description or diagram embodies concepts of space, time or matter, and leaves the thinker with what Whitehead called the sense of "misplaced concreteness". For my own part, I am convinced of the wisdom of Tyrrell's dictum, "There is no more fundamental way in which reality inheres in anything finite, than as an *aspect* of something which lies a step nearer to the absolutely real". The diagram used in Chapter 9 to convey the conception of individuals and their relatedness on different significant levels is obviously imperfect, but it is an attempt to convey the fact that the world of ultimate reality lies far above, and that successive worlds or strata as we move downwards are "aspects of" or "creations of" the one higher. We saw at the time that analysis of what we meant by perception of a material object led us to the conclusion that the whole supposedly material world is a construction of Mind.

The diagram below is not to be taken precisely or literally (certainly not spatially), and is intended only to be an indication of a way of thinking about the human self. The concentric circles represent different worlds, or levels, or planes of experience. They are of increasing remoteness from the ultimately real (6), as we move outwards. The flask-shaped loop represents an individual whose structure participates in all these worlds of varying significance. The level on which the individual is aware is determined by the flat termination.   This may be withdrawn from the physical level where it normally remains in the waking state.   In certain forms of clairvoyance it is withdrawn to the ætheric level ; in other clairvoyant states, farther still.   In light dreaming a measure of diffused awareness probably exists on the ætheric and astral levels ; in deep, dreamless sleep awareness is probably withdrawn to the mental level or thereabouts.   No memory of awareness on this level can be recovered in the waking state by an ordinary person.   The withdrawal of awareness to more interior levels than this is characteristic of mystical experience.

It is the level on which awareness is focused which determines what world will be described as objective : experience on levels interior to this will then be described as subjective.   This distinction is one of great

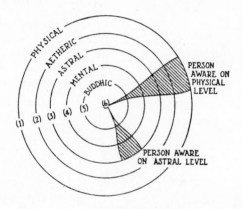

convenience, but it does not correspond to anything significant in the levels themselves : it describes only the relationship of an individual to these levels or worlds.

The shape of the individual loop is drawn to isolate different extents of each level, and illustrates thereby the different degrees of evolutionary development of the self on the several levels.   On the buddhic level, for example, little development is yet found in the ordinary person—though quite obviously individuals differ enormously.   I picture the ætheric world as a bridge-world having properties such as Professor Price describes intermediate between those of matter and mind.   (We are talking like this for the sake of clarity, having admitted that, on ultimate analysis, we believe the material world to be but an aspect or construct of mind.)   There are actually no clear-cut dividing lines or circles such as we have drawn in the diagram ; but many gradations as we proceed inwards.   Thus it would seem likely that in the projection of consciousness the vehicle may correspond to a cleavage—i.e., a circle—at many points in the region "ætheric-astral", and according to the particular point, so different types of experience outside the body may be forthcoming. The level (3) marked "astral" (which seems rather a strange term, though widely used) is commonly supposed to be the level of cleavage at death of the physical body : the "astral body" then becoming the outermost vehicle of consciousness and the "astral world" is then normally objective. There is obviously a good deal of unverified speculation here, but as long as the diagram is not pressed too far or taken for more than it is, I find this general scheme of some help in facing the enormous complexity of the self. In Chapter 12 we shall look in more detail at the scheme.

11

MATERIALISATIONS, PSYCHO-KINESIS AND POLTERGEIST PHENOMENA

" And behold, there arose a great tempest in the sea, insomuch that the boat was covered with the waves : but he was asleep. And they came to him and awoke him saying ' Save, Lord : we perish '. . . . Then he arose, and rebuked the winds and the sea, and there was a great calm. And the men marvelled saying ' What manner of man is this, that even the winds and the sea obey him ? ' "

MATTHEW VIII, 24–7.

" . . . . The super-normal means to us no more than the extension of the [actual] world beyond the point to which we are able to see. The boundary of the world of sense is to us a subjective barrier, whereas to the materialist it is an objective barrier."

G. N. M. TYRRELL.

" It is no longer possible to consider the human being as an aggregate of thought-producing mechanism. The evidence compels admission that we are in presence of a dynamo-psychic focus whence emanate manifestations of a power whose limits we cannot define."

EUGENE OSTY.

THE earlier chapters of this section have been concerned with ψ-faculty on its cognitive or receptor side—i.e., with knowledge which the mind could acquire or experience other than through the channels of sense. In the present chapter we have grouped together three types of phenomena which all have this in common : that they exhibit ψ-faculty on its motor or active side—i.e., they exhibit mind moulding or moving matter without the use of muscles. The phenomena of apparitions, on the theory which we have advanced, have, indeed, introduced us to the possibility of this.

The term " materialisation " is used to describe the appearance of matter of some kind, capable of scattering light, and thus being perceptible to the eye, and capable of a measure of resistance to touch. Such matter may apparently originate from the body of a certain type of medium and can be moulded by mind into forms, or used to carry out movements of an intelligent kind. The term " psycho-kinesis ", or briefly the P.-K. effect or telekinesis, is used of controlled experimental work in which material objects are caused to move by mental means. The so-called poltergeist phenomena are spontaneous uncontrolled examples of objects being thrown about senselessly, disturbing noises produced, and so on, without a known physical cause. We shall consider these phenomena in the above order.

I. MATERIALISATION: PHYSICAL MEDIUMSHIP

There is not, I think, anything inherently impossible in materialisation or psycho-kinesis. Thouless and Wiesner recognised the existence of ψ_κ as well as ψ_γ (vide p. 134), the former representing the function by which mind impresses the brain to move the body's musculature. We have made frequent use of the concept of a psychic æther through which mind has presumably its *modus operandi*—and we have moreover looked at the evidence for apparitions. It is not, then, on *a priori* grounds that we need approach this field of enquiry with some reserve. The reserve which most observers and students undoubtedly do feel is due to the large amount of fraud which has been associated with so-called physical mediumship. We must not allow ourselves on these grounds to be prejudiced against reliable evidence obtained under rigorously controlled conditions by competent observers. If even 99% of supposed data were proved fraudulent, the 1% which was true would remain of profound importance for our understanding of the kind of world we live in. This field of enquiry is certainly not one in which the ordinary person can experiment to any advantage. All the resources of a suitably equipped laboratory, which include infra-red cameras and telescopes, wire-recorders and electrical controlling circuits, should be available to the investigator. Despite all the fraud which has been reported, there can be no reasonable doubt that some most extraordinary para-normal physical phenomena have taken place. Competent observers, such as Dr. Schrenk-Notzing, Dr. Osty, Dr. Geley, Sir William Crookes, Mr. Harry Price, Professors Flammarion, Richet and Driesch, have expressed their conviction of this—and none of them was easy to convince. They were fully alive to the possibilities of fraud, and took most stringent precautions to circumvent it. It would be impossible, nor is it necessary here, to present at length the findings of these investigators. It is proposed to select a few illustrations and comments from half a dozen sources as a sample of data derived under reliable conditions.* References to original sources will permit the reader to study the field fully if he so desires.

* I am indebted to A. W. Osborn's *The Superphysical*, Chapter XIII, where more detail is given, for much of this information (Ivor Nicholson & Watson, 1937).

Eusapia Palladino. Of this famous medium, who lived in Naples, Dr. Hereward Carrington says : " Every group of scientific men that ever experimented with Eusapia knew very well that she would defraud them if the chance were given her to do so." The phenomena which took place seemed largely beyond her control, and, when at their best, were so completely beyond all possibility of normal production that Richet says : " All the men of science without exception, who experimented with her, were in the end convinced that she produced genuine phenomena." Dr. Carrington says, " I had sat with dozens of ' physical mediums ', every one of whom had turned out to be fraudulent. Yet I became thoroughly convinced of the genuineness of her phenomena, and so stated." He has given an account of them in several books.* Take, for example, this fragment :

> " Eusapia being securely held, hand and foot outside the cabinet, I have gone into the cabinet during the height of the séance and taken hold of the small séance table. . . . I could see across the table—see that nothing was visible there—yet an invisible being of some sort wrestled with me for the possession of the table, and finally succeeded in throwing myself and the table completely out of the cabinet."

Billowing curtains, levitations, floating objects in the air, and other such phenomena were obtained under conditions precluding fraud.

Rudi Schneider. Mr. Harry Price made a very rigorous examination of this Austrian medium in his own well-equipped laboratory of psychical research in 1929–30.† Under rigid test conditions, of which he says, " No one could possibly give a valid unfavourable report of any séance—no one can say the phenomena are produced fraudulently ", extraordinary para-normal phenomena were observed. No less than ninety-nine persons, including professional magicians, philosophers, scientists and others, witnessed these things at various times. Mr. Price says :

> " Cold breezes were felt by everyone; violent movements of the pair of curtains (hung separately, weight 9 lb. 14 oz.) which billowed and waved over the sitters' heads from time to time; movements and levitations of the luminous waste-paper basket (weight $7\frac{1}{2}$ oz.) and the coffee table (weight 7 lb. 10 oz.); the ringing of bells and twanging of a toy zither even in mid-air; . . . the emergence from, and withdrawal into the cabinet of ' hands ' and ' tubes ', some perfectly formed."

* *Eusapia Palladino and her Phenomena* ; *Story of Psychic Science*, pp. 206–21, etc.
† Harry Price : *Rudi Schneider : a Scientific Examination of his Mediumship* (Methuen, 1930).

The medium occupied a chair outside the cabinet, about five feet distant, and was immobilised by mechanical and electrical means. *Osty's Experiments with Rudi Schneider.* In 1932, in Paris, Dr. Osty made experiments in his own laboratory to test Schneider's ability to move an object by para-normal means. The object to be moved was protected by an infra-red beam falling on a photo-electric cell, and it was arranged that if this beam were obscured through any cause, a bell would ring. The bell did ring, sometimes for half a minute or more, and when this happened flashlight photographs showed the medium sitting in the usual position, fully controlled. They also showed nothing visible in the path of the infra-red beam. Whatever obstructed the beam was not a solid obstacle—and whatever its nature, it faded away under the influence of ordinary light, for lateral illumination of the beam stopped the bell ringing. The object was not often moved, and the researches were concentrated on the obscuring factor. The bell was replaced by a quick-period galvanometer and photographic recording drum, so that detail of the obscuration could be observed. A very significant fact was observed. When the beam was partially obscured, the galvanometer spot of light moved in sympathy with the respiratory rate of the entranced medium. These were recorded on the same photographic drum. The correlation was checked again and again. Some invisible substance with appreciable infra-red absorption appeared to be produced—and its production was shown to be associated with the physiological process of respiration in the medium.

Anna Rasmussen. Professor Winther of Copenhagen studied this medium for fifteen years and published a monograph on the subject.* Mr. Harry Price had no doubt of the genuineness of her phenomena, which took place in full daylight or bright electric light. In Professor Winther's laboratory a specially stout concrete pillar on a concrete floor supported a glass chamber in which were suspended a number of pendula of different lengths, the bobs being made of different materials. Price said : †

> " I have seen Anna Rasmussen's externalised energy move these pendulums at my request, although no person was less than a yard distant from them. These pendulums would swing or stop to order ; would change their course ; swing at right angles to one another, and announce the time of day by tapping the glass, etc. No ordinary external physical force could have affected these pendulums, and a steam roller crossing the concrete floor would not have moved them by vibrations set up."

* " Experimental Enquiries into Telekinesis ", *Jour. Amer. Soc. P.R.* Jan.–May 1928.
† Quoted from A. W. Osborn : *The Superphysical*, p. 184.

Marthe Beraud. Professor Richet investigated this medium with considerable thoroughness.* Later, Baron Schrenk-Notzing † conducted independent experiments with the same medium over a period of four years. The most thorough physical examination of the medium was made, and under conditions precluding fraud, clothed in a special close-fitting garment from head to foot, a white-looking substance (so-called " ectoplasm ") which became moulded intelligently into forms and figures, exuded from the medium's mouth in a deep trance. Photographs of these will be found in both books. In 1910, Dr. Gustave Geley ‡ had investigated the same medium with similar results. He affirmed, " I do not say there is no trickery. I say there was no possibility of trickery. Nearly all the materialisations took place under my own eyes and I have observed their genesis and development."

Franck Kluski was a non-professional Polish medium, of good education, who was investigated by Richet and Geley jointly. The so-called ectoplasm issuing from his body was moulded into the forms of hands, feet, etc., by unknown forces, and the idea was that irrefutable proof of this would be obtained if the " ectoplasmic limb " dipped itself into a bath of molten paraffin wax. A waxen glove could thus be made and if the ectoplasmic limb then de-materialised, the wax glove would remain behind intact as evidence. Richet's account is as follows :

> " Geley and I took the precaution of introducing, unknown to any other person, a small quantity of cholesterol into the bath of melted paraffin wax placed before the medium during the séance. This substance is soluble in paraffin wax without discolouring it, but on adding sulphuric acid it takes a deep violet-red tint : so that we could be absolutely certain that any moulds obtained should be obtained from paraffin provided by ourselves. . . . During the séance the medium's hands were held firmly by Geley and myself on the right and on the left so that he could not liberate either hand. The first mould obtained was of a child's hand, then a second of both hands (right and left) and a third of a child's foot. The creases in the skin and the veins were visible on the plaster casts made from the moulds.
>
> " By reason of the narrowness of the wrists, these moulds could not have been made from living hands ; for the whole hand would have had to be withdrawn through the narrow opening at the wrist. Professional modellers secure their results by threads attached to the hand which are pulled through the plaster. In the moulds here

* Professor Richet : *Thirty Years of Psychical Research* (William Collins & Sons, 1923).

† Schrenk-Notzing : *Phenomena of Materialisation* (Dutton, 1920).

‡ Dr. G. Geley : *Clairvoyance and Materialisation* (T. Fisher Unwin, 1927).

considered there was nothing of the sort; they were produced by a materialisation followed by a de-materialisation."

If the reader desires further evidence, he might care to study the reports of F. W. H. Myers on the scholarly Stainton Moses, which were only published after the latter's death.* If he is not by this time thoroughly bewildered, he might care to read the extraordinary account of " Rosalie ", a little girl who materialised apparently in flesh and blood at a séance. If Harry Price,† who had as much experience of mediumship as any man living—and knew all the tricks—had not himself vouched for it, few people would, I think, be able to accept it.

2. DISCUSSION OF THE DATA

No one surveying the records of these experiments and observations for the first time—especially the complete original accounts— can feel other than a sense of extreme bewilderment. In everyday life we know well that these things do not happen, and it is hard to bring our minds to accept such data even though obtained by men of exemplary character and great experimental competence, under the strictest conditions. Personally, I think we have no option : we must accord to these men the same confidence which we give to astronomers, atomic physicists and others, whose careful observations we shall never have the opportunity of verifying for ourselves. The fact that these physical phenomena are not commonplace does not in any way diminish their importance for our understanding of the nature of the world. Let us therefore try to fit them into our thinking.

The phenomena of materialisation are not, I suggest, different in kind from those of apparitions. In the séance room, in the presence of a medium who has a loosely-knit type of aetheric body, such forms constructed or moulded by mind in the extracted aetheric material assume a " density ", so to speak, which attracts a sufficient amount of ordinary chemical matter to enable them to scatter light and become clearly visible. The measure of solidity or impenetrability which such forms possess—as shown by the formation of wax moulds—need not imply the presence of much chemical matter. It can be accounted for by fields of force such as we know the psychic aether in the aetheric body can sustain. (We must remind ourselves again that even when an ordinary object is held on the hand, the pressure sensation arises from the inter-action of electromagnetic fields

* *Proc. S.P.R.*, Vols. IX and XI.
† Harry Price : *Fifty Years of Psychical Research* (Longmans, Green & Co., 1939).

between two almost "empty" structures.) I venture to suggest that if ever some "ectoplasm" is placed in a test tube it will collapse when the medium emerges from trance, as a child's balloon does when the string is loosened, and will leave behind nothing but the merest film of body proteins. The psychic æther which was the vehicle of the mental forces which sustained and moulded the form presumably finds its way back largely into the medium's body. There is no doubt that Mind is both creator and artist, expressing itself through what it creates; but, as we saw in Chapter 9, these forms lack permanence; they can be sustained only for a limited time. It is not at present of importance to know which mind is the operative one. It may be the mind of the sitter, the mind of the medium, a discarnate mind, or the combined effort of more than one mind.

Remembering that the psychic æther is a bridge between mind and matter, that it is the medium through which ψ_κ is operative, we here have the basis of psycho-kinesis—i.e., the movement of objects. By such means we can conceive of material objects being lifted into the air or thrown about, or floating down gently, of curtains billowing out as though in a wind, and of levitations. We have at least in the psychic æther a medium capable of sustaining mental-cum-physical forces and operating on matter in a "para-normal" manner. The ætheric forms may not always have enough chemical matter associated with them to be visible (as in Dr. Osty's work with Schneider), although the infra-red absorption may still be appreciable.

It has been suggested by Geley, Osborn and others that the process of construction of materialised forms in the séance room, while a little amateurish, is not substantially different from that associated with creation and growth in Nature. How do we suppose a physical body is built? Why does a leaf or flower grow to the size, shape, colour and symmetry-pattern which in fact it does—and to no other? When repair of a wound takes place, why are the form and outline of the original pattern so closely followed? Perhaps the so-called "astral" body is a dynamic, precise and persistent thought-form, which, through the medium of the ætheric body-structure which it directly creates, in turn moulds the body of ordinary matter to its form. The difference between the normal processes of growth in Nature and these para-normal processes may be only a difference of degree. The normal process is comparatively slow, and the resulting material form has a considerable measure of persistence in time: the para-normal process is comparatively rapid and the resulting forms contain relatively little matter and are evanescent. Geley * has drawn a number of analogies between these two fields, and it

* Loc. cit., pp. 180–1.

may be that in some distant future the problems of biology will be illuminated, if not solved, by research in this strange psychophysical region.

It is easy to speculate. Every thoughtful investigator in this field must realise that we are only at the beginning of our enquiry. It is all too easy to endow this *tertium quid*, which we have called a psychic æther, with all those qualities which will account for observed data. What we need is a programme of research to secure that a minimum is postulated and a maximum correlated. I think it is also clear that we shall not get very far until a number of well-educated, scientifically trained persons develop their own clairvoyant faculty. If a number of competent clairvoyants independently observed the same phenomenon—e.g., a séance or a living organism—and their testimony agreed, we might begin to collect a body of reliable information on a more significant level than that of ordinary physical observation.

3. PSYCHO-KINESIS. DR. RHINE'S WORK

The laboratory over which Dr. J. B. Rhine presided began its earliest experimental work in P.-K. in 1934, but, with considerable wisdom, his experimenters refrained from announcing their results until 1943, when they believed their accumulated data had established the effect beyond question. Rhine has given an interesting account of the development of this work in a recent book,* and D. J. West †has made a critical survey of these results. While critical of specific points, West's conclusion is " the case for P.-K. does not seem to be challengeable : it is probably even more clear-cut and conclusive than the case for E.S.P. itself ". In the simplest and earliest experiments the procedure consisted in willing a randomly thrown dice to come to rest with a chosen face uppermost. Assuming no bias in the dice, the probability of any face appearing is 1/6, and the results of a large run of throws are thus capable of statistical evaluation. By making each face in turn the target for an equal number of throws, the effect of possible bias can be eliminated. Sometimes a pair of dice were thrown simultaneously, and a large number of throws with the aim of a high score (eight or more) was followed by an approximately equal number of throws aimed at a low score (six or less). The probability of each of these is 5/12. It is obvious that the dice could not possibly be biased so as to give an excess of both high and low scores unless the score of sevens was appreciably deficient. I

* *The Reach of the Mind*, Chapters VI, VII, and VIII (Faber & Faber, 1948).
† *Proc. S.P.R.*, Vol. 47, p. 281 (1945).

shall quote only one experimental result to illustrate the kind of results obtained. (The score of sevens was not below expectation.)

Aim of Experiment.	Number of Throws.	Dice Score Deviation.	Critical Ratio.
High score . .	5,904	290	7·65
Low score . .	5,220	−140	3·92

The third column shows the actual deviation was 290 *more* than it should have been (namely, 2,460 on the laws of chance) when the *aim* was a high score; while it was 140 *less* than it should have been (namely, 2,175) when the *aim* was a low score. The critical ratio is a mathematical factor which estimates the significance of the result—and it is customary to assume that when it exceeds about 3, the deviations are quite beyond such as it would be reasonable to ascribe to chance. Incidentally, the *difference* of the two deviations gives a critical ratio difference of 8·26, a result of extremely high significance.

I shall summarise below with brief comment some of the interesting results of investigation of the P.-K. effect by Rhine and his colleagues.

1. Marked and very characteristic " decline " effects were invariably found. Thus in a given run of twenty-four throws of a dice, the scoring was highest at the beginning of a run. In second and third runs it also markedly diminished. To maintain a good scoring rate some change in conditions was necessary—either a different person, different dice, a different manner of throwing, or some other factor. Although the reason for the decline effects is not understood, they are an invariable characteristic of the P.-K. effect, and their demonstrable presence is regarded as a strong part of the evidence for P.-K. It will be recalled that similar effects were found in E.S.P.

2. By the use of mechanical devices for throwing, the possibility of human manipulation was eliminated without interfering with the P.-K. effect.

3. Experiments with the number of dice thrown together, ranging through 1, 2, 6, 12, 24, 48 to 96, showed that the best rate of scoring was with the largest numbers. If the causation was a physical force we should/have expected this effect to be the opposite—i.e., we should suppose that the larger the mass to be moved the less effective would be its control. Experiments with dice of varying size do not show that the smaller dice were more effective. The provisional conclusion must be that mass and volume are not determining factors—but it is the mental factors of novelty and interest which are important.

4. Tests with dice of varying shapes, sharp corners, round corners, etc., worked equally well, again supporting the view that the controlling force is not physical.

5. Tests on the effect of distance from the dice up to 25 feet show no change. The attitude of the person towards proximity or distance—i.e., his expectation of success or otherwise—was found to be important.

6. The effect of mental distraction is pronounced. In one experiment of sixty runs (each of twenty-four dice) an investigator scored a deviation of fifty-eight above the chance expectation. In a subsequent sixty runs, when deliberately distracted by another person, he went below chance expectation.

7. Drugs appear to have the same general effects as were found in E.S.P. (see p. 140).

8. Hypnotic suggestion directing concentration on the target face of the dice sent the scoring rate down, but suggestions of relaxation and making the test playfully improved the scoring above the pre-hypnotic level.

Clearly research in the field of P.-K. is only in its infancy, but it seems possible to draw some tentative conclusions. The two most obvious ones are, first, that P.-K. does not appear to be physical in its character—i.e., the causative forces do not act as we should expect physical forces to do, whereas mental factors, such as interest, novelty, distraction and mood, on the other hand, do seem significant. Secondly, all the evidence about E.S.P. and P.-K. is so similar as to suggest that they are very closely related phenomena. They may, indeed, be two aspects of the one process, as the notation ψ_γ and ψ_κ implies. In the one we have the sensory type of phenomenon of matter affecting mind (clairvoyance); in the other the motor-type of phenomenon of mind affecting matter (P.-K.).

Rhine has argued that one implies the existence of the other. Thus to influence the fall of the dice by bringing a force to bear on it at a point of space and time, he suggests E.S.P. must be used to provide knowledge of its correct application. The visual sense is obviously inadequate to this task. It seems, therefore, that E.S.P. : P.-K. (or $\psi_\gamma : \psi_\kappa$) is the mode of inter-action of Mind with the material world. When it happens indirectly but precisely through a physical body, we call it normal; when it happens directly but with far less precision, we are surprised, and call it para-normal. If it seems strange that Mind can influence the fall of a die, let us remind ourselves that every time we move an arm or a leg, Mind influences a lump of physical matter. One may be more highly organised than the other, but in principle is there any difference?

Our postulate of a psychic æther is of a medium or structure through which the above functions operate in the matter–mind relationship. It may be an organised "world" of comparable complexity in its organisation to the world of matter or the world of mind, even though functionally it is only a bridge between the two latter. To its many other properties it looks as though we must add the possession of forces and a type of energy of its own. Or is it a transformer of some unknown Energy of Mind into the Kinetic Energy of the physicist? We shall leave the further discussion of this until we have surveyed the dramatic and spontaneous phenomena classified as " poltergeist ".

4. POLTERGEIST PHENOMENA

The term " poltergeist ", which has passed into ordinary English usage, comes from the two German words : *polter*, to knock, rattle or bluster, and *geist*, a ghost or spirit. The sense of the word is thus " a boisterous, noisy, racketing spirit ". The phenomena—like those of haunting, for example—are fortunately not common but are well attested. The reader who desires to assess for himself how good the evidence is, should read a book such as that compiled by Harry Price.* He will find gathered together documented evidence and reports covering well-known cases over a period of some centuries. After vigorous criticism and discounting as much as possible, I think the evidence is good enough to establish this strange group of phenomena which it is natural to regard as a spontaneous uncontrolled form of psycho-kinesis. The accounts of the happenings each have their own peculiar features, but in general they show a remarkable similarity : unexplained noises, such as footsteps in empty rooms and corridors, loud bangs upon doors, sounds as of furniture being dragged about, blows or raps upon the floors or beds, objects inexplicably flying about and breaking. There are, however, a number of other effects which have been witnessed by responsible persons—such as the controlled type of flight of the objects, the appearance and disappearance of objects in locked and sealed rooms, the production of heat and cold and incendiary effects, etc.—which are of importance in relation to any theory of the phenomena.

As regards the acoustical phenomena, it is obvious that they fall into two classes—para-normal and normal. Thus if a loud noise appeared to originate from an empty room, we should count it as the former ; but if it came from a locked room where a bed was found

* Harry Price : *Poltergeist over England* (Country Life, Ltd., 1945).

overturned, we should count it the latter. Our problem is then what overturned the bed ? As an example of para-normal noises, we take an extract from the accounts of the haunting of the Epworth Parsonage in Lincolnshire (Dec. 1716–Jan. 1717), occupied by the famous Wesley family. I extract the following from Mrs. Wesley's written account to her son John :

> " Once coming up after dinner, a cradle seemed to be strongly rocked in my chamber. When I went in, the sound seemed to be in the nursery. When I was in the nursery, it seemed in my chamber again. One night Mr. W. and I were waked by some-one running down the garret stairs, then down the broad stairs, then up the narrow ones, then up the garret stairs, then down again, and so the same round. The rooms trembled as it passed along, and the doors shook exceedingly, so that the clattering of the latches was very loud.
> " Mr. W., proposing to rise, I rose with him, and went down the broad stairs hand in hand to light a candle. Near the foot of them a large pot of money, seemed to be poured out at my waist, and to run jingling down my night gown to my feet. Presently after we heard the noise as of a vast stone thrown among several dozen of bottles which lay under the stairs ; but upon our looking no hurt was done. We returned up into the nursery where the noise was very great. The children were all asleep, but panting, trembling and sweating extremely."

Our view is that all this type of para-normally produced noise comes under the same explanation as that of apparitions and hauntings, the phenomena are of the auditory instead of the visual type, and this is the only difference. Harry Price makes the interesting statement that " nearly half of all reported cases of hauntings exhibit poltergeist characteristics ". We therefore invite the reader to look again at Chapter 9, Sections 7 and 8. All that is said there can be applied directly to the understanding of these para-normal *auditory* phenomena. I have no doubt that a wire-recorder or tape-recorder would demonstrate the same *physical* characteristics in para-normally produced, as in normally produced, sounds. In the diagram of Section 6, a would be a subsistent " event " and d the perceived noise. In Section 7 the equation we wrote down would become : Physical Event = Subsistent Event + Sense-Data. In Section 8 all that we said of haunting is immediately applicable, and need not here be repeated. We may adopt the purely psychometric theory—that a persistent dynamic memory or a focus of bottled-up energy in the psychic æther is the proximate cause, but that the phenomena can only manifest through the release of this energy when a person of the right telepathic affinity comes into the neighbourhood. As previously indicated, a very simple extension of this view takes us to a " spiritistic " theory, if we suppose, for example, that the original agent's mind maintains this focus of bottled-up energy. It is difficult to see, however, what purpose could possibly be served, or what advantage gained, by the monotonous repetition for months of useless noises by a surviving intelligence. This repetitive, almost mono-ideistic type of action suggests rather the activity of a broken-off fragment of Mind—if such a concept may be allowed. For the present we will defer discussion of the essential nature of the " poltergeist " to consider other significant phenomena apart from the auditory ones.

The most characteristic and dramatic of these are the psycho-kinetic group. I quote by way of illustration a few lines *—they are typical of all the accounts.

> " Then went candle-sticks and other brasses : scarce anything remaining in its place. After this the glasses and china were put down on the floor for fear of undergoing the same fate, they presently began to dance and tumble about, and then broke to pieces. A teapot that was among them, flew to Mrs. Golding's maid's foot and struck it. . . . A ham that hung in one side of the kitchen chimney raised itself from the hook and fell down to the ground. . . . All the family were eye-witnesses to these circumstances as well as other persons, some of whom were so alarmed and shocked that they could not bear to stay."

There is one significant observation—for which the evidence seems good—that projected objects do not necessarily move in the sort of trajectory to be expected under the action of an initial impulse and a gravitational pull. Price himself was a witness in the Borley Rectory phenomena of the flight of a red glass candlestick down the well of the staircase, the candlestick having been just previously seen by him on the mantelpiece of the Blue Room upstairs. Needless to say, no person was upstairs. This flight must have involved at least two turns round corners. There is also the observation of Dom Richard Whitehouse and two other witnesses in Borley Rectory, of a bottle " poised in mid-air within a foot or so of the kitchen ceiling. It remained there for a second or two and then fell with a crash on the floor before us." † Such observations, if we accept them, suggest that the psycho-kinetic activity is at times more one of transport than projection, or shall we say of guided rather than free flight. The importance of the effect is obviously this : that we are not dealing merely with the effects of a simple mechanical impulse, such as the explosive release of an initial amount of energy might cause ; we are dealing with some force or energy directed spatially with a measure of intelligence or purpose—however primitive.

Associated with the projection of objects from one place to another

* *Poltergeist over England*, p. 150.   † Loc. cit., p. 20.

there is the so-called phenomenon of " apports ".   By this is meant
the passage of one object through the supposed impenetrable matter
of another—such as the appearance of objects in, and disappearance
of objects from closed and sealed rooms.   Cases of this were reported
by Rev. L. A. Foyster, who with his wife and family occupied Borley
Rectory for five years and witnessed many hundreds of para-normal
events.   I do not think the evidence for this is as good as for most of
the other things.   If, however, it should prove to be an absolutely
authentic phenomenon, I do not think it should present us with any
problem of a radically different kind from those already discussed.
We should bear in mind, for one thing, the equivalence of matter
and energy—and the evidence we already have of remarkable energy
production, under conditions precluding a normal physical explanation.   On the other hand, we should remember that apparitions
(interpreted as physical), and discussed in Chapter 9 (7), pass through
other physical objects and appear and disappear in closed spaces.
The evidence we have already discussed in the earlier part of this
chapter for temporary materialisation, followed by de-materialisation,
should also prepare us to consider as equally possible—if equally
mysterious—de-materialisation followed by re-materialisation.   From
the viewpoint of common sense such doings are incredible because
they are not a part of familiar experience.   We are concerned, it is
true, with an unfamiliar field, but it is one which is likely to be of the
greatest importance in understanding the real nature of the familiar.
Our primary concern should therefore be not with beliefs, however
widely held, but with evidence.

It is true that the properties of a four-dimensional space would
account immediately for the possibility of appearance and disappearance of objects from enclosed three-dimensional space.   This type
of explanation, by invoking the geometry of a space of higher
dimensions (as Dunne did in another connection), is not, I think, at
all helpful : indeed, it may be misleading if it causes us to suppose
that in a generalisation of physical concepts, rather than in penetration
to a higher level of significance, is a clue to understanding of the world.
On the other hand, the kind of sketch of the nature of the material
world presented in Chapter 9 (6) suggests that the function of Mind
is so all-embracing, as far as so-called Matter is concerned, that such
questions as materialisation and de-materialisation are aspects of one
of its most basic activities.   Happily for mankind, the knowledge
necessary to achieve this consciously is not generally available, but
the *a priori* possibility seems indubitable.   We have seen Mind in its
cognitive aspect unfettered by Space and Time : is there reason to
suppose that it is wholly a prisoner in its creative and kinetic aspects ?

Apart from the kinetic effects, there are very well-attested thermal effects associated with some poltergeists. Price has devoted a chapter of his book * to " Poltergeist Incendiaries ". In the famous Borley Rectory case, the Rev. L. A. Foyster reports in his diary a visit one day from his neighbours, Sir George and Lady Whitehouse. While they were there a fire broke out in an unused bedroom. The skirting-board at one place was described as " glowing red ". Another peculiar feature of the Borley case was the existence of a cold spot—apparently at times some 10° C. below its surroundings, according to investigations by a Cambridge group of observers. These thermal effects are of particular interest from the standpoint of the energy production involved.

Auditory phenomena can, as we know, be very impressive, and " leave nothing to the imagination ". This is primarily, however, because the human ear is a superlatively sensitive instrument. In point of fact, sound is a very " attenuated " form of energy. I do not suppose that all the sound emitted by enthusiastic crowds at a football final would provide enough energy to make a cup of tea. As regards potential energy, I calculate that the work required to lift a ton weight through about 30 feet against gravity would just about make a cup of tea. In other words, the special interest of the thermal phenomena arises from the fact that heat is a " concentrated " form of energy. The existence of a " cold spot " offers no solution of the problem of the origin of the energy involved in poltergeist effects. For obscure reasons, it may be that some of the effects are most easily produced by heat energy abstracted from the air, but of course the production and maintenance of such a cold spot require the constant expenditure of an equivalent amount of energy by the poltergeist. The problem of the source of this energy remains on our hands. The production of heat required to create incendiary effects is considerable : where does it come from ? It is probably wisest to say simply that we do not know. I propose, however, to make the not unreasonable assumption that every level of significance (i.e., each world of phenomena) whether physical, ætheric, or mental, has its own type of energy, and that under certain circumstances transformation from one level to another may take place. I think there are some pointers in this direction, which I shall proceed to discuss.

1. One of the most striking features of the poltergeist phenomena is that in an overwhelming majority of cases a young person seems to be the unconscious agent of the effects. In 95% of cases it is a young girl; in 5% a boy or youth, says Price. Moreover, sexual change or shock seems to be frequently associated either with the

* Loc. cit., Chapter XXVII.

beginning or the cessation of the phenomena. Puberty and adolescence are thus the periods favourable to the effects. Price * informs us that Eleonora Zugun's power vanished overnight with the first appearance of the menses ; that the Schneider brothers were brilliant about puberty, but the effects waned as adolescence advanced ; conversely, that Stella C.'s power became marked with sexual maturity ; that in the case of Esther Cox, the phenomena which lasted a year were initiated by nervous shock following attempted sexual assault, and that moreover they attained their greatest strength every twenty-eight days. He quotes Professor Thirring of Vienna, who experimented with Willi Schneider, and remarked that the psycho-kinetic phenomena were always much stronger when a sympathetic female was the principal controller. Price also tells of an interview with the husband of Frieda W., a young Austrian medium, who informed him that at the height of his wife's sexual excitement in their early married life, ornaments would sometimes fall off the mantelpiece in their bedroom ; also that during menstruation the physical phenomena of mediumship did not occur. I think we may conclude that there is strong evidence of some relationship between poltergeist phenomena and physiological activity—especially the activity of sex, in which physical and emotional factors both play a part.

The phenomena of physical mediumship, as we have suggested in Section 2, arise from some peculiarity of state or structure of the medium's ætheric body. It may be that this particular state is accentuated at or about the time of puberty or adolescence, when the ætheric body is probably in a phase of change and development, just as is the physical body. We do not suggest that the young person is the originating cause of the poltergeist effects, but rather is the possessor of an ætheric body by means of which a dammed-up reservoir of psychic energy can find release and discharge. The young person chances to be the temporary possessor of a means of converting the psychic energy (whether mento-emotional or ætheric, we do not know) into physical energy which is dissipated in the kinetic effects we have discussed.

2. The remarkable poltergeist phenomena associated with Jean Baptiste Vianney, Curé d'Ars, 1786–1859, are, I think, another pointer in the same direction. Gerald Heard † describes him as an " innocent, powerful, unintellectual saint ". He was for many years given to extreme ascetic practices : fasting, self-scourging and

---

* Loc. cit., Chapter XXX.
† I am indebted to Gerald Heard's *Preface to Prayer*, pp. 68–76 for this information (Cassell & Co., 1945).

allowing himself very little sleep. On the mental and emotional side of his nature, he gave himself to intense prayer for his " flock ", believing that in this way and through his physical sufferings he was atoning for their sinfulness. For years, then, his ætheric body was being subjected to a " battering " from both the physical and mental sides. Poltergeist phenomena began to make their appearance : loud noises were heard, his furniture moved round the room, and all the familiar effects were found. In addition, he developed a marked extra-sensory faculty. He remarked to a friend about raising money for charitable purposes, " One can get anything one wants if one fasts and watches enough ". Gerald Heard comments, " He was generating an immense force, as a dynamo generates power out of the otherwise imperceptible continuum ". Heard also says with considerable insight of this phenomenal outpouring of excess energy, " The source of the ' leakage ' must be looked for in what we may call the psycho-physical belt of the mind-body, and not in the specifically spiritual ". This harmonises with the general picture we have formed. It may well be that there is a natural energy circulation in the ætheric body as various clairvoyants have described,* and that the austere practices of the Curé d'Ars stimulated the intake of such energy to a degree that it had to find release beyond its natural function. This it did by a process of conversion into physical energy and dissipation of the latter through the movement of objects.

3. I find another pointer in a paper of Dr. John Layard,† which describes from the standpoint of Jung's psychology the cure of a psychopathic case by Dr. C. A. Meier, who was Jung's chief assistant. The view which Layard puts forward is that poltergeist phenomena may sometimes subserve a definite purpose—which is curative—by release of the energy created by tension of conflict in the deeper levels of an individual mind. (Here again we have the conception of a transformation of energy from one level to another.) Moreover, just as it is characteristic of ψ (that is of certain mental levels), that to convey information to consciousness it uses symbols—visual, auditory, etc., so in some circumstances, Layard's view is that it may use *objects* to convey a message. Hence arise poltergeist effects. The conditions in a personality which necessarily precede such phenomena are, according to Layard, " situations of extreme tension when the two poles of the personality are trying to join, but cannot ". Of the Curé d'Ars, Layard remarks that he was well aware of the message contained in the poltergeist phenomena which assailed him for over thirty-five years and which he interpreted as a

* E.g., Payne and Bendit : *The Psychic Sense*, pp. 79 ff. (Faber & Faber, 1943).
† ψ-phenomena and Poltergeists : *Proc. S.P.R.*, Vol. 47, p. 237 (1944).
I

conflict between powers of good and evil in his person—a conflict he never fully resolved. We shall not discuss further this fruitful Jungian hypothesis, but return to the specific case recounted of which the climax was as follows. The patient had, in a trance-like state of mind, been making a journey through the city, each phase of which was for her the symbolical unravelling of her conflict. At a certain time, just when the patient in her wanderings had penetrated to the centre of her conflict, a very loud report was heard by the doctor in his consulting-room. He left his dining-room and rushing over to investigate the noise, he discovered that a Gothic wooden bench nearly 500 years old, had split down its entire length. It had a massive seat (150 cm. by 3 cm.) and the smooth clean split was 2 to 3 cm. in breadth. This case and its interpretation gave rise to much critical and sceptical comment, into which it is not necessary to enter here. I present it only as another pointer towards the view that poltergeist phenomena provide a mode of release of accumulated energy on the mento-emotional level through its transformation into physical energy.

As to the nature of the poltergeist, there is no sound reason for supposing that a malicious or boisterous " spirit " is involved. The data are consistent with the view that the entity involved is a mental fragment expressing a group of primitive ideas or actions, but associated with a bottled-up reservoir of emotional energy. This seems to have a persistence in time—attached frequently, as in hauntings, to some building or locality. Only a person of the right telepathic affinity can become aware of it, and only a peculiar type of ætheric body can become the means of release of this pent-up energy by transforming it into physical energy. When this energy is completely discharged, the " poltergeist " is no more. In the case of the Curé d'Ars, the psychic reservoir was constantly being re-charged by his ascetic practices.

5. SOME SPECULATIONS

The hypothesis we have advanced to account for psycho-kinesis and its dramatic uncontrolled form in poltergeist phenomena is that we have a transformation of energy from one modality (psychical) to another (physical). It is a tempting starting point for many specu-lations. The sporadic, uncontrolled form seems generally to depend on a chance peculiarity of the structure of the ætheric body of an adolescent. It seems at least possible that some individuals of an advanced type may have knowledge of how to effect this transforma-tion of energy at will in a controlled manner, and we do not know what limits, if any, there are to such a process. I took the liberty of prefacing this chapter with a very remarkable example of this. Such powers have generally been attributed to persons of outstanding spiritual achievement, and in the light of our present knowledge—fragmentary though it is—we may be less disposed to regard them as wholly legendary than did our scientific predecessors. Through much ancient philosophical literature—Kabbalistic, Hermetic and Indian—persists the traditional belief that if the real " name " of a thing is known to a man, the powers inherent in that thing are under his control. It is a strange idea, very persistent, and perhaps by its very nature one that cannot be precisely expressed in words. It may, however, be another way of saying that an individual who has at his disposal the immense creative energies of the mental level and knows how to use his ætheric vehicle as the transformer and channel of these energies, can control in no small degree the physical world. As we have several times mentioned, the theoretical possibility of this should occasion no surprise to the person whose philosophy sees the material order as derived from, and an expression of, Mind in action.

I venture also to refer to a particular form of Indian yoga known as *kundalini* yoga. It appears to be a psycho-physical technique, involving certain breathing rhythms and forms of mental concentration, the aim of which is to arouse the so-called *kundalini* power. According to its exponents, this power lies latent at a centre near the base of the spine, but when aroused effectively it vivifies certain *chakrams* or centres in the ætheric body which are the keys to well-developed psychical faculty. (In our terminology this means ψ-faculty would become fully accessible and controlled by the will.) In addition, the individual is said to experience an enormous vitalising of the physical body to a degree which, if not properly prepared for, may be dangerous and destructive. Our Western physiology and psychology of course know nothing as yet of these matters : they are consigned, if they have been heard of at all, to the realm of superstition (along with psychical research and other such questionable matters). It seems to me probable that in this particular form of yoga the East has developed a technique of effecting the transformation of energy from one modality to another. The result is not, however, primarily the development of power over inanimate Nature, but the development of the fullest potentialities of the physical and ætheric bodies.

I venture also to comment on a matter which comes much nearer home : the maintenance of the physical health of the body and the *modus operandi* of certain types of healing. I shall do so very briefly and categorically—for it is a vast subject—in order to make one or two points relevant to the subject of psycho-kinesis. The preservation of the body in health as a smoothly working machine is certainly achieved through a large number of inter-related physiological and biochemical mechanisms, but behind these, and controlling them through the ætheric structures, are certain levels of the individual mind. The mind is kept informed by ψ_γ (or E.S.P.) and controls the physiological mechanisms through ψ_κ (or P.-K.). When things go wrong and physical symptoms appear, we are beginning to realise that the cause of the dis-function may be on any level of the self. The causation may be on the physical level (e.g., a bacterial or virus invasion), on the ætheric level, or on several different sub-levels of the mind. Although in the present state of our knowledge, alleviation of the physical symptoms may be the most that can be done (i.e., by therapy on the physical level), there can be no doubt that in the future a more fundamental therapy will always treat the patient on the level of the causes—not of the symptoms. It is, for example, a noteworthy achievement of medicine to maintain the diabetic in good health by the administration of insulin which his pancreas fails to secrete. It will be for the future to discover at what level of the patient (ætheric, mental, buddhic, etc.) control and direction of the responsible cells in the pancreas has failed. When this is known, a radical therapy will be possible. All this is a preliminary to comments which I desire to make about two different types of healing associated with these deeper levels.

There is some extremely good evidence, which it is quite impossible to disregard,* that a certain type of prayer of an intercessory kind may have extraordinary therapeutic power. I suggest for consideration that what may be happening in cases of this kind, is akin to the building up of telepathic rapport between the minds of the agents (i.e., persons praying) and the mind of the patient, resulting in sufficient stimulation of the latter to undertake with renewed energy the processes of healing and repair. The patient is helped on the mental level to help himself—and in some cases there may even be a transmutation of mental energy into physical.

There is a rather different kind of healing involving physical contact of the hands of the healer with the body of the patient. I suggest here that the healing forces are operative at the ætheric level, which becomes now the level of rapport. The mind of the patient is not now involved, but the mind of the healer acts psychokinetically through the ætheric body of the patient to stimulate the body of the patient towards health.

* See, for example, Alexis Carrel: *Man the Unknown*, Chapter IV; Howard Somervell: *After Everest*, Chapter XXVIII (Hodder & Stoughton, 1936); L. D. Weatherhead: *Psychology, Religion and Healing* (Hodder & Stoughton, 1951).

Chapter

12

THE COMPLEX STRUCTURE OF MAN

Not Chaos, not
The darkest pit of lower Erebus
Nor aught of blinder vacancy, scooped out
By help of dreams, can breed such fear and awe
As fall upon us often when we look
Into our Minds, into the Mind of Man—
My haunt, and the main region of my song.

WORDSWORTH.

" As the self existent pierced the openings of the senses outward,
one looks outward not within oneself. A certain thoughtful
person, seeking immortality, turned the eye inward and saw the
self."

KATHA UPANISHAD, IV, 1.

" If we think that our nature is limited by the little wave of our
being which is our conscious waking self, we are ignorant of our
true being. The relation of our life to a larger spiritual world
betrays itself even in the waking consciousness through our
intellectual ideals, our moral aspirations, our cravings for beauty,
and our longing for perfection. Behind our conscious self is our
secret being without which the superficial consciousness cannot
exist or act. Consciousness in us is partly manifest and partly
hidden. We can enlarge the waking part of it by bringing into
play ranges of our being which are now hidden. It is our duty to
become aware of ourselves as spiritual beings, instead of falsely
identifying ourselves with the body, life or mind."

RADHAKRISHNAN (from *Eastern Religions and Western Thought*).

He who knows others is wise;
He who knows himself is enlightened.

THE TAO TÊ CHING.

THIS is a subject so vast and overwhelming that, like a tree, its roots
ramify into the soil of all the sciences and its branches spread into
the empyrean of all the mysteries. Tennyson believed that could
he but fully understand the " flower in the crannied wall " he would
have the key to both God and man. No doubt we must grant poetic
licence here, as also in the judgment which sees in Man the measure
of all things ; but it is probable that the latter is the best clue we have.
For if the nature of Man does not in some degree partake of, and
reflect, the ultimates, how can he know anything of them at all ? If he
cannot discover divinity within himself, where in the sweep of space

and time shall he look with any hope of success ? All problems of the Universe and of the nature of knowledge therefore come back to Man himself, and in so doing throw light on his own structure.

The data of psychical research, which we have examined in the preceding chapters, have a very important contribution to make to the subject.

1. THE CONTRIBUTION OF PSYCHICAL RESEARCH

All the evidence points to a conception of the Self as a hierarchy, an impression which it was attempted to convey through the diagram on page 239. A brief review of the steps which led to this picture may be useful. Telepathy has shown us a whole world of Mind operative without essential dependence on matter. It has revealed the existence of mind-to-mind relationships not limited to the present moment nor apparently affected at all by space. All the data lend support to Bergson's conception of the brain as an organ of limitation of the mind. Clairvoyance introduced us on the sensory side, and psycho-kinesis on the motor side, to the relationships between matter and mind, and this led to the postulate of a psychic æther as an intermediary between the two. To understand object-reading this hypothesis seemed a necessity, and the psychic æther seemed also involved fundamentally in the phenomena of hauntings, apparitions and of materialisations. We do not therefore hesitate to incorporate an ætheric structure in Man's own synthesis. Of this we shall say more later. The level or world of Mind has its own sub-levels or strata, as was clearly shown by the phenomena of apparitions, where they were described by Tyrrell as playing roles like the author, producer and stage carpenter of a play. Some such subdivision or stratification of Mind (or a more complex one) is supported also by the nature of dreams, mediumistic trance and hypnosis, and by the subjective impressions of artists and others seeking to bring to birth in form the creative inspirations rising up from a more profound level of the self. The region or field of psychical phenomena extends over the whole range from matter to deeper mind : beyond this we pass into the field of mystical experience. Viewed thus in broadest outline, we can see Man as a synthesis of principles or vehicles of growing significance, and widening powers, as we approach towards his essence which is one with the ultimate reality.

2. THE ÆTHERIC OR "VITAL" BODY

It seems to me that the fact of clairvoyance (Chapter 6 (7)), to explain which we assumed a modification of the psychic æther associated with a material object, and on the other hand the fact of object-reading, which indicated the modification by a mind of the psychic æther linked with an object, provide grounds for expecting to find in Man a highly organised ætheric structure. For here is a region of psychic æther subjected continuously to the influence of a physical body and to the influence of a mind where these are linked in that close relationship characteristic of living things. From the recognition of the plausibility of such a structure or body, to a detailed description of its " anatomy " and " physiology ", is naturally a big step. Such descriptions as we have are necessarily derived from the descriptions of sensitives who can withdraw the focus of awareness to this level, which they then claim to see as objective. We must regard these descriptions with some reserve : at the same time, it is remarkable to find that some of the ancient knowledge of the Hindus is in broad general agreement with them. The student who desires a restrained and very reasonable introduction to this subject, should read *The Psychic Sense* by Payne and Bendit.*

The ætheric body appears to be very much a field of energy streams and forces inter-penetrating the dense physical body and extending a little distance beyond it (where it is " seen " as an aura).† Two important circulations are described, one nutritive ‡ and the other sensori-motor. Of the former we shall here say no more than that it is concerned with the intake and output of a type of energy from the ætheric world of which we know little, and which orthodox physiology does not as yet recognise. The sensori-motor circulation is intimately related to the physical sensation and action of the ordinary body, and also to the sensori-motor activity of the ætheric body (i.e., ψ-faculty). It is the latter which is of particular interest to us now. According to clairvoyant perception and to many ancient works on yoga, the ætheric body has a number of centres or " *chakrams* " which are like vortices or whorls with the apex located in the region of the spinal cord and the wide end terminating on the surface of the body. These centres are said to have each a dual function, receptive and motor. The receptive function is analogous to special-sense activity of the physical body ; in other words, these centres are the organs of extra-sensory perception. The motor functions corresponding to muscular activity of the physical body are

---

* This little book which is the fruit of collaboration between Dr. and Mrs. Bendit (he a well-qualified psychiatrist, and she an excellent sensitive), seems to me a pioneering work of great value in relating clairvoyant observations to the more familiar data of psychology and medicine.

† Vide W. J. Kilner : *The Human Atmosphere* (Kegan Paul, 1920).

‡ Vide A. E. Powell : *The Etheric Double and Allied Phenomena* (Theos. Pub. House, 1930).

little understood, but have to do with effects of the psycho-kinetic type, the passage of matter through matter (apports) and so forth. Extra-sensory perception of different quality is regarded as associated with the activity of different *chakrams*. There is one in the region of the solar plexus associated with psychic " feeling " or clair-sentience, one in the cardiac region associated with insight and intui-tion, one in the throat region connected with clairaudience, another at the level of the eyebrows, closely related to the pituitary gland and associated with clairvoyance, and another near the vertex of the head, linked with the pineal body and associated with spiritual enlighten-ment. (The Egyptian *uraeus* and the Brahmin caste-mark placed on the forehead are two symbols of the pituitary centre, and the pyramidal projection over the vertex of the head in Buddhist sculpture is a symbol of the last of these centres.) There are also other *chakrams* not apparently associated with E.S.P.

There is a close linkage between the central ends of the *chakrams* and the autonomic nervous system—but all this detail of the relation-ships of the physical and ætheric body is beyond the necessity of our examination here.* All that we desire to draw attention to, is that there is a considerable amount of detailed clairvoyant observation— which at present we must necessarily view with reservation. The paramount necessity of checking and counter-checking such data is obvious. It is neglect of such data which seems to me unfortunate, for they unfold to us the possibility of a new world of structure and function, and suggest a field of exploration compared with which the voyagings of Columbus are but a child's outing.

3. THE MENTAL STRUCTURE

What is the Mind ? We cannot hope to obtain a full answer by intellectual cogitation, for this is expecting Mind to explain itself. We should do well to remember that it is but another instrument of the self (even as is the physical body). It has an inner window opening on to the self at what we have called the buddhic level, and it has an outer window opening on to the ætheric structure and via this on to the physical body. Continuing the metaphor, we may add that it has side-windows opening out into the world of minds with which it is in relationship through ψ.

There is at least one matter on which most students of Mind agree : that there are various levels or strata through which inspira-tions pass to find form and embodiment. We have already recognised this in trying to understand apparitions where we used Tyrrell's

* Payne and Bendit : *The Psychic Sense*, Chapter IV, is a good account.

descriptive metaphors of "author", "producer", and "stage-carpenter" for three of them. The stage-carpenter was the active agency adjacent to the ætheric world, and the producer or mid-mind levels were peculiarly those of ψ-relationship between the agent's and percipient's minds.

In Upton Sinclair's book * an interesting subjective description is given by Mrs. Sinclair, the percipient, of the process by which she came to "see" clairvoyantly pictures in sealed envelopes. Her working hypothesis comprises (a) the conscious field (which has to be made blank as a preliminary), (b) the subconscious (from which thought—memory-trains and associations are *normally* thrown up into the conscious field), (c) a deeper zone which can acquire the knowledge desired. In addition, there is something which orders the effective state of mind and supervises it—which can (1) terminate it at will, (2) recognise the point at which it will pass into sleep, (3) issue the order as to what is desired. Mrs. Sinclair gives in detail a method she found effective in achieving the essentially relaxed state of body and mind: this is not relevant here. The point is that the deep level to which the order is given is capable of throwing up the desired picture wholly or partially on to the grey blank screen of the conscious field. Guesses and memory-ghosts from the intermediate subconscious region also tend to interpolate themselves on to the screen. By a study of the successes, the partial successes and the failures, Mrs. Sinclair came to recognise the different "feeling" associated with a true vision as distinct from the subconscious guess. She says :

> "There was of course always in my consciousness the question 'Is this the right thing or not?' When the true vision came, this question seemed to receive an answer 'yes', as if some intelligent entity was directly informing me. This was not always the case. At times no answer came, or at least if it came, it was obscured by guesses. . . . The subconscious answers questions, and its answers are always false; its answers come quietly like a thief in the night. But the deep mind answers questions too, and these answers come not quietly, but as if by inspiration, whatever that is—with a rustling of wings, with gladness and conviction."

As another ray of light on the mind's structure I quote from Æ (George Russell), the Irish mystic, poet and artist.† He is endeavouring to account for the nature of poetic inspiration.

> "I was in some profundity of being. There was neither sight nor sound, but all was a motion in deep being. Struggling desperately

---

* Upton Sinclair: *Mental Radio*, Chapter XXI (T. W. Laurie, 1930).
† Æ : *Song and its Fountains*, p. 72 (Macmillan & Co., 1932).

to remain there, I was being dragged down to the waking state, and then what was originally a motion in deep being broke into a dazzle of images which symbolised in some dramatic way the motion of life in that profundity. And still being drawn down there came a third state in which what was originally deep own-being, and after that images, was later translated into words. This experience I told to Yeats who said he had had an identical experience of the three states."

It is interesting to note again the broad recognition of three levels or zones within the mind, although it is not unlikely that there are functionally many different regions. In the present state of our ignorance it seems that three are as many as we can recognise.

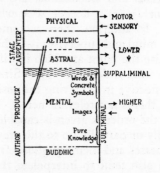

In another passage * Æ is speaking of dreams.

" The seer in dreams is apart from the creator. It is not unreasonable to surmise an intellectual creator able to work magically upon psychic substance. Sometimes indeed at the apex of a dream I have almost surprised the creator of it peering in upon me as if it desired by these miracles to allure me to discovery of itself."

We shall venture to use a diagram as an aid to thought, emphasising again that it is not to be taken as a cut-and-dried scheme, but only as a hint at a type of relationship which is of course not spatial at all. As previously suggested, objectivity and subjectivity are taken to be wholly determined for the individual by the level on which consciousness is focused. We might almost regard the vertical lines of the diagram as the boundary walls of a well, with the surface level of the water as the level of consciousness. In the waking state the water is brimming at the top—a clear, unruffled surface giving a sharp, clear objectivity to the physical world. All below this is then called subjective. The good sensitive can withdraw the water-level and keep the surface clear and unrippled—so that for such a one the ætheric and emotional and mental worlds may have clear objective

* Loc. cit., p. 21.

reality. In sleep we do something similar, but the water-level is rippled (i.e., consciousness is not focused, but diffuse), and permits no more than fragments, often distorted and disjointed, to be remembered afterwards. From Æ's description it is clear that he had kept consciousness clearly focused almost down into the deep-mind region. He identified himself with the seer, but had he been able to go a little further, he would presumably have known himself to be the creator.

Part of the Willett scripts, studied critically by Lord Balfour,* throw light on this subject. Edmund Gurney is communicating, and I shall quote a few statements which may be considered in relation to the diagram.

> " The transcendental self [i.e., our buddhic level and beyond it] might be referred to in a rough-and-ready manner by terming it the subliminal of the discarnate.
> " Take the persisting element [i.e., the discarnate self] which will be largely composed of subliminal with a vital percentage of supraliminal and call that blended consciousness if you will . . . discarnate supraliminality, and you will get as deeper strata the transcendental self. . . . Back of that again lies something I dimly reach after and you would call it ' the Absolute '."

In another remarkable passage dealing with the relation of the individual to the Absolute the communicator says:

> " It's the Absolute on its way to self-consciousness. . . . There is an analogy between the supraliminal and the subliminal, and the individual-rooted-in-the-Absolute and the Absolute."

Again and again Balfour returns to the nature and status of the various centres (our zones) in the subliminal mind. The question as to whether they are analogous to separate selves in a telepathic relationship, or different aspects of one self, is constantly canvassed. The most direct answer given is " Ranges of varying depth ", and, after repetition of the question, the answer is: " It's *One*: and an enlightening point of view—I think it is—is to conceive of it as allied and distinguishable—I missed a word—and then grouped round one nucleus." The difficulty of transmission of these metaphysical ideas through the sensitive is quite obvious, but I think there is no doubt that the communicators regard the " centres " or " levels " of the subliminal as by no means autonomous, but parts of one self. I do not think any questioning of this would have arisen but for the extraordinary phenomena of split personality.† I have expressed the

---

* *Proc. S.P.R.*, Vol. 43, pp. 290–314.
† The reader interested in these psychological abnormalities will find an account of the Sally Beauchamp case in *Proc. S.P.R.*, Vol. 19, p. 410, and the Doris Fischer case, Vol. 31, p. 30.

view that this is a type of dissociation with no direct relevance to the levels of the subliminal, which we have been discussing. It represents, I think, fission or fragmentation of another type, which I can best illustrate by vertical fissures in the diagram (where one is shown on the left-hand side). The communicators, indeed, say:

> " If you're going to confuse any of this with the whole question of secondary and tertiary personalities and their respective memories of each other, you'd be making a mistake. Those are cases of dislocation, imperfect and often pathological."

There is an interesting passage where Gurney is endeavouring to explain the sequence of events in communicating through Mrs. Willett. It is extraordinarily similar in its concepts to those of Æ's first passage. I quote a few sentences only:

> " I'm going to call that deepest portion, nearer to the transcendental self, say, H. Well, the H-self (of the sensitive) and I, agree on what we want—what I want—to get transmitted, and which the H-self normally, in its own H-ness, through its own cognitive faculties can know. . . . The H-self will touch the uprushable self just the grade below the uprushable, and the uprushable and the grade below will receive the knowledge from H. But in getting it into the uprushable focus as it were, it will know that a sort of crystallisation often through symbolism must be arrived at; and we will imagine, if you like, that that having been foreseen both by me and the H-self, we determined upon what sort of crystals to aim at. . . . Then comes that moment of binding when the self that lies in juxtaposition to the uprushable . . . passes it on to the uprushable point in such a state as to make uprush possible. It then rushes out as words spoken or written, or dreams, or never-to-be-denied moments of prescience. . . ."

In another suggestive phrase the communicators describe the supraliminal as " largely the result of attention to what pays ".

The part which I habitually think of as myself (the supraliminal) is the " central receiving station " of consciousness, and as the level of consciousness is raised or lowered (like the water in the well), I become aware of different levels of myself. Could we call this variable level the " retina " of consciousness ? To use such an analogy is probably dangerous. One is conscious all the time of using spatial imagery to describe relationships which are not spatial, and they may have as little applicability as the use of sound to convey the conception of colour to a blind man. To use the intellect to understand the mind brings us up against the inherent limitations of the instrument. Does this mean, then, that we can never hope to understand fully the nature of Mind ? I, for one, do not think so : but our deeper understanding will only come through contacting a level of the self behind Mind. This is probably done in certain forms of yogic trance and certain mystical states of illumination. But even so, we must be prepared for the possibility that such knowledge as a developed individual may obtain of himself cannot in its very nature find much expression in the symbolism of language. It may find a little more in poetry than in prose, and a little more in music than in both these; but, though incommunicable on the level of intellect, it is not necessarily incommunicable on the deeper buddhic level, where we may expect to find an increasingly intimate web of relationships.

This, however, takes us into the subject-matter of the next section of the book.

SURVIVAL OF DEATH: THE PROBLEM

Mysterious Night! when our first parent knew
Thee from report divine, and heard thy name,
Did he not tremble for this lovely frame,
This glorious canopy of light and blue ?
Yet 'neath a curtain of translucent dew,
Bathed in the rays of the great setting flame,
Hesperus with the host of heaven came.
And lo ! Creation widened in man's view.

Who could have thought such darkness lay concealed
Within thy beams, O Sun ? or who could find,
Whilst flower and leaf and insect stood revealed,
That to such countless orbs thou mad'st us blind !
Why do we then shun Death with anxious strife ?
If Light can thus deceive, wherefore not Life ?

BLANCO WHITE.

Life, that dares send
A challenge to the end
And when it comes, say, " Welcome, Friend ".

R. CRASHAW.

" The thought of death l eaves me n perfect peace, for I have a
firm conviction that our spirit is a being of indestructible nature :
it works on from eternity to eternity ; it is like the sun, which
though it seems to set to our mortal eyes, does not really set, but
shines on perpetually."

GOETHE.

IT can, I think, truthfully be said of F. W. H. Myers, famous
author of that classic *Human Personality and its Survival of Bodily
Death*, that no man desired proof of this more passionately than he,
and no one laboured harder to attain it. There is a story told of
Myers that, finding himself seated one day next to a distinguished
business man in circumstances that called for conversation, he
thought he would try to find out what the latter's idea of a life after
death was. The business man, however, quickly steered the conversation away. Myers tried again, but once more met with no
success. In the end he was reduced to putting the question directly,
" What do you suppose happens after death ? " The other looked
rather embarrassed and said, after an awkward pause, " We shall

enter into the joy of the Lord, I suppose. But why bring up such an unpleasant subject ? "

I doubt if more than one or two per cent of those who believe that they will survive death would give any more illuminating answer to the same question. Religious-sounding clichés largely concealing fear or ignorance would probably be found in the majority of replies.

We are told by Bede that when the monk Paulinus was at the Court of Edwin, King of Northumbria, in A.D. 627, endeavouring to persuade him to accept Christianity, the King was in two minds about it until one of his warriors spoke :

> " The present life of man upon earth, O King, seems to me in comparison to the time which is unknown to us, like to the swift flight of a sparrow through that house wherein you sit at supper in winter with your ealdormen and thegns, while the fire blazes in the midst, and the hall is warmed, but the wintry storms of rain or snow are raging abroad without. The sparrow, flying in at one door and immediately out at another, whilst he is within is safe from the wintry tempest : but after a short space of fair weather he immediately vanishes out of your sight, passing from winter into winter again. So this life of man appears for a little while, but of what is to follow or what went before we know nothing at all. If therefore this new doctrine tells us something more certain, it seems justly to deserve to be followed."

Edwin was, in fact, persuaded to accept the new teaching, and built the first York Cathedral. We should not infer from this that Christianity once had something to offer which it subsequently lost, but rather that answers which satisfy the questionings of one age prove wholly unsatisfying in the thought-climate of another. In this scientific age we are not concerned with *beliefs* but with *knowledge* ; we have rejected the sanctions of authority for those of understanding. This is all to the good. It is better that we should suffer and grow through our own adventure and discovery than remain as children in a paradise of dreams. I have quoted Bede, however, to remind us that a warrior of the seventh century and a Northumbrian king had longings and hungers like our own when faced with the mysteries of Life and Death. There is a moment which comes to all men when they look for the last time on features they have loved, now still and unresponsive. Nothing seems so utterly dead as this frail temple of mortality from which the tenant has departed. It is then that we hunger beyond all else to know whence the bright spirit has flown. Can we *know* ? How gladly would the questing mind in such an hour exchange much consolation for a little reliable knowledge.

I am far from supposing that Reason and the application of the Scientific Method are the only means of gathering knowledge.

Those who study the next section of this book will see unfolding vistas of the higher self which can apprehend Truth in virtue of its own intrinsic nature.   But since for most of us these ranges are not at present accessible to the will, we must use to the fullest extent the powers we have on the level of Mind.   Because the change involving death of the body takes place on a lower significant level of reality than that of Mind, there can be no doubt of the adequacy of the Mind's powers, if fully used, to provide us with a complete solution of our problem.   What progress we have made in this direction, it is hoped to survey in this chapter.

I. THE NATURE OF SURVIVAL

Mr. G. N. M. Tyrrell has reminded us on several occasions *
that the answers which can be given to most of our biggest questions depend on the background of thought from which they emerge. When therefore we pose the question, " Shall I survive the change called death ? " much depends on the concept of " I "—the self. This we have endeavoured to describe in Chapter 12.   Death means that the physical body is no longer serviceable as an instrument of the self, for the exploration of, and the response to, a physical environment.   It is therefore discarded.   It never was the self, as the common man is prone to think : it was an instrument of the self created by it—an ambassador or representative of it in foreign territory.   With the death of the body presumably the ætheric structure may vanish, or possibly the lower substratum of this ; for our chief knowledge of it suggests that its function is largely that of a bridge between lower-Mind and the Physical Body.   If the latter goes, the bridge is no longer needed.   Thus we shall assume that the " astral " vehicle (see Figure, p. 239) forms the new " body " of the self. *The astral environment or level of reality then becomes for the self an objective world.*   It is the new world of appearance in the after-death state, and it conveys to the common sense of beings on that plane the same appearance of being " real " as the world of matter does to the ordinary man on our present one.   Doubtless there will be materialists and idealists in that world also : there will be the sceptics and scientists who will tell their fellows it is the *only* reality, and the questing few who will urge the necessity for a deeper exploration if Truth is to be found !

The image-making faculty of the mid-mind levels is now probably incorporated in the outer bodily structure and accessible to the will, so that vistas of creative activity in modifying and beautifying the

* E.g., *Apparitions* : Myers Memorial Lecture, pp. 120–2.

environment unfold before the self. The creative faculty (Tyrrell's
" stage-carpenter "), which in Chapter 9 could but rarely sustain an
apparition for a short time, should now have free exercise within
the limits of the laws and of the basic world-structure sustained
by the World-Mind on that level. The arts should flourish, for
they will be built into the structure of life and not be peripheral,
as on the physical level.

The ψ-faculty, in the absence of the limiting effect of the brain,
should now become freely accessible as a mode of communication,
giving awareness of events in wide ranges of space and time. Again
—though this is speculative—there will probably be the necessity for
senses in the astral body, to canalise and concentrate the ψ-faculty
for intimacy of acquaintance with the near environment. It is, of
course, difficult not to transfer our material common-sense concepts
to this higher level and formulate a picture of existence incorporating
all the richness of sense-data (probably enormously extended)
together with freedom from the grievous limitations of a physical
body. In doing so we *may* be making a mistake—but my own
inclination is to think that we are not, for several reasons. 1. Some
indications are available to us from what we already know of the
structure of the self. Our inferences from these, though *very
limited*, are not going to be widely astray. 2. We have indications
in Chapter 10 of experiences outside the physical body which
suggest pseudo-sensory perception, though greatly widened in scope,
and embodiment in finite forms, though far less restricted in
freedom of movement. A close study of these cases is very illuminating.* 3. Both worlds—the material and the astral—are worlds
of " appearance ". From the standpoint of higher-Mind, which is
still subjective to denizens of these worlds (see Figure, p. 239), they
are both worlds of dream or relative illusion. Their limited measure
of reality is sustained by, and is only an aspect of, the higher, and
of the two, the material is the more removed from reality. Now,
space, time and finite form are creations and impositions of higher
mind. We should therefore expect to find them still controlling
—though probably with less domination—the astral world, as they
do the material world.

By " survival of the change called death " in our initial question
we therefore mean : will the whole hierarchy of the self continue
in its richness of being when the body disintegrates ? Shall I, this
centre of consciousness which I know myself to be, with all my
higher faculty of Love, of Creativity, of passionate hunger for Beauty

* Cf. also Tyrrell's views in *Science and Psychical Phenomena*, pp. 277–80
(Methuen & Co., 1938).

and Truth, with my essential memories and my gathered harvest of wisdom (small though it be) : shall I continue in unbroken communion with those I love and with these values ? This is at heart the question we really want answered—and put in this form it takes us far beyond the realm where psychical research alone can give us complete information. Indeed, it is perfectly obvious that the answer has been implicit in our assumption of an ascending hierarchy of levels of reality in the self. Clearly the existence of the more real cannot depend on that of the less real : the very opposite is true. Putting aside the larger question for the present, let us endeavour to discover how much psychical research has established by the experimental method.

2. THE PROBLEM OF PROOF

What do we mean by " proof " of survival ? It would be well if we asked ourselves precisely what sort of evidence we should be prepared to accept as proof, and then we can see if it is obtainable. Suppose an honest medium claimed that he (or she) was in communication with an intimate friend of ours who had died, what would satisfy us that the claim was true ? Let us take the much simpler case : a friend is believed to be on one side of an impenetrable screen and we are on the other. It is opaque, and somewhat distorts the voice, although conversation is still possible. How should we identify our friend ? We should undoubtedly be able to do so through the myriad subtle emotional, intellectual and moral distinctions which make each individual unique. I think we should particularly make use of (a) mannerisms or idiosyncrasies of thought, speech or action; (b) specific memories and interests which were shared; (c) reactions, emotional, intellectual and spiritual, to circumstance—which would reveal the underlying character. The problem with a medium is much more difficult : she is not an impersonal screen, but unconsciously adds to and colours all communications. Moreover, this is not all. It is unquestionable that in mediumistic trance the sensitive frequently achieves telepathic rapport with the sitter and in these circumstances may be " mind-reading ". In other words, the memories shared with the " dead " friend, and perhaps with no other living person, may have been unconsciously drawn by the medium from the sitter's own mind and presented through the medium back to the sitter. Thus telepathy between the living, and not communication from the " dead ", may be the source of intimate information and impressive memories. Even mannerisms or idiosyncrasies of the friend allegedly communicating may have been drawn by the medium from the subconscious memory of the sitter. Suppose the " dead " friend—through the medium—correctly informs the sitter of some unusual happening which will occur to him within a week, this may be precognitive faculty of the medium's deeper mind. Suppose X informs Y that he proposes to leave a message in a sealed envelope in safe custody, and that after his death, should he die first, he will endeavour to communicate its nature to Y. Suppose this was done accurately : would it prove the survival of X ? There would certainly be a reasonable presumption of it, but we have at least to recognise two theoretical possibilities. (1) That the clairvoyant faculty of the medium " read " this document, learning of its existence telepathically from Y. (2) That the message of X leaked telepathically into the subconscious of Y and remained there latent—i.e., never rising into Y's consciousness. The medium obtained it telepathically from this source. If X decided to leave a message in cypher and transmit after his death the key which would enable it to be decoded, this would be better evidence of survival in that (1) would be eliminated.

We see, then, that much intimate matter believed known to only two people, or much impressive information which might at one time have been assumed as only within the compass of a discarnate mind, has to be recognised as available to incarnate minds through the exercise of ψ-faculty. It is rather an ironical situation, for the evidence of psychical research has brought to us a recognition of the vast sweep of Mind, of its extraordinary powers not tied down to one point of time and space, and in doing this has shown it to be most improbable that Mind depends on matter for its ability to exist and function. Never has the survival by Mind of the death of the body seemed so probable, on the basis of evidence, yet never has conclusive experimental proof of survival been so difficult to secure. If we knew definitely what are the limits beyond which extra-sensory faculty cannot operate, it would be possible to devise a conclusive experiment ; but we do not know these limits.

We have surveyed some of the legitimate criticism which sees in the exercise of para-normal faculty by a medium an alternative explanation to communication from discarnate minds. We shall now look briefly at some of the experiments and tests designed to make the para-normal-faculty theory look less and less plausible.

3. BOOK TESTS

Book Tests originated with the mediumship of Mrs. Osborne Leonard, who goes into a deep trance, in which she is ostensibly controlled by a little Indian girl called "Feda". This matter is discussed later in Section 5. Feda purports to control the physical organism of Mrs. Leonard and pass on messages from persons on the other side. Here is an example :

Sitters : Miss Radclyffe-Hall and Lady Troutbridge.* "Feda" indicated a certain row of books in Miss Radclyffe-Hall's flat (where Mrs. Leonard had never been) and said that on p. 14 of the fifth book from the left something about half-way down the page gave her a feeling of heat; it might be heat like a hot fire, or it might be great anger spoken of as heat. The book indicated had not been read or opened by the sitters. Its pages had thirty-three lines. On line 16 of p. 14 occur the words "ardent patriot". Incidentally on line 15 of p. 15, almost adjacent when the book is closed, occurs the word "bonfire".

"Feda" ascribes this information to clairvoyance by the communicating spirit, but of course clairvoyance by the mind of the medium or the sitters or a combination of both of these is a possibility. I give one other illustration—the most interesting and impressive I have read.

Sitter : Lady Pamela Glenconner.† One of her sons, Edward Wyndham Tennant, known within the family as "Bim", had been killed in the Battle of the Somme in 1916. His father, Lord Glenconner, was extremely interested in forestry and planned and tended the forest areas on his own estates with great care. Lady Glenconner writes :

> ". . . During walks through the fragrant woods, when expressions of admiration or delight in the lovely scenery arose, how often would the depressing verdict be uttered by the ' Master of the Trees ' that the young shoots were being ruined by the ' beetle '. ' You see all those quirks—those sudden bends in the new growths ? Those show the beetle has got at them. You wouldn't see the damage to the young trees as I do, and it's the greatest pest we have to deal with . . .' and much more of the like in conversation. So familiar was the theme to the family that ' Bim ' has been known to say to his mother *sotto voce*, ' See if we get through this wood without hearing about the beetle '. If his father was unduly pessimistic about something ' Bim ' would say ' All the woods have got the beetle '."

We have here a homely instance of a family joke, something trivial but peculiarly characteristic of "Bim". In a sitting with Mrs. Leonard in December 1917 the control "Feda", after giving other

* *Proc. S.P.R.*, Vol. 30, p. 339 (1919).
† From *The Earthen Vessel*, by Lady Pamela Glenconner (John Lane, 1921).

messages, said "Bim now wants to send a message to his father. This book is particularly for his father. Underline that, he says. It is the ninth book on the third shelf, counting from the left to right, in the bookcase on the right of the door in the drawing-room as you enter; take the title and look at page 37." The book indicated was in fact *Trees* (by J. H. Kelman), and on page 36 at the bottom, leading on to page 37 were the words, "Sometimes you will see curious marks in the wood; these are caused by a tunnelling beetle, very injurious to the trees. . . ." Lady Glenconner says, "Had a chance observer been present when we traced this test, he would have said, 'This is no mourning family, these are happy people', and he would have been right".

The alternative explanation to this would be that the medium (*a*) derived this convincing characteristic of "Bim" telepathically from the mind of one of the sitters, (*b*) exercised an extraordinary power of clairvoyance to find an appropriate illustration of it. Because we do not know the limits of ψ, we cannot say these are impossible achievements. These examples will serve to illustrate the idea of book tests. Their implications have been discussed by many competent researchers,[*] but I do not think we can say more than that they are most impressive evidence for the fact of clairvoyance, and a reminder that available to Mind there is a power of gathering detailed knowledge of the kind particularly desired which any librarian might envy! It is not, of course, unreasonable to suggest that clairvoyance of this quality *may* be available to the discarnate mind more extensively than to the incarnate mind tied up to a material brain.[†] This supposition is reasonable enough—but we are concerned here with *proof* of survival, and we must admit that book tests do not help us in this.

4. PROXY SITTINGS

If a person who possesses memories of his deceased friend sits with a medium, telepathy may quite naturally be advanced as the source of the medium's information. Where a stranger or a friend sits on his behalf with the medium—someone who knows no more of the deceased person than merely the name—we make the telepathic explanation much more difficult. To retain it we should have to assume that the medium (*a*) derives from the mind of the sitter the

---

[*] *Proc. S.P.R.*, Vol. 31, p. 242; Vol. 33, p. 606; Vol. 40, p. 129; etc.

[†] This should not be underestimated. Consider, for example, the Gordon Davis case of Dr. S. G. Soal (*Proc. S.P.R.*, Vol. 35), where clearly a medium showed precognitive clairvoyance of a remarkable kind.

name and whereabouts of the person on whose behalf he is sitting, and (b) derives from the mind of this distant person knowledge about the deceased one. The necessity to postulate indirect linkage of this kind starts to undermine confidence in the adequacy of the telepathic theory. Those who desire to study the results obtained will find plenty of material available. The Rev. C. Drayton Thomas has given an account of twenty-four such sittings with Mrs. Leonard as medium.* More impressive, and perhaps more valuable to the student, is a particular case (that of Bobby Newlove),† in relation to which Mr. Thomas held eleven sittings with Mrs. Leonard. He had received a letter from a Mr. Hatch of Nelson, Lancs, asking him if he would endeavour to obtain information about Bobby, aged 10, who had recently died of diphtheria and was his step-daughter's son. The information which Mr. Thomas was able to send to Mr. Hatch finally convinced the latter that Bobby had established his identity. This information included an intimate knowledge of Bobby's home, his surroundings, his friends, etc., including—and this is interesting—information not in the mind of Mr. Hatch but which he was able subsequently to verify. This is of some importance, for Mr. Thomas had taken Mr. Hatch's letter to his first sitting with Mrs. Leonard, and if we accept psychometry as factual, the handling of this letter would have made possible a degree of mental rapport between Mrs. Leonard and Mr. Hatch. Among this information was a reference to a broken stile on a walk which Bobby liked. Mr. Hatch later discovered from a friend that a stile had been there, but was removed shortly before Bobby's death. Another remarkable piece of information was details of a route to a place where Bobby played frequently for some weeks prior to his death. This place was unhealthy by reason of two drain-pipes and it was suggested that Bobby's illness may have derived from this. Many who read Drayton Thomas's detailed account will probably decide that the simplest explanation is that which assumes the survival of Bobby, and that he communicated directly or indirectly through Mrs. Leonard. Others will take the view that telepathic rapport having been established with Mr. Hatch (unknown, of course, to him), the clairvoyant faculty of the medium applied to his home and neighbourhood—with perhaps a flash or two of retrocognition —will account for these data.

It is again clearly a matter of balancing relative probabilities : there are some who feel an explanation based on survival is much more probable, and vice versa.

* *Proc. S.P.R.*, Vol. 41, p. 139.
† Ibid., Vol. 43, pp. 439–519 (1935).

5. THE PROBLEM OF MEDIUMSHIP

It is impossible to discuss the evidence for survival without considering the nature of mediumship. It is not a subject which is easy to deal with briefly, for the attempt to unravel its nature has been the subject of many papers and several books. (References to some of these are given in footnotes and will indicate sources of fuller information.)

We have already made clear the general conception of the self as a synthesis or hierarchy of principles or vehicles, recognising that on each of these levels there is a whole world of significant phenomena shared by the corresponding principles of other individuals. We have suggested that objectivity and subjectivity are terms relative to the individual, depending on the particular level on which the consciousness is focused for the time being. Wherever this is temporarily found is the growing point of the psyche, and on this level is made a sharp distinction between the world which seems external and is held in common (objective) and the worlds of the interior levels which seem private (subjective). A " medium " or " sensitive " is a person who can at will withdraw consciousness in some degree to a level interior to the normal waking one, and at the same time keep open a channel of communication with the latter, usually through writing or speaking. There are two general methods of study of mediumship available : (1) that which has been adopted by the Society for Psychical Research over the last sixty years, which is the method of objective analytical study of trance data and conditions, and (2) the use of highly developed clairvoyant faculty to " see " what is happening. It is, of course, true that the interpretation of what is " seen " is involved in the latter, but the chief difficulty is that there are so few persons with this faculty developed to the necessary degree. As an example of the second method of study I quote briefly from the findings of Phoebe Payne,* who (apart from poltergeist mediums) makes a practical classification of mediums into five groups.

1. The medium who uses unconscious self-hypnosis. There is here no evidence of any external influence. There is a genuine degree of trance, but the phenomena are obviously crude impersonations or dramatisations carried out by a level of the subliminal mind. It adopts the role of an actor and plays

* Phoebe Payne : *Man's Latent Powers* (Faber & Faber, 1938). A recent study of trance phenomena has been published by Dr. and Mrs. Bendit (née Payne), *This World and That* (Faber & Faber, 1950).

one part after another—from General Booth to Queen Victoria —expressing sentiments the origins of which are not difficult to trace. The process is probably often compensatory for limitations in everyday life.

2. The medium who works in a semi-conscious state under partial control. This is not, as previously, characterised by the up-welling of thought-forms from within, but is described as the overshadowing of another personality. It appears as a " gradual superimposing of the mental and emotional bodies of the control upon those of the medium and the result is like a double exposure of a film or plate ". On other occasions the linkage appears to be telepathic. Mrs. Bendit herself experimented at one time with this form of trance and has given a most interesting subjective appraisal of it.

" My ordinary consciousness of people and environment was still there but a long way off, and an increasing acuteness of perception began to manifest. This awareness extended in two directions: into the outer world with a strange penetration into people's thoughts and emotions and a greatly enhanced range of knowledge, and into the inner worlds so that their details became as clear to my perception as the physical plane. . . . My own small thinking went on as an aside without any conscious volition and did not in the least interfere with the theme which was being expounded . . . my ordinary personality was . . . manipulated by something very much bigger . . . to me infinitely more an influence than a person."

I think it is in Mrs. Bendit's mind an open question whether this " control " is really a distinct and presumably discarnate being or an up-welling of influence from the more central self. Possibly sometimes the one, sometimes the other is true.

3. The completely controlled or dead-trance medium. This is a comparatively rare type, in which the medium's own self withdraws from the physical-ætheric vehicles in its astral body, and these vehicles are controlled by a quite different mind. The transformation thereby effected is sometimes remarkable—even the appearance of the face as well as the character and atmosphere are of a different personality.

4. The receptive but self-controlled psychic who remains self-conscious and directs his own psychism at will. In terms of the corresponding activity of the ætheric body, Mrs. Bendit says that the solar plexus *chakram* is no longer the main active centre, but that the heart and throat centres become active. She says further that " the better the education and moral development of the sensitive, the finer will be the quality of his

work, because it is almost impossible to transmit information with which there are no corresponding ideas in consciousness ".

5. The psychic using his own powers without extraneous aid. This is the fullest development of the preceding type, except that the head *chakram* of the ætheric body is now dominantly used. Of this type Mrs. Bendit says :

> " To him psychism is an art which he practises assiduously, as a dancer or musician practises in order to perfect technique ; it is the background against which he sees the whole drama of life . . . he lives naturally in several worlds at once except when he chooses to close his own psychic doors."

Mrs. Bendit's classification (based on her own psychism) is valuable, and, as far as I can see, conflicts at no point with the more general conclusions arrived at by the other method. If we are to advance substantially in our knowledge of this field, it will have to be through the development of a sufficient number of first-class psychics whose observations can be used as checks one against the other. This is a thoroughly scientific procedure.

Among the mediums subjected to very prolonged study by distinguished members of the Society for Psychical Research I shall refer briefly to two : Mrs. Piper and Mrs. Willett. The first of these is probably to be classified as Type 2 or possibly 3 at times, and the second, Type 4 in Mrs. Bendit's scheme.

Mrs. Piper was an American woman whose phenomena were studied for about twenty-five years—between 1886 and 1911. A brilliant, exhaustive and critical study of the whole of her record was made in 1915 by Mrs. Henry Sidgwick.* Two conclusions were accepted by all the responsible investigators—that Mrs. Piper displayed super-normal knowledge in her trance, and that this was not acquired by fraudulent means or wholly derived telepathically from the mind of the sitter. From where, then, was it derived ?

It should be explained for the benefit of those who are not familiar with these phenomena that when a medium loses consciousness and goes into a trance, another intelligence usually begins to speak through the medium (or use the medium's hand to write). This is called the medium's " control " or " guide ", for he manipulates the medium's organism. He acts as a go-between, and professes to hand on to the sitter the words of the communicator or communicators—the deceased person or persons with whom the sitter desires to be in touch. A medium may have one control or several.

* *Proc. S.P.R.*, Vol. 28 (1915). This comprises over 600 pages. Tyrrell, in Chapter XII of *Science and Psychical Phenomena*, has given a very brief survey.

The underlying idea is that the manipulation of the medium's organism requires some skill and practice : hence the role of a " control " who takes charge. In the early years of Mrs. Piper's mediumship there were a number of such controls, who called themselves " Chlorine ", Mrs. Siddons, Johann Sebastian Bach, Longfellow, Commodore Vanderbilt and Phinuit (the chief). In the years 1892–7 a new control appeared—George Pelham, a lawyer who had recently died and who had been a friend of Dr. Hodgson, an eminent investigator. From 1897 to 1905 a new group of controls, calling themselves the " Imperator Band ", appeared : these had formerly been controls of the English medium, Stainton Moses. Finally, after Dr. Hodgson's death in 1905, there appeared a Hodgson control. These controls all claim to be discarnate spirits. The main questions to which we want answers are these. Are these controls what they claim to be ? Is there any evidence that any spirit independent of Mrs. Piper at any time controlled her organism ? If not, what is the interpretation of these controls ? As to the communicators who speak via the controls, are they the spirits they purport to be ? These are the questions, upon satisfactory answers to which hangs the issue of communication between the living and the dead. Space does not allow us to do more than weigh the answers which those most competent to judge themselves formed. Dr. Richard Hodgson studied Mrs. Piper's mediumship for about twelve years.* His earlier report had been one of guarded scepticism. I shall quote from his later one :

> " In my previous report . . . I urged that there were almost insuperable objections to the supposition that such deceased persons were in direct communication with Phinuit, *at least in anything like the fullness of their personality :* but it seemed to me a hypothesis that should be continually borne in mind, that there might be some actual communication through Mrs. Piper's trance, but that the communication has been subject to certain unavoidable limitations. . . . [later] At the present time I cannot profess to have any doubt but that the chief communicators to whom I have referred in the foregoing pages are veritably the personalities that they claim to be, that they have survived the change we call death, and that they have directly communicated with us whom we call living through Mrs. Piper's entranced organism."

It was the evidence furnished by George Pelham (G. P.), who communicated—as a direct control—for several years after his death, which finally convinced Dr. Hodgson. I quote from his report on this :

> " Nor has he [G. P.] failed in the recognition of personal friends. I may say generally that out of a large number of sitters who went as

strangers to Mrs. Piper, the communicating G. P. has picked out the friends of G. P. living, precisely as the G. P. living might have been expected to do. (Thirty cases of recognition out of at least one hundred and fifty who have had sittings with Mrs. Piper since the first appearance of G. P. and no case of false recognition.) He has exhibited memories in connection with these and other friends which are such as would naturally be associated as part of the G. P. personality, which certainly do not suggest in themselves that they originate otherwise, and which were accompanied by the emotional relations which were connected with such friends in the mind of G. P. living.

"At one of his early communications G. P. expressly undertook the task of rendering all the assistance in his power towards establishing the continued existence of himself and other communicators, in pursuance of a promise of which he himself reminded me, made some two years or more before his death, that if he died before me and found himself 'still existing,' he would devote himself to proving the fact; and in the persistence of his endeavour to overcome the difficulties in communicating, as far as possible, in his constant readiness to act as amanuensis at the sittings, in the effect which he has produced by his counsels—to myself as investigator, and to numerous other sitters and communicators—he has, in so far as I can form a judgment in a problem so complex and still presenting so much obscurity, displayed the keenness and pertinacity which were eminently characteristic of G. P. living."

It must be admitted that such appropriate reactions to various friends are a subtle and very impressive psychological feature. It is difficult to see what better evidence than this could be expected.

On the other hand, Mrs. Henry Sidgwick, after her lengthy study of all the evidence, came to the conclusion that the controls were probably dramatised phases of Mrs. Piper's own consciousness. The "hypnotic self" was impersonating a number of characters successively: they were not considered to be co-existing secondary personalities such as occur sometimes in abnormal psychology. When it is recalled that some of these purported to be Julius Cæsar, Moses (of the Old Testament), George Eliot and "Imperator", supposed to be a very exalted spirit, but who talked vaguely and even immaturely, few intelligent people will think Mrs. Sidgwick's conclusion lacked considerable justification. She holds a similar opinion of the "communicators".

It is an extraordinary position: there is enough good evidence in the case of G. P. to convince able men like Dr. Hodgson and Sir Oliver Lodge of his genuineness as a communicator and control, and there is enough nonsense in general to make Mrs. Sidgwick conclude that the controls, in spite of all their asseverations, were dramatisations of part of Mrs. Piper's subliminal mind. I think we must come to the only possible conclusion: that expressed in the simple form already discussed the whole issue has been over-simplified. If we insist on " either/or " with unsatisfactory premises we are liable to find ourselves in a dilemma. Professor William James, who studied the Hodgson control of Mrs. Piper, believed that the processes were much more complex than those of the simple assumptions involved in the terms " control " and " communicator ". He said :

> " Extraneous ' wills-to-communicate ' may contribute to the results, as well as a ' will-to-personate ', and the two kinds of will may be distinct in entity, though capable of helping each other out. The will-to-communicate in our present instance would be, on a prima facie view of it, the will of Hodgson's surviving spirit ; and it can make fragmentary gleams and flashes of what it wishes to say mix with the rubbish of the trance talk on this side. The two wills might thus strike up a sort of partnership and reinforce each other. It might even be that the will-to-personate would be comparatively inert unless it were aroused to activity by the other will. . . ."

The fact is that the will-to-communicate may often be there ; but to suppose that the trance material is wholly of this origin, or not at all of this origin, is to present extreme alternatives. Mrs. Sidgwick recognises frankly, " If the whole dramatic form were play-acting, it might still be the framework in which veridical communications come to us." I think we are also prone to forget the possibility that just as the medium withdraws consciousness from his normal state and loses awareness of the waking world in order to function as a medium, there may be some corresponding displacement of consciousness necessary on the side of the communicator. This may place him temporarily out of touch (wholly or partially) with *his* environment, and immerse him in the limitations of a normal human outlook, or even of a dream state. To achieve a poised state neither too projected nor too withdrawn may be a matter of great difficulty. It is possible that if a communicator retains his normal human state too closely, his possibility of communication is weak and wavering ; if he departs too far from his norm, communication lines may be good but he may have nothing convincing to say because he is immersed in a dream-like state. It would seem likely that G. P. achieved considerable facility in maintaining the necessary conditions on his side, and it is equally evident that others were much less successful. It cannot be pretended that this is a very satisfactory conclusion : I think so far as trance mediums—the Types 2 and 3 of Mrs. Bendit—are concerned, we do not know enough to generalise. A particular instance may give convincing evidence of the survival of a particular personality. I should be disposed to accept Hodgson's judgment about G. P. Many other instances of "communicators" through the same medium may be most unconvincing, and yet remarkable flashes amid a lot of nonsense may suggest to us the possibility that there is a will-to-communicate in the background.

The mediumship of Mrs. Willett is of quite a different kind from Mrs. Piper's, being characterised by her retaining a consciousness of self. It covers a period of about twenty years (1908–28), and a most valuable analytical study of it has been made by the Earl of Balfour.* In its earliest form it was automatic script in a hand-writing which differed from that normally characteristic of Mrs. Willett. The earliest communicators purported to be F. W. H. Myers and Edmund Gurney, but subsequently there joined them Henry Sidgwick, S. H. Butcher, A. W. Verrall and another whose anonymity is preserved. These names constitute, of course, the brilliant and scholarly group to whose enterprise the founding of the London Society for Psychical Research was due. Early in 1909 Myers and Gurney indicated in the script that they were going to attempt a new type of communication ("I don't want her to develop into a second Piper "). Thus " Myers " wrote :

" I am trying experiments with you to make you hear without writing, therefore as it is I Myers who do this deliberately, do not fear or wince when words enter your consciousness, or subsequently when such words are in the script. On the contrary it will be the success of my purpose if you recognise in your script phrases you have found in your consciousness. I know this must be for a while disconcerting and be filled with the fear of that eternal S.S. [subliminal self] which I hope we have succeeded in dethroning to some extent. Therefore be agreeing to be disconcerted and do not analyse whence these impressions which I shall in future refer to as Daylight Impressions—come from, they are part of a psychic education framed by me for you. . . ."

Balfour speaks in his report of silent D.I.s where the message is remembered and written down, or spoken D.I.s where it is taken down verbatim at the time by a sitter. Script combined with this became the most usual form of Mrs. Willett's developed medium-ship. Her own subjective account is very interesting. In a letter to Mrs. Verrall dated September 27th, 1909, she writes :

" I got no impression of *appearance*, only character, and in some way voice or pronunciation (though this doesn't mean that my ears hear you know !). That is always so in D.I. I don't feel a sense of ' seeing ', but an intense sense of personality, like a blind person perhaps might have—and of inflections, such as of amusement or

* *Proc. S.P.R.*, Vol. 43, pp. 43–318 (1935).

emotion on the part of the speaker. If you asked me *how* I know when E. G. is speaking and not F. W. H. M., I can't exactly define, except that to me it would be impossible to be in doubt one instant— and with E. G. I often know he is there a second or two before he speaks. . . . I then sometimes speak first . . . . To me, by now there isn't anything strange in D.I.s except when I try to explain anything about them ; then I realise suddenly they are unusual ! But otherwise it gives me no more sense of oddness to be talking to these invisible people than it does to be talking to my son for instance. But I don't think I mentally visualise any sort of ' appearance ' with regard to them—it is as ' minds ' and ' characters ' that they are real to me, and yet *not at all* intangible or not-solid realities. . . ."

In contrast with the Piper trance phenomena, not only does Mrs. Willett retain a degree of consciousness of the self throughout, but also there are no " controls ". She is in her own person in touch with the communicators, who are the small select group referred to. The substance of the communications discussed by Earl Balfour includes much detail of the *modus operandi* of the process. Expressed in broadest terms, it is a telepathic process between the minds of the communicator and the medium, and the details of this are discussed in many scripts. The scripts of Mrs. Willett also cover discussions of telepathy, inspiration, the structure of the self and other metaphysical questions which clearly sometimes did not interest Mrs. Willett, but were wholly commensurate with the interests and the intelligence of the alleged communicators. A student of Lord Balfour's paper will feel the atmosphere of scholarship and of research which was so characteristic of the persons who purport to communicate, when they were alive on earth. Lord Balfour's judgment of the scripts is " they show a power of thought on difficult and abstruse subjects which, knowing Mrs. Willett as intimately as I do, I certainly should not have expected from her normal self ". Mrs. Willett was a well-read and intelligent lady but not particularly interested in the psychological and metaphysical problems which are discussed so constantly in the scripts. What judgment, then, shall we pass on the status of the communicators ?

In the introduction to his paper Lord Balfour, speaking of survival and the possibility and reality of spirit communication says, " My personal belief, arrived at after much study and reflection, leans strongly in favour of an affirmative answer." He also informs us that the scripts which he has been free to use are only a selection from the total, and that

" It would be impossible to do justice to the argument in favour of spirit communication on the basis of the Willett phenomena without violating confidences which I am bound to respect. . . . If I had before me only those Willett scripts to which I have been referring, I frankly admit that I should have been at a loss whether to attribute them to subliminal activity or to a source entirely outside the personality of the medium. . . . But having before me the whole of the Willett scripts, and being in a position to compare them with the scripts of other automatists of our group and with facts known to me but not known to Mrs. Willett herself, I am personally of opinion that they contain evidence of supernormally acquired knowledge which no mere subliminal mentation will suffice to account for."

It seems clear that the private scripts must have contained intimate memories, and a wealth of mannerisms and characteristics of these scholars, some of whom Lord Balfour had known intimately. The fact that he was able to come to the conclusion he announced is one which must carry very great weight.

6. THE EVIDENCE OF CROSS-CORRESPONDENCE

No résumé of the various lines of experiment which have contributed evidence relating to survival of death would be complete without some account of Cross-Correspondence. Its peculiar interest lies in the fact that ostensibly it is a type of experiment devised and conducted by the group of distinguished friends, Myers, Gurney, Sidgwick, Butcher and Verrall, who in their lifetime contributed so much in the field of psychical research. The experiment was made possible through the fact that four ladies who were deeply interested in the work of psychical research had developed considerable facility in automatic writing. These were Mrs. Verrall, Mrs. Holland, Mrs. Willett and Mrs. Salter. The idea underlying Cross-Correspondence is this. Suppose an incident or a theme characteristic, let us say, of the deceased F. W. H. Myers appeared in an automatic script, it might be claimed by the critic that it had been drawn from the medium's own subliminal mind or derived by her telepathically from the minds of other living persons who knew Myers. Suppose, however, that Myers (whom we will postulate as surviving) divided his message into phrases and fragments, sending some of these through the script of one automatist and some through the script of a second and of a third. These fragments, which to the automatists would seem meaningless and incoherent, if pieced together skilfully by an independent person would show purpose and planning by a mind independent of the automatists. Evidence that such experiments were being attempted began to appear in scripts from 1907 onwards. Some of the more highly developed themes contain a wealth of classical and literary allusions which demanded from the solvers of the puzzle a like knowledge combined with considerable ingenuity.

It is not proposed to illustrate this here, but the student should study a case or two for himself.* The chief criticisms which have been levelled against the obvious interpretation of this remarkable series of experiments are these. (*a*) That the pattern and design found in the scripts were illusory and that the data were, so to speak, forced into the supposed theory. (*b*) That the originating mind was Mrs. Verrall's (she being a classical scholar), and that in some obscure way fragments leaked over from her subliminal mind to those of her fellow automatists. To examine these possibilities experimentally, a dummy cross-correspondence experiment was devised,† but no support for these criticisms was obtained from it. Moreover, if the suggestion that Mrs. Verrall's subliminal mind was the source of the experiments is seriously entertained, it is remarkable that at the time of the supposed " leakage " no indications of the same theme occurred in her own automatic scripts. It cannot also be overlooked that the Cross-Correspondence phenomena did not cease after Mrs. Verrall died in 1916. This criticism, moreover, attributes to the *subliminal* mind a degree of ingenious purpose, planning, and distribution for which we have no other evidence.

Mrs. Sidgwick cautiously said of the Cross-Correspondence experiments, " I myself think that the evidence is pointing towards the conclusion that our fellow-workers are still working with us ". It is also very impressive to find that those who for many years were most closely involved in the solution and ordering of the Cross-Correspondence material, notably Mr. J. G. Piddington and the Earl of Balfour, endorsed the opinion expressed by Mrs. Sidgwick.

7. IMPORTANT OPINIONS ON SURVIVAL

Each student of the evidence must decide for himself what is his verdict about Survival. He is not limited to two contrasting judgments " proven " or " not proven ". He may think it not proven and improbable ; he may think it not proven but probable —in which case he will adopt it as a working hypothesis—or he may be confident it is proven—in which case he has found for himself an answer to one of Life's most heart-searching questions and should feel both relief and gratitude.

* Chapter 17 of G. N. M. Tyrrell's *Science and Psychical Phenomena* will give an impression of the work, or *Evidence for Personal Survival from Cross-Correspondences*: H. F. Saltmarsh (Bell & Co.).

† *Proc. S.P.R.*, Vol. 36, p. 526.

Expert witnesses may help us to arrive at our verdict. In any
case, we should hear what they have to say before we decide. The
names I quote are all distinguished by their critical caution and
intelligence, and—what is most essential—the persons have in all
cases spent many years of their life in first-hand study of the data.

Professor Charles Richet, who died in December 1935, was Professor of Physiology in the University of Paris. He was a Nobel
prize-man for his work on anaphylaxis and a world authority on
nutrition in health and disease, as well as a man of wide cultural
and literary interests. He was a careful experimenter and observer,
and no one would doubt that when Richet was satisfied as to a fact
it could be relied upon. For a considerable part of his life he was
profoundly interested in the field of psychical research, and he became wholly convinced of the facts of (1) cryptesthesia (his term to
cover telepathy, clairvoyance and precognition), (2) telekinesis (his
term for psycho-kinesis), and (3) the appearance of ectoplasm (i.e.,
the materialisation phenomena). He admitted these things, because
he was an honest and courageous observer, and could do no
other.* He theorised very little about them. He saw that they
were wholly apart from the orthodox scientific picture of the world,
and he was oppressed by a sense of our abysmal ignorance. " We
have understood nothing," he said, " absolutely nothing, of all these
phenomena ", and he felt it would be for the future to try to formulate hypotheses about them. He was a personal friend of F. W. H.
Myers and his wife, and of Sir Oliver Lodge : they exchanged many
friendly visits and discussed their differing views. To the end he
remained an agnostic so far as Survival was concerned. He could
not break away from conclusions which as a physiologist he felt
compelled to draw from the data of this field, which he considered
" established by innumerable proofs, a narrow, rigorous parallelism
between intellectual functions, otherwise called memory, and the
brain ". He continues : " I cannot believe that memory can exist
without the anatomical and physiological integrity of the brain.
Whenever there is no more oxygen, whenever the temperature is
either too low or too high, when there are a few drops of atropine,
or morphine or chloroform introduced into the blood, whenever
the course of cerebral irrigation is stopped—memory alters and
disappears." In his public utterances he maintained to the end
a materialist position, but Sir Oliver Lodge has told us that in
private he confessed " he was sometimes nearly bowled over by the

---

* *Thirty Years of Psychical Research* (Macmillan & Co., 1923) is the title
of the English translation of his great work *Traité de Métapsychique*. (See
a review by Sir Oliver Lodge : *Proc. S.P.R.*, Vol. 34, pp. 70–106.)

K

evidence [of Survival] ". Sir Oliver quotes from a letter written to him by Richet in July 1932 in which he says, " I am going to publish a book entitled ' The Great Hope '. And without being resolutely spiritist in the sense of Conan Doyle and Allan Kardec, I am approaching insensibly to your ideas."

H. F. Saltmarsh, who died in February 1943, was a man of great practical and business ability which he placed at the disposal of the Society for Psychical Research. He had also an interest in philosophical questions and had made contributions from time to time to the *Proceedings.* Two booklets are his—on Foreknowledge, and Cross-Correspondence—and he had made a careful first-hand examination of the mediumship of Mrs. Warren Elliott.* The themes which interested him most were the basic ones : the nature of the human self, and the nature of time and causation. In two of his papers, " Is Proof of Survival Possible ? " (Vol. 40) and " Ambiguity in the Question of Survival " (Vol. 46), he showed his deep and critical interest in this theme. It is of particular interest, therefore, to have a quotation provided by W. H. Salter from a letter Saltmarsh wrote to a friend bereaved in the war : †

> " I suggest that we are wrong in identifying the ' me which I now recognise as myself ' as the total true me. The first of these two ' me's '—call it for brevity the superficial me—is a composite being, largely composed of elements derived from the physical body ; it is ephemeral, seeing that the compound will be broken up at death and one set of elements, viz., the physical, dispersed. . . . I do not believe in the survival of the superficial me, nor do I desire it. . . . In honesty, I must confess that I am not completely convinced that there is any survival at all. I am inclined to think there is, but am not quite sure."

Sir Oliver Lodge, who died in August 1940, was a distinguished physicist. In the early years of this century he arrived at a conviction of the fact of survival and maintained it consistently throughout his long life. Thus, towards the end of his book *The Survival of Man,* first published in 1909, he writes : ‡

> " We find deceased friends—some of them well known to us and active members of the Society while alive—especially Gurney, Myers and Hodgson—constantly purporting to communicate, with the express purpose of patiently proving their identity and giving us cross-correspondence between different mediums. We also find them answering specific questions in a manner characteristic of their known personalities and giving evidence of knowledge appropriate to them.

* See *Proc. S.P.R.,* Vol. 39.
† *Proc. S.P.R.,* Vol. 47, p. 154.
‡ *The Survival of Man,* Chapter 26 (Methuen & Co.).

" Not easily or early do we make this admission. In spite of long conversations with what purported to be the surviving intelligence of these friends and investigators, we were by no means convinced of their identity by mere general conversation—even when of a friendly and intimate character, such as in normal cases would be considered amply and overwhelmingly sufficient for the identification of friends speaking, let us say, through a telephone or a typewriter. We required definite and crucial proof—a proof difficult even to imagine as well as difficult to supply.

" The ostensible communicators realise the need of such proof just as fully as we do, and have done their best to satisfy the rational demands. Some of us think they have succeeded. . . ."

There is no need to repeat similar statements which were maintained with conviction to the end of his life. The student will find an exposition of his views in a friendly answer to Richet's position in *Proc. S.P.R.*, Vol. 34, pp. 113–29 (1924), and in several of his books.

Mrs. Henry Sidgwick (1845–1936) was associated closely with the Society for Psychical Research from its beginning. No name was held in higher esteem by its members and no critical judgment more valued than hers. The record of her own researches and critiques by Alice Johnson * is an impressive one. When, at the age of 87, she was made President of Honour, her address was read to the Society by her brother, the Earl of Balfour. At its conclusion he added these words,

" May I be allowed before we separate to add one or two sentences of my own ? . . . Conclusive proof of survival is notoriously difficult to obtain. But the evidence may be such as to produce *belief*, even though it falls short of conclusive proof. I have Mrs. Sidgwick's assurance—an assurance which I am permitted to convey to the meeting—that, upon the evidence before her, she herself is a firm believer both in survival and in the reality of communication between the living and the dead."

W. H. Salter has written : † " The great impression which this declaration made among all who heard or read it lost nothing from the general and well founded belief that this assurance was fully shared by the speaker."

F. W. H. Myers died on January 17th, 1901, leaving behind him as his legacy to the world two volumes on *Human Personality* which have become a classic. He was a Fellow of Trinity, Cambridge, a very good classical scholar and a minor poet : had he chosen to do so, he could have made a name in English letters. It is perhaps

---

* *Proc. S.P.R.*, Vol. 44, pp. 53–97 (1936).
† Ibid., Vol. 47, p. 251 (1945).

fitting to close the list of expert witnesses with him.   Sir Oliver
Lodge, an intimate friend, said of Myers :

" His was a keenly emotional nature.   What he felt, he felt
strongly; what he believed, he believed in no half-hearted or conventional manner.   When he doubted, he doubted fiercely; but the
pain of the doubt only stimulated him to effort, to struggle; to know
at least the worst, and doubt no longer.   He was content with no
half-knowledge, no clouded faith, he must know or he must suffer,
and in the end he believed that he knew. . . . In the strength of that
belief he looked forward to perennial effort and unending progress :

> " Say could aught else content thee ? which were best,
> After so brief a battle an endless rest,
> Or the ancient conflict rather to renew,
> By the old deeds strengthened mightier deeds to do ? "

Sir Oliver Lodge continues :

" I never knew a man so hopeful concerning his ultimate destiny.
He once asked me if I would barter—if it were possible—my unknown
destiny, whatever it might be, for as many æons of unmitigated and
wise terrestrial happiness as might last till the secular fading of the sun,
and then an end.   He would not ! "

Since his scientifically stated conclusions are in his volumes for
all to read, I think we might allow Myers to give his judgment in
his own verse :

> Nay when all suns that shine, together hurled,
> Crash in one infinite and lifeless world :
> Yet hold thou still, what worlds soe'er may roll,
> Naught bear they with them master of the soul ;
> In all the eternal whirl, the cosmic stir,
> All the eternal is akin to her ;
> She shall endure, and quicken, and live at last,
> When all save souls has perished in the past.

8. CONCLUSIONS

The student who has followed this survey so far may be disposed
to speculate whether with the passing of the years, the pursuit of
more research and the accumulation of an overwhelming mass of
reliable data, the truth recognised by a few may not become the
possession of the many.   If by the possession of truth is meant
intellectual assent to a proposition as having high probability, the
answer is possibly yes.   But we cannot really possess anything we
do not love : nor can truths that really matter to us be other than our
own discovery.   Such truths, which affect our destiny and all that
we value, we cannot accept on any authority but that of our own

deepest self.   In poets and great artists and mystics the voice of the deeper self speaks clearly and authoritatively : for most of us it speaks occasionally and faintly, so that we crave also the support which the laborious mind can give us.

For myself, I can only say that my intuition, such as it is, supports Myers, and my attempt to evaluate the data of psychical research and form a critical judgment leads me to conclude that if survival of death is not rigorously proven, it is nevertheless established as of that high order of probability which, for practical purposes, can be taken as the same thing.

Rabindranath Tagore, poet and philosopher, once wrote to his friend C. F. Andrews :

> " My mind must realise itself anew.   Once I give form to my thought, I must free myself from it.   For the time being it seems to me that I want absolute freedom to create new forms for new ideas. I am sure physical death has the same meaning for us—the creative impulse of our soul must have new forms for its realisation.   Death can continue to dwell in the same sepulchre, but Life must increasingly outgrow its dwelling-place ; otherwise the form gets the upper hand and becomes a prison.   Man is immortal ; therefore he must die endlessly.   For Life is a creative idea ; it can only find itself in changing forms."

This I believe to be one of the truest and most inspired things ever said about Death.   To sum up : we have enough trustworthy evidence to anticipate our survival of the change called death.   If our conception of the Self as a hierarchy is true in broad outline—as I believe it is—we have enough to anticipate a great deal more.   For myself, Birth and Death seem to be respectively the great Exile and the great Returning Home.   I expect, when the immediate shock of change is over, to find myself with a body familiar to me (because it has always been a possession without my realising it), in a country from which come thronging back to me welcoming echoes of old familiarity.   It will still be a world of Appearance ; but since one veil at least will then have fallen from the face of Truth, I shall expect to find myself more responsive to her Eternal Beauty as I set out again—a pilgrim on the endless Way.

PART III

THE DATA OF MYSTICAL EXPERIENCE

Chapter

14

TYPES OF MYSTICAL EXPERIENCE

We have dreamed dreams beyond our comprehending,
Visions too beautiful to be untrue ;
We have seen mysteries that yield no clue,
And sought our goals on ways that have no ending.
We, creatures of the earth,
The lowly born, the mortal, the foredoomed
To spend our fleeting moments on the spot
Wherein tomorrow we shall be entombed,
And hideously rot,—
We have seen loveliness that shall not pass ;
We have beheld immortal destinies ;
We have seen Heaven and Hell and joined their strife ;
Ay, we whose flesh shall perish as the grass
Have flung the passion of the heart that dies
Into the hope of everlasting life.

SIDNEY ROYSE LYSAGHT (from " Horizons and Landmarks ").

" From the Unreal lead me to the Real ; from Darkness lead
me to the Light ; from Death lead me to Immortality."

A HINDU PRAYER.

THE world of trees and rocks, tables and chairs, is for the ordinary
unreflective man the one real world. There may have been some
excuse for the materialistic philosophy of the nineteenth century
which supported this, but the discoveries of modern physics in the
twentieth century themselves have undermined that outlook. The
solidity of the material world has proved illusory : it can be resolved
into particles and energy. In certain circumstances the particles
themselves dissolve into energy of radiation, and this label proclaims
our inability to say any more. We only *think* the material world is
solid and coloured and extensive in space and time because of the
sort of special senses and minds which we possess. These select
for us the qualities of the world we know. A bird's world, a fish's
world, an insect's world, must be wholly different to their consciousness because their minds and special senses are different from man's.
I think we must admit that their respective world-pictures are each
true within the limits of the perceiving instrument, but are all
extremely incomplete and fragmentary. It may be argued that
Man, as the highest mammal, has a wider concept of the world than

297

any other creature : but this affords no grounds for assuming that man's ordinary picture of the world is itself more than a very partial and limited one. Reality, we may safely assume, is a vast, almost unknown continent, and all we know of it is the little bit of beach upon which we have been stranded by " that immortal sea which brought us hither ". We may well ask " What are we ? " and " What is our relationship to this many-sided reality ? "

The data of psychical research, which we have surveyed, have introduced us to new levels or worlds of phenomena lying behind the material order of appearance. These levels have extended, strata upon strata, below the physical surface of things, through a closely related mediating region labelled " ætheric ", into the deep mind. Such a penetration has been, as we have realised, into regions of deepening significance—that is, we have travelled nearer to the ultimate reality. But always behind the things known has been the knower, behind the things seen the seer, behind the various instruments of the self—that Self whose very nature is consciousness. There may be some students who, weighing the evidence of psychical research, are completely satisfied as to the existence of Mind in its own right, but see the self as a body–mind complex and recognise no Self apart from this. To these, the data of mystical experience present an inescapable challenge.

On the evidence already considered, however, we think it desirable to differentiate between Mind as an instrument, and a deeper level which we have called buddhic, where the user of the instrument seems to have his centre of consciousness. We shall call this user the Ego : it is the centre of individuality. It is that which grows and develops by the use of his instruments and by the whole adventuring forth into terrestrial experience. We shall regard the Ego as the lower self—an outpost or ambassador of the higher Self which in its true nature is essentially divine and rests beyond the flux and change of time and form. The evidence for this will be found in the remainder of this book. But before we proceed to consider it, there is, we would point out, a wealth of personal experience—subjective though it may be—which shows to us deeps beyond the Mind. No man, however distinguished be the quality of his mind and however good his technique, can say " I will now sit down and write a great poem, or compose a great symphony, or make an important discovery ". There is a level deeper than Mind from which all inspirations and all creative insights arise, and Mind but gives these insights form, and technique gives them permanent expression. When we respond to the greatness of these things, whether found in truth or in music or any of the arts, it is not because our minds have

weighed their merit and pronounced them worthy to be appreciated,
but because our own buddhi recognises immediately and intuitively
the old authentic quality. " There is a verge of the mind ", says
William James,* " which these things haunt; and whispers therefrom mingle with the operations of our understanding, even as the
waters of the infinite ocean send their waves to break among the
pebbles that lie upon our shores."

I. WHAT IS MYSTICISM?

It is not easy to define mysticism, and even less easy to classify
satisfactorily the great variety of mystical experiences. We shall
therefore do no more than attempt to suggest what we understand
by it. The rest of this chapter will present the evidence for mystical
experiences and will, we hope, convey to the reader a sense of their
significance.

We have been compelled by our analysis to interpret the universe
on different levels of significance : the physical, the ætheric, the mental, the buddhic, and so on. Man himself participates in these
interwoven levels. When a man discovers that one level is rooted
in a higher one—that is, is sustained by it, and understood because
of it—and discovers this, not as a result of thought or cogitation,
but as a completely convincing fact of *immediate experience*—this is a
mystical experience. It is a state of insight—not derived through
the mind at all—but a state which is completely illuminating, convincing and satisfying to the feelings. By " immediate experience "
the philosophers mean unexpressed awareness, the perception of
an object or experience before it has been expressed in words.†

It is as though, to use Browning's metaphor (quoted on p. 31),
the light of Reality is dimmed for us by many obscuring screens
one around another like garments superposed. Each screen
separates one region or world of significance from the rest. These
screens between Reality and Appearance the Eastern philosophies
call Maya. They prevent us from understanding the true nature
of the world. In mystical experience, some or perhaps all of the
screens become more transparent, and then the greater light reveals
the obscure region on the outer side of the screen to be but part of
the more highly illumined region on the inner side. Whenever in
the presence of the less real a screen is removed or becomes transparent, and the more real breaks through, illuminating and absorbing

* *Varieties of Religious Experience*, Lectures XVI and XVII.
† E.g., John MacMurray : *Interpreting the Universe*, Chapter I (Faber &
Faber, 1933).

the former, we have the essence of mystical experience. The varying
depths of such experience, if one may pursue the metaphor further,
are such as might correspond to the removal of screen after screen,
so that in the profoundest experience even the region farthest
removed from reality is seen to be an aspect of, and one with the
Reality itself. The many become the one. " God in all " is the
key to mystical experience. At any level those who can dissolve
the veils of Maya find only the Divine, and have temporarily realised
themselves as a part of the great Unity.

In all mystical experience the sense of separateness, of individuality,
is to a great degree lost. In the state of illumination, that which is
known seems to merge with the knower, so that there is an intimate
unity between them. In the profounder mystical experiences this
results in a sense of unity with the All. Jesus expressed on many
occasions such insights as " I and my Father are one ", and " Ye shall
know that I am in my Father, and ye in me, and I in you ". This
undoubtedly is the source of the most profound affirmations of
Hinduism : " That art Thou ", and " The Atman is the Brahman "
(The Higher Self is one with the Supreme Being). It is doubtless
also the origin of the supreme Buddhist realisation " The dewdrop
slips into the shining sea ". If we interpret this as an affirmation
that individual lives count for nothing and finally slip back into an
infinite reservoir of life from which they sprang, we are seriously
in error. The mystical experience of unity behind this affirmation
is not spatial and could be as accurately portrayed by saying " The
shining sea slips into the dewdrop ". It is not surprising, therefore,
that Evelyn Underhill * attempts to define mysticism as " The art
of union with reality ".

How does mysticism fit into the general picture of the self which
we outlined in Chapter 12 and illustrated in the diagram on p. 239.
Would it be true to say that the sensitive who can withdraw the focus
of attention from an outer level and focus it on an interior one thereby
has a mystical experience ? I should not assent to this. Such an
experience would be psychical, but not necessarily mystical. The
characteristic of mystical experience is not determined by the level
on which awareness is focused, but by the quality of the experience
on that level. It is true that since some screens of Maya have been
left behind by the withdrawal of awareness to an interior level, the
direction of approach is towards reality. But the interior level on
which awareness is focused is also a world of " appearance ", and
whether the experience on that level is commonplace (i.e., appropriate
to that level) or mystical, will depend on whether the interior screens

* Evelyn Underhill : *Practical Mysticism for Normal People* (J. M. Dent).

remain unchanged or whether they become transparent so as to allow the greater illumination of the Real to break through. Mystical experience is clearly a possibility on any level, provided the interior screens become thin or transparent; but there is no reason for supposing that this is more likely to happen for the sensitive whose awareness is focused on the " astral " level, for example, than for the ordinary person whose awareness is on the ordinary material level. Psychism is thus to be regarded as experience natural and appropriate to an interior level in which awareness is focused. Mysticism is experience which results from the thinning of the veils which hide the light of reality. This may occur on any level. No sensitive, in my opinion, is able to focus awareness beyond the mid-mind levels and retain the capacity for communicating such knowledge. Any withdrawal of awareness to what we have called the buddhic level or beyond may probably be classed as " mystical " without doing violence to our exposition, for the light of Reality must shine there with considerable brightness. In the most profound mystical experience where the withdrawal of awareness is to the innermost levels, " subjective " and " objective " are indistinguishable terms. The Knower and the Known are one in the unity of consciousness.

The examples which follow in some cases contain psychical elements, but I regard them as mystical because of the significance they held for the experiencers. They conveyed to them a message of " value " : they felt that through them they had deeper insight into the nature of Reality. It is important, of course, to remember that the formulation of the experience in words is necessarily an imperfect attempt made afterwards by the mind to capture and understand it. All who have experienced such states constantly tell us that they are beyond their power to express : they can only hint at them. To be known for what they are, they must be experienced. William James points out that in this respect mystical states have a closer analogy with states of feeling than with states of knowledge. To know what love is, one must have loved : all the descriptive analysis in the world cannot really convey the knowledge to one who has not himself experienced it. To the classification of mystical experiences in the three sections which follow, little weight is to be attached. It is an attempt for the sake of convenience to arrange a representative selection of experiences in three groups of ascending significance— but of this we can only judge by their admittedly inadequate formulation in words. What we may with apology call the slighter mystical experiences are often new experiences of the familiar world whereby it is " seen " to be a garment hiding so much more. With further thinning of the veils, life and forms not perceptible to the physical eye appear : the universe is seen to be living and of the essential nature of light, beauty and joy. The meaning and purpose of existence become all clear and illumined, so that doubts no longer trouble and problems no longer exist—although the meaning and purpose are not an intellectual formulation. With increasing penetration of the light of Reality, less and less can be remembered or expressed, but those mystics who have known this experience try to tell us of the sense of infinite wonder and joy which lingers with them and the sense of union with something far greater than themselves.

These words are but introductory : it is desired that the following illustrations should speak for themselves. Their interpretation we shall attempt in the next chapter.

2. EXPERIENCE RECOLLECTED AS THOUGH ON THE LEVEL OF LIFE AND FORM (I SEE)

Case 1. From Payne and Bendit : *The Psychic Sense*, pp. 183–4 (Faber & Faber, 1943).

" I was sitting on the seashore, half-listening to a friend arguing violently about a matter which merely bored me. Unconsciously to myself, I looked at a film of sand I had picked up on my hand, when I suddenly saw the exquisite beauty of every little grain of it : instead of being dull, I saw that each particle was made up on a perfect geometrical pattern, with sharp angles, from each of which a brilliant shaft of light was reflected, while each tiny crystal shone like a rainbow. The rays crossed and recrossed, making exquisite patterns, of such beauty that they left me breathless.

" I was used, at odd intervals, to seeing the invisible counterpart of minute objects, but this was quite unexpected and fascinating. Then, suddenly, my consciousness was lighted up from within and I saw in a vivid way how the whole universe was made up of particles of material which, no matter how dull and lifeless they might seem at first sight, were nevertheless filled with this intense and vital beauty.

" For a second or two, the whole world appeared as a blaze of glory. When it died down, it left with me something I have never forgotten and which constantly reminds me of the beauty locked up in every minute speck of material around me."

Case 2. From Lady Acland : *Good-bye for the Present*, pp. 162–3 (Hodder & Stoughton, 1935).

" It had been a good day, with that sort of goodness that accounts for the way so many English folk-songs break into runaway choruses of ' Fol-de-riddle-ido '. We had been out by ourselves gathering primroses—rather uncommon flowers in our countryside, but we had found them in plenty in the places we remembered from last year. There was nothing going on in Milly's head except a sort of ' Fol-de-riddle-ido ' feeling as she let her eyes rove here and there, and saw the oaks in their light dressing of golden-bronze, the ash-trees still obdurately gaunt, the nimble lambs and their muffled-up old mothers, the fields and grey walls, and the path winding up past the stables to her home on the hillside. All at once, quite without prelude, an astonishing radiance welled up on all these familiar things and in the child herself. They were no longer just themselves, separate objects with edges of their own; they were that radiance, and the radiance was unbounded, glorious love. Often Milly had said to herself in vexed perplexity, confronted with the Deity of the church and the little pious books : ' I wish, oh, I wish, I could actually see God, just for one minute, then perhaps I would understand.' Now, quite clearly and unforgettably, without haste or surprise, she said : ' Why, I am seeing God—I could be seeing Him all the time! I am seeing right into God. He is seeing right into me.' Even the little girl Milly was aware that this in-seeing cannot last as an incident in time. For once, a prayer of her very own, not quick with fear, broke out in her heart : ' Please God, don't let me forget.' And she knew that the answer was as real as her prayer ; that, even if this in-seeing should never be hers again, the remembrance of it will belong to her for ever."

Case 3.   From Mary Austin : *Experiences facing Death*, p. 24 (The Bobbs-Merrill Co., 1931).

" I must have been between five and six when this experience happened to me. It was a summer morning, and the child I was had walked down through the orchard alone and come out on the brow of a sloping hill where there was grass and a wind blowing and one tall tree reaching into infinite immensities of blueness. Quite suddenly, after a moment of quietness there, earth and sky and tree and wind-blown grass and the child in the midst of them came alive together with a pulsing light of consciousness. There was a wild foxglove at the child's feet and a bee dozing about it, and to this day I can recall the swift inclusive awareness of each for the whole—I in them and they in me and all of us enclosed in a warm lucent bubble of livingness. I remember the child looking everywhere for the source of this happy wonder, and at last she questioned—' God ? '— because it was the only awesome word she knew. Deep inside, like the murmurous swinging of a bell, she heard the answer, ' God, God. . . .'

" How long this ineffable moment lasted I never knew. It broke like a bubble at the sudden singing of a bird, and the wind blew and the world was the same as ever—only never *quite* the same. The experience so initiated has been the one abiding reality of my life, unalterable except in the abounding fullness and frequency of its occurrence."

Case 4. From Richard Jefferies : *The Story of My Heart*, p. 199 (Longmans, Green & Co., 1891). This classic by a nature-mystic is full of passages such as the following :

" I was not more than eighteen when an inner and esoteric meaning began to come to me from all the visible universe, and indefinable aspirations filled me. I found them in the grassy fields, under the trees, on the hill-tops, at sunrise, and in the night. There was a deeper meaning everywhere. The sun burned with it, the broad front of morning beamed with it ; a deep feeling entered me while gazing at the sky in the azure noon, and in the star-lit evening.
" I was sensitive to all things, to the earth under, and the star-hollow round about ; to the least blade of grass, to the largest oak. They seemed like exterior nerves and veins for the conveyance of feeling to me. Sometimes a very ecstasy of exquisite enjoyment of the entire visible universe filled me." *

Case 5. From John Buchan : *Memory-hold-the-Door*, pp. 120–1 (Hodder & Stoughton, 1940).

" In South Africa I recovered an experience which I had not known since my childhood, moments, even hours, of intense exhilaration, when one seemed to be a happy part of a friendly universe. The cause, no doubt, was largely physical, for my long treks made me very fit in body ; but not wholly, for I have had the same experiences much later in life when my health was far from perfect. They came usually in the early morning or at sunset. I seemed to acquire a wonderful clearness of mind and to find harmony in discords and unity in diversity, but to find these things not as conclusions of thought, but in a sudden revelation, as in poetry or music. For a little, beauty peeped from the most unlikely wrappings and everything had a secret purpose of joy. It was the mood for poetry had I been anything of a poet.
" Looking back I find my South African memories studded with those high moments. One especially stands out. I had been ploughing all day in the black dust of the Lichtenburg roads, and had come very late to a place called the eye of Malmani—Malmani Oog— the spring of a river which presently loses itself in the Kalahari. We watered our horses and went supperless to bed. Next morning I bathed in one of the Malmani pools—and icy cold it was—and then basked in the early sunshine while breakfast was cooking. The water made a pleasant music, and near by was a covert of willows filled with singing birds. Then and there came on me the hour of revelation, when, though savagely hungry, I forgot about breakfast. Scents, sights and sounds blended into a harmony so perfect that it transcended human expression, even human thought. It was like a glimpse of the peace of eternity."

* Similar experiences will be found in Elizabeth Myers : *A Well Full of Leaves* (Chapman, 1943). Also see Kenneth Walker : *The Circle of Life*, p. 30 (Jonathan Cape, 1942).

Case 6. From C. F. Andrews : *Letters to a Friend*, pp. 25–6 (George Allen & Unwin, 1923). This experience was described by Rabindranath Tagore to his friend Andrews. He was standing on a verandah watching the sun rise above the trees in Free School Street, Calcutta. He said :

" . . . as I was watching it, suddenly, in a moment, a veil seemed to be lifted from my eyes. I found the world wrapt in an inexpressible glory with its waves of joy and beauty bursting and breaking on all sides. The thick shroud of sorrow that lay on my heart in many folds was pierced through and through by the light of the world, which was everywhere radiant.

" That very day the poem known as *The Fountain Awakened from its Dream* flowed on like a fountain itself. When it was finished, still the curtain did not fall on that strange vision of beauty and joy. There was nothing and no one whom I did not love at that moment. . . . I stood on the verandah and watched the coolies as they tramped down the road. Their movements, their forms, their countenances seemed to be strangely wonderful to me, as if they were all moving like waves in the great ocean of the world. When one young man placed his hand upon the shoulder of another and passed laughingly by, it was a remarkable event to me. . . . I seemed to witness, in the wholeness of my vision, the movements of the body of all humanity, and to feel the beat of the music and the rhythm of a mystic dance."

This mystic mood lasted for seven or eight days, and when he decided to accompany his brothers to Darjeeling, it was with the hope that he might have an even fuller vision amid the magnificence of the Himalayas. When he got there the vision left him, and he says :

" . . . That was my mistake. I thought I could get at truth from the outside. But however lofty and imposing the Himalayas might be, they could not put anything real into my hands. But God, the Great Giver, Himself can open the whole Universe to our gaze in the narrow space of a single lane."

Case 7. From C. E. Raven : *Good News of God*, p. 50 (Hodder & Stoughton, 1943).

" The healing came when with the sudden closing in of darkness the perspective became a silhouette, and the wide horizon of the fenland narrowed down to the small circle of the lamp. You know how in that little world every leaf and reed-blade takes on value ; how one becomes aware of ranges of beauty and interest normally ignored. So it was then. But out of the wealth of detail there was for me a drop of water in the axil of a teazle-leaf—a drop of water, and in it all the fullness of God. Our little lives, our fret and pain, so tiny and yet so tremendous. A drop of water and the presence of God."

Case 8. From W. L. Wilmshurst : *Contemplations*, p. 142 (J. M. Watkins). The account of this experience is abbreviated below. It can only have taken part of a minute of time, for it began in a village church during the singing of the " Te Deum ", and when it ended the anthem was still being sung. It is of great interest as showing a progressive development in profundity. The person who experienced it had had no previous psychical or mystical experience, and writes as follows :

" My thought began to contrast the modest praises uttered in this humble place in the outward world, by its crippled organ, the puny voices of this juvenile choir and handful of villagers with the stupendous unimaginable pæans which must needs be heard above when ' all angels cry aloud, the heavens and all the powers therein '. Whilst thus reflecting I caught sight, in the aisle at my side, of what resembled bluish smoke issuing from the chinks of the stone floor, as though from fire smouldering beneath. Looking more intently I saw it was not smoke, but something finer, more tenuous—a soft impalpable self-luminous haze of violet colour, unlike any physical vapour, and for which there was nothing to suggest a cause. Thinking I experienced some momentary optical defect or delusion, I turned my gaze farther along the aisle, but there too the same delicate haze was present. . . . I perceived the wonderful fact that it extended farther than the walls and roof of the building and was not confined by them. Through these I now could look and could see the landscape beyond. . . . At a single visual act, and without need of glancing from one point to another or from this object to that, the building I stood within and the whole landscape were in view. . . . I saw from all parts of my being simultaneously, not from my eyes only. . . . Yet for all this intensified perceptive power there was as yet no loss of touch with my physical surroundings, no suspension of my faculties of sense. A momentary doubt as to whether I was experiencing faintness or passing out of the body was solved by a grasp at the pew-back before me and by nudging, as if inadvertently, the arm of the person at my side. Thus satisfied of my physical bearings, I gave myself up with a pleasurable curiosity, to await developments. I felt happiness and peace—beyond words.

" Upon the instant the luminous blue haze engulfing me and all around me became transformed into golden glory, into light untellable. . . . The golden light of which the violet haze seemed now to have been as the veil or outer fringe, welled forth from a central immense globe of brilliancy. . . . But the most wonderful thing was that these shafts and waves of light, that vast expanse of photosphere, and even the great central globe itself, were crowded to solidity with the forms of living creatures . . . a single coherent organism filling all space and place, yet composed of an infinitude of individuated existences . . . I saw moreover that these beings were present in teeming myriads in the church I stood in ; that they were intermingled with and were passing unobstructedly through both myself and all my fellow-worshippers. . . . The heavenly hosts drifted through the human congregation as wind passes through a grove of trees ; beings of radiant beauty and clothed in shimmering raiment. . . .

" But this vast spectacle of mingled heaven and earth was succeeded by an even richer experience; one in which everything of time and place and form vanished from my consciousness and only the ineffable eternal things remained. . . . And as the point of a candle-flame leaps suddenly upward when an object is held just above it, so the flame of my consciousness leapt to its utmost limit and passed into the region of the formless and uncreated to tell of which all words fail. . . . For a few moments of mortal time, which are no measure of the intensity of the spirit's experience in the world immortal, all consciousness of my physical surroundings was withdrawn. . . .

" Eventually, while thus rapt, the remembrance of the outer world from which my consciousness had been transported returned to me, like an old half-forgotten memory. This world and my recent surroundings were exhibited to me, but at a most remote distance, as when one looks out upon a scene through a reversed telescope. . . . Without shock or violence the consciousness which had been so highly exalted relapsed and sank to its normal limits and became readjusted to physical conditions; the spirit was returned to its fleshly sheath as a jewel is replaced in its casket after use and locked away. Once more I was standing in the church, perfectly well and unmoved. I feared lest some physical collapse had occurred and created a scene. Happily no external sign of this terrific visitation had occurred; no one was aware that anything had happened. Only a few moments could have been occupied by an experience in the spirit, of which the incidents were so vivid and the details so numerous that my memory still fails to exhaust them. The singing of the ' Te Deum ' had not concluded. The words that first fell upon my reawakened ears were those of the moving cry raised for all here exiled in the flesh, ' O Lord, save Thy people and bless Thy heritage. Govern them and lift them up for ever. Make them to be numbered with Thy saints in glory everlasting.' Had those around me who sang those words been lifted up with me, they too would have known that, although a veil was before their face, they were already numbered with the saints in the Eternal Eye; they would have seen that the everlasting glory was about them at that moment and continually."

It would be possible to enlarge this selection almost indefinitely. Those who are familiar with the Irish poet, artist and mystic George Russell (Æ), know that his writings * are full of visionary beauty. He seemed to have almost constant awareness of a world lying within the garment of Nature which showed to him its secrets. There have, no doubt, been many greater poets than he, but I do not know of any whose poetry sustains so constantly the magical quality of revealing a world of significance not far away and trying to break through. Here are a few lines † of Æ's prose :

" Has not earth been tender towards us ? Are not sunlight, twilight, colour, form, element, melted into meanings so that they

* See especially *The Candle of Vision, Song and its Fountains* and *Collected Poems* (Macmillan & Co.). † *The Avatars*, p. 147 (Macmillan).

seem but voices out of that ever-living nature? Does not the very air we breathe seem at times to be the Holy Breath? Are we not for ever passing into what we contemplate? Have not solid earth, stone and hill become at times transparent to us? . . . Do we not at times go out from ourselves, our being expanded, so that we seem to mix with the life in nature as if we permeated it and had come together in the infinite yearning of centre and circumference for each other? In that so-mingling of natures the gates of the heart are unbarred for there is nought to defend."

Speaking generally, this describes the kind of experience known to the nature-mystics, and the beauty of the English countryside as seen through the eyes of its poets has made no mean contribution to this treasury. Their standpoint has been the world they know, but at least one veil, and sometimes one veil after another, has fallen away from the light of Reality, and shown to them the Highest irradiating the lowest, expressed through it, created by it, and living in it.

3. EXPERIENCE RECOLLECTED AS THOUGH ON THE LEVEL OF MIND AND BUDDHI (I KNOW)

Sometimes the mystic's vantage-point has not been the world of sense-data but the world of Mind. In some cases the mood has been one of extreme frustration, or desolation, or despair, when suddenly a veil has fallen away and the resulting illumination has changed everything. In other cases the mood has been one of serenity, and like a lightning flash out of a clear blue sky there has come a moment of illumination in which all problems seem to have been resolved. The attempt afterwards made by the mind to formulate what has been known is seldom successful, but for the experient the revelation has indubitable authority, and in some cases has changed the whole course of life, and the subsequent attitude to events.

Case 9. From Vera Brittain: *Testament of Friendship*, p. 325 (Macmillan & Co., 1940). This book is a tribute to the author's friend Winifred Holtby, whom Robert Lynd described as " one of the noblest women of her age ". She died at the age of thirty-seven. She had been told at the age of thirty-three by a London specialist that she might not have more than two years to live. Her health had made it necessary for her to lay down her work and take refuge in the country. Her whole spirit was in rebellion against the bodily weakness which made impossible the life of useful activity for which she was otherwise so well equipped. Walking up a hill feeling tired and dispirited, she came to a trough outside a farm-yard. The surface was frozen over, for it was a cold spring morning, and a number of lambs were gathered round trying in vain to drink.

" She broke the ice for them with her stick, and as she did so she heard a voice within her saying ' Having nothing, yet possessing all things '. It was so distinct that she looked round startled, but she was alone with the lambs on the top of the hill. Suddenly, in a flash, the grief, the bitterness, the sense of frustration disappeared ; all desire to possess power and glory for herself vanished away, and never came back. . . . The moment of ' conversion ' on the hill of Monks Risborough, she said with tears in her eyes, was the supreme spiritual experience of her life. She always associated it afterwards with the words of Bernard Bosanquet on Salvation :

" ' And now we are saved absolutely, we need not say from what, we are at home in the universe, and, in principle and in the main, feeble and timid creatures as we are, there is nothing anywhere within the world or without it that can make us afraid.' "

The voice—as a voice—is unimportant. The recollecting mind described the vehicle of insight in this way. The essential thing is the experience, which gave her an indubitable glimpse into the nature of reality, capable of changing in an instant despair into confidence and rebellion into acceptance.

For some, music has provided the favouring condition when for a moment the magic door has swung open. William de Morgan has told how in a mood of depression and despair he listened to a symphony of Beethoven and found healing. This music became for him at that moment a vehicle of insight into the real nature of the world, and he said to himself, " If reality is like that, I have no cause to be anxious or afraid." A more recent, and profounder experience is given below.

Case 10. From Warner Allen : *The Timeless Moment,* pp. 31–3 (Faber & Faber, 1946). The experience interpolated itself between two successive notes in Beethoven's Seventh Symphony and involved no conscious hiatus in listening to the music. The writer distinguishes between the mysterious event itself (union with God), the phase of Illumination which immediately followed, and the final phase of Enlightenment in which it is recollected and interpreted afterwards. He describes the recollected experience thus :

". . . I closed my eyes and watched a silver glow which shaped itself into a circle with a central focus brighter than the rest. The circle became a tunnel of light proceeding from some distant sun in the heart of the Self. Swiftly and smoothly I was borne through the tunnel, and as I went the light turned from silver to gold. There was an impression of drawing strength from a limitless sea of power and a sense of deepening peace. The light grew brighter, but was never dazzling or alarming. I came to a point where time and motion ceased. In my recollection it took the shape of a flat-topped rock, surrounded by a summer sea, with a sandy pool at its foot. The dream scene vanished and I am absorbed in the Light of the Universe, in Reality glowing like fire with the knowledge of itself, without ceasing to be one and myself, merged like a drop of quicksilver in the Whole, yet still separate as a grain of sand in the desert. The peace that passes all understanding and the pulsating energy of creation are one in the centre in the midst of conditions where all opposites are reconciled."

The stage of Illumination he could only attempt to convey thus :

" Something has happened to me—I am utterly amazed—can this be that ? (*That* being the answer to the riddle of life)—but it is too simple—I always knew it—it is remembering an old forgotten secret— like coming home—I am not ' I ', not the ' I ' I thought—there is no death—peace passing understanding—yet how unworthy I—."

Case 11.   From R. M. Bucke : *Cosmic Consciousness*, Introduction and pp. 73-4 (E. P. Dutton & Co.).

Dr. R. M. Bucke (born 1837, died 1902) was a remarkable man. In his youth and early manhood he had five years of thrilling adventure in Canada, which included experiences as a miner and prospector.   From one such experience he narrowly escaped with his life, and had to have the whole of one foot and part of the other amputated owing to frost-bite.   He graduated with distinction through the McGill Medical School and became one of the foremost psychiatrists in Canada.   He was elected President of the Psychological Section of the B.M.A. in 1888, and in 1890 President of the American Medico-Psychological Association.   He was a close friend of Whitman, whom he greatly admired.   At the age of thirty-five he had the mystical experience which coloured his whole subsequent life and led to the book *Cosmic Consciousness*, published just before his death.   In it he develops the theme of mystical experience as corresponding to a new level of consciousness, as far above the self-consciousness of ordinary men as self-consciousness is above the " simple " consciousness of the animal.   This work of Dr. Bucke earned the warm praise of William James as " an addition to psychology of first-rate importance ".   Not the least valuable aspect of his contribution is the challenge it offers to those who are disposed to class the phenomena of mysticism with psychopathic manifestations of the human mind.   Bucke was not only Superintendent of the Provincial Asylum for the Insane at Hamilton, Ontario, he was also Professor of Mental and Nervous Diseases at Western University (London, Ontario).   It is scarcely to be supposed he would have allowed a personal experience to have profoundly influenced his life and researches for thirty years had he not been persuaded of its transcendent importance. Here is the account of his experience :

> " He and two friends had spent the evening reading Wordsworth, Shelley, Keats, Browning, and especially Whitman. They parted at midnight and he had a long drive in a hansom. His mind, deeply under the influence of the ideas, images, and emotions called up by the reading and talk of the evening, was calm and peaceful. He was in a state of quiet, almost passive enjoyment.
>
> " All at once, without warning of any kind, he found himself wrapped around, as it were, by a flame-coloured cloud. For an instant he thought of fire—some sudden conflagration in the great city. The next [instant] he knew that the light was within himself.
>
> " Directly afterwards, there came upon him a sense of exultation, of immense joyousness, accompanied or immediately followed by an intellectual illumination quite impossible to describe. Into his brain streamed one momentary lightning-flash of the Brahmic Splendour which has ever since lightened his life."

As a result of this personal experience and his study of similar experiences of others, he came to believe that the general characteristics were these. The introduction is frequently through a subjective light or haze. There follows an ecstatic emotional state characterised by love, joy, peace and bliss beyond anything previously felt. Then comes an intellectual illumination—which is described thus :

> " Like a flash there is presented to his consciousness a clear conception (a vision) in outline of the meaning and drift of the universe. He does not come to believe merely ; but he sees and knows that the cosmos, which to the self-conscious mind seems made up of dead matter, is in fact far otherwise—is in very truth a living presence. . . . He sees that the life which is in man is eternal, as all life is eternal; that the soul of man is as immortal as God is; that the universe is so built and ordered that without any peradventure all things work together for the good of each and all; that the foundation principle of the world is what we call love, and that the happiness of every individual is in the long run absolutely certain. . . . Especially does he obtain such a conception of *The Whole* or at least of an immense *Whole* as dwarfs all conception, imagination or speculation springing from and belonging to ordinary self-consciousness, such a conception as makes the old attempts to mentally grasp the universe and its meaning petty and ridiculous."

Added to this, or rather as a part of it, is a profound sense of immortality—something which has for the experiencer the same simplicity and certainty as the knowledge " I am ".

Case 12. From H. G. Wells : *The Bulpington of Blup*, p. 78 (Hutchinson & Co.). In his book *First and Last Things* (London, Constable, 1909, p. 60), Mr. H. G. Wells writes, " At times, in the silence of the night and in rare lonely moments, I come upon a sort of communion of myself and something great that is not myself. It is perhaps poverty of mind and language obliges me to say that this universal scheme takes on the effect of a sympathetic person—and my communion a quality of fearless worship. These moments happen, and they are the supreme fact of my religious life to me; they are the crown of my religious experience." In 1933 he wrote a novel which attributes to one of the characters a moment of mystical experience. This is described with such insight that one is tempted to believe it may have been Wells' own later experience.

" As he watched these changes the miracle happened. The sunset was there still, but suddenly it was transfigured. The weedy rocks below him, the flaming pools and runlets, the wide bay of the estuary shining responsive to the sky, were transfigured. The universe was transfigured—as though it opened itself out to him, as though it took him into complete communion with itself. The scene was no longer a scene. It was a Being. It was as if it had become alive, quite still, but altogether living, an immense living thing englobing himself. He was at the very centre of the sphere of Being. He was one with it.

" Time ceased. He felt a silence beneath all sounds; he apprehended a beauty that transcends experience.

" He saw his universe clear as crystal and altogether significant and splendid. Everything was utterly lucid, and all was wonder. Wonder was in Theodore's innermost being and everywhere about him. The sunset and the sky and the visible world and Theodore and Theodore's mind, were One. . . .

" If time was still passing, it passed unperceived, until Theodore found himself thinking like a faint rivulet on the melting edge of Heaven. This he realised quite clearly was the world when the veil of events and purposes was drawn aside, this was the timeless world in which everything is different and lovely and right. This was Reality.

" The sun sank into the contours of the island, softened in shape as though it were molten, broadened down to an edge of fire and was lost. The sky burned red and grew pale.

" Something was ebbing away from him, receding from him very rapidly, something he would, if he could, have retained for ever. The stupendous moment was passing, had passed and he was back in the world of everyday. He was roused by the mewing of a seagull. . . . He turned his face homeward.

" He felt he had made some profound discovery. He had been initiated. He knew. But did he know? What was it he knew? He had no words for it. . . . The glow remained a living light in his mind for several days, albeit a fading glow, and then it became a memory. It became a memory from which the vividness had faded altogether. He knew that it had been a profound and wonderful perception, but less and less could he recall what precisely it was he had perceived."

Case 13. From William James : *Varieties of Religious Experience*, 1902, p. 392 (Longmans, Green & Co.).

In several pages of these famous Gifford Lectures, Professor William James gives examples of mystical experiences obtained under anæsthesia. The subject was a gifted woman to whom ether was administered as an anæsthetic for an operation. The last " dream " before regaining consciousness is described below by this lady, who says it was " most vivid and real " to her.

" A great Being or Power was travelling through the sky, his foot was on a kind of lightning as a wheel is on a rail, it was his pathway. The lightning was made entirely of the spirits of innumerable people close to one another, and I was one of them. He moved in a straight line, and each part of the streak or flash came into its short conscious existence only that he might travel. I seemed to be directly under the foot of God, and I thought he was grinding his own life up out of my pain. Then I saw that what he had been trying with all his might to do was to *change his course*, to *bend* the line of lightning to which he was tied, in the direction in which he wanted to go. I felt my flexibility and helplessness, and knew that he would succeed. He bended me, turning his corner by means of my hurt, hurting me more than I had ever been hurt in my life, and at the acutest point of this, as he passed, I *saw*. I understood for a moment things that I have now forgotten, things that no one could remember while retaining sanity. The angle was an obtuse angle, and I remember thinking as I woke that had he made it a right or acute angle, I should have both suffered and ' seen ' still more, and should probably have died.

" He went on and I came to. In that moment the whole of my life passed before me, including each little meaningless piece of distress, and I *understood* them. *This* was what it had all meant, *this* was the piece of work it had all been contributing to do. I did not see God's purpose, I only saw his intentness and his entire relentlessness towards his means. He thought no more of me than a man thinks of hurting a cork when he is opening wine, or hurting a cartridge when he is firing. And yet, on waking, my first feeling was, and it came with tears, ' Domine non sum digna,' for I had been lifted into a position for which I was too small. I realised that in that half hour under ether I had served God more distinctly and purely than I had ever done in my life before, or than I am capable of desiring to do. I was the means of his achieving and revealing something, I know not what or to whom, and that, to the exact extent of my capacity for suffering.

" While regaining consciousness, I wondered why, since I had gone so deep, I had seen nothing of what the saints call the *love* of God, nothing but his relentlessness. And then I heard an answer, which I could only just catch, saying, ' Knowledge and Love are One, and the *measure* is suffering '—I give the words as they came to me. With that I came finally to (into what seemed a dream world compared with the reality of what I was leaving), and I saw that what would be called the ' cause ' of my experience was a slight operation under insufficient ether, in a bed pushed up against a window, a common city window in a common city street. If I had to formulate a few of the things I then caught a glimpse of, they would run somewhat as follows :

" The eternal necessity of suffering and its eternal vicariousness. The veiled and incommunicable nature of the worst sufferings ;—the passivity of genius, how it is essentially instrumental and defenceless, moved, not moving, it must do what it does ;—the impossibility of discovery without its price ;—finally, the excess of what the suffering ' seer ' or genius pays over what his generation gains. (He seems like one who sweats his life out to earn enough to save a district from famine, and just as he staggers back, dying and satisfied, bringing a lac of rupees to buy grain with, God lifts the lac away, dropping *one* rupee, and says, ' That you may give them. That you have earned for them. The rest is for ME.') I perceived also in a way never to be forgotten, the excess of what we see over what we can demonstrate."

The first part of the dream experience is characteristic of dreams. The bodily sense of pain is woven into the dream and made the symbolic vehicle of truth. The climax comes when all symbolism is left behind and she is able to say, " I *understood* . . . this was what it had all meant ". Note the profound sense of significance it had for the dreamer who could say afterwards, " I realised that in that half-hour under ether I had served God more distinctly and purely than I had ever done in my life before, or than I am capable of desiring to do ".

Case 14. *An Arabian mystic.* This expression in poetry of a mystical experience has been translated by Sir Cecil Spring-Rice. It shows the same fading away of the sense of separateness into boundless being where the Knower and the Known become one. A voice from Heaven calls to him :

> " Behold I call my creature, even thee
> The poor, the frail, the sinful and the sad ;
> And with My glory, I will make thee glad ;
> Come unto Me, My friend, come unto Me ! "
> Even so the voice from heaven I heard, and came
> And veiled my face and plunged into the flame.
> Last night I lived a mean and abject thing
> Content in bondage, glad and prison-bound,
> With greedy fingers blindly groping round
> For such brief comfort as the hour might bring.
> Today I am the North wind on the wing
> And the wide roaring of the clamorous sea,
> And the huge heaven's calm immensity,
> And all the bloom and music of the Spring.
> I lived and loved. Now is it life or death
> Here in this vast world wherein I move ?

How when the winds of heaven are my breath,
And the great sun the eye whereby I see ?
I live not in myself, only in Thee.
Last night I loved. This morning I am Love.

4. EXPERIENCE BEYOND EXPRESSION

All mystics have discovered that behind the façade of appearance, behind the world of everyday life, there are worlds of being compared with which the former is unreal and " dead ". The experiences already presented clearly indicate the existence of many such worlds or levels of closer approach to reality, and it is difficult to be analytical and say where one world of significance ends and another begins. In terms of our simile of the many screens round the light of Reality, it is as though these screens, beginning with the outermost, gradually become thin and dissolve away in deepening mystical experience. At a certain depth of penetration the Self feels itself " at home " in a world of being rather than of becoming, a world with a timeless and eternal quality about it.

One instant I, an instant, knew
As God knows all. And it and you
I, above Time, oh, blind! could see
In witless immortality.*

It is a state in which the sense of multiplicity and separateness is lost, so that the mystic feels that he has at once discovered his true Self and that he is one with all Selves and with the Divine. Such experiences can seldom be sustained long nor can they be commanded. It is as though the outer man has had access, for a moment only, to the inner citadel of the Self, and seen its glory.

Yet ever and anon a trumpet sounds
From the hid battlements of Eternity ;
Those shaken mists a space unsettle, then
Round the half-glimpséd turrets slowly wash again.†

All those who, even for a moment, have glimpsed this ineffable world have longed all their waking days to recapture the experience. We may, I think, surmise that it is a state of being of which full and continuous awareness is the goal and destiny of Man. It is that which Man, the pilgrim, exiled in space and time, may hope someday to attain through his struggle, suffering and seeking.

We have remarked that the profounder mystical states are seldom

---

* Rupert Brooke's poem, " Dining-room Tea ", is a moving example of one such moment of mystical insight.
† Francis Thompson : *The Hound of Heaven.*

long-sustained nor can they be commanded. We should perhaps qualify both statements, for history bears witness to the fact that there have been men on earth who have achieved full Enlightenment. These are men who have a fully conscious knowledge of the unity of their own Self with the Divine Self. They are men who can at will withdraw the veils from the light of Reality which is within themselves. Their retention of these veils is a free choice so that they may help mankind on the level of its greatest need.

5. THE CULTIVATION OF MYSTICAL EXPERIENCE

The cases presented in this chapter have been spontaneous examples of mystical experience. Such experiences in their profounder forms are felt by those who have had them to be the goal of all man's striving—states of being so perfect, exalted and satisfying—that if they could be sustained constantly, the only adequate descriptive term would seem to be " union with God ". The Christian mystics use the terms " Unitive Life " and " Beatific Vision ". The Hindus use the term " Moksha ", the Buddhists speak of " Nirvana ", but all are referring to a state of being which no words can express. It is clearly a state of being with which the essence of the higher religions is deeply concerned, for it may be properly regarded as the goal of all such religious aspiration. If a definition of religion be thought necessary, we might perhaps propose that of William James : " The feelings, acts, and experiences of individual men in their solitude, so far as they apprehend themselves to stand in relation to whatever they may consider divine."

The question then arises for us : can Man himself *do* anything to achieve mystical experience, or is it some act of grace beyond Man's control or influence ? The truest answer would seem to be that while the profounder mystical experiences are certainly beyond ordinary man's willing or commanding, and in that sense are given, nevertheless the fulfilment of certain conditions favours these experiences. It is because of this that the " contemplative life " has always had its place of honour in the religions of the world ; for freed from preoccupation with the things of sense, so that certain disciplines of the mind and soul can be followed, it has been generally believed that the aspirant may reach a point where he can receive the supreme vision. The Christian contemplatives have their own description of the Way. They distinguish three stages. (1) Purgation, which is a moral purification. It is the renunciation of greed in all its aspects, whether love of gain, love of fame, or love of pleasure. (2) Proficiency, in which all fear goes, and positive powers and virtues take possession of the self. (3) Union, the final stage in which ignorance of the nature of the self, of time and of existence departs, and enlightenment or the unitive life is born.

Case 15. *The Blessed Angelico of Foligno*. It is appropriate to close this collection with a few experiences of a Christian mystic of the thirteenth century. She was born in 1248, some twenty-two years after the death of Saint Francis. She became the founder and leader of a group of Franciscan Tertiaries who vowed themselves to poverty and self-knowledge and spent their lives in charitable works. The hard years of progressive renunciation and spiritual search have been described by Evelyn Underhill.* They were years holding much of intense mental and physical agony, and were not without morbid psychological manifestations, but she came through in the last twelve years of her life (dying at the age of sixty-one) to " profound inward peace ". All who came into contact with her recognised the spiritual quality of her nature. She was able to write such things as these :

" I beheld the ineffable fullness of God ; but I can relate nothing of it, save that I have *seen* the fullness of Divine Wisdom, wherein is all goodness. . . .

" All that I say of this, seems to me to be nothing. I feel as though I offended in speaking of it, for so greatly does the Good exceed all my words that my speech seems to be but blasphemy. . . .

" The eyes of my soul were opened and I beheld the plenitude of God, by which I understood the whole world both here and beyond the sea, the abyss, and all other things. . . . And in this I beheld nothing save the Divine Power, in a way that is utterly indescribable, so that through the greatness of its wonder the soul cried with a loud voice saying, ' The whole world is full of God.' Wherefore I understood that the world is but a little thing ; and I saw that the power of God was above all things and the whole world was filled with it. . . .

" After I had seen the power of God, His will and His justice, I was lifted higher still ; and then I no longer beheld the power and will as before. But I beheld a *Thing*, as fixed and stable as it was indescribable ; and more than this I cannot say, save that I have often said already, namely, that it was all good. And although my soul beheld not love, yet when it saw that indescribable *Thing* it was filled with indescribable joy, so that it was taken out of the state it was in before and placed in this great and ineffable state. . . . But if thou seekest to know that which I beheld, I can tell thee nothing save that I beheld a Fullness and a Clearness. . . . Thus I beheld a beauty so great that I can say nothing of it save that I saw the Supreme Beauty which contains in itself all goodness."

Behind the popular forms of the Eastern religions—Hinduism, Buddhism, Taoism, etc.—there is a psychological technique known

* Evelyn Underhill : *The Essentials of Mysticism* (J. M. Dent).

as yoga practised by the few. The term yoga comes from a Sanskrit root which is that from which the English word " yoke " is derived. It constitutes a discipline by which the lower self (or Ego) is joined to the higher self (or spirit). In other words, it is a technique designed to lead to the conscious union of the human self with the Divine. The methods will be discussed later, in Chapter 17. All that we wish at present to affirm is that there are paths to man's goal on which, if he wills to do so, he may enter. Radhakrishnan * has expressed it thus :

" The oldest wisdom in the world tells us that we can consciously unite with the divine while in this body, for this is man really born. If he misses his destiny Nature is not in a hurry; she will catch him up someday and compel him to fulfil her secret purpose."

* Radhakrishnan : *Eastern Religions and Western Thought* (O.U.P.), p. 26.

Chapter

15

THE INTERPRETATION OF MYSTICAL EXPERIENCE

Oh, miracles of sight and thought and dream !
You do but lead us to a farther gate,
A higher window in the prison wall
That bounds our mortal state :
However far you lift us we must fall.
But lo ! remains the miracle supreme,—
That we, whom Death and Change have shown our fate,
We, the chance progeny of Earth and Time,
Should ask for more than Earth and Time create,
And, goalless and without the strength to climb,
Should dare to climb where we were born to grope ;
That we the lowly could conceive the great,
Dream in our dust of destinies sublime,
And link our moments to immortal hope.

SIDNEY ROYSE LYSAGHT.

Not thus has God ordained it ; nay, but He
To silent hearts is present silently ;
He waits till in thee perish pride and shame,
Sense of thyself, and all thy thoughts of fame ;
Then when thy task is over, His begun,
He leads thy soul where all the Arts are one—
Leads to His shrine, and has of old unfurled
To chosen eyes the wonder of the world.

F. W. H. MYERS.

I. THE PROBLEM OF CREDIBILITY

I DO not know what impression the fifteen selected examples of mystical experience leave on the mind of the critical reader. They might have been multiplied many times. I believe, however, we have looked at a representative selection from which we can safely draw general inferences, and that additional examples would but confirm these inferences.

I imagine some critical readers with the approach characteristic of scientific method will think as follows. In Natural Science we gather our sense-data together, we check and counter-check them, and we use our minds to order them, to formulate hypotheses and finally to discover underlying laws. In psychical research we have, by and large, done the same thing, although at the present early stage of research we are but groping to discover the laws, and our hypotheses are necessarily very tentative. In the field of mystical experience we seem to enter a different world, to which the scientific method is inapplicable. Certain persons have subjective experiences which are profoundly significant for *them*, but how can *we* tell whether they are not deluded ? These experiences cannot be repeated at will; they cannot be subjected to critical examination by the minds of others. What authority can they possibly have for persons who have not experienced them and cannot test them ? Are we not now leaving the solid ground of verifiable things for the shifting sands of subjectivity ? Such questions demand careful consideration at this stage.

We have already discussed the limitations of the scientific method in Chapter 5. The views there expressed partially answer these questions. The fact is that there are huge tracts of experience to which the scientific method cannot be applied. Let us be very clear about this, and not suppose that because this is so, any doubt is thrown on their existence or importance. A person may say " I feel a pain " or " I feel remorse ". No one can disprove such an affirmation : the person involved can alone say what he feels. There may, of course, be objective evidence in speech or conduct which can be regarded as lending support to, or leading to doubt of, his statements—but not doing more than this. We cannot doubt, however, that feelings do exist in spite of the impossibility of external proof or disproof of their existence in others. We must, and we do, take account of them. We do not say, " We cannot demonstrate that feelings exist in other people and moreover, people who say they have feelings are possibly deluded ". The reason is that we know we ourselves have feelings, and that they are different from, but quite as real a part of ourselves as our intellectual processes. A precisely similar argument should apply to those who tell us they have had certain mystical experiences. Proof or disproof of the truth of such statements by others is out of the question, and if there is reluctance to recognise them, it is presumably on the unconvincing and illogical grounds that we have not had such experiences ourselves.

Those of us who have not had first-hand experience are called upon to make up our minds as to the credibility of these things. Personally I find two features very impressive.

1. Those who have had the more profound type of mystical experiences, no matter in what age or to what race or creed they have belonged, tell us the *same* fundamental things : the sense of separateness vanishes in an all-embracing unity, there is certain knowledge

of immortality, there is an enormously enhanced appreciation of values, and there is knowledge that at the heart of the universe is Joy and Beauty. This unanimity of testimony is quite remarkable.

2. Those who have known such an experience are always profoundly impressed by its significance as a revelation of truth. There is from then onwards, not the satisfaction of an intellectual answer to life's ultimate questions, but a serenity born of the knowledge that all is well, and that the secret purpose of the universe is good beyond all telling.

> I am a wanderer: I remember well
> One journey, how I feared the track was missed,
> So long the city I desired to reach
> Lay hid; when suddenly its spires afar
> Flashed through the circling clouds; you may conceive
> My transport. Soon the vapours closed again,
> *But I had seen the city. . . . ٭*

It is, of course, always possible to suggest that good and sincere people who claim to have had mystical experiences are self-deluded. The implication of such a suggestion is that truth can be distinguished from error by counting heads : that the experiences of the majority are in some way a " norm " and the departures of a minority from this are *ipso facto* abnormal and suspect. The number of good artists in the community is only small : why do we not look at these and call them queer and abnormal ? In fact, we look at great Art and realise that it tells us something of the nature of a reality beyond the senses but mediated through them. We say the artist has the gift of insight—and wish we had it too. The number of good musical composers or of poets in the community is only small, but we do not call them queer and self-deluded. We listen to the music or the poetry : it speaks to us of a world beyond that of our senses and tells us something of the nature of reality. We say they have a gift—and wish we had it too. Should we be less just to the mystics ?

The mystics claim to have had an experience which in its deeper forms is incommunicable in words—but they unite in bringing back the sense of certain overwhelming convictions about the nature of things. To some of us these are a revelation of the nature of reality. We make an inner response such as we make to great art or music : we feel reality *ought* to be like that. Why should we not add : they have a gift, which we wish we had too ?

When we analyse what " self-delusion " amounts to, our thoughts turn either to the wish-fulfilment type of belief beloved of psychoanalysts, or to the dissociated systems of ideas characteristic of

٭ Robert Browning : *Paracelsus.*

L

schizophrenia. I consider that we may rule out the latter as having any relation to true mystical experience. We find in the greater mystics no delusions of grandeur, but always a great humility, and often even a reluctance to talk of an experience which has been sacred to them. Far from being a disintegrating experience unfitting its possessor to cope with life, it is integrating in a high degree, enabling its possessor to face life with the serenity and confidence born of insight. There is a delightful story told of Sri Ramakrishna, the charming and childlike Indian saint whose teachings and personality have inspired so many others in modern India. From the evidence available it seems probable that he entered frequently during his life into some of the profounder mystical experiences. The story * is that, hearing of his sanctity, two eminent pundits went to visit him to elicit his views, and to subject them to careful examination and analysis. Greatly impressed by what they heard, they solemnly declared in his presence that he must be an Avatar—an incarnation of the Divine. Ramakrishna is said to have received this announcement with indifference—and with childlike simplicity to have said, " Just fancy!—Well, I'm glad it's not a disease. . . . But, believe me, I know nothing about it."

It is quite true that in certain forms of delusional insanity the patient reports visions, voices, the obsessing sense of a mission, the feeling of control or influence by powers other than the self, and so on—all of which can be found in certain cases associated with mystical experience. William James † has pointed out that such states of insanity are, however, pessimistic, not optimistic, in their emotional content, menacing and dissociative, not joyful and integrative. The fact is that all experiences, thoughts, feelings and creative inspirations have to pass, in the course of finding expression, through a certain part of the mind. (We discussed this in Chapter 12 (3).) So also have dream-material and all the repressed memories and dissociated morbid systems of ideas which arise in the course of psycho-analysis. The common venue need not imply a common source. Imagination and Memory, for example, may look alike; but their sources are quite different. It is certainly true, as William James has said, that what comes must be " sifted and tested and run the gauntlet of confrontation with the total context of experience ". The affirmations of the mystics have no intrinsic authority in virtue of which we are obliged to accept them. All that is Truth authen-

* Christopher Isherwood in *Vedanta for the Western World*, p. 16 (George Allen & Unwin, 1948).
† William James : *Varieties of Religious Experience*, p. 417 (Longmans, Green & Co., 1943).

ticates itself in the end by evoking a response from a depth of ourselves beyond our mind. It is, of course, quite possible for the sceptic to maintain that our purest longings and highest aspirations are part of a vast delusional system. I would only add the comment that I have yet to discover the sceptic who holds this view with the same sense of utter conviction as that which the mystics possess of their truth. The sceptic is uncertain, they are certain. In this rarefied region of Truth's domain we can only see what we have fitted ourselves to see by love and self-discipline.

The most reassuring evidence that mysticism has no necessary connection with psychopathic states of mind is found by looking at the personality, character and influence upon others of some of those who are known to have had the most profound mystical experience. Consider Gautama the Buddha, the Chinese sage Lao-Tse, St. Paul, St. Augustine, Plotinus (of whom Whittaker says he is " the greatest individual thinker between Aristotle and Descartes "), Dante, Jelalu'ddin Rumi (the Sufi poet), John Yepes (known as St. John of the Cross), Ruysbroeck, Kabir (the weaver-mystic of fifteenth-century India), Jacob Boehme, Honoré de Balzac, Walt Whitman, etc. If such men, whose personalities so profoundly impressed their contemporaries, and who contributed so enormously to the world's treasury, were self-deluded or psychopaths, we suggest that the world could do with many more of them ! Their " delusion " is preferable to our sanity. No doubt a number of mystics exhibit mental eccentricities, instability, morbid states and sometimes neurosis—but so do a number of artists, musicians, scientists, philosophers and critics, and we must not be unfair in our judgments.

The suggestion that perhaps the mystics are self-deluded in the sense of " discovering " their own wish-fulfilments (i.e., seeing what they want to see, and finding what they want to find) will not stand examination. If the reader will look again at the examples in Chapter 14, he will note the unexpectedness of the experiences, the passivity of the experiencer in the presence of something other than the self and the completely new sense of revelation it brings. If there is something of wish-fulfilment about these, it is certainly obvious that there is also a very great deal more. " Suddenly, in a moment," said Tagore, " a veil seemed to be lifted from my eyes." " Suddenly, in a flash," said Winifred Holtby, " the grief, the bitterness, the sense of frustration disappeared." " Something has happened to me—I am utterly amazed . . . yet how unworthy I," said Warner Allen. " I *understood*—this was what it had all meant. . . . I realised that in that half hour under ether, I had served God more distinctly and purely than I had ever done in my life before, or than I am capable of desiring to do," said another. " The gate was opened to me, that in one quarter of an hour I saw and knew more than if I had been many years together at a university," said Jacob Boehme, the inspired shoemaker-mystic of Görlitz, Germany. Dr. R. M. Bucke, the eminent Canadian psychiatrist, claims that he learned more within the few seconds during which the illumination lasted than in previous months or even years of study, and that he learned much that no study could ever have taught. The illumination itself continued not more than a few moments, but its effects proved ineffaceable ; it was impossible for him ever to forget what he at that time saw and knew ; neither did he, nor could he, ever doubt the truth of what was then presented to his mind. (Although recounted in the third person, the description is by Dr. Bucke himself.)

If these persons were deceived or deluded in the experience of life which brought to them the greatest sense of inner conviction and certainty, I think we may as well come to the despairing conclusion that nothing can be known, and all may be delusion. For my own part, I think we must evaluate the expressions of mystical experience —if we have the capacity to do so—as we evaluate great art or great music. We make to these things a response—not with our minds and feelings alone, or even chiefly with these, but with some deeper part of our essential nature, which echoes back to our conscious self that this is an insight into Reality. If we cannot make this response let us be honest and sincere about it : but let us not deny that other equally sincere people may respond to reality in a way which we cannot. Although my temperament excludes me, I fear, from mystical experience of other than a very slight kind, I am profoundly relieved to read of the deeper experiences of others. To hear that Reality is knowable from the lips of some great sage, to be assured by great seers that the spirit of man belongs to an eternal world, and yet to know of none like ourselves who have ever experienced this —who can turn to us and say, " I am now as certain of this, as of the fact that I exist "—would be a matter for the gravest misgiving. Happily we are reassured by facts of experience, and these are as relevant to the structure of the world as the facts of experiment.

2. THE PROBLEM OF INTERPRETATION

If the reader will look again at what I have called, with apology, some of the slighter forms of mystical experience, he will notice certain features in common. (a) The illumination or radiance which is seen to infuse everything " without " is felt to come from

" within ". (b) The sense of belonging to a new and greater unity is always felt. That which is seen forms a part of a larger whole. (c) The emotional tones are always supremely attractive : pulsing light, livingness, joy, peace, happy wonder. Through them, and interwoven, is an enormously enhanced sense of the supreme values, and the most adequate description usually seems to the experiencer to be a " revelation of God ". (d) Words fail to express the experience, and the terms used are known to be only symbols and analogies.

These features are all illustrated by the previous examples.

(a) " Suddenly my consciousness was lighted up *from within* and I saw " (Case 1). " An astonishing radiance welled up on all these familiar things and *in the child* herself " (Case 2). " Earth and sky and tree and wind-blown grass, *and the child in the midst of them* came alive together with a pulsing light of consciousness " (Case 3). " I was aware that in reality the feeling and the thought were in me, and not in the earth or sun " (Case 4). " Suddenly, in a moment, a veil seemed to be lifted from my eyes. I found . . ." (Case 6), etc.

(b) " They were no longer just themselves, separate objects with edges of their own ; they *were* that radiance . . ." (Case 2). " I can recall the swift inclusive awareness of each for the whole—I in them and they in me and all of us enclosed in a warm lucent bubble of livingness " (Case 3). " Scents, sights and sounds blended into a harmony so perfect that it transcended human expression, even human thought " (Case 5). " I seemed to witness in the wholeness of my vision the movements of the body of all humanity " (Case 6). " All was an ocean of life—a single coherent organism filling all space, yet composed of an infinity of individuated existences " (Case 8). Cases (11), (12) and (14) reveal the same sense of unity in a greater whole.

(c) " The whole universe . . . filled with this intense and vital beauty " (Case 1). " The radiance was unbounded glorious love." The little girl's spontaneous reaction was " Why, I am seeing God —I could be seeing Him all the time " (Case 2). In Case (3) we have a precisely similar reaction. John Buchan writes of Peace and Joy and says of his experience : " The world was a place of inexhaustible beauty, but still more it was the husk of something infinite, ineffable and immortal, in very truth the garment of God." All the examples, according to the depth of insight and the measure of ability to express it, convey the same moving sense of infinite significance.

Before considering the last feature—of the failure of words to express mystic experience—let us weigh the three features illustrated.

(*a*) The awareness is lit up from within, and this lights up all that is regarded as being without. The reader will perhaps look again at Browning's metaphor of the lamp of Reality swathed round by many obscuring screens (Chapter 14 (1)). This parable of the self—which is the best we can find—provides a natural place for all three features of mystical experience. We have suggested that the obscuring screens of Maya which surround the lamp prevent us from seeing clearly in the outer regions, and thus from understanding the true nature of the world. But in mystical experience it is as though these screens become more transparent, and when it is flooded by the greater light, we see the world as a new revelation. "Truth is within ourselves," as Browning says,—and

> to know,
> Rather consists in opening out a way
> Whence the imprisoned splendour may escape.

(*b*) The sense that all the visible, tangible world is a part of a larger whole and is apprehended as having an underlying unity, finds a clear place in Browning's parable. The obscuring screens separate worlds or planes of diminishing reality, as we go outwards from the central light. But whenever, standing in the dimness of the outer world, a veil is temporarily removed or a screen dissolves away, we see the fuller light of the Real illuminating the darkness of the world where we stand—and this world is then realised as only a part of a larger whole. It is absorbed into the more real world with the dissolving of the screen.

Bradley, in his famous work *Appearance and Reality*, has said the same thing.

> " Nature viewed materialistically is only an abstraction for certain purposes, and has not a high degree of truth or reality. The poet's Nature has much more. Our principle that the abstracted is the unreal moves us steadily upward. It compels us in the end to credit Nature with our higher emotions. The process can only cease when Nature is quite absorbed into spirit, and at every stage of the process we find increase in reality."

(*c*) How utterly satisfying it is to know that, in spite of all appearances in the familiar world, nevertheless when *this* light shines it is all seen to be good—unutterably good. In the dimness of our normal state of consciousness we see strife and struggle, suffering and injustice, evil and torture, anguish and failure. But when the veils are withdrawn in a moment of insight, the mystics, with no dissentient voice, speak of the omnipresent overflowing Joy at the heart of things, of " unbounded glorious Love ". Thus Whitman speaks of " The ocean filled with joy—the atmosphere all joy !

Joy, joy, in freedom, worship, love! Joy in the ecstasy of life: enough to merely be!" Evelyn Underhill remarks: "The dies which the mystics have used are many . . . but the gold from which this divine coinage is struck is always the same precious metal, always the same Beatific Vision of Goodness, Truth and Beauty."

Even a single limited and partial experience contains so much that is wonderful and satisfying that its recipient can write thus:

> "I know nothing of the ecstasy of the mystics except for one illuminating personal experience. A flash of insight not induced by first love, religious fervour or mental or spiritual auto-intoxication, but unsought, surprising—a split-second of Time containing all Time, not so much a vision of beauty and harmony, but the certain knowledge that they existed. The briefest moment, yet so illuminating and life-giving that it still seems more vivid than all the days and years of my life. The best description I can find is that it was a marriage of the mind with the universal mind (whatever that is)— satisfying and complete. . . . A man fortunate enough to have had such an experience could never go down to his grave with bitterness, for he has tasted and, what is more important, knows that he has tasted the height and the depth and the fullness of life." *

Those who have followed these views of the nature of mystical experience will, I think, find that it is a natural extension of, and certainly not out of harmony with views expressed much earlier on the nature of ordinary perception. Thus in Chapter 5 we said: "The plain man's world and the physicist's world (X in our diagram of the round tower) are not regarded as illusions, but as having a degree of reality arising from the fact that they are aspects of something which is more real. It is on this deeper level (Y in our diagram) that the more real essences of things are supposed to exist, and that all perception really takes place." The process of perception was considered again, and illustrated in the diagram in Chapter 9 (6). The recognition that this is the nature of perception (an activity within the mind) makes it easy, I think, to conceive that an inner illumination may change the whole significance of the thing perceived. Some forms of insight or intuitive knowledge may indeed be represented by a process like that illustrated on the right-hand side of the diagram (p. 206)—but lifted up a step, so as to relate the world of values to the world of the mind's potentialities. Such insight would give immediate access to knowledge—not the indirect access involved in the use of our senses. We shall not pursue these psychological aspects further. It is more important for our philosophy of life that we should rightly evaluate the data

* Letter by H. P. Shapland to Warner Allen, quoted by permission from Warner Allen: *The Happy Issue*, p. 28 (Faber & Faber, 1948).

of mystical experience than that we should understand exactly how
these experiences arise.

3. THE PROBLEM OF EXPRESSION.   SYMBOLS

It has been already pointed out that after the immediate illumination of a mystical experience is over, the mind attempts to
clothe in words its feeling–memory of the experience, and also its
interpretation of its significance.   How far can this be done ?
Again and again in attempting to express such experiences in words
for the benefit of others, the narrator expresses a sense of the inadequacy of language.   Thus in Case 12 : " He felt he had made
some profound discovery.   He had been initiated.   He knew.   But
did he know ?   What was it he knew ?   He had no words for it. . . ."
Those who bring back a few clear and certain convictions, as in
Cases 11 and 13, equally feel the crippling limitations of language.
Dr. Bucke speaks of " an intellectual illumination quite impossible
to describe " and of a conception of " an immense Whole [such] as
dwarfs all conception, imagination, or speculation springing from
and belonging to ordinary self-consciousness ".   As the mystical
experience of Case 8 deepens in character, a point is reached where
" all words fail ".   So also St. John of the Cross writes of a mystical
state called the " union of love ".

> " We receive this mystical knowledge of God clothed in none of the
> kinds of images, in none of the sensible representations, which our
> mind makes use of in other circumstances.   Accordingly in this
> knowledge, since the senses and the imagination are not employed, we
> get neither form not impression, nor can we give any account or
> furnish any likeness, although the mysterious and sweet-tasting
> wisdom comes home so clearly to the inmost parts of our souls.   Fancy
> a man seeing a certain kind of thing for the first time in his life.   He
> can understand it, use and enjoy it, but he cannot apply a name to it
> nor communicate any idea of it, even though all the while it be a mere
> thing of sense.   How much greater will be his powerlessness when it
> goes beyond the senses."

All words are symbols enabling us to communicate with each
other.   We have some words which are symbols of sense-data.   If
the words " green apple " are uttered, they will bring to the mind of
the hearers (provided they know the English language) the idea of
certain sense-data.   We have words for feelings such as fear, anger,
patience, sympathy, and these when uttered convey certain ideas to
the hearers because they, too, have experienced these feelings and
associated them in memory with the appropriate sounds.   We have
words for the highest values we know : beauty, truth, goodness and

love, and to one who has recognised these values the uttering of the word will convey the idea of the value. But here we are beginning to see already that a word of rich content to one person may be empty, or of little significance to another person, because his experience cannot fill it with content. It is clear that mystical experience is only communicable in terms of the lower analogies of values or of those still lower, of ideas or feelings. Even then, the only persons who will adequately appreciate the experience are those who have themselves known it. The rest of us can only attempt to extrapolate * upwards from the richest content which such values, ideas and feelings have for us, to the unexperienced wonder of mystical experience. It is the sense of the inadequacy of all symbols and analogies as representations of God, which has led to parables such as the following :

A student went to a great Indian sage and said, " Reverend sir, teach me Brahman ". The sage remained silent, and the student said again to him, " Reverend sir, teach me Brahman ". He still remained silent. When asked by the student a third time, he said, " I do teach thee Brahman. I am silent."

Of our highest values, truth, beauty, goodness and love, their expression in the symbolism of words is often felt to be so inadequate as to be a degradation. Thus D. G. Rossetti in his sonnet " Silent Noon " says :

> So this winged hour is dropt us from above.
> Oh ! clasp we to our hearts, for deathless dower,
> This close-companioned inarticulate hour
> When twofold silence was the song of love.

So in the presence of great beauty we do not want to talk, we want to worship.† Walt Whitman wrote in " Leaves of Grass " :

> When I undertake to tell the best I find I cannot,
> My tongue is ineffectual on its pivots,
> My breath will not be obedient to its organs,
> I become a dumb man.

Such expressions as are found in mystical literature, " a dazzling darkness ", " the formless Form ", " the unstruck music of the infinite ", " the cloud of unknowing ", " the teeming desert ", which can mean nothing to the person who has had no experience to which they correspond, show the inadequacy of language to express

---

* " Extrapolate " is a mathematical term. If a smooth curve is extended beyond the limit of observed data and a value thus determined, this is the term employed. Erigena spoke of God as the " extrapolated goal of the migratory instinct of the human spirit ".

† See Rupert Brooke's poem " The Voice ".

the experience. We have already suggested that Art, which strives
to express values, is perhaps a more effective language, but we know
ourselves to be in a region where all these things are but symbols of
something higher and greater, as the shadows cast on the back of
Plato's cave assured the prisoner of a truer and wider life of which
they were the representations.

4. THE PROBLEM OF THE VEILS. MAYA

Those who have thought much about the structure of the self (and
therefore about the structure of the world) have expressed in a
variety of ways the central idea of Browning's parable of the imprisoned splendour, which is the one Reality. Veil after veil
reduces the light, until in the physical world on which we focus our
awareness, we are living in the dim twilight not of unreality, but of
that which is farthest removed from the ultimately real.

G. N. M. Tyrrell has said, " There is no more fundamental way
in which reality inheres in anything finite than as an *aspect* of something which lies a step nearer to the absolutely real ".

" Mysticism ", says Nettleship, " is the belief that everything in
being what it is is symbolic of something more."

" Every truth ", says Isaac Penington the Quaker, " is shadow
except the last. But every truth is substance in its own place,
though it be but a shadow in another place. And the shadow is a
true shadow, as the substance is a true substance."

Dean Inge * says :

> " It is a mystical doctrine to which Plotinus gives great importance,
> that all creativity is the result of contemplation. The One by
> contemplating itself produces the world of spiritual reality (the
> ' intelligible world '). This in turn by contemplating the One
> generates the world of Soul ; and Soul, by contemplating the
> ' Intelligibles ', generates the world of phenomena. Each product
> is inferior to its archetype, which it resembles as far as it can. Every
> creator then creates, so to speak, with his back turned."

Radhakrishnan † expresses the point of view of Hindu thought.
" The objective world exists. It is not an illusion. It is real not
in being ultimate, but in being a form, an expression of the ultimate.
To regard the world as ultimately real is delusion." He quotes the
great Indian philosopher Samkara in warning us against the temp-
tation to regard anything not completely real as utterly illusory.

---

* W. R. Inge : *Mysticism in Religion*, p. 159 (Hutchinson).
† Radhakrishnan : *Eastern Religions and Western Thought*, pp. 31, 86,
etc. (O.U.P.).

" The world has empirical being which is quite different from illusory existence."

I think the reader will see that these thinkers are all striving to express difficult metaphysical views which the parable of the lamp illustrates. What, then, *are* the veils which hide the light of reality and which appear to dissolve in mystical experience ? Why are they there, and whence do they arise ? Indian philosophy has a useful term Maya for such veils which stand between the less real and the more real. Unless we are aware of Maya we mistake a part for the whole, an aspect for the thing itself, the dim light of our present awareness for all the light there is. The answer to these questions takes us right into the heart of that most profound problem—the structure of the human self.

All that psychical research could tell us about this was represented in simple terms in the diagram on page 266. Some of the veils to which we have referred may be regarded as the horizontal lines there drawn. The data of mysticism show us that behind the buddhic (or intuitive) level there are depths of the essential self, doubtless also curtained by many veils from that central essence which we have called the lamp of reality—the imprisoned splendour. This essence is the Spirit of man, called the Atman by Indian philosophers. It is the true Self, the real " I " : it is immortal and divine, if the recollected experience of the greatest mystics is true. For the sake of clarity at this stage, let us accept all the risks of over-simplification and express the facts (crudely and spatially) as follows. The zones shown in our diagram constitute collectively the empirical self, the individual personality, the Ego—the self which ordinary people believe themselves to be and with which they identify themselves. If asked to locate their sense of selfhood, their " centre of gravity ", it would be placed somewhere in the zone of mind. The highest mystical experiences show that the Spirit of man, his true Self, lies beyond this and is normally veiled from the Ego. The Ego thinks *it* is the light of the self : it does not know that all its light is borrowed from and sustained by the true Self. Just so, primitive man saw the moonlight streaming down on the earth and did not realise he was seeing the pale reflection of rays from an invisible sun. Somewhere about the mental-buddhic level is what Gerald Heard has frequently called in his books the " strangulated consciousness " which cuts off the Ego from the Self. We should call it a dense veil in our parable. The essence of mysticism is the glimpsing of the true Self by the Ego, and in this experience we come for a moment to know our true divine nature. The experience is so overwhelming and wondrous that, as we have seen, all language fails to capture the memory. The highest state of consciousness is called by the Indian sages *samadhi*. They speak of *savikalpa samadhi* in which the Ego has become absorbed in the true Self, the ultimate or perhaps the penultimate veil having gone. In this state of consciousness the " I " sense remains, though not separate from God, who is known in his personal aspects—Creator, Father, Friend, the Beloved. In the higher *nirvikalpa samadhi* no sense of " I " remains. There is complete blissful unity in the One, the Impersonal, the Absolute.

The person who enters into true *samadhi* returns from it changed by the experience. Although on his return to normal waking consciousness he regains the sense of the Ego, there is no longer any egoism. It is then but the servant of the true divine Self, its exiled outpost in space and time, and it knows itself to be this. Such an individual lives serene amid the turmoil of change and chance, for he has seen God in all things and all things in God. Radhakrishnan * has attempted to describe *samadhi* thus.

> " The conscious division and separation of the self from the divine being, the object from the subject, which is the normal condition of unregenerate humanity, is broken down. The individual surrenders to the object and is absorbed by it. He becomes what he beholds. The distinction between subject and object disappears. Tasting nothing, comprehending nothing in particular, holding itself in emptiness, the soul finds itself as having all. A lightning flash, a sudden flame of incandescence, throws a momentary but eternal gleam on life in time. A strange quietness enters the soul ; a great peace invades its being. The vision, the spark, the supreme moment of unification or conscious realisation, sets the whole being ablaze with perfect purpose. The supreme awareness, the intimately felt presence, brings with it a rapture beyond joy, a knowledge beyond reason, a sensation more intense than that of life itself, infinite in peace and harmony."

It is clear from all that the mystics tell us that our normal level of conscious living is no more than a state of drugged somnolence, of dreaming or of sleep-walking, compared with this high level of super-consciousness. While we are dreaming, the dream-experiences seem real to us : we do not question their validity, nor do we remember our waking state. To the man who has wakened up, the dream experiences have vanished. They are impermanent, and have been swallowed up by the greater reality of the waking state. In the waking state we experience all the clash of opposites : good and evil, happiness and misery, success and failure. From the higher standpoint of the mystics these latter experiences are unreal, or have at most a very limited degree of reality, and all religion

***

* *Eastern Religions and Western Thought*, p. 50 (O.U.P.).

exhorts us to wake up from our pitifully ignorant state of suffering and struggle to know the world as it really is. The world of the opposites seems the only reality to us because of the veils of Maya, and when we ask ourselves what these are, the only answer seems to be " Ignorance ". The primary ignorance, the densest of the veils, is that which leads us to identify ourselves with our Ego. We remain thus as ignorant of our true nature, the Divine Self, as the dreamer is of his waking self, which he has forgotten—perhaps not quite forgotten. For just as in dreams distorted fragments may arise which are reminiscent of waking experience, so in our ordinary life we hear at times alluring whispers of something we greatly desire but do not possess. The quest for inward happiness lures men on : it is really the call of their Divine Self for recognition, but men do not know it, and plunge into the world of the opposites hoping to find it. Craving and desire are the expressions of the Ego's search for happiness where it cannot permanently be found. Hence it is that the seers all point to discrimination and detachment as the way of spiritual progress : discrimination between the less real and the more real, and detachment from those things which cannot in their nature bring lasting satisfaction. There is much truth in the saying, " The incentive to all action is the search for Happiness, and the only difference between the saint and the sinner is that the former searches the direct way and the latter the indirect way." * †

To two of our questions we shall defer answers. Why the veils of Maya are there at all, involves us in speculation on the meaning and purpose of human life (see Chapters 19 and 20). How the veils may be penetrated or dissolved away—in other words, the way of attainment or self-realisation—is a question of the greatest practical importance, and we shall deal with this in Chapter 17.

5. THE PROBLEM OF THE ONE AND THE MANY

On the physical level we all feel the intense solitariness of individuality. There are you, and here am I. You can never know what it is like to be me, nor can I ever know what it is like to be you. As though to emphasise this, or at least symbolising it, our bodies are all discrete and well-defined entities separate in space. Your body and mine cannot occupy the same region of space at the

---

* *The Initiate* by His Pupil (Routledge).

† Lucid accounts of the ideas expressed in a condensed form in this section will be found in articles in *Vedanta for the Western World*, pp. 110, 160, 417, 437, ed. by Isherwood (Allen & Unwin), and also in Radhakrishnan's valuable book *Eastern Religions and Western Thought*. Both these are warmly commended to the student.

same time. It seems probable (vide Chapter 13 (1)) that in the after-death state (the " astral " world) we are still in a world of forms, a world of objectivity interpreted by the mind as it tries to understand it as existing in a kind of space and time. From what we learned of the nature of Mind through psychical research, it was apparent that while individual minds undoubtedly exist, there is on a certain stratum of the mental world a network of relationships. We find that minds are in communication with each other, provided a certain quality of affinity exists. More significant, however, than the in-creasing facility of *communication* as we move towards the real, is the increasing sense of *relationship* with all life which deepening mystical experience brings to the one who experiences it. We drew attention to this in Section 2. It is as though from that Sun which is the One, a myriad rays shine forth which are the myriad created forms. At a great distance—far away from the Sun of Reality—they are all separate and discrete, but as they are traced back towards the Real, their unity in the common source is apparent. The unanimity with which the mystics refer to this experience and the bearing which it obviously has on what philosophers call the problem of the " One and the Many ", make it worth while to look at the meaning of the term " individuality ".

Tyrrell * has pointed out very cogently that our habits of thinking about objects distributed in space make us prone to think that indi-viduality somehow springs out of the spatial separateness of our bodies, whereas, he says, " selfhood is an intrinsic character, irre-solvable and not derivative from anything else ". On the principle that each significant level reflects an aspect, or is a shadow of some-thing more real on a higher level, we can assume that something akin to mental separateness also exists. But we have previously remarked that something akin to mental relatedness also exists to a marked extent on this world-level. The striking thing about apparitions (vide Chapter 9) was that there, a collaboration of the mid-mind levels of two selves produced something which was not-self.

Speaking of these mid-mind levels, Tyrrell says :

> " They show this ' I-ness ' quality, not as something which is either there or not there, but as something which can be present in *degree*. In the personality, the mid-level centres possess in some degree *both* the qualities of selfhood *and* of otherness from self ; and it looks as if the higher we go in the personal hierarchy, the more selfhood we find and the less otherness. At the head of the hierarchy the pure subject of experience is unthinkable, while the normal self is an enigmatic compound of pure self with the lower personal elements, and by no

* *Proc. S.P.R.*, Vol. 44, p. 7 (1936) ; Myers Memorial Lecture on *Apparitions*, p. 77 (1942).

means a stable compound. We must, I think, look upon our personalities as at once partaking of selfhood and providing an internal environment for self."

It has been suggested that perhaps our individuality lies in the separateness of our mental content or, more correctly, in the uniqueness of our mental content. No two persons have just the same memories or experience : does this constitute the nature of individuality ? We might imagine, perhaps, that two discarnate selves completely share their memories with each other, but would this make them indistinguishable ? I think not, for even in yogic trance, when the mind is completely still and unused, there is still the silent experiencer, the intuitive self. Even in two individuals holding all memories and experiences in common, there would still be at least the possibility of different reactions to the experience. It is, however, apparent that as we penetrate towards the true spiritual essence of individuals, the things which can be fully shared increase, and the things which cannot be shared decrease. When the limit is reached, when the root of " I " is experienced, as in the profoundest mystical experience, the overwhelming discovery is made that this root of " I " is united to all other " I's ", for all are united in God. This sublime truth has found expression in the deeper insights of all the great religions.

Thus from Christianity we have " Christ is All and in All ", " In Him we live and move and have our being ", " I am the Vine : ye are the branches ", " I and my Father are one ". Alice Meynell writes : *

Access, Approach
Art Thou, Time, Way and Wayfarer.

Radhakrishnan writes : †

> " The fundamental truths of a spiritual religion are that our real Self is the supreme Being, which it is our business to discover and consciously become, and this Being is one in all. The soul that has found itself is no longer conscious of itself in isolation. . . . It is the soul's experience of the essential unity with the whole being that is brought out in the words ' Thou in me, and I in Thee '."

Hinduism makes the great affirmations " That art Thou " and again " The Atman (i.e., the true Self) is the Brahman (i.e., the Supreme Being) ".

There is a story ‡ of a Swami, a very great soul whom a Mahomedan mutineer stabbed severely. The Hindu mutineers caught

* Poem " I am the Way ".   † Loc. cit., p. 32.
‡ *Complete Works of Vivekananda*, Vol. II, p. 84 (Mayavati Memorial Edn.).

and brought the man to the Swami offering to kill him. But the Swami looked up calmly and said, " My brother, thou art He, thou art He! " and expired. " Inasmuch ", says Gerald Heard, * " as they did it unto the least of these the brethren of Eternal Life they did it to the Eternal Life in themselves."

Sri Krishna Prem † writes :

> " Gone is the sense of a separate finite self, with its individual gains and losses, its personal hopes and fears, and in its place comes the experience of the One Atman, abiding in all beings, of all beings as eddies in that all-pervading ocean of bliss."

Alan Watts ‡ says that the Buddha's doctrine of no-self is simply the denial that the Self is individual, that it belongs in any way to particular human beings. He translates a famous Buddhist text thus, " Be such as have the Self as your lamp, Self as only refuge." This divine essence the " Self " is the same Self in all, and is comparable with the Christian doctrine of the Holy Spirit—God immanent.

The problem as to what constitutes individuality remains on our hands. We agree that individuality does not reside in bodily separateness, nor yet in uniqueness of mental content, and we may ask ourselves whether at any level of approach to reality its origin is apparent. I do not think there is any such point until we get back to the unity in the divine Self. It is as though we are the myriad thoughts of God, as a myriad beams may originate from the one Sun. Plotinus § would have us preserve the truth of individuality without losing sight of unity. Porphyry, his great disciple, said "Particular souls are distinct without being separate ; they are united to each other without being confused, and without making the universal Soul a simple aggregate."

It is clear that all our language is riddled with spatial concepts and it is probably difficult to do more than suggest by some sort of lower analogy, what is the higher and fundamentally inexpressible truth. Perhaps the individual human consciousness, the sense of " I "-ness is an irreducible and fundamental thing, and the increasing sense of unity as we penetrate towards reality is a unity of *relationship*. I think we can find useful analogies for this on many levels—being careful not to press them too far. There is on the material level the relationship of atoms in a molecule. The atomic nuclei remain

* *Preface to Prayer*, p. 111.
† *The Yoga of the Bhagavat Gita*, p. 56 (J. M. Watkins, 1948).
‡ Alan W. Watts : *The Supreme Identity*, p. 42 (footnote) (Faber & Faber, 1950).
§ W. R. Inge : *Philosophy of Plotinus*, Vol. I, p. 213 (Longmans, Green & Co., 1929).

intact, but the external structures are interlocked to form a new and larger whole. Take the human body. The billions of cells are united into functioning organs and the various organs into a still greater whole through which runs a principle of co-operation and unity. The unity is one not of structure and function, but of relationship. On the level of mind we have the unity of relationship of many varied memories held without confusion within a single mind. In art we have the unity of relationship of pigments forming a painting or of notes forming a piece of music.

The poet * may sing :

> Thou art less than a spark of his fire,
> Or a moment's mood of his soul :
> Thou art lost in the notes on the lips of his choir
> That chant the chant of the Whole.

The mystic would say not " lost " but " found " : found one with the Whole.

* W. Watson : " Ode in May ".

Chapter

16

IMPERISHABLE THINGS

" As I get older my poetry seems to be less revelation out of the psyche than the summing-up of whatever wisdom the outer mind had gathered.   But almost the last poem which seemed to me to come out of the genie in the innermost with the old authenticity, made promise that no precious thing would be lost, and when we went inward to our own immortal, we would regain all that Time has taken away."

> Be not so desolate
> Because thy dreams have flown,
> And the hall of the heart is empty
> And silent as stone,
> As age left by children
> Sad and alone.
>
> Those delicate children
> Thy dreams, still endure.
> All pure and lovely things
> Wend to the Pure.
> Sigh not.   Unto the fold
> Their way is sure.
>
> Thy gentlest dreams, the frailest
> Even those that were
> Born and lost in a heart-beat
> Shall meet thee there.
> They are become immortal
> In shining air.
>
> The unattainable beauty,
> The thought of which was pain,
> That flickered in eyes and on lips
> And vanished again ;
> That fugitive beauty
> Thou shalt attain.
>
> Those lights innumerable
> That led thee on and on,
> The masque of time ended,
> Shall glow into one.
> They shall be with thee for ever
> Thy travel done.
>
> Æ (*Song and its Fountains*).

I. CHANGE AND THE CHANGELESS

THERE are few themes to which the poets revert more frequently and with greater poignancy than the transience of earthly things.

The theme is one which finds an echo at some time or other in all human lives—the " heart-break over fallen things ", the melancholy remembrance of all loveliness that passes away, and which we would fain clasp to us for ever.

Some of the poets express it as they look back to the days and home of childhood, when life was happy and carefree and " full of kindly faces ". They range from Thomas Hood, with the simple pathos of his lines :

> I remember, I remember
> The house where I was born,
> The little window where the sun
> Came peeping in at morn ;

to the lament of R. L. Stevenson * on viewing again his childhood's home. In his memory

> Fire and the windows bright glittered on the moorland ;
> Song, tuneful song, built a palace in the wild.
> Now, when day dawns on the brow of the moorland,
> Lone stands the house and the chimney-stone is cold.
> Lone let it stand, now the friends are all departed,
> The kind hearts, the true hearts, that loved the place of old.
> Spring shall come, come again, calling up the moorfowl,
> Spring shall bring the sun and rain, bring the bees and flowers ;
> Red shall the heather bloom over hill and valley,
> Soft flow the stream through the ever-flowing hours ;
> Fair the day shine as it shone on my childhood—
> Fair shine the day on the house with open door ;
> Birds come and cry there and twitter in the chimney—
> But I go for ever and come again no more.

A generation of soldier-poets—Rupert Brooke, Julian Grenfell, Wilfred Owen and others—have likewise shown us the poignancy of the feelings of hosts of young men who loved sunshine " and the colours of the earth " and perished in the slaughter of the world-wars, almost before they had entered upon their heritage.

Many poets have mused upon the pathos of mortality. Gray's famous elegy written in a country churchyard contrasts the continuing life of the country with the transient lives of those who now sleep beneath its rugged elms and yew-trees' shade. Wordsworth † has given us one of the greatest odes in the language by his reflections on the glory which has passed away from the earth—the same world which to boyhood's eyes was " apparell'd in celestial light ". He knows that he can never again have that carefree, light-hearted

* " Home no more Home to me."
† " Ode on Intimations of Immortality from recollections of early childhood."

sense of oneness with Nature which childhood's hours brought to him, but affirms that his love for her has been deepened by his meditations upon the transience and suffering of the human heart.

> Though nothing can bring back the hour
> Of splendour in the grass, of glory in the flower;
> We will grieve not, rather find
> Strength in what remains behind;
> In the primal sympathy
> *Which having been must ever be ;*
> In the soothing thoughts that spring
> Out of human suffering;
> In the faith that looks through death,
> In years that bring the philosophic mind.

Wordsworth came to feel certain deep intuitions of the self as the " fountain-light of all our day " and " the master-light of all our seeing ". But it must be admitted that not all our poets viewing human life have found this haven. There is the unutterable sadness of W. B. Yeats' lines :

> The years like great black oxen tread the world,
> And God the Herdsman goads them on behind,
> And I am broken by their passing feet.

Kipling, looking at the rise and fall of civilisations, compares their transience to that of flowers, and describes in one of his poems * the blindness with which every generation of men continues to imagine it is building something which will evade the destroying hand of time.

The most poignant poetry describes " with tenderest taciturnity " the emotions of the human heart when its friends depart. We have the heartache of all humanity in Tennyson's lines :

> Break, break, break,
> On thy cold grey stones, O Sea!
> And I would that my tongue could utter
> The thoughts that arise in me.
>
> O well for the fisherman's boy,
> That he shouts with his sister at play!
> O well for the sailor lad,
> That he sings in his boat on the bay!
>
> And the stately ships go on
> To their haven under the hill;
> But O for the touch of a vanished hand
> And the sound of a voice that is still!

* " Cities and Thrones and Powers."

> Break, break, break,
> At the foot of thy crags, O Sea!
> But the tender grace of a day that is dead
> Will never come back to me.

Every poet has expressed this in his own language—none perhaps
better or more often than Walter de la Mare.* His melancholy
notes, his delicacy and restraint, are perhaps unsurpassed in the
poetry of change. Robert Lynd has called him the poet of " love
shackled with vain-longing—vain-longing for lovely things that pass,
for love that passes ". He says to us:

> Look thy last on all things lovely
> Every hour. Let no night
> Seal thy sense in deathly slumber
> Till to delight
> Thou have paid thy utmost blessing;
> Since that all things thou would'st praise
> Beauty took from those who loved them
> In other days.

The reader will, I think, agree that the poets are but expressing the
universal sense of change. Two thousand five hundred years ago,
the Buddha saw this very clearly—that bodies, sensations, perceptions, thoughts (and he taught, these are not the self)—all are impermanent. He saw the root of all human suffering and all evil in
" desire " (i.e., in emotional attachment to the things which are
transient and must therefore pass away). The basis of his philosophy of life is rooted in this universal experience of transience and
flux, and his religious teaching was to show men how to escape from
it to that inward peace which is permanent. This has been the aim
of all great teachers—however variously it has been stated. Five
hundred years after the Buddha, Christ made the same offer to men,
" Come unto me, all ye that labour and are heavy laden, and I will
give you rest ". All men of insight have known it was possible—
having discovered it for themselves—the changeless amid the
changing, the Eternal in the midst of Time, the One amid the Many.
Wordsworth clearly sensed it:

> Even such a shell the universe itself
> Is to the ear of Faith; and there are times,
> I doubt not, when to you it doth impart
> Authentic tidings of invisible things;
> Of ebb and flow, and ever-enduring power;
> And central peace, subsisting at the heart
> Of endless agitation.

* Among many others some of the finest examples are: "The Quiet
Enemy", "Old Ben", "Away", "Farewell", "Goodbye", "What",
"Unregarding", "All that's past", "Haunted" (vide *Collected Poems*
(Faber & Faber)).

All such insights are mystical. They cannot be demonstrated, they can only be experienced. The cry of questing human minds is : are these things true? There is, in the end, no other proof than that which we discover for ourselves by treading the path of spiritual Attainment or Self-Realisation. All that philosophy can say is that these insights are not implausible, that they do not conflict with reason, and at most, that they might be expected to be true.

2. TIME: THE DECEIVER *

All change takes us back to that fundamental mystery—the nature of Time. The imperishable implies something coexisting with, but not dependent on Time (i.e., which is Eternal). Let us be quite clear that " Eternal " does not mean lasting for ever in time : it is the quality of those things which are ultimately real and are rooted in a level outside Time. Dean Inge has expressed it thus, " ' Eternal ' is the expression of permanence of value amid the changes of Time ". Both Plato and Plotinus express the view that Time is the shadow or symbol in the phenomenal world, of Eternity, which is the quality of the real world. Both feel that " Time resembles it as far as it can ". I find my own view of Time cannot go with confidence beyond that portrayed in Chapter 7, but my philosophical affinities are with Plotinus and the Neo-Platonists, of which in our own day W. R. Inge has been the leading exponent.†

Lotze has reminded us that some part of the mind is necessarily outside the flow of temporal succession or it would be impossible to survey events within the specious present. Both Kant and T. H. Green recognised also that the sense of succession in time could only arise because a part of the self was outside this succession. Inge says, " It is because the Soul is in its deeper self outside the time-series that it regards the fleeting shows of phenomenal life as either vain or tragic, and identifies itself willingly with those parts of experience which can defy ' the wreckful siege of battering days '." Plotinus assures us that " nothing which truly is can ever perish ". What we really want to know is, how much of ourselves is in this

---

* I owe this appellation to my friend Dr. Weatherhead. Time has been called by poets " the refreshing river ", " the ever-rolling stream ", and by philosophers " the form of the will ". We have heard of the " bird of Time " and Time's " winged chariot ". But to the mystic it is part of Maya and a deceiver. St. John of Patmos in his vision saw a state in which " There shall be Time no longer " (Revelation x, 6).

† The philosophically-inclined reader might care to read *God and the Astronomers*, or the two volumes of *The Philosophy of Plotinus*, by W. R. Inge.

category ? For practical purposes I think we must reduce the question to that which survives the change we call death.

Does memory survive this change ? This question has been answered implicitly in the affirmative in Chapter 13, and if the reader will study again the data there presented, he will agree that the establishing of the survival of personality was dependent upon the survival of memory—for which the evidence was very strong indeed. Apart from this, there is, I think, much good evidence that while the *recall and expression* of memories is (while we are incarnate beings) through our brain mechanism, memory proper is itself the " stuff " of the mental world to which our minds respond. Consider, for example, the fact that at the point of death, when the linkage of mind and brain is presumably loosening, the self sometimes surveys with a wealth of detail and vividness, memories which had fallen into the " unconscious ". Here for example is part of a letter * written by a person who was nearly drowned at the age of fourteen :

" Only for a few seconds was I conscious of sinking. Then, dropping ever so rapidly through a pale green world through which hazily and with terrific speed all the events of my life seemed to whirl around me. Crowds of people hurried about me. All I had ever known was flung into this great whirl. The green was gradually fading and a golden light came suddenly and clearly illuminated each particle of the memory.

" Here the memory of events became *so clear that they were re-experienced.*

" Yet all the time, even in episodes unconnected with them, there were crowds of people. The final images before regaining consciousness *were amazingly complete with such a wealth of detail*, even to sunlight on a blade of grass, the willows in bloom, the hum of bees among the catkins, and the acrid dampish odour of the black earth covered with decaying willow twigs. These were details of my life when I was five years old.

" I remember as particularly vivid the impressions of a nurse with whom I had lived for two years at this time."

This vividness and detail is far from what would be expected if memories were stored in brain-tissue. Lapse of time did not seem to impair the intrinsic vividness of the memories at all, and it is difficult to see how this can be the case if changing brain-tissue is their vehicle. Injury to the brain may, as we know, result in so-called " loss of memory "—by which we mean inability to *recall* these memories at will. The brain-mechanism of recall is then obviously damaged, but subsequent restoration of the memories shows

---

* A. W. Osborn : *The Superphysical*, p. 54 (Ivor Nicholson & Watson).

the latter to be themselves unimpaired. I do not think this evidence is logically conclusive against the materialist view of memory, but it seems to me to be heavily weighted against it. The direct evidence of the memory of surviving personalities (Chapter 13) is, I think, conclusive and unchallengeable. With the retention of memory, we can affirm that the mind, and hence *a fortiori* all that really makes us what we are, cannot be touched by the change we call death.

The fact is that we are too much slaves of sense-perception. We are hypnotised by space and by time—the forms under which we try to understand the outer world. We live in a dream from which the only way to wake up is to take the ancient path of self-realisation. All those who have found their feet upon it and travelled a little way have seen the material world differently. They have seen that though outward forms are constantly changing, this is but a sign of the rich ever-active Eternal Life within, and that we ourselves are a part of that Life and can lose nothing that we love or cherish.

> " The illusion from which we are seeking to extricate ourselves is not that constituted by the realm of space and time, but that which comes from failing to know that realm from the standpoint of a higher vision. We are at length restored to consciousness by awakening in a real universe, the universe created by the One Mind as opposed to that perversion of it which has been created by our egocentric selves. We then see the visible world as the expression of the immanental life of God, the Divine in manifestation. In relating ourselves to it we live objectively within the sphere of the Presence, just as we live in that Presence subjectively in the depths of our mystical being. And in the properly integrated personality the two processes have become one." *

Dean Inge has expressed the same truth in the words, " The value of natural objects is not that they remind us of something that they are not, but that they help us to understand something that they in part are."

It is not that space and time and sense-perception are illusions, but rather that, rightly viewed, they are clues—pointers to so much more. But from time to time, under the stars at night or on a mountain top, at sight of some great natural beauty or perhaps of a lovely human face, we momentarily awake, and the feeling that we are in the presence of a great mystery sweeps over us, bringing with it a mood of deepest worship. It is then we are beginning to sense reality—the one reality to which all mystical experience and true religion bear witness, in knowledge of which standeth our Eternal Life, and to serve which is perfect freedom.

* Lawrence Hyde : *The Nameless Faith*, p. 59 (Rider & Co., 1950).

3. THE WORLD OF VALUES

All the great minds in philosophy recognise the existence of Values. Here are two expressions of view on which we may ponder:

" Of the things in space and time we say, this thing is outside that, they cannot coincide and amalgamate; this thing comes after that, the former must disappear before the latter arrives. But our minds tell us that there is a large class of objects of which these statements are not true, and the meanings of which are incommunicable in these terms. These things do not interfere with each other. They are alive and active, but they are neither born, nor do they die. They are constant without inertia, they are active but they do not move. Our knowledge of this order is as direct and certain as our knowledge of the spatio-temporal order, and we have an idiom to express that knowledge." *

Or again :

" Our life has value only because and in so far as it realises in fact that which transcends time and existence. Goodness, beauty and truth are all there is which in the end is real. This reality, appearing amid chance and change, is beyond these and is eternal. . . . For love and beauty and delight, it is no matter where they have shown themselves, there is no death nor change. These things do not die, since the Paradise in which they bloom is immortal. That Paradise is no special region, nor any particular spot in time or place. It is here, it is everywhere where any finite being is lifted to that higher life which alone is waking reality." †

The supreme values which we know are Goodness, Truth and Beauty. By Goodness is not meant here a state of moral achievement, nor a quality of integrity which is in constant conflict with evil. Such a use of the word " goodness "—and it is the common one—belongs to the ordinary phenomenal world of the conflict of the opposites. It is rather Love in its essence and fullness which is meant by the supreme value " Goodness ", and we shall use this term. These three values which are spaceless and timeless authenticate themselves. They are not, so far as we can see, symbols or shadows of a reality lying behind themselves on a still higher level of significance. They mediate to us directly, not indirectly, the nature of Reality. They constitute together the white light which shines outwards through all the veils of Maya from the imprisoned splendour within. These beams pierce to the outermost limits of the world of nature, and when we pass them through the prism of our mind's analysis, we find in the spectrum only Love, Truth and Beauty.

Of these supreme values we can say with complete confidence,

* W. M. Urban : *The Intelligible World*, p. 267 (Macmillan & Co., 1929).
† F. H. Bradley : *Essays on Truth and Reality.*

they are imperishable. They are the very stuff of reality, as the mystics find when they penetrate farthest into the centre of being which is their own spiritual essence. But on all lower levels, on all the planes of being, mental, astral and physical, the Values find a measure of form and embodiment, and whenever we discern this we are happy. We are happy for a moment because our exile is forgotten and our homesickness is assuaged by these echoes of the life of our own deeper being. A little later the forms which embody the Values we have loved pass away. They change and perish with the passage of time : it is then we need to reassure ourselves that nothing which we truly value is ever lost. The embodiment may change and pass, but the essence of all we have cherished is imperishable.

Of natural beauty, its transience and fadingness lend an under-current of melancholy to our most exalted moments. The daffodils by Ullswater which gave Wordsworth his moments of ecstasy—moments of which the memory returned to refresh his commonplace days—themselves perished within a month. The " incomparable pomp of eve ", the sunset sky which has held us spellbound in adoration, fades into paler colour and is lost in the oncoming night. Never again will that sunset speak to the eyes of men : it has vanished for ever. W. H. Davies has reminded us that " a rainbow and a cuckoo's song may never come together again ", and Mr. de la Mare that

> beauty seen of mortal eyes
> Immortal habitation has
> Though beauty's form may pale and pass.

All of which is true : but it is not merely true in the sense that we are a part of all we have met, that all experience has made us what we are, and that all our memories are an imperishable possession. There is a truth profounder than this : that in the depths of our being we never do lose anything we have ever valued.

The poet who wrote " Daisy " also wrote :

> All which thy child's mistake
> Fancies as lost, I have stored for thee at home :
> Rise, clasp my hand and come.

Of all the Victorian poets, Browning saw this most clearly. He expresses it fiercely in " Rabbi Ben Ezra ".

> Fool ! All that is, at all,
> Lasts ever, past recall ;
> Earth changes, but thy Soul and God stand sure :
> What entered into thee,
> *That* was, is, and shall be :
> Time's wheel runs back or stops ; Potter and clay endure.

He expresses it with complete confidence in " Abt Vogler ".

> Therefore to whom turn I but to Thee, the ineffable Name ?
>   Builder and maker, Thou, of houses not made with hands !
> What, have fear of change from Thee who art ever the same ?
>   Doubt that Thy power can fill the heart that Thy power expands ?
> There shall never be one lost good !   What was, shall live as before ;
>   The evil is null, is nought, is silence implying sound ;
> What was good, shall be good, with, for evil, so much good more ;
>   On the earth the broken arcs ; in the heaven, a perfect round.
>
> All we have willed or hoped or dreamed of good, shall exist ;
>   Not its semblance, but itself ; no beauty, nor good, nor power
> Whose voice has gone forth, but each survives for the melodist
>   When eternity affirms the conception of an hour.

If the transience of the forms which Beauty inhabits is a source of melancholy to our earth-bound eyes, this is surely not less true of the forms we love.   A person A affirms that he loves B.   Which B does he love ? B was once a baby, later a child, then a youth or maiden.   He (or she) passed on to adult life, through the years of middle age and on to old age with its infirmity.   The forms of B were always changing, so that someone who knew the child might, after many years, fail to recognise the man or woman.   When we ponder on this, it is clear that the forms which change are not really in themselves the object of love at all.   These are but transient expressions of an underlying self which is the real object of love. We love the forms because they are symbols, expressions of something in the deeper self that we hold in common.   Sex is such a symbol on the physical level of the union on a deeper level of two selves.   Often degraded in a world which mistakes appearance for reality, and symbols for all that there is, sex nevertheless remains itself unsullied, a reminder of the primal ecstasy of Life, a faint echo on the physical plane of one of the supreme values of which we may hope to know more as we pass inward.   F. W. H. Myers speaks of this :

> And Love ? thine heart imagined, it may be,
> Himself the Immortal here had lodged with thee ?
> Thou hadst clomb the heaven and caught him in the air,
> And clasped him close and felt that he was fair ?—
> He hath but shown thee, when thou call'dst him sweet,
> His eyes' first glance, and shimmer of flying feet,—
> He hath but spoken on his ascending way,
> One least word of the words he hath yet to say,—
> Who in the true world his true home has made
> With fair things first-begotten and undecayed,—
> Whereof thou too art, whither thou too shalt go,
> Live with Love's self, and what Love knows shalt know.

TO EACH HIS WAY

" All the Buddhas point the Way, but each one must tread every step of it himself."

BUDDHIST SAYING.

" By whatsoever path you come to Me I shall welcome you, for the paths men take from every side are Mine."

LORD KRISHNA (in the *Gita*).

Thou art the Way.
Hadst Thou been nothing but the goal,
I cannot say
If Thou hadst ever met my soul.

I cannot see—
I, child of process—if there lies
An end for me,
Full of repose, full of replies.

I'll not reproach
The road that winds, my feet that err.
Access, Approach
Art Thou, Time, Way and Wayfarer.

ALICE MEYNELL.

MANY of my readers will have read the short story of H. G. Wells which he called " The Door in the Wall ". A few years before Mr. Wells' death a friend of mine said to him, that of all his books and writings, which had given him great pleasure, he thought he liked best " The Door in the Wall ". Mr. Wells appeared to be rather moved, and said, " I think that is my own favourite too."

It is the story of a man who attained high position and success, who once as a child found his way through a green door in a sunlit wall into a garden. It was not an ordinary garden; it was another world, alluring, beautiful and completely satisfying to heart and mind. He had to leave it: he was compelled to—and found himself again, a little boy weeping on the pavement of an ordinary street. Though he searched long and diligently, he could not find the door again. On six occasions in his life, at wholly unexpected moments, the door was once more offered to him. On each occasion he chose to pass by, and it is interesting to observe these occasions. On the first of them he was entering on the busy preoccupations of school life. Life was becoming systematised. External disciplines were limiting his freedom and the word " duty " was beginning to have meaning. It was easy to run past the green door, with every reason to believe that he could find it again when he wanted to. The second opportunity was offered on his way to a scholarship examination that would lead to an Oxford career. The attractiveness of academic knowledge, the broadening field of interest in the thoughts of men in the sciences and the arts—these allured him, and he passed on. On the third occasion he passed by because of pride arising from his concern for what others would think. He speaks of " an appointment in which my honour was involved ". On the next two occasions of opportunity the imperative claims of duty and life held him. On the first he was called to the House of Commons for an important division ; on the second he was hurrying to say good-bye to his father, who was dying. All good things in themselves, be it noted. On the sixth occasion the attraction of worldly honour and distinction held him : to have gone through the little green door then would have cost him his place in the reconstructed Cabinet. We observe that in all these circumstances there was nothing discreditable in his choice. Reason could offer sound support to his decisions, which were made according to the canons of good common sense. Yet how easily we conceal the truth from ourselves ! We say " We have no time ", and forget that we have all the time there is. At every stage of life, from youth to age, we can find the most cogent excuses for ourselves, and the good is constantly the enemy of the better. We are too often like children who want both the penny and the toffee-stick. We want the security of the familiar, and we also want Truth. We want worldly success, and we also want spiritual understanding. We want power, and we also want peace. We have to learn that throughout life we must choose again and again between one good and another good, and that we cannot have both.

The story of " The Door in the Wall " reminds us of the Supreme Good that calls to us from time to time, of a world of Reality close to our familiar one, but from which we are shut out save when, on certain occasions, the door is offered to us. We can hurry past it in the eagerness of youth. We can forget about it in our University days, when all the thrill of discovering new worlds of knowledge fills us. We can be content without it when love and marriage and children are all-absorbing and when we are competing with others for position and power. It returns at intervals to haunt us in the forties, when we have discovered our limitations and know how few of the dreams of youth will ever be fulfilled. We are always free to pass by the little green door: it is offered to us when we least expect it, and we are never compelled to enter in. Yet no good thing ever comes to us, save as we sacrifice what, to us, is a lesser good. And the Supreme Good demands from us all that we have. There is in man the cry of the heart for the Eternal, the hunger of the soul for God, the longing of the Ego for the Self, and it comes to haunt us just when we think we are safest.

I have written this chapter to show the ways which men have taken in their spiritual questing. This questing for Truth is much like the ascent of a mountain peak up which run a number of paths from different sides. Some climbers take one path and some another, but if they keep ascending they will come closer to their fellows who are on different routes, and they may hope to meet them on the summit, where all paths converge.

1. WHAT IS MEANT BY REALISATION?

The interpretation we have made of mystical experience (Chapter 15) has shown us our goal, and we are now concerned with the way to it. This may be, and has been, expressed in different ways. We have spoken of the Lamp of Reality: the true Self which is Divine, swathed in veils of Maya and obscured from our Ego or empirical self, which is in the dimness of the World of Appearance. From this standpoint the practical problem is the dissolving of the veils of Maya—the opening of a way " whence the imprisoned splendour may escape ". Expressed otherwise, it is the realisation, not in theory but in experience, that the Ego with which we are normally self-identified is not the true Self. Again, it may be described as the achievement of a new state or quality of consciousness, such as in the highest mystical experience has been glimpsed but could not be sustained for long. These are all different ways of trying to express the same thing, and all are rather imperfect ways, as many thinkers have pointed out.* Whenever we say " How can *I* attain this state or achieve this experience ? " we are really denoting the Ego by the personal pronoun " I ". We know, of course, from the nature of mystical experience, that the Ego is submerged, lost, surrendered in such experience; or, to put it in another way, the consciousness of our true Self is then the only reality, and this alone *is*. Our true Self (the Atman of the Hindus) is one with all Selves

---

* Vide Alan W. Watts: *The Supreme Identity* (Chapter V) (Faber & Faber, 1950). I am indebted to this writer for his understanding and clear exposition.

and all are one in the Divine Self.   In other words, this Self is eternal and infinite : it does not need to " attain " anything, it fully realises everything always.

This is a paradoxical situation : the Ego cannot expect to realise the Supreme, and the true Self realises it always by its very nature. We must try to reframe our question.   Probably it should run more like this, " What can the Ego do to facilitate its own surrender and disappearance, thus leaving the light of the true Self undimmed and in full possession ? "   Even this is not an unexceptionable form of the question, but it probably gives the right conception.   All the verbal difficulties arise because, as Watts has pointed out, there are really two different languages involved : the language of religion and the language of metaphysics.   The language of religion is the language we commonly use when we speak of knowing God (God is regarded as a possible *object* of knowledge), or of attaining spiritual enlightenment (the goal is placed in the future).   In the language of metaphysics, which is concerned with ultimate truth, not relative truth, God cannot be an object of knowledge.   He is one with the subject which knows.   For this subject, which is eternal and real, time has no meaning : full realisation is always present.   The language of religion, which is essentially practical, bringing ultimate truths as far as possible into relationship with our finite space-time conditions, is necessarily only an analogy or a symbolic expression of the higher truth.

We have asked the question, " What can the Ego do to facilitate its own surrender and disappearance, thus leaving the light of the true Self undimmed and in full possession ? "   Can we suggest an answer by considering a familiar analogy—that of an actor, who is both a private individual with a full life of his own, yet on the stage plays a part in which for a time he is absorbed.   Let us speak of Henry Irving playing " Hamlet " (Irving is the Self and Hamlet the Ego).   Hamlet does not appear on the stage apart from Irving, to whom he owes his temporary presentation, but Irving's existence does not depend on Hamlet.   Irving lives a " real " life, of which Hamlet knows nothing.   But to present Hamlet on the stage, Irving temporarily forgets his private life, and lives in the part he has created.   Irving may choose to stop playing Hamlet—he may, indeed, choose to play Lear—but the choice is Irving's, not Hamlet's.   If we frame the question " What can Hamlet do to facilitate his own surrender and disappearance, thus leaving Irving unlimited and in full possession of the stage ? " we see that Hamlet can do nothing ; the choice is Irving's, for he alone is " real ".   If we go on to ask why Irving plays Hamlet or any other part at all, we ask analogically a question which takes us into the heart of the ultimate mysteries. In spite of all we have said of the Self—of its infinite and eternal nature—there must be some gain to it by its temporary absorption in an actor's part : that of the Ego on the stage of space-time. What this gain may be we shall venture to consider in a later chapter. We must not assume that nothing is gained in enrichment of the Self : to do so is surely to reduce the whole temporal process to meaninglessness. I sometimes think that from our finite mental viewpoint what we characterise as infinite and eternal may not, in the strict metaphysical sense, be so at all. These terms may stand for a quality of consciousness so far beyond anything we know that the words " infinite " and " eternal " seem the only ones adequate. But how do we know that this is not the starting point for a new and still profounder type of consciousness of which we can form no conception ? If this be doubted, it does but suggest that we have not grasped, and cannot hope to grasp, what these words really mean.

The conclusion that the Ego can do nothing seems dismal, until we appreciate that the truth in this statement is of the same order as that the Ego does not really exist. The fact is, *for practical purposes*, best expressed by saying that a part or aspect of the Self is immersed in, and lives through the Ego's life. Moreover, all the Ego's strivings and seeking and aspiring are really expressions of the immersed Self's promptings.

This chapter is intended to be practical and relevant to our human situation. We shall therefore use the analogical language of religion, and not that of metaphysics, in what follows. The explanation we have made should help the reader to understand that this formulation is only an aspect of truth. It should also show the futility of trying to persuade others to go along a road for which either by temperament or spiritual growth they are not fitted. If the Self prompts each Ego, it is, in its wisdom, trying to move it along that path which *in the end* will bring it surely to the goal. To suppose that the way which is best for one is best for another, is the tragedy of all those narrow sectarian outlooks which have no metaphysic and no mystical insight, and which suppose that the little mole-hills on which they stand so triumphantly are the mountain peaks of Truth.

There are certain traditional ways which men have taken, and we shall describe these as though they were clear-cut and different from each other. In practice, however, there can be few individuals who do not combine in varying proportions the techniques and outlooks of several of these varying paths.

2. THE WAY OF ACTION (KARMA YOGA)

The life of Action is traditionally regarded as contrasting with the life of Contemplation, and in very broad outline we may say that the former accords more closely with the Western temperament and the latter with the Eastern temperament. There are some who would say that Christianity is essentially a practical religion, peculiarly adapted to the Western extraverted life. They would point out that love and service are its key-words, love to God expressed through love to man, as its two greatest parables, those of the Prodigal Son and the Good Samaritan, bear witness. There are those who would say that Hinduism by and large is introverted, that it is so concerned with the Beyond which is Within, that it neglects the here-and-now, especially in its social implications. Such judgments leave so much unsaid that they are probably misleading and unwise. We must not forget that in Christianity we find considerable detachment from the world enjoined upon its followers in such words as these, " Seek ye first the Kingdom of God and His righteousness ", and " Lay not up for yourselves treasures upon earth where moth and rust doth corrupt . . ." Likewise we should not forget that the great Hindu classic, the *Bhagavad Gita*, is outstanding in its advocacy of Action :   " All action originates in the Supreme Spirit which is Imperishable, and in sacrificial action the all-pervading Spirit is constantly present." " Therefore do thy duty perfectly, without care for the results ; for he who does his duty disinterestedly attains the Supreme." It is of no value to discuss whether one Way is better than another : each man who treads a Way suited to his temperament with diligence and complete sincerity is fulfilling the purpose of his incarnation.

If sometimes the devotee of the Way of Action is tempted to think the Way of Contemplation is more direct and heads straighter for the spiritual goal, he may take comfort in three things.

1. It is the Way the higher Self is leading him, and to doubt it is to doubt the highest Wisdom. If, caught in the busy round of duty and action, one longs to be a hermit or vice versa, it should be remembered that on a profound level the Self has chosen (within certain limitations imposed by the laws of Karma) the circumstances and external setting which, rightly reacted to, offer the individual his best opportunity of spiritual attainment.

2. It is the mark of the highest spiritual achievement completely to redeem the lowest. It may perhaps be an easier step to leap from the plane of the quiescent Mind through contemplation into realisation of God, but it is a still greater achievement

M

to achieve full enlightenment on the plane of matter and action. Indeed, there can never be full enlightenment until it is found and retained on every level of consciousness. The greatest Mystics have always shown the way here: they have seen the struggling millions of Earth sunk in ignorance and suffering, as brothers and sisters of their own who have lost or never found the Way. The mystic has known that they cannot rise to where he is unless he comes down to help them on their level, and he has come. As Gerald Heard* has said, "They do work supremely for others because there is no private salvation; the whole of life is one immense company of unlimited liability."

3. There is no level on which the mystic experience is not possible. To those with eyes to see, God is all and in all. Evelyn Underhill† has expressed it thus:

"There are in His universe no fences between the 'natural' and 'supernatural' worlds; everything is a part of the creative Play of God, and therefore—even in its humblest details—capable of revealing the Player's mind.

"The willing acceptance of the here-and-now as a means of representing supernal realities is a trait common to the greatest mystics. For them . . . all aspects of the Universe possess equal authority as sacramental declarations of the Presence of God."

Thus Jesus saw His Heavenly Father "making His sun to rise on the evil and the good, and sending His rain on the just and the unjust", and said, "My Father worketh hitherto, and I work." Most of His parables were concerned with action, and in one of them He specifically rebukes those who leave their talents unused. The charter of good works never received more august support than on an occasion when two disciples of John the Baptist, who had come to determine His credentials, were told to return with the words, "Go and tell John the things ye do hear and see—the blind receive their sight and the lame walk, the lepers are cleansed and the deaf hear, the dead are raised up, and the poor have good tidings preached to them."

Krishna, likewise addressing Arjuna, says: "There is nothing in this universe, O Arjuna! that I am compelled to do; nor anything for Me to attain; yet I am persistently active. For were I not to act without ceasing, O Prince! people would be glad to do likewise. And if I were to refrain from action, the human race would be ruined; I should lead the world to chaos, and destruction would follow."

---

* Gerald Heard: *Preface to Prayer* (Cassell).
† Introduction to *Poems of Kabir*: translated by Tagore (Macmillan).

Let us examine, then, the Way of Action, observing first that up to a certain point we are compelled to act—no complete escape is possible. Actions on the physical plane bring their trains of consequences, and other action is then demanded from us. We do not, and cannot, altogether live in isolation : when we enter the human family we enter a realm of relationships. " Duty " has compelling meaning for us. We are bound in the iron circle of Necessity as well as by the golden circle of Love, and we cannot, while being true to ourselves, contract out of the obligations. The iron circle of Necessity is called in Eastern philosophy the law of Karma, but every religious and philosophical system recognises it in one form or another. War, illness, accident, bereavement—a hundred things may come upon us, *apparently* unrelated to our own past actions, which we could not by any normal foresight have avoided, and which call upon us to act or react. Let us realise this first of all : that it is only within certain limits, much more circumscribed, perhaps, in the typically Western life than in the Eastern, that we are free to act or withdraw from action. Although this material world is undoubtedly a world of Appearance only, and we are temporarily its prisoners, we cannot be indifferent to why it " appears ", and why for the time we are its " prisoners ". Something of great value must be potentially attainable through it, and our business is to find out what this is.

Let us first be clear what it is not. The value of the experience is clearly not primarily—and may not even be at all—in what is achieved on the physical level. Its value is primarily on the personality of the doer, and perhaps on other personalities. What happens to all the good works or achievements of men ? Ultimately they are superseded : time sweeps them away to become a part of the world-memory. But the choice that determined that a good thing should be done, and the effort of will, the courage and the fortitude which went into the doing of it—these are imperishable things ; for they have been built into the character of the doer. It was doubtless this truth which led Heard * to write : " Being therefore is all, and doing merely the symptom and sign of being, as body is the appearance of spirit."

The tragedy of the Western world is that Action, which might have been a spiritual Way, has become a goal. Valuable as a means, so long as we clearly understand it to be such, it has become an end in itself. Like a habit-forming drug, it has given rise to the incessant craving for more action. Once a material goal has been reached and a particular programme completed, other goals are specified and

* Gerald Heard : *The Third Morality*, p. 265 (Cassell & Co., 1937).

other programmes formulated. Some fancied goal above the material, such as leisure to create, to enjoy Nature, to think and meditate, at first the stimulus of endeavour, fades in the course of attainment, and more endeavour replaces it. The means have unknowingly become the end.

Pondering on this, A. C. Benson * wrote :

" Satisfied desire is the least contented of moods. . . . The work of each of us matters very little to the world, but it matters very much to ourselves that we should have some work to do. . . . This strange sense of escape which drives us into activity and energy seems given us not that we may realise our aims, which turn out hollow and vapid enough when they are realised, but that we may drink deep of experience for the sake of its beneficent effect upon us."

This, I think, is a sound conclusion, but it will not be very welcome to many good people who are earnestly struggling for social reform, believing that some day the ideal society will be achieved through the efforts of men of goodwill. Their goal they would describe as Utopia, or perhaps as the Kingdom of God *on earth*. In looking for a goal in history, on the material level, there is no solution of the riddle. Ends are to be looked for in the underlying spiritual order to which the material one is but a means. Ends are in the realm of consciousness, not of institutions.

A critical analysis of good works is called for. When the hungry are fed, when sick are cared for, when slums are abolished, when ideal government is achieved—what have you done? You have increased the comfort and material well-being of people and set them free from anxiety in relation to the struggle for the necessaries of life. You believe you have done what you can to provide the setting in which their happiness is possible. You have provided, perhaps, a more favourable opportunity for happiness to follow; but happiness is a state of mind which you cannot command in another. You may have alleviated your neighbour's suffering, you may have increased his opportunity of enjoyment, and these are all good things to do, so far as *you* are concerned. The only certain goodness is in the *doing*, however. These things you have done may lead the person for whom they are done to a little gratitude or greater kindliness, a step on the road of spiritual understanding; but it is equally possible they may not.

The fact is, of course, that with all the difficulties of life removed, and with nothing left to improve except the character of men, it is difficult to see how character itself would be improved. The

* A. C. Benson : *Escape, and other Essays*, pp. 13–16 (Smith Elder & Co., 1915).

principal value of all good works is in the opportunity they afford of expressing a relationship. This expression on the outer plane of becoming corresponds to the greater unity of selves on the inner planes of being.

In his stimulating Gifford Lectures,* Macneile Dixon reminded us that

> " This clash of opposites may have brought it about that we have a Universe at all, and that we ourselves its offspring are in being, that from this dark soil of conflict creation sprang. . . . But for these oppositions in nature and human life ' the world-wide warfare of the eternal Two ', nothing had taken place, all were sunk in a motiveless motionless stagnation."

In their absence, no longer would the world be a school for character, or, in Keats' phrase, " a vale of soul-making ". In A. C. Benson's words : † " It is important that we should strive with all our might to eliminate the baser elements of life, yet we must be brave and wise enough to confess how much our best happiness is born of the fact that we have these elements to contend with." The Utopian makes his mistake in placing his goal within the historical process. In so doing he is mistaking the function of a preparatory school for the infinite vistas of more real life on higher levels of being. The historical process simply provides a succession of spiritual opportunities.

Let us return to our question : what is this something of great value which is potentially obtainable through the Life of Action in the world of Appearance ? It is knowledge, pre-eminently self-knowledge, perhaps best described as Wisdom. The Way of Action does not ascend to the summit ; it merges into the Way of Knowledge at a certain level. Action is the out-working on the physical plane of our own deeper selves. In that sense and to that degree it is symbolic. Over and above the reactions forced upon us by karmic law, our choice of action is generally the reflection of our desires. We may act through greed or anger or fear, through the desire for comfort, power, fame or security ; or we may act through kindness, love, sympathy and understanding. The man who acts through love and understanding is not entangled in the world of action : it is a conscious expression of his nature. The great majority act because they desire something for themselves : it is the fruits of action which are alluring. It is for this reason that all the great religions teach us that we should act with discrimination (i.e., understanding) and with detachment from the fruits of action.

* W. Macneile Dixon : *The Human Situation* (1938), pp. 200–1.
† *Escape, and other Essays*, p. 19.

We should, indeed, do all the good we may, but desiring no recognition by others, and unconcerned with the final results. Thus the *Gita* says : *

> " In this world people are fettered by action, unless it is performed as a sacrifice. Therefore, O Arjuna ! let thy acts be done without attachment, as sacrifice only. . . .
> " He who can see inaction in action, and action in inaction, is the wisest of men. He is a saint, even though he still acts.
> " The wise call him a sage ; for whatever he undertakes is free from the motives of desire, and his deeds are purified by the fire of Wisdom.
> " Having surrendered all claim to the results of his actions, always contented and independent, in reality he does nothing even though he is apparently acting."

These truths are reiterated in many forms throughout the *Gita*. " Your interest shall only be directed to the deed—never to the fruits thereof." The same teaching runs throughout the words of Jesus. It is implicit in the parable of the Good Samaritan. In a parable of judgment based upon the doing of unselfish works we are told " Inasmuch as ye did it unto one of the least of these My brethren ye did it unto Me "—a statement of the most profound metaphysical implications, as we have seen. The " giving of a cup of cold water, in *My Name* " we are told is not without reward. As Marco Pallis † has said in an excellent booklet, " for the act to be effective it must be performed not for its own sake, but in the name of the All-giver and in imitation on the relative plane of the archetype of All-giving on the universal plane ".

Viewed from the standpoint of appearance only, from the " relative plane ", the work of men seems so largely a round of futility. " What are you growing oats for ? " said a visitor to the farmer. " To feed the horses, sir," he replied. " And why do you keep horses ? " he said. " To plough the fields," was the answer. " And why do you plough the fields ? " he asked. " To sow oats," said the farmer. It is a parable which represents life, where existence on the material plane is seen as an end in itself. So to regard it is to miss the great ends which life here can serve. Does it really matter from the point of view of Action as a spiritual Way whether a man ploughs a field or governs a kingdom, whether he peels potatoes or writes a book ? Browning said, " All service ranks the same with God," and Tennyson wrote in two lines of great insight,

* *Bhagavad Gita* : Chapters II, III and IV contain some of the world's highest wisdom.
† Marco Pallis : *The Active Life* (J. M. Watkins).

> For merit lives from man to man
> And not from man, O Lord, to Thee.

Merit, whether it be esteem, respect, honour or distinction, is a human appraisal. No man standing in the Hall of final Judgment will venture to say, " I was honoured of men, I received praise and distinction, I governed a kingdom, I became a cabinet minister, I wrote an important book, I was a great artist." He will be happy if he can say, " I did my best where I was : I finished the work you gave me to do."

3. THE WAY OF LOVE (BHAKTI-YOGA)

The Way of Action is, as we have seen, a discipline on the material plane. It involves renunciation of the fruits of action, an impartial attitude to success and failure as these are outwardly assessed. The Way of Love or Bhakti-yoga is a discipline on the emotional level. It is not a way of renunciation, but of expansion, and sages have regarded it as the most natural, and therefore the least difficult of the Ways. It is the way of loving devotion to God, and therefore is, or should be, the foundation of all religious life. This Way says, " Love ! love the Highest with complete devotion, and all that is ignoble will fall away." Such love ultimately finds God everywhere and in everything : in Nature and in human nature, in joy and in sorrow, in beauty and in ugliness—there is nothing that to the Bhakta does not speak of, and reveal, God, the great Lover.

> " He who experiences the unity of Life, sees his own Self in all beings, and all beings in his own Self, and looks on everything with an impartial eye.
> " He who sees Me in everything and everything in Me, him shall I never forsake, nor shall he lose Me." *

To the Bhakta (if a woman) the husband is not loved for the husband's sake, but it is the divine Self within him which is loved. So the wife is loved by the husband for the divine Self within her. Such is true of every relation of attraction on every level, though only the Bhakta is conscious of it. In the Christian tradition, St. Francis and St. Theresa are notable followers of the Way of Love. Sri Ramakrishna is an outstanding example of this in the Indian tradition.

Tagore has described how in one of his mystical experiences this universal sense of Joy and Love irradiated him. " Everyone, even those who bored me, seemed to lose their outer barrier of personality ;

---

* *Bhagavad Gita*, VI, 29, 30, or see 1st Ep. John, iv, for the same teaching.

and I was full of gladness, full of love, for every person, and every tiniest thing." It was said of Lao-Tse, the Chinese sage, that he " universalised his heart ", and this is what the Way of Love involves. Tagore * once wrote to his friend C. F. Andrews these pregnant words :

> " Real love is always a wonder. We can never take it for granted. Your love for me I accept with joy and thankfulness, and wonder to which account to put it. Perhaps every man has some worth unknown to himself, inspiring love through the cover of his self. It gives one a hope that truth is more than appearance, and that we deserve more than we can claim with apparent reason. Love is for the unlimited in us, not for the one who is loudly evident. Some say that we idealise him we love ; but the fact is that we realise through love the ideal in him—and the ideal is the real if we know it. We have the eternal contradiction in us that our worth unfolds itself through our unworthiness, and love can go beyond the process overtaking the ultimate truth. We could never be certain that we are more in truth than we are in fact, if we were not loved."

Love is, of course, primarily a matter of relationship. It begins in the region of duality and ends in the region of unity, and even on the human plane transforms the outlook on the world. To the ever-deepening love for God of those who tread this Way everything is transformed radically. In the end, Lover, Love and the Beloved are one. If " God is Love " is the highest truth, then the devotees of this path are clearly treading the direct way to the Supreme Unity.

4. THE WAY OF KNOWLEDGE

There are some whose temperament is not primarily devotional, and who are fundamentally more interested in things of the mind than in outer activities and relationships. The typical scientist and philosopher are in this group. It is not, however, recruited only from the more highly educated section of the community. There are many folk in all walks of life whose approach to problems is critical, analytic and scientific in temper. They long to *know*; the data of " revelation " are always suspect, and never easily accepted by them. They feel that their intellectual integrity is of primary importance, and at every stage of building a philosophy of life reason must offer its confirmation.

In Parts I and II of this book we have presented data and made an analysis which may commend itself to this temperament. The data of mystical experience, which we reviewed later, may have

---

* *Letters to a Friend*, ed. C. F. Andrews, pp. 47–8 (George Allen & Unwin).

convinced some readers that though all knowledge comes *through* the Mind, there are vast regions of awareness which the Mind cannot itself grasp, but with which a deeper part of ourself is in immediate contact. The most that the trained mind can do, when applied to the data of the outer world, is to order, co-ordinate and formulate theories. In other words, it provides us with an organised body of information and with theories and laws relevant thereto. All that we *believe* in this field, but say we " know ", is, of course, a matter of a high degree of probability. The further we use the mind as an instrument of analysis, the more we realise how little it can give us of certainty, how ineffective it is to provide us with indubitable answers to the questions which we most want answering. It is clear, then, that by the Way of Knowledge as a path to God is not meant any pursuit of academic " knowledge " such as we have gained through the normal use of the Mind in studying the outer world.

One of the main characteristics of mystical experience is the sudden breaking through into awareness of knowledge, convincing and certain and authoritative. It is knowledge of those things which we most desire to know ; it is knowledge of the real nature of the world, and it is always felt to be wholly good and completely satisfying. If we could achieve, or cultivate by any means, a state of consciousness in which such knowledge was an ever-present reality and possession, instead of being the fruit of rare and unheralded moments, we should indeed be on the path to Enlightenment. There have been many systems devised by which men have affirmed that it is ultimately possible to do this. All of them are forms of mental discipline, usually founded on a preliminary moral discipline or purification of character. The insights of mystical experience cannot be commanded, but it would seem that where the mind can be brought into a state of poised stillness, the deeper self is able, and often willing, to reveal itself in varying measure.

Every religion has its methods or techniques by which in differing degrees the mind is stilled and according to the capacity of the worshipper what are felt to be deeper insights and experiences emerge into awareness. All these techniques have much in common, and books introducing them to the general reader are given in a bibliography (*vide* Appendix). I propose here to give a brief account of only three of these. The first one to be described is the mental discipline associated with the yoga-system of Patanjali, which is one of the oldest in the world and has probably influenced all other Oriental systems. The second is a technique of self-observation possibly of Chinese origin. The third is the technique of prayer associated more particularly with the Christian mystics.

5. THE YOGA-SYSTEM OF PATANJALI

This is incorporated in one of six philosophical systems of Indian thought. The date of its origin is not known with certainty, but it is probably about 2,000 years old. The part of it which we shall attempt to expound here is a practice designed to bring the mind completely under the control of the will, so that it is then a really efficient instrument of consciousness. The yoga *sutras* of Patanjali are a very condensed account, and the Western reader certainly needs an interpretation and commentary. The best introduction is in my opinion, Geraldine Coster's little book, *Yoga and Western Psychology*.* Patanjali lists eight activities or practices which constitute his system.

1. Obedience to the moral law. This is particularly specified as including abstention from killing, lying, stealing, incontinence and greed, but includes a great deal more than a mere catalogue of negative virtues.
2. Obedience to the spiritual law. Particularly mentioned is " discipline ", by which is meant the achievement of mastery as distinct from slavery to the instincts and emotions, study, and an attitude of cheerful acceptance of life.
3. The practice of certain postures. These are designed to promote health of the body and to stimulate the " ætheric " body.
4. The practice of certain rhythms of breathing, believed also to affect considerably the ætheric body and to be capable of stilling mental processes.
5. The practice of withdrawal of mind from sensory phenomena—clearly a valuable preliminary to the elimination of distractions and to acquiring ability to concentrate.
6. Concentration.
7. Meditation.
8. Contemplation.

It is the last three of these which constitute the essential discipline, and which we shall now consider in detail. Concerning 3 we shall only remark that while the characteristic cross-legged (lotus) posture used in the East has advantages, such as erectness of the spine combined with stability of the body, it is not essential. The best

---

* Published by O.U.P. A recent valuable book is by Ernest Wood : *Practical Yoga* (Rider & Co., 1952). The reader who wishes to probe into authoritative accounts by Indian thinkers might consult *The Complete Works of Vivekananda* (Vol. I) ; or Radhakrishnan : *Indian Philosophy*, Vol. II, Chapter V.

posture for most Westerners is that which allows the body to be forgotten. The disadvantage of lying in bed or in an arm-chair is that sleep may supervene. Probably the best position is sitting upright in a chair of suitable height, with both feet planted firmly on the ground. The spine may be easily maintained erect when a position of balance (leaning neither forward nor backward) is found. Concerning 4 we shall only remark that certain breathing rhythms are an aid to quietening the mind. For example, half a dozen slow and deep respirations will be found by most people to assist in reaching a state of mental quietness. If more complicated procedures are attempted it is important to study some text-book and follow the instructions carefully.* It should be understood that these are not essential, but only potential aids to the mental discipline we are about to consider.

The basis of these rests on the easily verified observation that our minds are not under the control of our wills and have consequently become inefficient instruments. We do very little real thinking, and most of our mental states are coloured by emotion which we do not recognise as present. Moreover, our restless minds are never still, but ideas and pictures float across the screen of awareness constantly. This restless panorama has been described as busy-mindedness: it is as though the mind had the characteristics of a butterfly flitting inconsequentially from flower to flower.

If the reader doubts this, let him try a simple experiment. Let him try to hold one thing, and one thing only, steadily in the focus of his mind for about half a minute. Failure is almost certain: he will have been surprised by another invading thought before he has had time to challenge it and turn it out. As an alternative experiment, let the reader decide to hold his mind free from any thought for about half a minute, and the same failure will probably result. His experience may be somewhat as follows.

The command " Peace, be still " is issued to his mind. The act of addressing this perhaps raises the question as to how he can ascertain if it is obeyed. Speculations follow, and suddenly realising that he is thinking, he repeats the original command. Perhaps he keeps repeating it, and then he recognises that the repeated directions are thoughts, and once more he starts again. He now makes a determined effort to throw his mind out of action: once more he finds he is thinking, perhaps about the task of concentrating and how to do it. Then he thinks of thinking, and what it is. He suddenly realises he is getting nowhere, and grimly starts again. He

* E.g., Yogi Vithaldas : *The Yoga System of Health* (Faber & Faber) ; or F. Yeats Brown : *Yoga Explained* (Gollancz).

now finds he is perhaps thinking of not thinking. By this time he realises that his mind is a seething mass of concepts jostling each other to capture his attention, and wondering what to do with these unruly mental children, the gong strikes, and he confesses his failure.

One of the most fundamental steps in all mental disciplines is to be able at will to still busy-mindedness and to be able to hold the mind free from thought for as long as desired, *without strain*. When this can be done, a most important step has been taken. The mind in this state has been compared to a candle-flame in a windless place, or to the placid surface of a pool on which the ripples have died down so that the clear depths beneath can reveal themselves. This state of mind can then be used for a further leap forward into " active contemplation ". In practice it may be found easier to approach this stage in steps—and these are through the practice of concentration and meditation.

In the practice of concentration a subject for thought must first be selected. What it is does not matter—perhaps an orange, a four-pointed star, a colour, a rose. The concentration should be on a simple thought. If, for example, a primrose is to be the object of thought, take either the shape, or the colour, or a simple visual image combining the two. The person must not think *about* it, or allow memory trains of association to develop. Moreover, the mental attitude must not be one of grim determination. The mind, like the body, must be relaxed and unstrained. It is safe to say that for many weeks or months the results will be meagre, but all experienced travellers on this road tell us that perseverance is slowly rewarded. Again and again the mind, which wanders easily, has to be brought back to its object of concentration.

In this stage of practice there are four factors involved. There is the will directing experience, there is the mind, there is the object of thought and there are the distractions. The distractions may have their origin from without (as from sense-data), or from within (as intruding ideas thrown up by the subconscious mind), but in a sense these are both from different levels of the mind itself. The practice of concentration, when it is finally successful, leaves three factors only : the will, the mind, and the object of thought. The next step into which it merges imperceptibly is one in which the sense of effort diminishes, until finally the mind appears to become one with the thought. This is called meditation by some. From this stage it is apparently possible either to pass easily into a passive, dreamy, unproductive state akin to mediumistic trance, or to pass into an active creative state which is the desirable climax. This last state, which is called by some writers meditation, and by others contemplation, is a poised state of consciousness. The mind is not active, it is still and placid. A deeper level of the self throws its searchlight of wisdom on that which it is desired to contemplate, and profound insights and intuitive knowledge become available. A greatly enhanced sense of freedom, power and knowledge is realised. When this stage of achievement is attained, the student will need no instructions from others : he can find out the further way for himself. In any case, it is probably impossible to express in words directions for going further. There are, however, some words of advice which masters of this path have left for others who would follow.

It is quite possible to acquire and develop at this stage considerable psychic powers (called in Eastern philosophy " siddhis "). The person whose aim is spiritual development is generally wise to leave them alone. It is not that in themselves they are wrong, any more than physical powers are wrong. But to acquire power is to undertake new responsibilities for which the moral order of the universe will hold a man responsible. Too often the fascination of such power has led to arrest in spiritual progress, and sometimes to actual decline. Steiner announced what he called the golden rule of occultism : for every step taken in the acquirement of such powers, take three in the perfecting of your own moral character. The Buddha taught his disciples that they should be by-passed. They have to do with knowledge and action on another level of " appearance " only, and the seeker for reality should not be side-tracked.

A special type of concentration, less to be commended to the general reader, is the use of *mantrams*. This is any word or phrase such as " Pater Noster " or " Ave Maria ", or the Greek Orthodox prayer, " Lord Jesus Christ, Son of God, have mercy ", which is constantly repeated many hundreds of times. In the end a sort of automatic process is set up in which the mind apparently becomes one with the object of thought. In a brief flash, when the state is shattered, there is the possibility of a moment of illumination before the Self and Ego restore the normal relationship. This technique is one which might be appropriate to monastic conditions, but one not inherently likely to strengthen the mind's powers of concentration thus rendering it a more efficient instrument of analytical thought in ordinary life. Moreover, if successful, it affords but a transient experience, valuable as that may be to the seeker.*

* A little volume with a good deal of valuable, practical advice, which is based on the Buddhist approach, is *Concentration and Meditation* (pub. by The Buddhist Lodge, London).

6. A TECHNIQUE OF SELF-OBSERVATION

This technique is based upon the fact that our true Self (or rather that part or aspect of it which is concerned with the individual) is ordinarily not recognised to be what it is. As we said in Section 1, it is partly immersed in, and lives through the Ego's life. All the Ego's strivings and seeking and aspiring are really expressions of the immersed Self's promptings, but we identify ourselves with the Ego, and do not know our true nature. To use our former simile, it is as though Irving had quite forgotten his real nature and supposed he *was* Hamlet. This technique, one might say, consists in self-remembering while continuing to play Hamlet. It corresponds to a division of attention—so that one part of Irving remembers himself and views objectively the other part playing a role. Alan Watts * in an account of this practice says :

" It is the ability to retain one's normal and everyday consciousness and at the same time to let go of it. That is to say, one begins to take an objective view of the stream of thoughts, impressions, feelings and experiences which constantly flow through the mind. Instead of trying to control and interfere with it, one simply lets it flow as it pleases. But whereas consciousness normally lets itself be carried away by the flow, in this case the important thing is to watch the flow without being carried away."

This is clearly a different thing from mere mind-wandering, because of the detached, uncritical observation of the stream. The determined practice of this detachment ultimately reveals to the person that behind what at first seems an artificial process there *is* a part of the Self which is always an observer of the stream and not immersed in it.

Watts stresses that although the process is one in which the Self distinguishes itself from the stream of mental experience, it *accepts* it (i.e., it allows it to continue as before and does not repudiate it). The infinite always includes the finite, but through this practice it does so consciously, not unconsciously.

In a strange but interesting book † P. D. Ouspensky makes reference to a practice virtually identical with this. He has described his subjective experience of it, and says that he came to realise that he had had moments of self-remembering (without knowing it at the time) from childhood upwards. In such times " he " had stood momentarily in wonder at the strangeness of " himself " being there

* Alan W. Watts : *The Supreme Identity*, p. 176 (Faber & Faber, 1950).
† P. D. Ouspensky : *In Search of the Miraculous*, pp. 117–21, 141–51 (Routledge & Kegan Paul).

in that place at that time. In times of great emotional crisis he observed sometimes a similar detachment as though a part of the self remained aloof and the other part acted or participated in events. He remarks that the memories which could really be recaptured with almost the vividness of present experience were those where an act of self-remembering had been coincident with the external event. Ouspensky's teacher, Gurdjieff, taught him that there were four states of consciousness. The lowest of these is sleep. The second state is the " waking " state, in which men have the *illusion* of clear consciousness, but which, in his view, is little more than a drugged or sleep state. The third state, in which few men live except in occasional moments, is of real self-consciousness (i.e., of self-remembering). The fourth state is of full enlightenment, in which things are known as they really are. He maintains that the way to the fourth state is through the third, and that in the great majority of men, who are only in the second state, the third will occur only occasionally in flashes.

I had a friend, an unusually gifted man, who died a few years ago. He had undertaken both the mental disciplines I have outlined. The following notes of his may be of some help to others.

" A man should subject himself continuously to the discipline of self-observation, and guidance in this respect is given below. The man who does so will in the end find himself in tune with the infinite powers and perceptions of his Intuition by which he will be guided rightly through the most difficult situations of his life. Intuition is the wisdom of the pure consciousness, and embraces all that has been learned and assimilated as wisdom through the prior existences of the soul or self. It is eternally struggling to inform the self-aware consciousness and cause it to make judgments in conformity with the former's sense of right and wrong. The judgments of the Intuition are infallible, but the power of the Intuition to enforce its judgments is limited by the nature of the bodily instrument with which it is associated.

" Here, then, is direction for the student :

" 1. He must propound to himself with affirmative and assertive iteration the idea that the goal of his aspiration (maximum self-knowledge, self-control and self-development) is of infinitely greater value than the attainment of any worldly ambition, and is worthy of any sacrifice. Thereby he will cultivate willingness to subordinate lesser things to the greater, and to renounce what needs to be renounced to reach the goal.

" 2. He must continuously supervise the play of his emotional experience in order to break down the habit of responding automatically to his feelings and emotions. Immediately he becomes aware of any feeling (say of anger) he must refuse to submit to it before studying it objectively, whereupon he can deliberately choose whether to be angry or not. By so doing he will quickly realise that he (his spirit or self) and his emotions are separable, and with practice he will acquire ability to objectify and control his emotions at will. Thenceforth all his sensational and emotional experience will become increasingly perceptible by his spirit as objective experience, and will become increasingly amenable to deliberate rejection or acceptance by reference to his alert and unimpassioned self-consciousness. By constant practice he will become able to discard at will the sense of identity with experience, and to replace it with an exalting sense of aloofness, power, and freedom.

"3. He must sedulously labour to cultivate right emotions—in particular a sincere sympathy for all mankind. The evocation of useful emotions is not more difficult than the control and elimination of unprofitable emotions. No emotions are less profitable and more hurtful to the spirit than the emotions of aversion and hate. They can be eradicated by acquiring knowledge of their underlying cause, by the practice of disidentifying self with experience, and the cultivation of a desire to replace them with opposite emotions, such as sympathy and love. Objectification of hate and aversion brings to awareness the fact that the spirit only experiences these emotions when and while it allows itself to be identified with them. If the spirit withdraws itself from them and examines them, even for a moment, for that moment it is a spectator and not an experiencer. The spirit may become re-identified with the experience. But it has been free, if only for an instant, and it can be free again—for ever if it wills.

"4. The student must practise returning to the consideration of every emotion to which he has submitted and with which he has become automatically identified, after the emotional tumult has subsided. If the emotion has been of an exhausting nature (e.g., passionate anger), he will find himself eager to forget it and disinclined to review it. Examination of the cause of his reluctance to review the experience will reveal the existence of a sense of shame for having surrendered to the emotion (identified himself with it), together with a vague consciousness that he could have resisted effectually had he been sufficiently alert at the critical moment when a choice between resistance and submission might have been made.

"On further research he will become fully and clearly conscious that a choice (to submit or to resist) actually was presented. It occurs at the first moment of consciousness of the call of the emotion. Every man can remember several occasions when he refused to identify himself with some emotion (i.e., refused to submit to it) by reason of an external influencing circumstance. Many men, for example, find little difficulty in maintaining placidity under sharp provocation if another person is present whose respect they covet; yet instantly they give way to anger under less provocation if no such person is present. Those same men would probably choose not to be angry if they practised recollectedness and thereby had developed spiritual alertness. The virtue of recollectedness is that it can provide a subjective restraint at least equal in strength to that of any external influence.

" When he ignored the moment of choice, so that instead of choosing to be angry or not to be angry he responded automatically to the impulse to anger, he did something of which afterwards he is ashamed. On enquiring what part of him is ashamed, he will find that his body is not capable of shame, but his spirit is very capable of shame, and is ashamed. On seeking to know why his spirit is confessedly ashamed, he will learn that it is not because he gave way to anger; it is because he did not exercise his spiritual prerogative of self-government, but allowed his body-machine (mind) to govern him. This is the practice of recollectedness. It must be practised until it becomes a habit. Nor should the student be deterred from the practice by the subtle fear that in endeavouring to liberate himself from one habit (the habit of automatic response to emotion) he may be contracting another, for it is only by forming the habit of breaking chains that the spirit will at length become entirely free. Before the goal is reached, all habits must be broken, meanwhile it is better to be ruled by good habits than bad. For good habits are less difficult to break than bad, and new than old. These exercises lead towards self-awareness, and this gives the spirit power to detach itself from identification with experience.

" 5. He must weave all the above exercises into the transactions of his daily life in the manner that a carpet-maker weaves the coloured threads of pictures into the texture of a rug. Thereby he will acquire strength and spiritual beauty, even should he fail to reach his goal."

7. THE TECHNIQUE OF PRAYER

Prayer may be regarded as the supreme practice of the religious life. Whereas the previously mentioned practices may, in the broad sense, be described as psychological, the practice of prayer at least assumes a theistic outlook. God is regarded as knowable and the object of man's highest aspiration. Both roads, as we have seen, will in the end lead the true follower to the highest experience—which is the same, whatever terms be used to describe it. The Christian mystics have described three stages on the way. They have called them Purgation, Proficiency and Completion (or the Unitive Life). The first stage is chiefly concerned with moral discipline (i.e., with the alteration of conduct). This consists in the elimination of all that is undesirable and futile in one's mode of living and the acquirement and strengthening of all the virtues. Proficiency is the stage of deeper activity, the changing of character and its evolution through high prayer and contemplation. The final stage—the Unitive Life—has probably not been attained by one man in a million : it is the approach to Enlightenment, the goal of all living, the consummation of all our striving and aspiring—Union with God.

In the stage of Purgation, with which most of us are concerned, prayer is the means of progress, and four types of prayer are characteristic of ascent through this stage : (1) vocal prayer ; (2) mental prayer ; (3) affective prayer, or prayer of the will, and (4) the prayer of Simplicity or Simple Regard. It will be interesting to note the marked parallels between these and the yoga practices previously described.

In vocal prayer the use of words can have no other function than to assist in concentration. The elimination of distractions and the avoidance of mental wandering are effected to a considerable extent by the use of words. The collects and classic written prayers of the Church are designed by their form to focus the mind on the idea of God. When this is done effectively, the second type, mental prayer, may be used with advantage. Words now are few—they are charged with depths of meaning, until at last they seem poor symbols of profound reflections of wonder, awe, reverence and love —all directed towards God. On these we then desire to dwell, for they are inexhaustible in significance. As these meditation trains revolving round the central idea of God exhaust themselves through their inadequacy (a process which Gerald Heard suggests may take a year) the third type of prayer begins to take its place. Thought images are now discarded and leave in their place only " the naked intent of the will ". This obviously corresponds to one-pointed concentration of the yoga-system, with the idea of God as the object of aspiration. Entry upon this third type of prayer usually has an emotional or " affective " phase when the self is moved by intense longing for the infinitely desirable (" As the hart panteth after the water-brooks, so panteth my soul after thee, O God "). The emotional phase should give place to a quieter desire based on Love and Wonder and a sense of the Numinous. He is the supreme Love and Beauty and Truth to which the will in silence urges the self. This passes with time into the fourth type of prayer of Simple Regard. Here the one-pointedness is held without strain of any kind, and a sense of Immanence grows. This clearly corresponds to the stage of meditation proper of the yoga-system, or even to the entry upon contemplation. With the practice of the prayer of simple regard, the first stage of the mystic way passes slowly into the second stage of Proficiency. The sense of the Immanent presence of God which arises in the prayer of Simple Regard now begins to permeate all times and activities of life. With the entry upon Proficiency another " quality of the will "—a power other than the surface will—is said to come into play. Gerald Heard says : " The surface will is not so much being superseded as merged and fused in a comprehensive Will." This again is very reminiscent of the Self now being able to disidentify itself from the stream of experience, not critical of the latter, but knowing that in a real sense it causes and includes the latter. (These are the comprehensive Will and the surface Will.)

The stage of Proficiency has been described in detail by the Christain mystics. It also has its own types of prayer—but we shall not attempt to summarise these here.* It would be presumptuous to suppose that anything more than the merest indications of prayer's possibilities can be given in a brief section such as this. It is, however, interesting to trace the correspondence of technique between East and West, and to reflect that thousands of years ago the hermits and forest-dwellers of India found a way to God not very different from that of the Christian saints, and not unrelated to that which the Western city-dweller may use if he wills.

For whether men sit on the snowy heights of the Himalayas or toil on the torrid plains of India, whether they participate in the busy life of London or hear

> the silence of the seas
> Among the farthest Hebrides,

they all have immortal longings in them, and their destiny is the same. " When I sit and meditate," said an Indian sage to his disciples, " gradually as I pass onward I raise my hand to the Ultimate Truth. Then I behold other hands coming from other parts of the world to rest upon the same shining Oneness. They, my brothers, are touching the same Truth as I. How can there be conflict between them and me ? "

" They shall come from the East and from the West, from the North and from the South, and shall sit down in the Kingdom of God."

* Gerald Heard's little booklet *Training for the Life of the Spirit* is commended as an excellent summary. His larger book *Preface to Prayer* will also repay study. (Cassell & Co., 1944 and 1945, respectively.)

PART IV

THE SIGNIFICANCE OF THE WHOLE

Chapter

18

PRE-EXISTENCE, RE-INCARNATION AND KARMA

" The child does not know the distant thunder of the deep he
goes to, which brings not a flutter to his heart that dreams. We
cannot awaken the dreamer or point out his fate. That is ordained
by the past, for the soul in its first kiss of the body renews an
ancient love ; and in this kiss, however gentle, are all the desires
which brought it back to the world."

Æ (in *Song and its Fountains*).

" Looking back on the past I have vivid sense of a being seeking
incarnation here, beginning with those first faint intuitions of
beauty, and those early dreamings which were its forerunners.
It was no angelic thing, pure and new from a foundry of souls,
which sought embodiment, but a being stained with the dust and
conflict of a long travel through time, carrying with it unsated
desires, base and august, and, as I divined of it, myriads of
memories and a secret wisdom. It was not simple but infinitely
complex, as a being must be which has been in many worlds and all
it has experienced has become a part of it. . . . It was a being
avidly desirous of life, while another part was cold to this, but was
endlessly seeking for the Spirit."

Æ (in *Song and its Fountains*).

> Hence, in a season of calm weather
> Though inland far we be,
> Our souls have sight of that immortal sea
> Which brought us hither ;
> Can in a moment travel thither—
> And see the children sport upon the shore
> And hear the mighty waters rolling evermore.

WORDSWORTH (*Ode on Intimations of Immortality*).

IT is probably true to say that a number of my readers have already
reacted to the title of this chapter * with some measure of emotional
interest or aversion. Some people seem curiously and almost instinctively interested in these topics, others, frequently religious-
minded people, feel antagonistic, as though some strange pagan
faith was subtly menacing their cherished beliefs. The average
thoughtful Western man has in general given little consideration to
these matters, although his reticence does not always match his

* I am indebted in this chapter to my friend A. W. Osborn's *The
Superphysical*.

375

knowledge. In any attempt to formulate a philosophy of life and endeavour to see meaning in our pilgrimage, these ancient beliefs cannot be lightly set aside. It is our duty to weigh them carefully, and without prejudice, in order to see if they illuminate for us tracts of experience which would otherwise remain dark and mysterious.

In so far as they are truths, it is fully recognised that they can only be relative truths (i.e., truths explanatory of experience in the world of appearance): but these are the only sort of truths we can hope to grasp with our minds. The mysterious character of Time itself always looms in the background of thought whenever we talk of the evolution of forms, or of consciousness, whenever we speak of a Way or a future goal. As long as we recognise this, we may safely go forward into our subject which concerns the great rhythms of Being and Becoming.

1. THE CASE FOR PRE-EXISTENCE

(a) We start from indisputable ground. Here we are on earth, going through a set of experiences in physical form along with millions of others. We were born into these conditions, into a particular nation and a particular family, without, so far as we are aware, having had any opportunity of choice in these matters. Let us look particularly at the tragic side of life, because this presents the thoughtful person with doubts and problems far more than does the attractive and happy side of life. We see children born into the world under the greatest variety of conditions. Some have sound, healthy bodies with good brains, keen, alert and capable, when fully matured, of sustaining great thoughts. Others are handicapped from the beginning with unhealthy bodies, blindness, deafness, disease and defective intelligence. For some the environment is one of security and affection, encouragement, culture and æsthetic interest; for others it is depravity, squalor and ugliness, and one of indifference or gross cruelty by the parents. For some, opportunity stands knocking at the door waiting to welcome and assist; for others it passes by, or knocks too late. Are these things just chance, or are they " planned by God " ? If neither of these alternatives is acceptable, what explanation have we to offer which carries with it the reasonable assurance that we live in a just world ? If God is just, and good and all-loving, the person who supposes each soul born into the world to be a new creation of God is faced with a real dilemma. There is no doubt that the conditions into which some souls are born preclude their proper development in this life. In some cases the physical body is a wretched tenement: consider the imbecile and the Mongolian idiot. In other cases the environment of fear, cruelty and brutality is calculated to crush and brutalise before the child's personality can possibly resist it. Is it conceivable that God is capable of doing something which any ordinary decent person would do all in his power to prevent or mitigate? The Christian, at least, should remember the words of Jesus, " If ye then, being evil, know how to give good gifts unto your children, *how much more* shall your Father which is in heaven give good things to them that ask Him? " The commonplace orthodox answer to this dilemma is quite frankly an evasion. It runs something like this. " Certainly there is inequality, but in the light of a future state there is justice too. Life, we must remember, is a handicap race. To whom much was given, from him much will be required. Shakespeares and Newtons must make good use of their talents. The idiots, the suffering and crushed must do their best, realising that God is just and merciful, that He only expects achievement commensurate with their talents, and that in the end all will have been found to be worth while." However true these affirmations may be, they do not face the problem, which is concerned not with compensations in a future state, but with an explanation of the present state. There is an obvious way out of the difficulty— namely, to abandon the idea that each soul born into this world is in some mysterious way a fresh creation of God. If we do so we need not assume that chance or accident is an alternative " explanation " of the gross inequalities at birth. We can take our stand on the Law of Cause and Effect, and say that all these grossly unequal conditions of birth and childhood are the results of prior causes. Since these causes are not by any means apparent in the present lives, this involves as a logical necessity the pre-existence of souls. It is then possible to affirm that we are the product of our past, that present circumstances arise as the result of self-generated forces in states of prior existence.

It is curious that in the West we have come to accept the Law of Cause and Effect without question in the scientific domain, but seem reluctant to recognise its sway on other levels of significance. Yet every great religion teaches this as part of its ethical code. " Whatsoever a man sows that shall he also reap." * In Oriental philosophy this is the great Law of Karma. Whatsoever a man sows, whether in the field of action or thought, sometime and somewhere the fruits of it will be reaped by him. As a boomerang thrown by a skilled person will move rapidly away to a great distance on a circular path, but finally returns to the hand of the thrower, so there

* Gal. vi. 7–8 ; see also Matt. vii. 2, 16–18.

is an inexorable law of justice which runs through the world on all these levels. There is no question of rewards and punishments at all: it is simply a question of inevitable consequence, and applies equally to good things and evil things. We must, moreover, remember that we are none of us isolated beings. We manifest in a web of relationships and are interlinked with persons both in this world and others, whose thoughts and actions affect ours, and whom we in our turn affect. We reap effects which others have sown, and we sow causes which influence others; but a justice which inheres in the ultimate nature of things—the Law of Karma—governs all.

Such a viewpoint is logical, and avoids the incredible supposition that God places one newly created soul in a position of advantage and another in a position of extreme disadvantage, and in effect tells them both to make the best of it. If we suppose that a man is born an idiot because of his activity in previous lives it may seem brutal, but let us be clear that it is not the explanation which is brutal, but the facts. Heredity, of course, is operative: no one denies this. It must, however, be seen as an effect as well as a cause. Looking behind the heredity, we infer, on this view, that the Law of Karma operates so as to direct or draw a person to be born to certain parents under certain conditions.

(b) The pre-existence of the human soul is also supported by the widely different degrees of spiritual achievement we find around us. There is a vast gulf between the spiritual quality of the best person we know and the worst, between the saint or sage on the one hand and a degenerate wretch on the other. It is so great a gulf that many consider it cannot be accounted for in terms of failure or achievement in one life-span of seventy years. It seems to me to represent a gulf quite as enormous as that which on the physical evolutionary level separates primitive and advanced forms of life. It suggests the probability that the two spiritual states are the culmination of very varying moral and spiritual struggle through a long past.

The same remarks apply equally to the chasms found in intellectual and artistic capacity. We have on the one hand a Plato, an Einstein, a Michael Angelo or a Leonardo da Vinci, and on the other we have the primitive tribesmen of equatorial Africa. It is wellnigh impossible to believe that the difference between the highest men of our race and the lowest is accountable in terms of one lifetime of effort in newly created beings. It suggests rather that these differences represent the result of ages of past achievement, striving and discipline in lives prior to the present.

(c) A special form of the previous argument concerns the appearance from time to time of infant prodigies. We have a Mozart or a Chopin composing symphonies of great musical maturity or playing an instrument with outstanding skill at an early age, when the teaching or environment are completely inadequate as explanations. We occasionally come across mathematical prodigies—mere boys who can perform elaborate mathematical operations without any adequate teaching or training. We are told of Sir William Hamilton, who started to learn Hebrew at the age of three, and

" at the age of seven he was pronounced by one of the Fellows of Trinity College, Dublin, to have shown a greater knowledge of the language than many candidates for a fellowship. At the age of thirteen he had acquired considerable knowledge of at least thirteen languages. Among these, beside the classical and the modern European languages, were included Persian, Arabic, Sanskrit, Hindustani and even Malay. . . . He wrote at the age of fourteen, a complimentary letter to the Persian ambassador who happened to visit Dublin ; and the latter said he had not thought there was a man in Britain who could have written such a document in the Persian language.

" A relative of his says, ' I remember him a little boy of six, when he would answer a difficult mathematical question, and run off gaily to his little cart.' Dr. Brinkley (Astronomer Royal of Ireland) said of him at the age of eighteen, ' This young man, I do not say *will be*, but *is*, the first mathematician of his age '." *

Genius at an early age cannot be conveniently ignored because of its rarity. It calls for an explanation. By recognising pre-existence, we may reasonably suppose that such outstanding gifts represent an overflow into the present life of great prior achievement in particular fields. In this connection we may recall Plato's theory of Reminiscence : the view that knowledge we acquire easily is " old " knowledge with which our enduring self has in a previous state of being been acquainted. On the other hand, knowledge which we find difficult to assimilate, or in which we lack interest, may be that which we meet for the first time. So, too, Intuition is possibly to be regarded as based on wisdom assimilated through the experience of past lives.

(d) The commonplace matter of family differences is one which must frequently create speculation. Physical differences and likenesses are doubtless covered by genetical laws, but differences of a profound kind in mental, moral and artistic characteristics sometimes occur, and remain quite inexplicable on biological grounds. This would not be unreasonable if we assume that each soul has a long

* Quoted in "The Ancient Wisdom" by A. Besant, from *North British Review*, September 1866.

past behind it, and was drawn to incarnate according to karmic laws in a family whose parents could provide him with the physical vehicle and environment most suited to his further development. It has been remarked that Johann Sebastian Bach was born into a family with a long musical tradition, but we need not infer from this that his genius could be accounted for by his heredity. Rather the view would be that his musical genius needed a special quality of physical vehicle and a certain environment for its satisfactory expression and further progress, and his soul chose, or was directed towards, parents capable of providing that opportunity. The soul determines the heredity, not the heredity the soul.

(e) In the field of personal relationships there are occasionally friendships and antipathies of a very marked kind where no psychological explanation seems to fit the facts. Cases of love at first sight, though necessarily suspect through being so much the stock-in-trade of the romantic novelist, may find an explanation on the lines indicated. They may represent the reaction to relationships which have pre-existed the present lives.

I have two friends who permit me to use their own experience here. The husband I will call A, and his wife B. Now in late middle life, they are an exceptionally cultured, wise and kindly couple. He is an important business executive, although chiefly interested in philosophy and those questions which are ultimate in our thinking and living. She is a cultured lady who had in earlier years some psychical sensitivity and more than one experience of a mystical character. B says that she had known from the days of her girlhood that she would, after long waiting, finally meet someone of great significance to her. In her own words, " It was a sudden welling-up from the subconscious, almost like an inner voice assuring me that no one in my then circle of friends was of any special significance for me, but that I should have to wait for a relationship of great importance, and not only would I have to wait, but I would have to wait a very long time." In the middle thirties A came from abroad and met B at a public function for the first time. This first meeting both intuitively recognised was of the greatest significance, and as they have now been married for over twenty-five years, their immediate intuition has been adequately tested. A year or two before meeting A, B had a curious experience in the form of a waking vision. This is her account of it.

" I suddenly lost touch with my surroundings and seemed to be in another place and period, which might have been medieval Britain, or some northern European country. I was lying in bed, and knew I was at the point of death. I had given birth to a child, which I knew I should never see. The room was very large indeed. Part of it, the living part, had an earthen floor. The bed I was lying in was at the top (near the door), and was on a raised platform.

" There was a great commotion outside. I knew my husband was there and that he was about to set out on a very dangerous adventure. He was undertaking a forlorn hope on behalf of his King, and the populace were cheering him. He came in to say good-bye to me, and knelt beside my bed, overcome with grief. We both knew we should not meet again alive. The parting was terribly poignant and when the vision departed I found myself weeping bitterly. I felt I had been through the dreadful experience once again.

" When the vision ceased, I was puzzled, because I knew no one who might have been the man. Later, on thinking it over, I wondered if a man I knew well might have been he, because when I first met him I had a very strong impression that I had known him well in a past life. I wondered, without any sense of conviction, if it might have been he.

" When I met A, I knew without a shadow of doubt that it was he and have never wavered in that belief since."

It is significant that this vision came to B with all the emotional force of a poignant memory.

(*f*) Finally, I think we should consider a viewpoint expressed by Plato in the *Phaedo*, that if souls be only supposed to come into existence at birth, their survival of death would seem to a philosopher improbable. We may express it positively thus : that if the nature of the soul is immortal (as Plato believed), an immortality which implies an infinite future also implies an infinite past. To accept the one without the other, as some appear to do, is a strange feat of mental gymnastics, the grounds for which are difficult to discover.

Such, I think, is the case for our pre-existence of this life.

2. THE IDEA OF RE-INCARNATION

If the case for pre-existence is considered a strong one, then the idea of re-incarnation presents no logical difficulties, whatever be the emotional reaction to it. What the soul has done once by the process of incarnation in a physical body, it can presumably do again. (By the term " soul " we mean that individualised aspect of the Self, including buddhi—the Intuitive self—and Higher Mind, all of which are regarded as immortal.) We should of course bear in mind that what is meant by the phrase " have lived before " is not that the physical form Raynor Johnson has lived on earth previously, but rather that Raynor Johnson is only a particular and temporary expression of an underlying immortal soul which has adopted previous and quite possibly different appearances. The power that builds forms in the world of appearance exists apart from the forms. Of this we have had much evidence already. We may reflect on the pageant of living things (Chapter 3), the power which builds an oak tree from an acorn, or a human child from a fertilised ovum. We may recall also the evidence of psychical research in Chapters 9, 10, and 11.

If the general conception of evolution be regarded as applicable to the soul as well as to the physical world, it is not either improbable or unreasonable that the soul should adventure forth into the physical world in a newly-built body to acquire further experience of the kind which this world can provide. The fact that the soul has done so once was presumably for adequate and compelling reasons, and whatever these are, it is apparent that more might be gained by a *series* of such incarnations.

The doctrine of re-incarnation has had a long history. Originating probably with the ancient sages of India, it found a fundamental place in both Hinduism and Buddhism. Among the Greeks it was taught by Empedocles, Pythagoras and Plato. Traces of it appear in the teaching of Philo of Alexandria and in several of the early Church Fathers. It was officially pronounced to be a heresy by the Council of Constantinople in 551. In the Roman world it seems to have appealed to Cicero and Seneca, and the poets Virgil and Ovid. The sixth book of Cæsar's *Gallic War* records that the Druids of Gaul taught this doctrine. In recent times it has been supported by Giordano Bruno and van Helmont, by Swedenborg, Goethe, Lichtenberg, Lessing, Herder, Hume and Schopenhauer (as a reasonable hypothesis), Lavater, Ibsen and Maeterlinck.* Of recent philosophers, the most weighty testimony is probably that of James Ward, Professor of Mental Philosophy at Cambridge, who supported it in his Gifford Lectures on the *Realm of Ends*. Professor McTaggart of Cambridge also argues for it in his work *Some Dogmas of Religion* (1906). Dean Inge, without wishing to be definite, confesses, " I find the doctrine both credible and attractive ". The English-speaking poets have toyed with this doctrine rather more than the philosophers. There are passages in Shelley, Wordsworth, Tennyson, Rossetti, Browning, Longfellow and Whitman which show their interest in it.

Thus Browning in a poem to Evelyn Hope, a girl who died at the age of sixteen, expressed his sense of an old friendship and an underlying bond:

* Authority for this list is from W. R. Inge: *God and the Astronomers* p. 290.

I claim you still, for my own love's sake!
  Delayed it may be for more lives yet,
Through worlds I shall traverse, not a few;
  Much is to learn and much to forget
Ere the time be come for taking you.

John Masefield has written:

I hold that when a person dies
  His soul returns again to earth;
Arrayed in some new flesh-disguise,
  Another mother gives him birth.
With sturdier limbs and brighter brain
The old soul takes the road again.

These names are sufficient, I think, to show that the doctrine of re-birth has commended itself to many thoughtful men. It need not be supposed to imply that re-birth takes place in any automatic way or with only a short interval between succeeding lives. There are occult schools of thought which lay claim to surprisingly detailed knowledge on such subjects, affirming as the source of their information teachings communicated by incarnate beings of very mature spiritual development.* Whether such claims have any factual basis is a matter of personal opinion, and I do not think my own is of more value than any one else's. I think the only safe guide is to blend critical caution with the tolerant spirit which is prepared to find truth in many strange places. A thoughtful friend of mine has said to me, more than once, that he keeps a mental shelf on which to place inconspicuously, ideas and theories which he does not find necessary for his present philosophy. Later, facts and data may demand one of these theories for their understanding, and he will then be prepared to take it off the shelf!

A widely accepted doctrine appears to present the view that after death of the physical body the individual has a life on some level of the " Astral " plane—perhaps for the equivalent of some hundreds of years, and that at the close of this a second transition with discarding of the astral body takes the self on to the mental plane where it lives a shorter and intenser life, still, however, in a body or form. Finally the deeper self, having absorbed all the value and wisdom of such experience, seeks again an adventuring forth into matter, and the " outgoing " process again sets in, leading ultimately to re-birth. All forms of the doctrine agree that it is Desire which again attracts the soul to earthly life. The Sanskrit word is *Trishna*

* The Theosophists are one such school. An exposition of their views will be found in books of Annie Besant or three books of A. E. Powell *The Astral Body, The Mental Body, The Causal Body*).

which means " thirst " for sentient existence. Re-birth result
from the pull or attraction of earthly love and desires. This being
so, it is clear that the cultivation of detachment and the elimination
of material desires are an essential element of the Eastern teaching
which seeks to show men how to leave the Wheel of Becoming and
be free from the ceaseless round of births and deaths.

We are, of course, here in a region of speculative thought, and
the ideas put forward are of the " revelatory " character on the value
of which each person must form his own opinion. In two interesting
books of Geraldine Cummins * which are the product of automatic
writing there are given communications purporting to come from
F. W. H. Myers, one of the distinguished scholars who founded
the London Society for Psychical Research. He made the following
writings :

> " As there are certain centres in the brain, so in psychic life there
> are a number of souls all bound together by one spirit, depending
> for their nourishment on that spirit. . . . It explains many of the
> difficulties that people will assure you can only be removed by the
> doctrine of re-incarnation. . . . Many soul-men do not seek another
> earth-life, but their spirit manifests itself many times on earth. There
> may be contained within that spirit twenty souls, a hundred souls,
> a thousand souls. The number varies. What the Buddhists would
> call the karma I had brought with me from a previous life is, very
> frequently, not that of my life, but of the life of a soul that preceded
> me by many years on earth, and left for me the pattern which made
> my life. . . . When your Buddhist speaks of the cycle of births, of man's
> continual return to earth, he utters but a half-truth. I shall not
> live again on earth, but a new soul, one who will join our group, will
> shortly enter into the pattern or karma I have woven for him on earth
> . . . You may say to me that for the soul-man, one earth-life is not
> enough. But as we evolve here we enter into those memories and
> experiences of other lives that are to be found in the existence of the
> souls that preceded us and are of our group. I do not say that this
> theory which I offer you can be laid down as a general rule. But
> undoubtedly it is true in so far as it is what I have learned and experi-
> enced.
>
> " The majority of people only re-incarnate two, three, or four
> times. By participating in the life of the group soul I perceive and
> feel the drama in the earthly journey of a Buddhist priest, an American
> merchant, an Italian painter—and I am, if I assimilate the life thus
> lived, spared the living of it in the flesh. You will recognise how
> greatly power of will, mind and perception can be increased through
> your entry into the larger self. You continue to preserve your
> identity and your fundamental individuality. But you develop
> immensely in character and spiritual force. You gather the wisdom

* Geraldine Cummins : *The Road to Immortality, Beyond Human
Personality* (Nicholson, 1932 and 1935 respectively).

of the ages not through the continual ' sturm und drang ' of hundreds of years passed in the confinement of the crude physical body; you gather it through love which has a gravitational pull and draws you within the memories of those who are akin to your soul, however alien their bodies may have been when they were on earth.

" There is no set law concerning re-incarnation. At a certain point in its progress, the soul reflects, weighs and considers the facts of its own nature in conjunction with its past life on earth. If you are primitive this meditation is made more through instinct—a kind of emotional thought that stirs up the depths of your being. Then the spirit helps you to choose your future. You have complete free-will, but your spirit indicates the path you should follow and you frequently obey that indication."

These are, to say the least, very interesting views.

3. SOME OBJECTIONS TO RE-INCARNATION

There is a number of questions which inevitably arise in the mind of anyone who seriously considers this subject.

Why do persons not remember their past lives? It is, I think, a reasonable reply to say that when we know how memory works we may hope to have an answer. The memory of events in our present life gets more and more sparse and uncertain as we go back to early years. Few people can recall much of the third year of their life, and almost certainly nothing of the second year of life. This datum of observation suggests that we ought not *normally* to expect to recover memories of pre-existent life, and their absence should not be taken as evidence against pre-existence. It may be remarked that under hypnosis extremely early memories have been recovered from the deeper mind, which must clearly store them somehow. All that we may deduce from this is that if the memories of pre-existent lives are in fact recoverable, we should only expect it to be possible in unusual circumstances or with a special technique.

The fact is that some persons have claimed to possess *memories* for which they cannot account in terms of their present life. Of course assertions prove nothing, and the sceptic will always enquire how the person distinguishes between memories and imaginations. I *know* that I had a holiday in Teignmouth over twenty years ago, and that this is a memory, and not an imagination, although I may have no corroborative evidence. All we can do, then, is to assess the weight to be attached to evidence by what we know of the character of the witness.

The lady B whose waking vision was described earlier in this chapter had also another fragmentary glimpse of what she felt to be

N

a memory of a previous life. In this glimpse A, her present husband, was a monk, and she and another person were young boys being taught by him. This fragment came a few years later than the first vision, and after she had met A.

Professor Lutoslawski, a Polish scholar, whose book *The World of Souls* favourably impressed William James, wrote, " For me the subjective certainty of pre-existence is parallel to the certainty of immortality. . . . I *know* that I have existed before this life, either on earth as a man, or elsewhere in similar conditions."

Krishnamurti, whose spiritual quality and insight have impressed all who have come into contact with him, said in 1931, " For me re-incarnation is a fact, and not a belief; but I do not want you to believe in re-incarnation. On the contrary, reject it; put it out of your mind; and remember only that as you are the product of the past, so you can control the future. You are master of yourself and in your own hand lies eternity." Such is wholly in the line of Krishnamurti's teaching, which is that nothing should be accepted on external authority: that the only authority is within the self. Moreover, he is constantly pointing people away from the Ego-centred, partial aspects of truth to the ultimate Truth which can only be known so far as the Self is realised.

D. G. Rossetti in a short poem called *Sudden Light* expresses a memory of the past.

> I have been here before,
>   But when or how I cannot tell:
> I know the grass beyond the door,
>   The sweet keen smell,
> The sighing sound, the lights around the shore.
>
> You have been mine before—
>   How long ago I may not know:
> But just when at that swallow's soar
>   Your neck turned so,
> Some veil did fall—I knew it all of yore.

Readers of John Buchan's delightful volume of reminiscence * may recall that he tells of three unusual experiences. " I find myself in some scene which I cannot have visited before, and which yet is perfectly familiar; I know that it was the stage of an action in which I once took part, and am about to take part again; I await developments with an almost unbearable sense of anticipation. And then nothing happens; something appears which breaks the spell." If there were not the subjective sense that the scenes were associated

---

* *Memory-hold-the-Door*, pp. 121–3 (Hodder & Stoughton).

with events in a *past* age, they might of course be interpreted according to Dunne's theory as recovered precognitive dream memories. As it is they appear more probably to be retrocognitive glimpses.

A very different objection sometimes raised to the theory of reincarnation, sees in the absence of continuity of memory of previous lives something unjust in the operation of the law of Karma. Thus the argument would run, if X, Y, and Z are successive lives on earth of the same individual, why should Z inherit happiness and suffering arising from causes in the life of Y or X of which he has no memory? I think the answer to this is that forgetting may have an important function to play in our development, as well as remembering. An analogy may help us here. A good mathematician can tackle a new problem presented to him, because he has at his command a knowledge of principles, a variety of mathematical processes and techniques, and skill in the use of them. Such equipment is the fruit of years of teaching and research, of trial and error, and of experience in solving other and perhaps simpler problems. Most of these will be forgotten, but what remains with him is not some thousands of details, but the fruits of his experience. This remains available to be drawn upon in facing any new situation. If memory retained all the myriad details with equal vividness, the fruits of experience might be hard to sort out with swiftness when required. It is probably much the same with the experience of the self in many lives. It is not that any detail is necessarily lost, but rather that in the interests of efficiency what remains available to us in a new life is the garnered wisdom of the past—the fruit of experience. This is the past which is of real value to us in facing new situations, and it *is* available to us as Intuition—the wise promptings of our higher self. It is doubtful if a detailed recollection of the experience of past lives would add anything of real value to this intuitional wisdom. It may possibly be that the higher self uses at least a part of the life between births for the assimilation of terrestrial experience and the distillation from it of wisdom.

At the same time, it is interesting to notice that there are a number of well-attested cases * of persons who appear to remember considerable detail of prior existences which are capable of verification. Bearing in mind all the possibilities of para-normal cognition, the re-incarnation hypothesis is by far the simplest one in some of these cases. Apart from what may be described as these rather rare and freakish cases, it would seem that some masters of the spiritual life do have available a knowledge of their own past. Krishna, speaking

* Vide an interesting book by Hon. Ralph Shirley: *The Problem of Rebirth* (Rider & Co., 1936).

to Arjuna, said, " Both you and I have passed through many births ; you know them not, I know them all." *

Another question sometimes raised about re-incarnation is " Why *here* again ? " Are there not other worlds, other significant levels, a whole universe of possibilities ? It may be so. It may also be said of our life here on earth that this planet is big enough for us to roam in, but we find that however far a man may travel, love and duty call him back to his own country and his own home again. Love is a cosmic principle of attraction, and if his spiritual kindred are involved in life on earth, these bonds and desires will draw him back to help them and to share their life. It is reasonable to assume that the cycle will continue with Earth as the magnet until the attaching bonds of desire are finally broken. In a poem dealing with the soul's progress F. W. H. Myers † expresses this nostalgic longing for Earth which he imagines the soul carrying with it.

> So, howsoe'er thy soul's fate bear her far
> Thro' counterchanging heaven and avatar,
> Still shall her gaze that earliest scene survey
> Where eyes heroic taught the heavenly way,
> . . . . .
> Where o'er themselves they seized the high control,
> Each at the calling of the comrade soul.
> . . . . .
> Ah Fate ! what home soe'er be mine at last,
> Save me some look, some magic of the Past !
> O'er deep blue meres be dark cloud-shadows driven ;
> Veil and unveil a storm-swept sun in heaven ;
> Cold gusts of raining summer bring me still
> Dreamwise the wet scent of the ferny hill.

4. THE LAW OF KARMA

We have already referred briefly to this Oriental doctrine, of which the Law of Cause and Effect as we know it in the material world may be regarded as a special case. Indeed, the Law of Karma is just this law applied to all the significant levels—of thought, desire and action. It is strange that our Western scientific tradition leads us to accept it so readily on the material plane, but that we are reluctant to recognise it on the others. I think it is because we profoundly believe that there is such a thing as human freedom—the freedom of the will to choose—and as we do not know within what limits this is operative, in order to safeguard our faith in freedom we

---

* *Bhagavad Gita*, IV, 5.
† " The Renewal of Youth " : from *Collected Poems* (Macmillan).

reject the potentially menacing doctrine of Karma. Yet the consequence of rejecting the reign of law on the levels of desire and
thought is inevitably to suppose that chance and caprice rule there.
To many of us this would seem most improbable, and we must be
prepared to consider carefully the relation between human and
karmic law.

If we look at history we find that " love of freedom " has played
no inconsiderable part. For this men have fought and died. Yet
again and again, after fighting to secure some environmental change
that they thought would secure them freedom, it has eluded them.
This is because the more important causes of bondage are within
men's hearts and minds, not outside them. We are prisoners of
our habits, of our fears, our desires, our hopes and our social interests.
We are prisoners of our climate of thought, our prejudices, our background of teaching, our mental limitations, our accepted political,
scientific, religious and philosophical beliefs. If to be truly free is
to live and act in accordance with our real inner nature (that of the
Self as distinct from the Ego), the fact is that freedom is a very rare
phenomenon. We are all prisoners, some perhaps tethered with a
longer rope than others, but none of us free except within the little
circle determined by the length of rope. For a large part of humanity
this circle is very small indeed, but people do not know it. They
cherish the illusion of choice and freedom of the will, and would be
offended to be told they were well-nigh automatons. The Ego, that
centre in the mind with which we falsely identify ourselves, is the
focus of all the patterns of thought and desire and action we have
built up. The real Self which alone has freedom gets very little
chance to exercise it because of the dominant Ego. At one extreme
there is what we may call " animal-man ", completely governed by
the Ego. Place him in a given situation and you might predict how
he would behave. He may imagine he exercises his will to choose.
His will has, in fact, little or nothing to do with it: he is governed
by the strongest desire at the time. At the other end of the scale is
" spirit-man ", the sage or saint, the truly enlightened man, whose
Ego only exists as the perfect vehicle of expression of his Self in the
lower worlds. He alone is free. Indian philosophy uses the term
moksha, or liberation, to describe his state. In between these extremes is the mass of humanity. Let us be clear, then, that inner
freedom is something which has to be earned and won (by ways which
we have attempted to describe in the previous chapter). The
Buddhist says we are bondslaves of Ignorance. Jesus proclaims the
same thing: " Ye shall know the Truth—and the Truth shall make
you free."

The patterns of thought, desire and action to which we have alluded, and which constitute our bondage, are but the consequences of the Law of Karma. This maintains that every thought and desire and action, though apparently over and done with, has consequences. These may be pleasant or otherwise; they may follow rapidly or be long delayed—perhaps until some other life. It is, then, what we *are* that creates for us the circumstances of our existence. These circumstances and events are attracted to us by karmic law. It is only within the limits which such law prescribes that we are free to act, desire or think. According to the way in which we do react in thought, word and deed to given situations, we neutralise or modify existent Karma. Each circumstance and event, tragic or happy, is attracted to us by what we have been and are, and in itself offers to us, by a right reaction to it, the opportunity of spiritual development.

It is perhaps not a misleading analogy to say that while the rules of football or cricket prescribe a framework within which the game must be played, they leave the player free within these limits to decide how and in what direction he shall send the ball. So it is with karmic law and the circumstances we have to meet. We must beware, however, of presuming to judge others, or of making any glib and facile deductions about past Karma from present circumstances. If individuals lived in isolation, the possibility of such judgments being right might be appreciable. We do not, however, manifest in isolation, but in a web of relationships. As Gerald Heard has said: " I cannot say to the deformed beggar, ' So you earned and so you are '. Neither he nor I has ever been, is now, or ever will be an absolute individual. We earn for each other both good and evil, and are earned for." As a consequence, exponents of the Law of Karma * have always maintained that there is a Karma of groups, nations and races, in which individuals inevitably participate.

Moreover, as a counter to any facile judgments, we should recognise that adverse and difficult circumstances may be an opportunity of great spiritual advance to noble natures, and who are we to judge that such a one may not have chosen poverty, hardship or insignificance for such a high reason?

There are some persons who feel antipathetic to the conception of Karma on the ground that it leads to fatalism. By fatalism we understand a philosophy of life which assumes that all that we experience arises from a destiny or powers outside ourselves which we can in no way influence or control. It makes human life the sport of destiny, and necessarily leads to resigned indifference or cynicism.

* E.g., A. Besant: *The Ancient Wisdom*, Chapter IX.

Such a philosophy is not a legitimate deduction from the idea of Karma, which says, rather, that there is no fate or destiny which we have not made and do not make for ourselves. We are today the product of our long past, and we shall be tomorrow what we make of ourselves today. Karma may be inescapable, but it is not unchangeable. The fatalist who stands on the river-bank and, seeing a person who cannot swim struggling in the water, says to his friend, a swimmer, " Let him alone : it is his Karma," is misunderstanding Karma. It may have been the man's Karma to tumble into the river, but it was equally a part of his Karma to do so when there was a man on the river-bank who could help him.

There are others who feel antipathetic to the idea of Karma because it suggests a cold impersonality about the Universe : a sort of machinery grinding out inexorable consequence. I do not see why this reaction should be the case. It is possible to believe in Love as the supreme governing power in the Universe and still to hold that on every significant level there is a reign of Law. A dependable universe is far more easily conceived as an expression of a loving power than a capricious universe. We do not think that the existence of a Law of Gravitation or of any of the Laws of Nature leads to a coldly impersonal universe, nor need we feel that the existence of Law on any significant levels does so.

5. IS THERE CHANCE OR ACCIDENT ?

Let us look briefly at what we often describe as the tragic and mysterious side of life. Here is a young man who, after years of study and discipline, has qualified himself to be a surgeon : he is suddenly blinded in an accident. Another young man out for a day's recreation is accidentally shot through the spine and will have to spend the whole of his life on his bed. Here is a child in a pram, when a slate is blown off a roof by a gust of wind and maims or kills it. Such examples of what we call " chance " or " accident " where no reasonable vigilance or foresight on the part of the victim could have prevented the occurrence might be multiplied. How do we fit these poignant happenings into our philosophy of life ?

It should, of course, be remembered that many things in life come to us in ways which are unforeseeable and apparently fortuitous, and that not all of these are unpleasant. They cover every kind of experience, from those we have most valued to those most disliked. Perhaps a chance meeting, a casual word or glance, a missed train, a shower of rain—a hundred such things—can sometimes affect the whole current of life. Whether there could possibly be a material world in which there were such possibilities for good, without also such possibilities for ill, is, I think, very doubtful. We must not lose sight of this when we are oppressed by the poignant, tragic things. There are two questions which demand an answer as we reflect on these matters :

1. Is there chance or accident, or do we regard these things as not affecting human life ? Are there perhaps only happenings, the causes of which are so numerous or remote that we cannot trace them ?

2. Is this life on earth *just* to individuals ? We may perhaps consider that, taking a broad view of human life, the happiness on the whole outweighs the unhappiness, but we still have the problem of justice to the individual on our hands.

Let us consider carefully what we mean by chance or accident. Henri Poincaré,* a distinguished mathematician and philosopher, has pointed out that what we call fortuitous phenomena may arise in several ways. If we knew precisely all the laws of Nature and the *complete* situation of the material universe at a given initial moment, then it would be granted that we could theoretically calculate the situation of the universe at any succeeding moment.

1. Suppose we do not know all the laws, this might be one source of unpredictability.

2. Suppose all laws are known, but that a slight inaccuracy in knowledge of the initial situation produces a large inaccuracy in the final situation. Again in practice prediction becomes impossible.

3. All the laws being known, suppose nevertheless the causes of an event are extremely complex and numerous, then prediction may be impossible. For example, the position of a particular grain of sand shaken up with many other grains.

4. All the laws being known, suppose we select what we believe to be all the relevant factors in the initial situation, but in fact neglect one factor which seems irrelevant but comes to play an important part. This may vitiate prediction.

I think this analysis by a mathematician helps us to realise that while for a sufficiently inclusive mind (the " Divine Mind ") there could be no such thing as chance, we must in practice recognise the existence of chance for our finite minds. By chance, we mean that which we cannot be expected to foresee or predict on the basis of our experience. We take, for example, the tile blown by a gust of

---

* Henri Poincaré : *Science and Method.*

wind off a roof and killing a child. There are numerous causes, such as the height and slope of the roof, the type of fastening of the tile, corrosion of the nails, fissures in the underlying wood, defective workmanship perhaps originating years previously, the direction and speed of the wind, which in turn is caused by distant temperature variations over the earth's surface, the location of the pram at this precise moment, etc., etc. From the practical point of view these causes are so numerous that we may properly describe the event as " chance " in the sense that we have defined this word (viz., an event we could not have predicted on the basis of our experience).

But now let us consider whether the events which here concern us (viz., events affecting human beings) are ever solely the product of material or physical causes. The answer is obviously No. Emotional and mental factors play a part. In the above example the defective fastening may have been due to a workman's forgetfulness or momentary interest in something else. The person wheeling the pram may have been influenced by innumerable desires (e.g., to look in passing shop-windows) or by innumerable thoughts (such as to perform another task before going out), all of which affected arrival at the particular place at the particular time. As soon as we recognise the influence of emotional and mental factors our knowledge of the telepathic inter-linkage of minds reminds us that numerous other living persons, as well as independent thought-forms, may have contributed to the event. We begin to see that we cannot possibly hope to assess or know of more than a small fraction of the relevant causes. At least we must view as not unreasonable the karmic hypothesis which presumably has its operative mechanism on the level of Mind. On this view it is what we *are* on the mental level which draws to us circumstances and events of a certain kind. There is, on this view, no such thing as accident or chance, but only the great karmic law of cause and effect operative presumably through telepathic means to attract and repel.

I think we have to make up our minds—and we shall do so doubtless according to our temperamental preferences—whether we say there is chance in the world affecting human lives, or whether we say that what *seems* like chance is governed by karmic law on another significant level. I think we can scarcely claim at present to have proof of this latter hypothesis, and if we adopt it, we do so as an act of faith. For my own part, I adopt it, believing that there is no fate, circumstance or event which in the last analysis we do not or have not created for ourselves (i.e., ourselves in relationship with others). I do not think this is either an optimistic or a pessimistic

o

view, and certainly not a fatalistic one. We are today what we have made ourselves through all the past, and we shall be tomorrow what we have been made by the past together with our present attitudes. To this we may add the conclusion to which we were led in Chapter 7 (p. 166), that on the psychic level, future states also may be the cause of present events. The pull of the future may contribute equally with the influence of the past to present events and circumstances. This is an impressive, and I think may be an encouraging, thought to some who are living in the shadow of loneliness, frustration, adversity or seeming tragedy. The relation between future and present may be as significant as between past and present. " It doth not yet appear what we shall be ", and the present may be what it is, so that a future may be what it shall be (and what on the deeper levels it already *is*).

We may appropriately turn to the second question. Is this life on earth *just* to individuals ? Should we expect it to be so if it is only a fragment of an infinite pilgrimage of the soul ? If we go into a theatre at one door, walk across its breadth, and pass out by the farther door, what we may see and hear enacted on the stage in that short time-interval may seem most puzzling—even unjust and tragic. But we do not know what has led up to this glimpse, nor what will follow it. It is surely equally probable that many a human life will be a problem and a mystery unless it is viewed in the setting of a larger whole which has preceded and will follow it. Justice is only a word applicable to the whole play.

It is not, I think, mere optimism, nor a pleasant form of wishful thinking only, but rather a reasonably based faith to share the confidence Browning expresses in " Rabbi Ben Ezra " :

> Grow old along with me !
> The best is yet to be,
> The last of life, for which the first was made :
> Our times are in His hand
> Who saith ' A whole I planned,
> Youth shows but half ; trust God : see all, nor be afraid ! '

Chapter

19

THE PURPOSE OF HUMAN LIFE

On! I have guessed the end; the end is fair,
    Not with these weak limbs is thy last race run;
    Not all thy vision sets with this low sun;
Not all thy spirit swoons in this despair.
    Look how thine own soul, throned where all is well,
        Smiles to regard thy days disconsolate;
    Yea; since herself she wove the worldly spell,
        Doomed thee for lofty gain to low estate;
    Sown with thy fall a seed of glory fell;
        Thy heaven is in thee, and thy will thy fate.

Inward! aye deeper far than love or scorn,
    Deeper than bloom of virtue, stain of sin,
    Rend thou the veil and pass alone within,
Stand naked there and feel thyself forlorn!
Nay! in what world, then, Spirit, wast thou born?
    Or to what World-Soul art thou entered in?
    Feel the Self fade, feel the great life begin,
With Love re-rising in the cosmic morn.
    The inward ardour yearns to the inmost goal;
        The endless goal is one with the endless way;
    From every gulf the tides of Being roll,
    From every zenith burns the indwelling day;
And life in Life has drowned thee, and soul in Soul;
    And these are God, and thou thyself art they.

        F. W. H. MYERS (*A Cosmic Outlook*).

THE most intriguing and fundamental problem is that of our very existence. Why are we a part of the cosmic process, and what are we doing here? There are 2,000 million people on the planet living out their little lives. Their average expectation of life is less than fifty years: another 2,000 million will then take their place. Whence and whither and to what purpose is this great terrestrial procession, which on a modest estimate has been moving for half a million years? Where are the thoughts and dreams, the hopes and fears, the work and sufferings of this multitude? Are they just " dead facts stranded on the shore of the oblivious years " ?

If we look up at the night sky, in which on a very clear night some 3,000 stars are visible to the naked eye, are we innocent enough to suppose that this is a spectacle arranged for man's benefit? If this is our simple assumption, may it not be suggested that the 20,000 million stars which we cannot see with the naked eye remain to be explained ? If our innocence is not of this quality, perhaps in our wisdom we have some clue to the immensities—space, time and matter ? A thousand questions can be asked which stagger the imagination and baffle the reason. Are we, then, beings with the capacity to ask such questions but with no means or hopes of finding answers to them ? I do not think so. Although the intellect is limited in the type of question it can answer and the type of answer it can provide, there is abundant evidence of the powers of a deeper self. This deeper self can probe the world which lies behind that of our senses, and offers to us not a clear-cut intellectual formulation by way of answer, but a profound conviction that (in words of William James) " the nature of reality is congenial to powers which we possess ".

We have now reached a point where we must look back at the way we have come in order to discover, if we can, pointers and clues to the meaning of human life.

I. THE INTELLECTUAL EVALUATION OF LIFE

When the present epoch comes to be assessed in the perspective of history, it seems at least likely that two things will impress the historian : the enormously accelerated rate of scientific discovery and consequent technological advance, and the singular way in which these advances were used for physical destruction. Of the prestige of science in our day there can be no doubt, and the release of atomic energy has given to physicists particularly a special aura of authority. It cannot, however, be too often stated that the most genuinely far-reaching discoveries and conclusions of modern physics will cause no flutter in either Chancelleries or Defence Departments, but that their philosophical importance is enormous. We have considered some of these conclusions about space, time and matter, in Chapters 2 and 5, and it is appropriate that we should remind ourselves of them again. There are some properties of Light which suggest that it exists as concentred particles or bundles of energy, while other experiments can only be understood if Light consists of waves. The same strange uncertainty was later found to exist about electrons, protons and even atoms, which, having been regarded unquestionably as particles, were yet found in some experiments to behave like waves. This strange irresolvable dilemma led physicists to abandon the idea that models based on our visual perception of large-scale phenomena were applicable to the atomic and intra-atomic region. In other words, modern physics no longer purports to say what is the ultimate stuff out of which matter, as we know it, is built. All that it claims to do is, with the help of mathematics, to correlate symbols of unknown entities and express relationships between these symbols. To those who remember the confidence which physics had half a century ago in its " ultimate particles ", and its belief that the material world-structure was a matter of complicated mechanism not beyond the power of mathematicians to resolve, the new outlook is revolutionary. It is gratifying and profoundly significant that the conclusions of physicists (based upon their own techniques) about the nature of the microcosm should accord so remarkably with the views of philosophers.

We may sum up the physicists' conclusions in a sentence : that space, time and material form, all of which are useful, and indeed basic concepts, in the large-scale world, are elusive concepts— probably of little value in explaining the microcosm. The philosophers have told us for a long time that space and time are mental conceptions or devices to assist in the correlation of our sense-data. They have told us that as far as the material world is concerned sense-data are the only things of which we are aware, and that the plain man's assumption (which was until recently also the physicists' assumption) that there was something " substantial " or " material " out there in space as the cause of these sense-data, is unnecessary. If there is such a substratum of objects as the source of these sense-data, such objects can scarcely be concrete; if they are, we can know absolutely nothing of them. If they exist, they must be mental in character. This leads us, then, in a general sense, to suggest that the relation between ourselves and what we call an " outside world " is substantially a relation of minds to mental objects. Such a relationship is akin to that between a person's mind when it is in hypnotic rapport with another waking mind and accepts as veridical the latter's creative thoughts. The outside world of objects may thus be regarded as originating in a sustained mental field created by the Divine Mind—with which our minds are in a kind of rapport. This is substantially Berkeley's position. Creation takes place first on the level of Divine Mind, and from this is projected outward into the world of sense-data, which is the reflection on a lower significant level of the greater reality which causes it.

Our finite minds also have their measure of creativity. They are to some extent free, and are sources of thoughts, ideas and emotions some of which pass outwards on the mental level to affect other minds (as in telepathy), while others lead to bodily activity. The creative power of man is, in the present stage of his development, largely on the material level and *indirect*. By this I mean that a man may create the thought-form of a table, but in order to create it as a material object (i.e., to create the aggregate of sense-data which we describe as a " table ") he must use his muscles and direct tools to shape it from wood. The " wood " is, of course, a group of sense-data maintained by the field of the Divine Mind which we must, however, suppose capable of local modification by the individual mind. Thus a man might saw and cut it to change its form, or burn it to change (though not to lose) its substance. It would, however, be impossible for the ordinary man to create a " table ", having what we call permanence and substantiality, purely by the processes of thought. His mental activity as the creator of special aggregates of sense-data (which we label material objects) is by the indirect method of muscular control and direction.

We would draw attention, however, to two rare but apparently possible modes of creativity available to our finite minds, on the material level. One is the direct action on matter by the transformation of psychic energy into the kinetic form, as we saw was possible in the phenomena of psycho-kinesis and poltergeist effects. The other is the creative process described in the production of apparitions, and again in connection with materialisation phenomena. Here we maintained that such created objects differ from ordinary material ones only in their comparative impermanence and in the relatively small amount of chemical substance involved. Happily, at present man in general has not got these powers at his disposal, but they are there awaiting future development if the evidence of psychical research is accepted

Just as man's highest creative achievements are at present *indirect* —embodied in art, sculpture, music and architecture, with all their beauties of line and form, rhythm and colour—it may well be that the world of Nature, wholly or in part, is the *direct* creation of higher intelligences and higher creative minds than ours. We have no grounds for assuming that man's mind is the highest product of the great evolutionary process, just because it is the highest mind animating a terrestrial physical body. There may well be a whole hierarchy of creative consciousnesses using minds as far in advance of man's as his is in advance of the amœba's or the worm's. Their creative activity on the mental level may be the source of the myriad varieties of living creatures. The half-million species of insects, for example, represent inventive ingenuity of a high order—inventive ingenuity which cannot be reckoned in the direct line of, and subserving the end of, man's own evolution. Is it unreasonable to suppose that these creations sometimes represent exuberant artistry, as we reflect on the butterflies and moths, and that at other times they represent countless experiments, curious and brilliant, in the production of thought-patterns and their working out in matter? These may indeed be some of the forms of Art open to orders of Intelligence a little higher than our own. Such thoughts were doubtless in the mind of Edward Carpenter * when he wrote:

> " Creation is a stupendous and perpetually renewed work of Art, an everlasting evolution and expression of inner meanings into outer form, not only in the great whole, but in every tiniest part. Nature is a great vehicle, an innumerable network and channel of intelligence and emotion. . . .
> " The intelligences which constitute the universe are doubtless of infinite variety and of infinite gradation in development. Some may find expression in a mere point of space, others may enclose a planet or a solar system. Some are harmonious and accordant together; others may be—as well we know—in violent mutual hostility or warfare.
> " Yet . . . all of them in the end and deep down must have a common purpose and object of existence—and in that thought there is liberation, in that thought there is rest."

As we look at the overall biological picture, we are driven to ask ourselves the question: Why is the trend of evolution towards the creation of organisms of increasing complexity? One or two million years ago Man had not appeared on the earth; 100 million years ago the first mammals had not appeared. Not only is the process one of increased elaboration of general structure, but it is in its later stages one of great elaboration of brain-structure. The empirical answer is, I think, obvious. It is to provide for increasing ranges of awareness. It is to provide an instrument increasingly more responsive and efficient for the growing expression of Mind. Both Mind and Body have been regarded as instruments on different levels of significance of consciousness which lies behind them, and we cannot but infer that in some sense (which we shall shortly define) the whole process of evolution subserves the individualisation and evolution of consciousness. One of the notable deductions which we felt obliged to draw from the facts of precognition (p. 166) was that, on the psychic level, future events (as well as past ones) may be the cause of present states. The pull of the future may be quite as important as the thrust of the past. It is a conclusion at which Smuts had arrived by a wholly different route and which he embodied in his philosophy of holism (p. 68). It is a fact surely of the utmost importance to any fundamental understanding of evolution, and to any attempt to ascertain the goal of this age-long process.

* *The Art of Creation*, pp. 33–4 (George Allen & Unwin).

2. WHY IS THERE A PROCESS OF BECOMING?

Many thinkers have remarked upon the differing qualities of con-sciousness found in living things. P. D. Ouspensky * in his unusual study of dreams found evidence which suggested that different organs of the body have a primitive type of consciousness associated with them. This is I think debatable, but that they have a primitive type of *mind* associated with them is, I consider, indubitable. Our definition of " living " was a state of association of mind with matter, and clearly the self-maintaining chemical processes of great complexity and efficiency which organs carry out, establish the presence of mind. We have seen also that apparitions and certain materialised forms manifest temporarily the properties of living things, but not the properties of consciousness. They are animated by thought-forms having a limited life and certainly a limited repertoire of actions.

As we look, however, at the pageant of living things in Nature, there is a point, perhaps ill-defined and uncertain to our observation, where the entry of a primitive type of consciousness seems to be manifest. We may call this simple consciousness. It is charac-terised by the fact that the knower, the knowledge and the object known all remain undifferentiated by the living creature. This quality of consciousness persists right up to the human level and is possibly found in some primitive tribes. There is here no sense of selfhood, no looking before and after ; the creature is just a receiving centre of sense impressions and the executant of unpremeditated and unplanned movements. The very young child shows only this type of response.

The second quality of consciousness characteristic of mankind may be called self-consciousness. The first sensing of self as dis-tinct from other-than-self is accompanied by fear. A sense of danger and menace to the self arises, and growth of the instinct of self-preservation shows when the transition to this second type of con-sciousness is beginning to take place. The sense of time arises, the subject or knower separates himself more and more from the world of objects. He builds up an Ego by processes and attitudes which are wholly self-centred and lead to his own security, comfort or power. The world of objects is considered to be there to minister to him. All aspects of resistance are there to be fought and over-come. There can be little doubt that the emotions provide the driving forces, and that struggle and conflict which we characterise as selfish and evil from our more advanced standpoint, subserve at

* *A New Model of the Universe* (1938), p. 281 (Kegan Paul).

this earlier stage the necessary purpose of self-definition.   From the vast sea-bed of simple consciousness the island peaks rise into the isolation of self-awareness and establish themselves.   This process of individuation is effected by struggle and conflict, by self-assertion and greed, by lust for power and cunning.   This total phase designed to establish an individualised ego may be regarded as the downward or descending arc in the great cycle of becoming.   When its lowest depths have been sounded and individualised human consciousness has been established, the slow climb up the ascending arc begins, and things which in the earlier phase were good now become evil and have to be discarded.   The terms good and evil are relative —they belong to this world of the opposites ; they are relative entirely to an individual's stage of development.   (We may believe there is an absolute Good knowable only by the fully evolved being, but we really need another word to avoid confusion with " good " which is the antithesis of " evil ".   There is no absolute Evil—and the absolute Good is beyond the world of the opposites which embraces good and evil.)   The average stage of humanity at present appears to be somewhere on the lower part of the ascending arc. We recognise the higher values, we pay tribute to the ideals of unselfishness, kindliness, self-sacrifice and generosity, but we fail so very frequently to realise them.   The convulsive wars of our age are perhaps the violent rearguard actions of humanity trying to ascend, but dragged back by the powerful elemental forces generated in the earlier phase of the descending arc.   It is remarkable that the opposing sides in these wars seek to justify their struggle by paying at least lip-service (and sometimes much more than this) to ideals of freedom, justice and goodwill.   This is not without significance, and shows that we are on the whole on the ascending arc.

In the van of humanity so far as its spiritual development (or evolution of consciousness) is concerned are the few whom we call mystics.   They have had glimpses, transient experiences, of a third quality of consciousness coming to birth.   They have all felt in this new stage that the knower, the knowledge and the known become one again, but it is a very different state from that of simple consciousness, because what is now known is Reality, not Reality swathed in veils of Maya.   This quality of consciousness has been given many names—cosmic consciousness, the mystic vision, the unitive life, etc.—but it is certain that these refer to one and the same thing which in its fullness and permanence constitutes Enlightenment.   It is the great returning home to God, with the God-like potentialities (which were there latent from the beginning in consciousness) now fully unfolded.

There are some who seem to find this cosmic process meaningless, for they say: " If God is perfect, what can the process add to His perfection ? " We reply: Why should perfection exclude change ? Why should perfection be thought of as static, not dynamic ? A rose-bud may be perfect as a rose-bud, and an open rose may be perfect as an open rose. If a great artist produces a perfect picture, is he precluded from producing another perfect one ? I think we seem to be in the region of paradox because we forget that the perfection of God is unlike any finite perfection : it is the perfection of the infinite, and this already includes all finite possibilities. The Hindu sages who spoke of the finite Universe as the " play " of God probably felt this intuitively. We may conceive of the Infinite Artist in the joy of His artistry for ever producing new forms; the Infinite Lover in the joy of His being for ever creating new objects for His love. The exfoliation of the Infinite can have no limits.

But, it may still appear to some that the process is meaningless. If God is All; if He is the central Self and we in our real essence are a part of that Self, as sunbeams are of the sun; if the imprisoned splendour in each self is divine, and therefore Infinite and Eternal too, what is the point in the whole cosmic process of Becoming ? The only answer I can offer is this. From the creature's standpoint it is the achievement of a new quality of consciousness, and from the Creator's standpoint it is a consequence of His nature as Love to provide this. It is obvious that we are moving here in the most specu-lative regions of thought and all our ideas may be nonsense. The sug-gestion I make is that the creative activity of God includes embryonic spiritual beings, entities having simple consciousness, which is, however, infinite and eternal. The maturing of these so that they come to *know* their divinity (which they already possess, but do not realise they possess) is perhaps the basis of the whole cycle of Be-coming. How can they know their infinity if they do not know the finite ? How can they know the meaning of immortality if they do not know mortality ? How can they know omnipresence if they do not know limitation ? This very special kind of knowledge of their own nature has to be won by an age-long process of descent into the prison of space and time and a gradual ascent therefrom, in which knowledge, and ultimately omniscience, is *won*. It seems that this final quality of consciousness has to be won in two stages. The transition from simple to self-consciousness results in the building up of an Ego, a tower from which to contemplate existence. This is, however, but a half-way stage, the achievement of which is to have established an individualised centre of consciousness, a sense of selfhood.   This, I believe, is for ever retained, but has to be redeemed from all that constitutes egotism, so that in the end the true divine Self shines forth from a new centre with God-like qualities.

An acorn retains all the potentialities of the oak from which it came, but they are latent and unmanifest until it is sown in the earth and subject to the forces and buffetings of the kingdom below it. From this it emerges, climbing into the light, to become ultimately another mature oak.   It is perhaps a faint analogy of the process of growth of embryonic spirit sown in the lower strata of mind and matter and subject to all the buffetings of experience.

One of the clearest summaries of the whole process of Becoming has been given by Edward Carpenter,* from whom I quote below.

" What then, it will be asked, is the object or purpose or use of our incarnation in this grosser body ?   Limitation and hindrance are part and parcel of the great scheme of the soul's deliverance . . . . These subserve the evolution of self-consciousness and of the sense of identity. It is obvious that diffused faculties and perceptions, however swift and powerful, could never have brought these gifts with them.   It was only by pinning sensitiveness down to a point in space and time by means of a body, and limiting its perceptions by means of bodily end-organs, that these new values could be added to creation—the local self and the sense of Identity.   All the variety of human and animal nature, all the endless differences of points of view, all diversity and charm of form and character and temperament must be credited to this principle. . . . And not only limitation but also hindrance. These things give an intensity and passion to life, and a power and decisiveness to individuality, the absence of which would indeed be sad.   As a water-conduit by limiting the spread of the stream and confining it in a close channel gives it velocity and force to drive the mill, so limitation and hindrance in human life stimulate the in-dividualised energy from which for good or evil, all our world-activities spring. . . . The vast and pervasive soul-stuff of the universe (in its hidden way omniscient and omnipresent), suffers an obscuration and a limitation, and is condensed into a bodily prison in a point of space and time—but with a consequent explosive energy incalculable. The Devil—diabolos the slanderer and the sunderer, the principle of division—reigns. . . . He builds up the actual, fascinating, tragic, indispensable world that we know.   Selfishness and Ignorance, the two great powers of discord and separation are his ministers ;   the earth is his theatre of convulsive hatreds and soul-racking passion. But this diabolonian process is only one segment of the whole.   After the long descent and condensation and imprisonment of the spirit in its most limited and inert and self-regarding forms, after its saturation in matter, and its banishment in the world of death and suffering, the rising curve of liberation sets in, and the long process

* Edward Carpenter : *The Drama of Love and Death* (George Allen & Unwin).

of its return. It is through love mainly that this second process works itself out. From point to point through unison with others, by absorbing something from their experience, by sharing a wider life, the spirit's manifestation grows. By this the great tree of organic life spreads upon the earth; by this each race stem multiplies its tissues and expands; by this the buds of human souls are formed; and by this the souls themselves are freed to independent life. . . . Each soul is a gradual rising to consciousness of the All-Soul; a gradual liberation and self-discovery of the divine germ within it. First the race-soul rising towards this consciousness, and then the individual souls thrown off, rising independently towards the same. . . . Love indicates immortality. No sooner does the human being perceive this divine nucleus within himself than he knows his eternal destiny. Plunged in matter and the gross body he had learned the lesson of identity and separateness. All that the devil can teach him, he has faithfully absorbed. Now he has to expand that identity, for ever unique into ever vaster spheres of activity—to become finally a complete and finished aspect of the One."

Similar ideas are expressed by the communicator purporting to be F. W. H. Myers in the remarkable automatic scripts of Geraldine Cummins.*

" The spirit or deeper mind which nourishes a number of journeying souls with its light, is a thought of God. This thought is individualised, but not in the human sense. It is individual in that it has a certain apartness from its Creator, the apartness of the created thing from the One who gave it life. These myriad thoughts or spirits begotten by the Mighty Idea, differ from one another; many of them, nearly all, before they control and manifest themselves in matter are crude, innocent, and incomplete embryos. They must gather to themselves numberless experiences, manifest and express themselves in uncountable forms before they attain to completion, before they know perfect wisdom, true reality. Once these are acquired they may take on divine attributes and pass out Yonder, entering within the Supreme Idea and becoming part of the Whole."

It is easy to be critical of the terms and analogies used, but we are obviously attempting to understand something beyond all our experience, and we should not expect to have more than clues or pointers to the direction in which we may look for truth.

C. C. Massey,† using dualistic terms, refers to the cycle thus:

" The object of the embodiment of the Spirit in matter is presumably that it may, by exercise and effort, attain to individual self-conscious mastery, so that all its actions may be self-determined and no longer due to automatic or involuntary response to suggestion

---

* Geraldine Cummins: *The Road to Immortality*, pp. 31–2.
† C. C. Massey: *Thoughts of a Modern Mystic*, p. 50 (Kegan Paul).

proceeding from the Spirit's environment. . . . What distinguishes
Spirit from Matter is that the one is an active, the other a passive
principle. This active principle evolves and emerges by *itself
disengaging itself* from the passive principle in which it is at first bound
up and imprisoned. It escapes successively *by its own activity*,
from the mineral into the vegetable, from the vegetable into the
animal—while in man its effort, which was before instinctive and
spontaneous only, becomes self-conscious. . . . Matter is its womb,
out of which it must grow by its own life."

We would again stress the imperfections of this kind of analogical
representation, but it hints at the truth that the whole process is a
progressive getting rid of the illusions engendered by this imprisonment in space, time and matter, so that the sense of oneness with the
all becomes a permanent conscious possession.   It has been always,
so to speak, a reality—but not appreciated.

It is in the light of this that we understand such teachings as these
of Æ, " Human evolution is the eternal revealing of the Self to the
selves ", or again, " Whatever makes us clutch at the personal,
whatever strengthens the illusion of separateness, whether it be the
possession of wealth, or power over the weak, or fear of the strong,
all delay the awakening from this pitiful dream of life by fostering
a false egoism."

> For are we not at home in Thee,
>   And all this world a visioned show ;
> That, knowing what Abroad is, we
>   What Home is too may know?

3. HOW, THEN, SHOULD WE LIVE?

In the light of our knowledge of the kind of universe in which we
live, and of what we know of ourselves and our destiny, what sort of
lives should we live ?   By what kind of living can we best advance
the great purpose of our existence ?   Is extra-sensory perception a
thing we should endeavour to cultivate in ourselves ?   Is the active
or contemplative life the more effective in spiritual evolution ?
These are practical questions which face us all.

Perhaps we may consider first the desirability of developing latent
psychic faculties.   As a matter of principle, since the upward path
is one of expanding consciousness, it cannot be other than right to
develop latent faculty.   Whether it is for a person the thing *most*
worth while doing is for each person to decide for himself.   One
person feels it worth while devoting much time and practice to the
art of painting, another to the art of music, another to the gathering

of knowledge of men and of books.   We all have to choose between many desirable things which all may involve the growth of different aspects of the self's powers.   There is perhaps one important point of difference between the development of psychic faculty on the one hand and artistic or technical faculty on the other.   The ordinary person with well-developed extra-sensory faculty would find two temptations constantly present and very strong: interference in other people's business, and psychical exhibitionism, or, as we vulgarly say, " showing off ".   It is safe to say that unless these two temptations were resolutely overcome, the possession of well-developed extra-sensory faculty would result in spiritual deterioration rather than progress.   It is for this reason that Patanjali lays great stress first on the development of character.   Rudolf Steiner, a distinguished occultist, has said, " It is right that a person should learn of the secrets of Nature only so much as corresponds to his own degree of development."   If a person therefore desires to know whether it is right to give time and effort to develop extra-sensory faculty, the safest way to find an answer is to probe into the determining motive. Is it love of power, or egotism, or mere curiosity ?   If so, the indications are unfavourable.   No one need assume, however, that the disciplines involved are easy.   In fact, the necessary qualities of perseverance and sustained zeal are a safeguard likely to deter many. In an extraordinary address on the powers of the mind Vivekananda * said :

> " I know very little of this science. . . . It took me thirty years to learn it ; thirty years of hard struggle.   Sometimes I worked at it twenty hours during the twenty-four ; sometimes I slept only one hour in the night ; sometimes I worked whole nights ; sometimes I lived in places where there was hardly a sound, hardly a breath ; sometimes I had to live in caves. . . . And yet I know little or nothing ; I have barely touched the hem of the garment of this science.   But I can understand that it is true and vast and wonderful."

From what we know of the structure of the self, it should be clear that developed extra-sensory perception will add to our avenues of gathering knowledge and to our power over the environment, but in itself will add nothing to spiritual growth or development.   It broadens but it does not deepen life : all depends on the use made of the increased knowledge and power.   Moreover, there is this also to be said : that at an advanced stage on the spiritual way paranormal powers become naturally available, since the greater achievement includes the lesser.   Probably for most this is the safest way for them to arise.

---

* *Complete Works of Swami Vivekananda*, Vol. II, p. 22.

I anticipate, however, that there will come a time when the Natural Sciences will make tremendous advances, not because of better instruments and apparatus, but because a few people have at the command of the will their vast, and at present little-used, psychic faculties. I anticipate, moreover, that within a few centuries the art and science of healing will be radically improved by the increased knowledge and increased powers that thus become available. Clairvoyant diagnosis will supplement, and to some extent replace, that of physical methods, and the mind-to-mind relationship of telepathy and the mind-to-body relationship of psycho-kinesis will to a considerable extent supplement and ultimately replace much of medicine and surgery as we now know them. The physical presence of the healer will moreover not be necessary ; a letter will provide the link which will make available the skill of the most competent trained minds, no matter where on the earth's surface they happen to live. These things may seem a Wellsian phantasy, but I am strongly inclined to regard the next epoch of man's development as that of his psychical unfolding.

Is there a " best " type of life ? At Gangotri, the source of the Ganges, a remote place of pilgrimage in the fastnesses of the Himalayas, there live, in conditions of the utmost simplicity, a number of Indian contemplatives. Their place of retreat is only accessible at a certain season of the year ; they are isolated at other times by the snows and the monsoon. They are engaged in exploring an inner world whose sublime heights and abysmal depths are more magnificent than those on which their outer eyes can look. The true Himalayas are the Himalayas of the Soul. These men are not misanthropes, or ignorant of another kind of life : some have been to Universities and some have taken part in public affairs. They have chosen to live thus—to forsake the comforts of the body and the companionship of friends, for a quest of the spirit.

We in the West find this difficult to understand. We have placed an undue emphasis on action rather than being, and we have, perhaps more than the East, missed our way. We need not have done, for action in the right spirit is *one* way. What I want to say is perfectly illustrated in an account given by D. G. Mukerji * of a visit to a sage, to whom he had been led by his brother. The author had lived for many years in the U.S.A. and was visiting India again after long absence, acutely conscious of the differing viewpoints of East and West. He describes his entry into the room where the sage was sitting.

* D. G. Mukerji : *My Brother's Face* . . ., pp. 62–4 (Thornton Butterworth, 1925). By kind permission of E. P. Dutton & Co., Inc.

". . . I felt the same sense of a strange power pervading the room.

" On the floor were seated two young ladies, an old gentleman, their father, and a young monk in yellow, crouching before the Maharshi as though bowed by his sanctity.

" The Holy one bade me be seated. ' I am glad ', he said, ' that thy feet pain thee. That will start the easing of the pain in thy soul.' . . . He turned to the others, ' What was I talking about ?—I remember— the hospital which is a punishment for doing good.' ' How could that be, my Lord ? ' questioned the old gentleman.

" ' Even thou, an old man, dost ask me that question also ? Well— it all began one day about eleven years ago. I, who was meditating with a brother disciple under a big tree, decided to stop meditating and care for a man who had fallen sick by the roadside. He was a lean moneylender from Marwar, and he had come to Benares to make a rich gift to some temple in order to have his way to Heaven paved in solid gold. Poor fellow, he did not know that all the flowery good deeds done to catch the eye of God will in the end become the bitter fruits of desire.

" ' I ministered to him until he recovered and could return to Marwar, to lend more money, I suppose. But the rascal did me an evil turn. He spread the news all along the way that if people fell sick near my big tree I took care of them. So very soon two more people came and fell sick at the prearranged place. What else could my brother-disciple and I do but care for them ? Hardly had we cured them when we were pelted with more sick folk. It was a blinding shower. I saw in it all a terrible snare : beyond doubt, I felt, if I went on tending the sick, by and by I would lose sight of God.

" ' Pity can be a ghastly entanglement to those who do not dis-criminate, and there I stood, with a wall of sick men between me and God. I said to myself, " Like Hanuman, the monkey, leap over them and fling thyself upon the Infinite." But somehow I could not leap, and I felt lame. Just at that juncture a lay disciple of mine came to see me ; he recognised my predicament and, good soul that he was, he at once got hold of a doctor and an architect and set to work to build the hospital. Very strange though it seems, other illusions co-operated with that good man to help him—the moneylender, the first fellow I cured, sent an additional load of gold and built the day clinic. In six years the place was a solid home of delusion where men put their soul-evolution back by doing good. Shiva, Shiva ! '

" ' But, Master, I notice that your own disciples, boys and young girls, work there ? ' I put in my question.

" ' Yes, like these two young ladies here, other young people come to me to serve God. Well, youth suffers from a delusion that it can do good. But I have remedied that somewhat ; I let them take care of the sick as long as their outlook on God remains vivid and un-tarnished, but the moment any of my disciples show signs of being caught in the routine of good works—like the scavenger's cart that follows the routine of removing dirt every morning—I send that person off to our retreat in the Himalayas, there to meditate and purify his soul. When he regains his God-outlook to the fullest, if he wishes, I let him return to the hospital. Beware, beware : good can choke up a soul as much as evil.'

" ' But if someone does not do it, how will good be done ? ' questioned the old gentleman in a voice full of perplexity.

" ' Live so,' replied the Master in a voice suddenly stern, ' live so that by the sanctity of thy life all good will be performed involuntarily.' "

It is impossible to suppose that any general answer is possible to the question " Is there a ' best ' type of life ? " There probably is, however, a best type of life for a particular individual at a particular time. The word " best " I take to connote that which offers to him or her the opportunity of spiritual development on the side where it is most needed. Since we regard the experiences of human life as a means to an end which lies far beyond it, we cannot suppose there is an absolutely best type of life here. We saw in Chapter 17 that there were different ways suited to many diverse types of person and many stages of development. The assumption by a busy Westerner that contemplatives who spend many hours of the day sitting apparently in a trance, are " wasting their time " or " doing nothing " is probably foolish and ill-informed. A person's circumstances may require from him just the discipline which that practice represents. (Moreover, it is possible that through telepathy and prayer, he may quite conceivably be exerting more influence on the thoughts and outlook of men than his critics dream.) Likewise it is foolish for the contemplative to regard all action as evidence of attachment to the world—the forsaking of reality for illusion. We are not called upon to judge the way of others but to follow our own with complete sincerity.

There is an Eastern word *dharma*, difficult to translate, but conveying the ideas of duty and obligation, a mission—through fulfilling which we can best develop. It may be said that each person has his own *dharma*, and it is the way of wisdom to learn that acceptance of it is a condition of both progress and happiness. By this is not meant indifferent resignation, but the cheerful attitude which says " I will not spend time complaining at the conditions of my life. I may try to change them—but I will not have a discontented mind. These conditions, by my right reaction to them, can minister as much to my spiritual development as others which I should much prefer. This is my *dharma* at present and therefore I accept it courageously." If our lot is cast in some busy and inescapable round of action, it is no good feeling frustrated and longing to be a contemplative. There are certain qualities we can win for ourselves in the busy round which perhaps we need very much to win to balance our character. When we have really won them we shall probably draw to ourselves a change of conditions and a different opportunity. Let it not be forgotten that to achieve peace amid peaceful surroundings is good, but to achieve it amidst stormy surroundings is greater. To achieve meditation on mountain heights in the East is good, but to achieve it in London is a greater thing. To find the presence of God in the Beyond is good, but to find it on Earth is a greater achievement.

We need constantly to remind ourselves that both pleasure and pain can be our teachers, and that we may progress and learn life's lessons as much from the evil as from the good. Grey of Fallodon,* in a letter to Katherine Lyttelton after the death of his wife, wrote four sentences which must have come from the depths of his own intuitive self, and which can speak to us all.

> " It is true that I am alone, but in that way I learn what sorrow teaches, and that is to the good. For instance, I ask, if Dorothy joined me again, should I be more or less loving now? And the answer is ' more loving '. I had learned all that happiness could teach me and now I have learned more, for sorrow and happiness both teach love, only each leaves so much untaught which only the other can give."

Love must be the greatest of all things, if through it and because of it God created all that is, so that we might in the end illustrate His perfection.

We have looked in this book at many questions, and found perhaps satisfying answers to none. But even to look fearlessly is to be strangely comforted. We live in a universe more wonderful than all our dreams : this at least seems clear. The faint and far-off voices that come to us seem wholly friendly. Most grateful are we for those, our kith and kin who have gone further, and tell us *out of their experience*, with a conviction it is difficult to doubt of

> That Light whose smile kindles the Universe,
> That Beauty in which all things work and move,
> That Benediction which the eclipsing curse
> Of birth can quench not, that sustaining Love
> Which through the web of being blindly wove
> By man and beast and earth and air and sea,
> Burns bright or dim, as each are mirrors of
> The fire for which all thirst. . . .

* G. M. Trevelyan : *Grey of Fallodon*, p. 148 (Longmans, Green & Co.).

APPENDIX

Books for Further Reading

Chap.

1.	*The Human Situation*	W. Macneile Dixon	Arnold & Co.
2.	*The Nature of the Physical World*	A. S. Eddington	Everyman
	The Universe Around Us	J. H. Jeans	C.U.P.
3.	*The Science of Life*	Wells, Huxley and Wells	Cassell & Co.
	Holism and Evolution	J. C. Smuts	Macmillan
4.	*The Mind in the Making*	James H. Robinson	Jonathan Cape
	Progress and Catastrophe	Stanley Casson	Hamish Hamilton
5.	*Philosophical Aspects of Modern Science*	C. E. M. Joad	George Allen & Unwin
	Grades of Significance	G. N. M. Tyrrell	Rider & Co.
6.	*The Reach of the Mind*	J. B. Rhine	Faber & Faber
7.	*Foreknowledge*	H. F. Saltmarsh	Bell
8.	*Supernormal Faculties in Man*	Eugene Osty	Methuen
9.	*Apparitions* (Myers Memorial Lecture, 1943)	G. N. M. Tyrrell	London : S.P.R.
10.	*The Projection of the Astral Body*	Muldoon and Carrington	Rider & Co.
	The Case for Astral Projection	Sylvan Muldoon	Aries Press
11.	*Poltergeist over England*	Harry Price	Country Life, Ltd.
12.	*The Psychic Sense*	Payne and Bendit	Faber & Faber
13.	*Human Personality*	F. W. H. Myers	Longmans, Green & Co.
	The Road to Immortality	Geraldine Cummins	Nicholson
14.	*Practical Mysticism for Normal People*	Evelyn Underhill	J. M. Dent
	Varieties of Religious Experience	William James	Longmans, Green & Co.
15.	*The Timeless Moment*	Warner Allen	Faber & Faber
	Mysticism in Religion	W. R. Inge	Hutchinson
	The Perennial Philosophy	Aldous Huxley	Chatto & Windus
16.	*Song and its Fountains*	Æ	Macmillan
	The Collected Poems	Æ	Macmillan
17.	*Yoga and Western Psychology*	G. Coster	O.U.P.
	The Secret Path	P. Brunton	Rider & Co.
	Way into God	R. G. Coulson	John Murray
	The Supreme Identity	Alan Watts	Faber & Faber
18.	*The Problem of Rebirth*	Ralph Shirley	Rider & Co.
	The Ancient Wisdom	Annie Besant	T.P.H.
	The Superphysical	Arthur Osborn	Ivor Nicholson & Watson
19.	*Eastern Religions and Western Thought*	S. Radhakrishnan	O.U.P.
	Preface to Prayer	Gerald Heard	Cassell

APPENDIX TO CHAPTER 2

THE ENCHANTED GROUND OF THE MICROCOSM

So far the outline of scientific ideas about the atom and its structure seems reasonable enough, and we are bearing in mind the warning that any model or picture of " what it looks like " is not to be taken too seriously. It is a concession to the prime importance to ourselves of our sense of vision as an organ of gathering the raw material of knowledge. The real knowledge is of certain laws or relationships between symbols, and these are expressed by mathematical formulæ. Very grave doubts have been growing, however, in the last twenty-five years whether any sort of model is permissible, for it is necessarily something that we visualise in space and time, and models have invariably led us into attempting to reconcile incompatible ideas. We shall try to show the non-technical reader very briefly how this came about, but it is as well to admit that the weight of the evidence can only be appreciated mathematically.

If the radiation—the heat and light—given out by a hot, black body is examined with a spectroscope, thermopile and galvanometer, it is possible to measure how much energy of each different wavelength is radiated. Experiment shows this to be a characteristic relationship which can be represented as a smooth-flowing graph. At the beginning of the present century Professor Planck was endeavouring to interpret these experimental data with the help of the then-known laws, which had been derived from a study of matter in bulk and radiation. He found it impossible to do so, but by introducing a completely new idea (namely that radiation could only be emitted by atoms of matter in " quanta " or energy-corpuscles), the difficulty was resolved. Quanta each contain an amount of energy dependent on the frequency (v) or colour, the amount of it being given by hv. Here h ($= 6 \cdot 55 \times 10^{-27}$ erg. sec.) was a constant new to physics and is now familiarly known as Planck's constant. The new conception differed from the old in that energy of radiation could on the new view only be absorbed or emitted by atoms of matter in discontinuous amounts, one quantum at a time : on the old view a continuous flow was believed possible.

When Bohr in 1913 was attempting to explain the hydrogen spectrum he used the same basic idea with brilliant success. Planck's constant made it inevitable that the hydrogen electron could only move in certain precise orbits. The innermost of these corresponds to the normal state of the atom, the other possible outer orbits are those into which it might be displaced by excitation in a discharge tube. When the electron is displaced to such an orbit and subsequently falls back into an interior one it throws off the balance of its energy as a quantum of radiation.

The constant h again proved the key to an understanding of atomic spectra, an extraordinarily complex field of enquiry, and similarly in 1918 and following years it proved the key to understanding molecular spectra. There could seemingly be no possible doubt that the light radiated from atoms and molecules was emitted in quanta or corpuscular " bundles " each containing energy $h\nu$. But this of course was quite at variance with the wave theory of light which visualised the radiation as moving away from its source in expanding spherical waves. There is clearly here an extraordinary *impasse*. Some optical phenomena such as interference and diffraction seem to demand a wave theory of light, others such as we have mentioned seem to demand a quantum or corpuscular theory of light. No attempts at compromise or assimilation of one group of data into the theory of the other has yielded any success. We have reached a most illogical position : wave or corpuscle, which is light ?

We can illustrate the gravity of the dilemma from a well-known phenomenon of physics called the photo-electric effect. Here, when light falls on a metal, electrons are ejected from the metal surface. The energy of emission of each electron is found to depend wholly on the frequency (or colour) of the light, not on its intensity or brightness. This fact is immediately understandable on the quantum theory of light, but is quite inexplicable on a wave theory. We can weaken the intensity of the light source to a point where a calculation shows that it would take hours for any atom to absorb enough energy from a wave-front to eject an electron. But in fact we find that even then some electrons are emitted immediately. There seems no doubt that the light *must* consist of quanta which are concentrated enough to enter individual atoms. When they do so these atoms can at once eject an electron.

As soon as we feel quite certain that light consists of highly concentrated quanta, consider the following experiment which makes us quite uncertain again ! If we replace the metal surface by a very narrow slit with a photographic plate some distance behind the slit, a diffraction image of the slit would be recorded. Suppose now we place another similar slit at the side of, and parallel to the first so that the light could go through both slits. We do not then find two separate diffraction images but an interesting interference pattern of alternating bright and dark lines on the plate. This is easily understood on the wave theory of light where the wave front strikes the two apertures and the two sets of ripples on the other side interfere with each other to produce this pattern. It would not matter how faint was the source of light, a sufficiently long time of exposure of the photographic plate should and does in fact reveal this pattern. But on the quantum theory how shall we account for it? The source might be so faint that the light quanta arrived individually at the slits. After agreeing that a quantum was so concentrated that one atom could absorb it, are we now going to say it is so large that it can divide itself between the two slits? If not, let it go through one of the slits. What awareness does it then have of the presence of a neighbouring slit in virtue of which it is compelled to take a different direction to the one it would take if this slit were absent?

When we come to this sort of *impasse* it is clear that there is some basic assumption at fault. Eddington has expressed it thus, " We must not think about space and time in connection with an individual quantum; and the extension of a quantum in space has no real meaning." The position seems to be this. Our studies of the properties of matter and electricity up to comparatively recent times involved large numbers of atoms and electrons. The laws of physics discovered over the years are the well-known classical laws, and space and time are reasonable and necessary concepts in this world of the macrocosm. The fundamental laws of the microcosm, however, seem to be very different: we are just beginning to probe into them. The classical laws, it seems, are the limiting forms which the quantum laws take in the region of high quantum numbers (which is our familiar world). We have no justification for supposing our large-scale laws and concepts are valid when transferred to the inside of the atom. What is valid there we shall have to discover by patient experiment and novel hypotheses, and Planck's constant h seems to be the important clue.

Before we consider what progress has been made to unravel these laws, let us look at another bypath of research in modern physics. We have seen to our embarrassment that light seems sometimes to behave like waves and sometimes like corpuscles—a feature which suggests strongly that models of " what light looks like " are in no sense valid. De Broglie made the suggestion that possibly those entities which have usually been regarded without question as corpuscular (viz., electrons, protons and even atoms themselves) might in some circumstances behave like waves! He developed this view mathematically with considerable ingenuity, showing that the wave-length associated with any particle would be h divided by the momentum of the particle. The only possible orbits for an electron going round a nucleus would be those in which stationary waves could persist (i.e., whose perimeters would be integral multiples of the wave-length). This prediction agrees completely with Bohr's earlier theory. Without discussing it further on the theoretical side we may say that numerous carefully conducted experiments showed what no one had hitherto suspected, that even our authentic corpuscles may sometimes behave like wave-groups! If we shoot a beam of *electrons* through a suitably narrow slit we find the same diffraction pattern as light would give. Shoot them through *two* parallel slits and we find the usual interference pattern! Indeed, a microscope has been constructed in recent years which makes use of a beam of high-speed electrons instead of a beam of light. The " view " has to be photographed, of course ; it cannot be seen by the eye.

It certainly looks as though whenever we enter the microcosm, the world of atoms, electrons, protons and light quanta, we are faced with the same dilemma. It is not merely a question of some peculiar mystery associated with the nature of light : it is a question rather of whether the fundamental assumptions with which we approached this field of the infinitesimally small, are applicable at all. Obviously if space and time as we know them are inadmissible concepts in the microcosm, it is absurd to postulate any model of these small-scale entities and the terms electron, proton, light-quantum, are really no more than x, y and z—symbols for unknowns. This attitude is so drastic that we naturally enquire whether it has any support from other evidence.

About 1925 this highly unsatisfactory situation in atomic physics was subjected to careful examination by several brilliant mathematical physicists. Heisenberg initiated this development which has come to be known as the New Quantum Theory. The attempt to provide a model of any sort is definitely ruled out by all these investigators, who content themselves by showing that there are several different mathematical methods which will unify and correlate the data of observation. In 1927 Heisenberg announced a principle now known as the Principle of Indeterminacy which bids fair to be one of the basic laws of the microcosm. It is not difficult to understand and we shall endeavour to expound it—for it seems to show what real significance Planck's constant h has in the microcosm. Any particle must have position and momentum (mv) according to our basic ideas. Heisenberg's Principle states that it is in the very nature of things impossible to know both of these with complete accuracy. The more accurately a particle's position can be determined, the less accurately can its momentum be determined, and vice-versa. It is expressed by saying mathematically: Error in determination of position multiplied by the error in determination of momentum equals h. It means, for example, that if, in an experiment, we could locate an electron to an accuracy of $\frac{1}{1000}$ of a millimetre, the inevitable error in simultaneously finding its velocity is about 1 kilometre per second. The reader may wonder why this principle should be a master key to the microcosm. Perhaps we can explain this in simple terms. Momentum $\times$ distance is a quantity called Action. Nothing at all can take place in the material world without Action being involved. This principle virtually gives us therefore the basic atom of action: it is none other than h, Planck's constant. Moreover, simple as it appears, this Principle of Indeterminacy can be applied to account for all our hitherto "contradictory" experiments: interference, diffraction effects, photo-electric effects, atomic and molecular spectra, etc. It is, in other words, a unifying principle of great power.

It may still seem to the reader a rather mysterious and academic idea to account for all these experimental data.* May we therefore put it this way. We are creatures built on a scale which is prodigious compared with atoms and molecules. In order to begin to understand our world we had to define three fundamental quantities, mass, length and time; an eminently reasonable thing to do. We defined standard units of these three things and then proceeded to measure the world and discover relationships which we call laws. Now instead of being built on this large scale, can we imagine ourselves of atomic size, with the microcosm for our native world? We are starting out to try to understand it, and we decide to begin by looking for reliable and constant things which seem fundamental, and which we can define. It is certain that length would never have been selected. Imagine someone suggesting a hydrogen atom as our standard measuring rod: in the very nature of things it couldn't keep still! If we started to look for it, and located it correct to 10^{-8} cm. (its own size), it would be observed slipping away at 540 metres per second. We should have to make use of a light quantum to find it, and this collision of the light quantum would set it moving rapidly! It is also quite certain that Time would not have been selected as a fundamental unit. Perhaps it has occurred to the reader that the hydrogen electron going round in its orbit would provide a natural and reliable clock. Alas, the

* The technical reader may be interested to consult *The Quantum Theory*: F. A. Lindemann (O.U.P.).

Principle of Indeterminacy quickly shows us that in the normal state of the hydrogen atom, the " action " performed when the electron goes once round is only h, so that we are, in the very nature of things, completely uncertain whereabouts in the orbit it is. It is equally everywhere! Of course it will be remembered that we really agreed to abandon models and orbits : they do not help us at all. The reader will then naturally ask : if distance and time seem to be indeterminate in this enchanted world, what constants or fundamentals might we have found with which to build our scheme of microcosmic physics ? It is difficult to answer the question, but it looks as though Numbers are still all right. The only other thing we can be sure of is this element of action h, of which one or more units occur in everything that happens.

Perhaps we can leave this strange world of the almost infinitesimally small with the realisation that with the exceptions just mentioned, none of our mental concepts—colour, position, shape, sound, resistance to touch, etc.—apply there. Indeed Space and Time which seem to dominate our familiar world are quite elusive in the microcosm. They are concepts which have proved very helpful to the understanding of our familiar world, and which we have ourselves introduced into it—but only because we found ourselves built on a very large scale compared with atoms and molecules.

INDEX

DATE DUE

DEC 11 85			
GAYLORD			PRINTED IN U.S.A.